IN THEIR FOOTSTEPS

Inspirational Reflections on Black History
for Every Day of the Year

Daryl Grigsby

12/14/07

to Maureen,

*Thank you
for your
support and
help over
the years!*

[signature]

![acta]

PUBLICATIONS

This book is dedicated to those in whose footsteps I follow:
my grandfathers Langston Fairchild Bate of Louisville, Kentucky,
and Harold Victor Grigsby of Nashville, Tennessee;

my grandmothers Clyde Easter Woolridge of Muskogee, Oklahoma,
and Lucille Oliver Dean of Gunnison, Mississippi;

and my parents, Russell Dean Grigsby and
Jacqueline Helen Bate Grigsby, both of Washington, D.C.

I also dedicate this book to my wife, Leslie Robinson Grigsby;

and to those who follow in our footsteps,
our daughters Lauren Alyssa Grigsby and Hillary Devon Grigsby.

IN THEIR FOOTSTEPS
Inspirational Reflections on Black History for Every Day of the Year
by Daryl Grigsby

Edited by Marcia Broucek and Gregory F. Augustine Pierce
Cover design by Tom A. Wright
Art work by Jihmye Collins
Text design and typesetting by Patricia A. Lynch

Scripture quotations are from the *Newly Revised Standard Version Bible*, copyright © 1989
by the Division of Christian Education of the National Council of the Churches of Christ in
the USA. Used by permission.

Text copyright © 2007 by Daryl Grigsby
Artwork copyright © 2007 by Jihmye Collins

Published by ACTA Publications, 5559 W. Howard Street, Skokie, IL 60077-2621,
(800) 397-2282, www.actapublications.com

Library of Congress Catalog number: 2007927592

ISBN: 978-0-87946-336-6

Printed in the United States of America by Versa Press

Year 15 14 13 12 11 10 09 08 07
Printing 15 14 13 12 11 10 9 8 7 6 5 4 3 2 First

CONTENTS

INTRODUCTION

My spiritual journey began in an evangelical Baptist congregation, moved through Black Nationalist Christian circles, transitioned through progressive political organizations, and has now settled in the Roman Catholic Church, where I serve as a leader of a black Catholic men's group in my parish. At each phase of my spiritual journey, I have been impressed with and moved by figures and events in black history that demonstrate the love, courage, faith and hope necessary for building peace, justice and community. At the same time, I have been struck by the relative absence of inspirational literature regarding the legacy of black spirituality. A walk down the aisle of a Christian bookstore or through the religion section of most secular bookstores will reveal very little of vast and diverse reservoir of black spirituality.

The primary purpose of this book is to correct this deficiency and to provide the reader with daily inspiration drawn from the richness of the black struggle for survival. In these pages Rosa Parks, Patrice Lumumba, John Coltrane, Maya Angelou, Steve Biko, Elizabeth Lange, and hundreds more ask that we all—of whatever creed, race, gender, ethnic background or political persuasion—follow in their footsteps in our own struggle for humanity.

Each day of the year in this book is graced with a person or event from black history, and the dates are usually not random or accidental. Most entries are listed on, or close to, the day the person died or the date of a significant event in his or her life or in black history.

It is my intention that you read each reflection on the actual calendar date, applying the legacy to your own life and struggles that day. Yet, the book can be read in whatever way benefits you. You can read the book straight through, skip around to entries that catch your interest, or use the book as a teaching tool in a classroom or for personal education. An index at the back of the book will help you find individual and organizational names and some repeated topics.

I hope that in these pages you will find people or events to which you are particularly attracted and that draw you into further study. The life stories of many of the lesser-known people in the book, such as Walter Rodney, William Sheppard, Maria Stewart, Henry Dumas, Jarena Lee and others, can offer inspiration and insights beyond what is written here.

I have researched the facts contained here extensively for six years, and have made every effort to cross-check factual information. There are literally thousands of facts contained here. Should you find an error, I ask both for your understanding and that you contact me through the publisher with your information.

In addition, there are many other individuals I could have included beyond the 366 contained here. If you are aware of other inspirational persons or events in black history, let me know of those as well. I already have a list that could form the basis of a future volume, and your additions would be welcome and taken seriously. For both errors and additions, please contact me by e-mail at acta@actapublications.com.

I have been a lifetime student of black history. Yet I have been greatly inspired through the research for this book. I have learned new things and been reacquainted with people I have neglected or forgotten. The courage, faith, generosity and perseverance of all of them have inspired me in many significant ways. It is my prayer you experience the same as you read, reflect and work to follow "In Their Footsteps."

Daryl Grigsby
Seattle, Washington

JANUARY

Barbara Charline Jordan

≣ The Emancipation Proclamation: "Forever Free"

The Civil War was not going as anticipated. Union casualties were mounting, and the Northern public was questioning the wisdom of war. President Abraham Lincoln needed something to breathe life into his bloody cause. In the fall of 1862, he found it. On September 22, 1862, Lincoln announced the Emancipation Proclamation, declaring: "That on the first day of January in the year of our Lord, one thousand eight hundred and sixty-three, all persons held as slaves within any state…in rebellion against the United States shall be then, thenceforward, and forever free…."

Since the Proclamation, historians have questioned Lincoln's commitment to black liberation. The lesson of the Emancipation Proclamation, however, lies not in Lincoln's motives, but in the actions of the slaves. The initiative of black folk made the Emancipation Proclamation possible, necessary and inevitable; Lincoln was merely the tool.

At the time of the Civil War, four million black men, women and children were enslaved in the South. They responded to their servitude with resistance: Jemy the African, Nat Turner, Denmark Vesey and Gabriel Prosser plotted and implemented revolution; Dangerfield Newby, Osborne Anderson, Lewis Leary and John Copeland accompanied John Brown in his war against slavery; Harriet Tubman and other conductors traveled the Underground Railroad to freedom. Countless more drew on faith, subterfuge, cunning and pride to survive the ravages of slavery. While Lincoln wavered and wondered, black folks stood firm. For the slaves, the Civil War was God's hand in history, God's judgment of slavery.

While January 1, 1863, may have been the legal beginning of the Emancipation Proclamation, freedom for slaves began every day they lived with dignity. President Lincoln proclaimed what black slaves already knew: One day they, their children and their grandchildren would be forever free.

The Emancipation Proclamation that took effect on January 1, 1863, is considered one of the seminal events of black history, formally marking the end of slavery and giving the Civil War a holy purpose.

≣ Donny Hathaway: "Someday We'll All Be Free"

Donny Hathaway loved gospel music. Even at the young age of three, he was singing in the gospel choir in his parent's church in St. Louis. Nurtured in the bosom of black churches in St. Louis and Chicago, young Hathaway was surrounded by the sights and sounds of gospel music; the emotional singing, heartfelt lyrics and wailing souls became the elements of his musical formation.

Hathaway's singing talent and piano skills earned him a Fine Arts scholarship to Howard University in Washington, D.C., in 1964, where his training enabled him to become a significant figure in black music. His influences on rhythm and blues—and the black freedom struggle—is profound. Current artists such as Alicia Keyes and others cite Hathaway as a major influence and inspiration.

While at Howard, Donny Hathaway met future singer Roberta Flack, and the two would later produce memorable duets in the 1970s. Yet, in many respects, Hathaway's legacy was established with his first recordings. In 1969 he and his roommate, LeRoy Hutson, wrote the classic song, "The Ghetto." Produced at the height of both the Black Power and Civil Rights Movements, "The Ghetto" was a penetrating look at life in urban black ghettos, a reminder and a call to action about poor living conditions that black people were trying to change. His 1970 album, *Everything Is Everything*, became for many the musical foundation of the fight for equality and justice. In addition to "The Ghetto," the album featured a classic rendition of Nina Simone's "To Be Young, Gifted and Black." Hathaway's gospel roots pulsate throughout the song, and hundreds of young black children were inspired to reach higher after hearing Hathaway sing of black pride.

By the time of his death in 1979, Hathaway had only recorded three solo studio albums. These three, however, along with his duets with Roberta Flack, were enough to make him one of the more influential and significant soul singers of the 1970s. His 1973 song, the emotional "Someday We'll All Be Free," was not only a revered work during its time but was most recently performed by Alicia Keyes at a post 9/11 concert.

On January 13, 1979, Donny Hathaway was found dead on the sidewalk beneath the open window of his apartment at Essex House in New York City. He had fought depression constantly during his life, and many believe his death was a suicide.

JAN 3　　　　≣ **Vincent Harding: "Black Power and the American Christ"**

Scholar, preacher, black activist and historian Vincent Harding exposed the subservience of American Christianity to racism. In 1967, the magazine *Christian Century* published his article, "Black Power and the American Christ," condemning the white church for its flag-waving support of American oppression, injustice and violence. Harding described how Africans first met the "American Christ" on slave ships, and how this same Christ had been used for two hundred years to bless slavery and justify the extermination of indigenous Americans. Harding charged that the American church had turned Jesus Christ into a deformed apologist for racism, intervention, discrimination and materialism. He credited black power advocates for exposing this ruse and reinterpreting Christ as one who stood with the oppressed.

Harding, however, did not merely critique white Christianity; he called on Christians of all races to follow the real Jesus:

> *It is we Christians who made the universal Christ into an American mascot, a puppet blessing every mad American act…. If he whom we call the Christ is indeed the Suffering Servant of God and man, what excuse can there be for those who have turned him into a crossless puppet, running away from suffering with his flaxen locks flapping in the wind.*

In a powerful call for justice, Harding urged,

> *Let us begin to pray that time may be granted us to turn from blond dolls to the living revolutionary Lord who proclaimed that the first shall be last and the last, first.*

Vincent Harding's article, "Black Power and the American Christ," appeared in Christian Century on January 3, 1967. Harding was the Director of The Institute of the Black World and has written numerous books, including Martin Luther King: The Inconvenient Hero.

JAN 4　　　　≣ **Maria Fearing: Free to Be a Servant**

Maria Fearing was born a slave in Gainesville, Florida, in 1833. From that shackled and unpromising beginning, she became a teacher, missionary and servant of God.

Like most slaves, she was forbidden to read or write; hard work in the fields and in the kitchen of the mistress were the only skills she "needed." Slavery, degradation and misery were all she knew, so when freedom came, it was hard to imagine life without a master. It did not take long, however, for Fearing to do something with her liberation. In 1866, at the age of thirty-three, she learned to read and write. With that accomplished, she worked her way through the Freedman's Bureau School in Talladega, Alabama. Through sheer discipline and self-determination, Maria Fearing became what most thought impossible: a girl born in slavery unbroken enough to achieve and excel.

Yet this was not all. During her time on the plantation and in the Freedman's School, Fearing became increasingly committed to her Christian faith. Although it started small, with almost a whisper, before long she was spending hours each day in prayer and Bible study. At times, in her personal devotions, she would hear a voice calling her to something greater, a mission beyond herself, and perhaps beyond her country. She read in the New Testament how the apostles traveled the world spreading the gospel, and she felt called to this. But where? Where would an ex-slave go to tell others about the blessings and riches of Jesus Christ?

Where else but Africa! Knowing her family had been taken from Africa, she decided to become a missionary there.

In 1889, when she was fifty-six years old, Fearing went to Africa as a missionary of the Presbyterian Church. She took her reading, writing and faith into the jungles of Africa and founded the Pantops Home for Girls, which became a shelter for girls who would have otherwise been enslaved, raped or held as ransom until their families returned with a quota of rubber from the plantations.

Maria Fearing overcame her own enslavement, subjugation and illiteracy to become a minister to the oppressed. She used her freedom not as license to meet her own needs but to become a servant.

Maria Fearing was one of the first Presbyterian missionaries who traveled to the Congo in the 1890s. Their work was so profound and lasting that for years the Presbyterian Church was the largest Protestant denomination in the Congo.

JAN 5   ≡ **Charles Mingus: Blues and Roots**

Many consider Charles Mingus to be the greatest bassist in the history of jazz, and he was an arranger, composer and producer of many classics of that great American art form. He was also a prophetic social critic, a complex man, at times violent, at times gentle. Few lived on the raw edges of life as Mingus did; his erratic behavior, violent outbursts and brilliant insights were legendary. He was a musical giant who fought mental disease his entire life.

In his autobiography, *Beneath the Underdog*, Mingus portrays a boy surviving turmoil at home, fights on the streets and sexual explorations at school. The personal traumas of his life were surpassed only by the ugliness of racist America. Exclusion, degradation and discrimination were common experiences, and Mingus absorbed the political and personal into his soul.

Mingus' anger, passions, faith and tenderness shine in his music. His intense personal pain and social exclusion resonate in his bass notes and compositions. "Haitian Fight Song," "Prayer of Passive Resistance," "Wednesday Night Prayer Meeting" and "Better Git Hit in Your Soul" reveal the anger of his protest, the pain of his heartache and his hope in the black church. His song "Better Git Hit in Your Soul" emulates a "holy roller" being filled with the Holy Spirit, virtually putting his listeners in the midst of a black church service. He wanted his audience to be "hit" in the soul, to be moved in the deepest parts of their being.

Love, bitterness, racism and liberation were all part of Charles Mingus' life, and through his music, Mingus' pain and passion become ours.

Musical giant Charles Mingus died in Cuernavaca, Mexico, on January 5, 1979, of amyotrophic lateral sclerosis (Lou Gehrig's Disease). His autobiography, **Beneath the Underdog,** *tells of his difficult life and encounters with racism.*

JAN 6 ≡ **Mamie Till-Mobley: "We All Can Be Better"**

Mamie Till-Mobley was nervous about her son's summer trip to Mississippi. Though Emmett looked forward to visiting his uncle Mose, Mamie was unsettled about how her son, so used to Chicago, would fare in racist Mississippi. She tried to block out any bad thoughts but was constantly nagged with worry. Early Sunday morning, the phone rang. Mamie answered, and the voice on the other end hesitated.

"I don't know how to tell you. Bo…." Bo was the family name for Emmett.

"Bo, what?" Mamie asked, her mind spinning.

"Some men came and got him last night."

With those words, Mamie's life was forever changed. Her son was her whole world; for years, it had been just him and her, and she had watched him grow from a sick baby into an inquisitive and responsible teenager. She was proud of him, of the way he helped children in the neighborhood, of how he brought his grades up and of how he was so mature around adults. And now, down in hateful Mississippi, "some men" had taken him away.

The story has been told often—how Emmett was accused of whistling at a white store clerk in Money, Mississippi. How that night, J. W. Milam and Roy Bryant kidnapped him, drove him to a barn and beat him with pistols, fists and tools. They tortured and taunted him all night, gouged his eye out, shot him and threw him in the river with a cotton gin fan around his neck. When the distorted body was returned to Chicago, no one could believe that the grotesquely misshapen body had once been a teenage boy.

Mamie Till-Mobley was paralyzed with grief; her life, her love, was gone. She demanded that the funeral be held with an open casket, for she wanted the world to see what racism had done to her son. Over seven thousand people attended Roberts Temple Church of God in Christ, and the swollen, inhuman face of Emmett Till became one of the catalysts for the Civil Rights Movement. After Till was lynched, Milam and Bryant bragged about their role, were acquitted by an all-white jury and, within days, sold the story of their confession to *Life* magazine. The brutal slaying of Emmett Till inspired many to fight to end racism and discrimination; thousands who attended the funeral or saw the photos later participated in the struggle for civil rights. Many historians say that Mamie Till-Mobley's decision to have an open casket for her son was crucial in energizing the later civil rights struggle.

After Emmet's murder, Mamie Till-Mobley fought her despair and sadness, even her thoughts of suicide. She became a teacher in the Chicago Public School District, where she encouraged hundreds of children with her message of hope.

She later wrote in the story of her life, *Death of Innocence*,

> *Hardly a moment goes by when I don't think about Emmett and the promise of a lifetime. You don't need to be reminded of the horror you have seen, even for a brief moment—in your boy's battered body….I am experienced, but not cynical….I am hopeful that we all can be better than we are. I've been broken-hearted—but I still maintain an oversized capacity for love.*

Despite suffering firsthand the consequences of violence, Mamie Till-Mobley maintained a faith in the human capacity for change. She continued to fight the demons of despair as she gave her time and love to Chicago's schoolchildren.

Teacher and activist Mamie Till-Mobley died on January 6, 2003, in Chicago, Illinois. Her beloved son, Emmett, was murdered on August 28, 1955.

JAN 7   ≣ Lawrence Ndzanga: "He Put His Whole Life into It"

The lone figure of Lawrence Ndzanga sat quietly in the dimly lit cabin in the deserted rail yard. The night was still, and the only sounds were distant cars and the language of night animals. Shortly after midnight, tired African rail workers limped through the door. Within an hour, perhaps a dozen had joined Ndzanga in the cabin. He had expected at least thirty, but the Rail Administration had threatened immediate termination for any worker with union ties. Since no African worker could afford to lose his job, people were afraid to come.

Despite the disappointing turnout, Ndzanga persisted in organizing South African rail workers, for black workers were treated little better than slaves. Without notice, their pay could be slashed or they could be transferred to a desolate outpost. Injuries were frequent and often severe, and blacks were given the most dangerous assignments. Injured workers were often fired without medical care or financial assistance. Ndzanga taught them how to use the grievance system, petition for their rights and join the union.

As a veteran organizer of the South African Railway and Harbour Worker's Union, Ndzanga knew well the hazards of his calling. But despite goon squads and spies, he managed to avoid detection and would often appear just when workers needed him most, becoming a legend among workers in the Transvaal.

Ndzanga and his wife, Rita, were known among black workers for their courage in standing against the railway bosses. Nothing frightened them. Though Ndzanga was detained, arrested, beaten and exiled, he never gave up. One black union leader told his comrades that "Ndzanga…put his whole life into it."

Eventually, the Railway Workers Union joined the militant South African Congress of Trade Unions (SACTU) to help bring dignity and better working conditions to black workers. Organizers such as Lawrence Ndzanga were the backbone of the South African workers movement and helped hasten the end of apartheid.

On January 9, 1976, Lawrence Ndzanga was murdered by the South African Security Police. He was being detained without trial under South Africa's dreaded Terrorism Act. His wife, Rita, was in prison at the time of his murder and was forbidden to attend his funeral. She was later released without charge.

JAN 8   ≣ Reverend Pauli Murray: Song in a Weary Throat

In her book *Song in a Weary Throat: An American Pilgrimage*, the lawyer, poet, activist, educator and priest Pauli Murray describes her life struggle. If she was at all weary, it was from her earnest fight for human dignity.

At Hunter College in New York City, she was one of only four blacks in a class of two hundred and forty-seven students. Overcoming every obstacle, she graduated with distinction. Believing that racial and gender equality were hidden in the promise of law, Murray went on to Howard University Law School. Foreshadowing the defiance of Rosa Parks, in 1940 Pauli Murray and her friend Adelene McBean refused to move to the back of a Greyhound bus.

In 1966, Murray and other women activists founded the National Organization of Women (NOW). Later that year, she left the Episcopal Church in protest of their persistent discrimination against women and blacks. Yet, as a long-time Episcopalian, she returned to help her beloved church. Convinced that Christ's gospel was essential to human liberation, Pauli Murray sought ordination as an Episcopal priest. On January 8, 1977, she became the first black woman ordained in the Episcopal Church.

Whenever Rev. Murray mounted the pulpit, black and female issues were at the heart of her sermons. She saw the church, the law, her writing—everything she did—as a means of ending human inequality, and she lived her belief that spiritual transformation was critical to social action and political change.

Rev. Pauli Murray was ordained on January 8, 1977, in the National Cathedral in Washington, D.C., the first black woman ordained by the Episcopal Church.

JAN 9   ≡ **Countee Cullen: "Yet Do I Marvel"**

Black artistic talent converged on New York City to create the miracle of the Harlem Renaissance. Langston Hughes, Jean Toomer, Zora Neal Hurston, Claude McKay, James Weldon Johnson, Gloria Douglas, Wallace Thurman and many others masterfully conveyed black life on canvas, in verse and with song. Many consider Countee Cullen the most brilliant writer of them all. Born in Louisville, Kentucky, adopted by a Methodist minister and his wife, Cullen burst on the literary scene with his poems "Color" (1925), "Copper Sun" (1927) and "The Ballad of a Brown Girl" (1927).

Cullen is most remembered in black America for his brilliant poetic creation, "Yet Do I Marvel." The great James Weldon Johnson considered the poem's climactic ending "the two most poignant lines in American literature."

In this classic poem, Countee Cullen inquired why God would allow such horrific black suffering. He wondered how survivors of the auction block, cotton fields and slave ships could still love from their hearts. He marveled that beauty could emerge from the curse of blackness, that rhyme and verse could emerge from the souls of a people considered subhuman, inferior and unclean. But he knew that they did because he had lived it.

Cullen embraced black life, wove it into verse and gave it back to the world. The gift of his poems—"Incident," "For a Lady I Know," "The Litany of the Dark People," "The Black Christ," to name a few—graced Harlem then and continue to inspire us now. Countee Cullen asked poets to sing their song of anguish, and he urged us to read the great black poets, so that we, too, could wonder about the "curious thing" of brilliant creativity in the midst of racism and pain.

Poet Countee Cullen died of complications from high blood pressure on January 9, 1946, in New York City. He was an important part of the Harlem Renaissance in New York City.

≣ Frederick McGhee: "Away with This Evil!"

Born a slave in 1861, Frederick McGhee was freed after the carnage of the Civil War. Using a combination of good fortune and hard work, he became a lawyer, a political activist and an outspoken proponent of equality. Eventually, his prominent voice caught the attention of Catholic Archbishop John Ireland, a powerful bishop and an advocate for racial equality. Ireland asked to meet with McGhee, and McGhee was shocked that a white man would reach out to black activists. He was so impressed, in fact, that he began to study Catholicism. McGhee felt that any faith that transformed a white man to such an extent was worth exploring. Influenced by Bishop Ireland's courageous stand for black rights, McGhee ultimately joined the Roman Catholic Church. As a new convert, he had a passion for the faith that only furthered his unquenchable thirst for justice and equality.

Just a few short years after his conversion, McGhee stood as a delegate and key speaker at the 1892 National Black Catholic Congress in Philadelphia. His address, "Our National Institutions," was a brilliant attack on segregated schools. As a trained lawyer and accomplished public speaker, McGhee was spellbinding. Convinced that as long as whites attended well-funded schools and blacks were restricted to impoverished leftovers, inequality would last forever, he spoke passionately for black equality. His faith had taught him a better future was possible. To the hungry lion of white supremacy, he declared, "Away with this evil!"

> We proclaim that all Americans are equal, but the common equality of man is but like the enchanted palace...and this system of separate schools is like the strong, hungry glaring lion.... Away with the evil of the caste school.

Frederick McGhee's speech began a movement by black Catholics to demand integration in Catholic and public schools. And his words were prophetic: The great Thurgood Marshall used similar language in 1954 to argue *Brown v. Board of Education*. Later, McGhee was to become one of the founders of the NAACP and a key leader in its legal attack on segregation.

Frederick McGhee was a prominent delegate and key speaker at the National Black Catholic Congress that began on January 5, 1892.

≣ Evangelina Rodriquez: Healer of the Poor

Nothing in the early life of Evangelina Rodriquez hinted at the greatness she would later attain. Evangelina was born poor, illegitimate and black in the Dominican Republic, a nation where any one of those characteristics foreshadowed a life of despair. Soon after birth, Evangelina was abandoned by her father, and when she was six, her mother died suddenly. Evangelina was taken in by her grandmother, Tomasina.

Despite her barren beginnings, Evangelina Rodriquez was wise beyond her years. The great Afro-Dominican poet Rafael Deligne recognized a future in the girl and persuaded Tomasina to keep her in school. Rodriquez grasped the opportunity and studied so diligently that she became the first Afro-Dominican woman educated in medicine. After receiving her medical degree in Paris, France, she returned home a specialist in gynecology and pediatrics.

Although her education offered a future of wealth and security, she chose the way of service and compassion. The anguish of her childhood enabled Rodriquez to embrace the pain of the poor and the outcast, and she provided free medical education for prostitutes, built a center for lepers and led night classes for illiterate peasants. She was often seen working with the poorest and sickest peasants in the Dominican Republic, without charge, donating both her money and time. Evangelina Rodriquez's selflessness became legendary on the island, and the work she started continues to this day.

Evangelina Rodriquez's service to the poor threatened the Catholic Church and the Trujillo dictatorship, and in 1946 she was beaten and tortured. She died on January 11, 1947, of injuries inflicted by dictator Trujillo's henchmen. Many of her family and friends abandoned her out of fear. Still, her work did not die, and today several clinics bear her name.

JAN 12   ≡ **Lorraine Hansberry: A Raisin in the Sun**

Lorraine Hansberry created *A Raisin in the Sun,* a classic theatrical production with profound societal implications. It was the first Broadway play written by a black woman, and it ran for an unprecedented five hundred and eighty-three performances, with Sidney Portier and Ruby Dee in the starring roles.

A Raisin in the Sun is a stunning replica of black lives stunted by racism, exposing its lingering destructiveness. The images that Hansberry created on the Broadway stage flowed directly from her life. Her father had won a legal battle against restrictive covenants, an achievement that enabled blacks to purchase homes in white areas. The victory was hollow, however, as bigotry chased her father to Mexico. The Hansberry family experienced the literal dislocation of racism, and Lorraine infused her play with that trauma.

Lorraine Hansberry was a playwright committed to transforming the world around her. Nina Simone, the great singer and a close friend of Hansberry, who attributed her own political awakening to Hansberry, wrote:

Lorraine was truly dedicated. Although she loved beautiful things, she denied them to herself because they would distract her from the struggle, which was her life. She wore no make-up, except lipstick, and had only five dresses. She said, "I'm pretty the way I am."

A Raisin in the Sun remains a testament to Hansberry's talents. Over the years, it has energized many activists and progressive leaders; high schools, colleges, community groups and theatrical troupes across America pay continual tribute to Hansberry by reenacting her work.

Lorraine Hansberry, author of "A Raisin in the Sun," the first drama written by a black woman to be produced on Broadway, died on January 12, 1965, in New York City.

JAN 13   ≣ **Sterling A. Brown: "Gittin' Stronger"**

At a time when black college graduates were rare, poet Sterling A. Brown earned a master's degree from Harvard University and went on to become a professor of English at Howard University for over forty years. During those four decades, Brown mentored Stokely Carmichael; the future president of Ghana, Kwame Nkrumah; actor Ossie Davis; the Marxist poet Amiri Baraka; and many others.

As a poet and a teacher, Sterling constantly drew from his roots, maintaining throughout his career that the folk wisdom and blues he heard in Virginia gave vitality to his pen. Although he had studied under America's most learned faculty, he once wrote, "My best teacher was the poor black folk of the South." Brown emerged from the rich soil of black culture, and he never allowed the dominant white world to corrupt his message.

In deed and word Brown exemplified the tenacity of black struggle, and his poetry honored his people. Perhaps no poem captures black strength as well as his classic, "Strong Men," which recounts the horrors inflicted on black men chained, sold, forced to hard labor, penned in factories, hemmed in slums and relegated to servitude. Yet, the poem ends in triumph. Brown gives honor to black men not destroyed by adversity but made stronger by the pain of their ordeal. Despite the slave trade, sharecropping, violence and degradation, these "strong men git stronger."

"Strong Men" expresses the marvelous legacy of Sterling Brown. The men and women he mentored at Howard continue to alter the face and fortunes of black America; likewise, the common people from whom he drew his strength continue on, "coming on…gittin' stronger."

Poet and professor Sterling A. Brown died on January 13, 1989, in Takoma Park, Maryland. He was a mentor of Stokely Carmichael, Kwame Nkrumah, Ossie Davis, Amiri Baraka and many others.

Abdias do Nascimento's contributions to Afro-Brazilian identity are so vast that his life seems the work of multiple persons. In 1937, when he was but twenty-three years old, Nascimento joined *Frente Negra Brasileira* (United Black Front) to advocate for black rights. Sixty years later, in 1997, he was re-elected to the Brazilian State Senate.

During those sixty years, Nascimento used the stage, literature, podium and legislature on behalf of Brazil's African descendants. He founded the *Teatro Experimental do Negor* (Black Experimental Theatre) where Afro-Brazilian theatre flourished for years. He later published *Quilombo*, a journal dedicated to black freedom.

At a time when some may have rested on such prestigious accomplishments, Nascimento was just warming up. He went on to convene the Afro-Brazilian Democratic Committee, became President of the National Convention of Blacks and organized the First National Conference of Brazilian Blacks. His work in these conferences led to mass movements that undermined much of Brazil's discrimination. Forced into exile in 1968, he still promoted black pride everywhere he traveled, lecturing on African history in the United States and Nigeria and teaching African culture upon his return to Brazil.

Yet, despite these impressive achievements, politics may have been Nascimento's most powerful tool for Afro-Brazilian equality. As a member of Brazil's House of Deputies and later its Senate, he worked tirelessly for the excluded. He passed the bill that created November 20 as National Black Consciousness Day in memory of the revolutionary leader Zumbi. He promoted affirmative action to remedy centuries of discrimination, created scholarships for Afro-Brazilian education and passed several laws to protect poor black Brazilians.

These brief sketches of Abdias do Nascimento are but a glimpse of his commitment, faith and generosity in the cause of black freedom. No wonder many scholars consider him the twentieth century's most complete African intellectual. If there were any justice, Nascimento would be a household name across the globe.

Few have duplicated the sheer artistic, literary and political output of Abdias do Nascimento. Each stage of his career—in theater, literature, teaching and politics—was founded on one purpose: the cultural and political elevation of Afro-Brazilians.

≡ Patrice Lumumba
Prime Minister of the Democratic Republic of the Congo

All of Africa seemed on the verge of collapse. As brutal as the Belgians were, many feared that their departure from the Congo would unleash anarchy, tribalism and bloodshed. On one front, the Belgians, having profited from the horrific treatment of the Congolese people, now plotted to undermine the new nation's independence. On another front, the United States' fear of Soviet influence led it to try to destroy any freedom struggle not beholden to free markets and corporate interests. And on the home front, while the Congolese people had longed to be free of Belgium, they now feared leaders who put tribal supremacy over national unity. The swirling drama of Congolese independence was almost frightening.

In the midst of this cauldron appeared the great Patrice Lumumba. Postal worker organizer and founder of the MNC (*Mouvement National Congolais*), Lumumba was a charismatic leader in the Congo. His love for black people and his passion for African unity were unparalleled, and the people knew it. In 1958, he attended the All-African People's Conference and met Kwame Nkrumah from Ghana. The two of them talked excitedly of Africa for Africans, of freedom for Ghana and the Congo, and of a gifted and culturally rich continent. Yet their desire did not blind them to the obstacles. They were only too aware that colonial interference, economic dependency and fragmented tribalism stood in the way of their hopes.

The year 1960 was a tumultuous time for Lumumba and the Congo. Patrice Lumumba was selected as Prime Minister of the newly independent Democratic Republic of the Congo, but his vision of unity among African nations and tribes soon conflicted with those who used division to promote personal or corporate gain. Lumumba stood firm, and he fought vigorously, but his charisma, eloquence and passion made him dangerous to those who benefited from a weak and pliable Congo. Reactionary Africans, the Belgian government and the United States' CIA conspired to have him silenced.

When the United Nations withdrew their protection from Lumumba, he fled for his life, but Congolese traitors, CIA operatives and Belgian troops tracked his every footstep. Col. Joseph Mobutu had him arrested and taken to Katanga province, where he was tortured and brutally murdered. The voice of African unity was gone.

Yet even in death, Lumumba was an inspiration. Future African freedom movements, from Zimbabwe to Angola to Guinea-Bissau, drew strength from his example. A continent away, in the United States, advocates of black freedom continue to evoke the memory of Patrice Lumumba, and he is one of the enduring symbols of Third World pride.

Prime Minister Patrice Lumumba was murdered on January 17, 1961, in the Katanga province. African soldiers shot him under orders of Belgian officers, and Belgian troops hacked his body to pieces, burned it in sulfuric acid and buried it in an unmarked grave in an attempt to forever destroy his power. Reactionaries in the Congolese military, Belgian agents and the CIA have been implicated in his murder.

JAN 16 ☰ Maya Angelou: "On the Pulse of Morning"

It was a beautiful morning. Winters in Washington, D.C., can be spectacular, as sunrise splashes pink and blue hues across the frozen earth, and this day was particularly buoyant, for it held the promise of a new president. William Jefferson Clinton was to be inaugurated, and his climb to the presidency brought great hope for the future. Yet none of us was prepared for what we heard that morning.

African-American poet Maya Angelou proclaimed, in her measured cadence, a stirring poem of human dignity. When she read her beautiful work, "On The Pulse of Morning," it was as if the entire country held its breath. Her brilliant poem swept us up in human history. She described our legacy of greed and violence, yet she celebrated an unquenchable hope in the future. She advised that our fate is not predetermined, that we have the power to change it. She proclaimed that, despite our history of darkness, ignorance and war, we still have the capacity to hope and to love.

Though Angelou herself was a victim of abuse and violence, to read any or all of her autobiographical works is to be exposed to the triumph of courage and faith. Her books *I Know Why the Caged Bird Sings*, *Gather Together in My Name*, *The Heart of A Woman* and *A Song Flung Up to Heaven* are testaments to the abiding power of hope. Angelou's call to us—no matter what obstacles we face, no matter who tells us what we cannot do or say—is to continue the struggle. She uses poetry, her own and that of others, to call forth what often lies dormant in us: our capacity to hope and to love. She tells us that the only thing lacking in our world is the fullest expression of our humanity, that the change needed most in our world starts with our own hearts and spirits, that with a revived hope and love we may all awaken to the "brilliant morning" she described.

When Maya Angelou finished reading that day, millions of us felt the elusive promise of love within our grasp. We sensed our power to create a world worthy of our calling. If only we could see and believe and do, if only…if only…we could say "Good Morning" to the dawn of redemption and justice.

Maya Angelou read her poem, "On the Pulse of Morning," at President Bill Clinton's inauguration on January 20, 1993, in Washington, D.C.

JAN 17 ≣ Barbara Charline Jordan: "My Faith in the Constitution Is Whole"

No one who saw it will ever forget the image: a black Congresswoman sitting in judgment on the President of the United States. But that was not quite all. For the first time in history, millions of Americans watched on television as a poised black woman was center stage. Few had ever heard such perfect diction, such fabulous articulation of personal conviction.

In 1974, while a member of the House Judiciary Committee, Barbara Jordan stunned America during President Nixon's impeachment hearings. Anyone near a radio or television can remember her confident voice:

When the Constitution of the United States was completed on the seventh of September of 1786, I was not included in that "We the people." I felt for many years that somehow George Washington and Alexander Hamilton just left me out by mistake. But through the process of amendment, interpretation and court decision, I have finally been included in "We the People." …My faith in the Constitution is whole. It is complete. It is total. I am not going to sit here and be an idle spectator to the diminution, the subversion, the destruction of the Constitution.

Barbara Jordan knew intimately the promises of the Constitution, for she had lived without its benefits. She grew up in a poor, segregated Houston neighborhood and had watched her grandfather eke out a living selling junk. Throughout high school, college and graduate school, she was the first black here, the only woman there, the often solitary one catapulting over every racist and sexist obstacle in her way. Jordan was the only black woman in her high school debate team, one of few women in law school, the first African American elected to the Texas Senate since Reconstruction and the first southern black woman elected to Congress. Such were the pioneering contours of her life, and she knew that the Constitution enabled her to climb such heights. She also knew that the document alone was not enough, that it took sweat, time and sacrifice to make the promises real.

Therefore, Nixon's disdain for the Constitution was an attack on the substance of Jordan's very life. She and others before her had worked hard to be counted among "we the people." Jordan would not allow the president or anyone else to subvert that which had enabled her to climb from the ghetto to the Congress.

Barbara Jordan's speech at the House Judiciary Committee on July 24, 1974, is remembered as one of the great orations in United States history. Its greatness lay not just in her eloquence but also in the deeds behind it. Her life, sacrifice and courage were sacramental proof that the Constitution works.

Barbara Jordan resigned from politics when she was 45, due to complications from multiple sclerosis. She was later named to the National Women's Hall of Fame, and is listed there along with other women such as Eleanor Roosevelt, Helen Keller and Rosa Parks. Barbara Jordan died at age 59 on January 17, 1996, in Austin, Texas.

JAN 18 ☰ Blessed Father Cyprian Michael Iwana Tansi: "Endowed with Virtue"

Iwana Tansi was one of the Nigerian boys who attended mission schools run by Catholic priests near their village. Unlike many, however, young Tansi eagerly absorbed the teachings of the church. Everyone who met him was struck by his seriousness about God. To him, God was everywhere—in the trees, in the fields and in everyone he met. The Catholic teachings that God's grace was in all things, that the sacraments—simple elements such as water, bread and wine, images, rosaries and statutes—were but physical indications of the spiritual reality, fit perfectly with young Tansi's view of God. He was enthusiastic about the Catholic faith and was baptized when he was nine. At his baptism he chose the Christian name of Michael. By the time he was sixteen, Michael Iwana Tansi began teaching classes at the mission school, and when he was twenty-two he entered the seminary to become a priest.

At age thirty-four, after twelve years of study and training, he was ordained a priest at the Catholic cathedral at Onitsha. When he was assigned to his first parish, Father Tansi unleashed his talents. He became known for his ability to combine spirituality and action; his prayer life was as vigorous as his ministry to others. He evangelized villagers, served the poor and sick, counseled those to be married, and gave freely of his time and talents to any in need.

When Catholic Bishop Charles Heery sought to establish a Trappist monastery in Nigeria, he believed Fr. Tansi to be the perfect candidate. Tansi's work embodied all of the practices the Trappists life: asceticism, poverty of spirit, chastity, prayerfulness and silence. Tansi agreed to the bishop's request and traveled to England for the intensive spiritual formation program to enter the Trappist order. When he was assigned to the Abbey of St. Bernard at Leicestershire, Tansi added Cyprian to his name. His brothers in the order soon witnessed the same devotion and prayerfulness he had displayed in Nigeria.

Cyprian Michael Iwana Tansi died before he was able to return to Nigeria as a Trappist monk, but the effects of his presence and ministry would linger for years. One observer wrote of him, "He proved himself endowed with virtue, devoted to responsibility and given over to piety, prayer and studies." For Fr. Tansi, active ministry and contemplative prayer were not separate; they were interrelated features of a life committed to God.

Father Cyprian Michael Iwana Tansi died on January 20, 1964, of an aortic aneurysm. He was buried at the monastery in England, but his remains were later transferred to his native Nigeria and buried at Aguleri, one of his parish assignments, where they remain today. He has been declared "Blessed" by the Catholic Church.

JAN 19   ≡ Harry Belafonte: "Daylight Come"

On January 19, 2002, Harry Belafonte was the guest speaker at St. Sabina Catholic Church in Chicago, Illinois. He talked of his lifelong struggle for human dignity, black equality and economic justice. In the span of a couple hours, Belafonte described his evolution as a human being, an artist and a proud black activist. What he called "the canvas of my youth" was in fact a remarkable story of how he rose from Caribbean roots, military duty and frequent wanderings to find his meaning and purpose in black struggle.

After being discharged from the Army, Belafonte met several Pullman Car workers, black men whose membership in The Brotherhood of Sleeping Car Porters made them politically astute and socially active agents of change. When they grew tired of Belafonte's constant questioning, they gave him a copy of W.E.B. DuBois' *Color and Democracy*. That book, says Belafonte, opened his eyes to the roots of racism, inequality and poverty, and he committed himself to social activism and political transformation.

Once Belafonte began his acting and singing career in the American Negro Theatre in Harlem, he had the great fortune of meeting Paul Robeson, which only deepened Belafonte's search for meaning: "I found in him a voice that led me to places I had never dreamed of. He became my mentor." Around this same time, Belafonte's music became a commercial success, launching a career that slowly blossomed into national fame. In his heyday, Belafonte was known as the King of Calypso, and in 1957 his albums outsold those of Elvis and Sinatra combined.

Belafonte is one of many artists who use art as a weapon for peace and justice. His signature work, "Banana Boat Song (Day-O)," which remains a popular song to this day, calls for justice in the poignant words "daylight come." He says:

> When I sing "The Banana Boat Song," most people see it as some whimsical, fanciful little tale that brings charm and delight to the listener. But to me, it's about a human condition that was very real to me as a child in Jamaica and very painful and very exploitative.

The work that had begun in the pages of *Color and Democracy* and in conversations with Paul Robeson deepened with time. Harry Belafonte was a solid supporter of Rev. Martin Luther King, Jr., and the Southern Christian Leadership Conference (SCLC), an advocate for the poor and ignored, and a peace activist. In recent years he has condemned the excesses of globalization; spoken out against U.S. intervention in Grenada, Panama and Iraq; and been active in work to end world hunger, Third World debt and militarism.

In an interview with Cornel West, Belafonte urges,

> Do not look upon struggle as some harmful, negative thing. Struggle has great glory and great dignity and great power and great beauty.... The more you discover through struggle the purer you become.

The life and the words of Harry Belafonte portray the fight for human dignity and remind us that sustained warfare requires sustained fighting.

Musician and actor Harry Belafonte has been at the forefront of countless struggles for equality, justice and peace, supporting the Civil Rights Movement, Nelson Mandela and the South African freedom struggle. His "We Are the World" concerts have helped relieve famine in Africa.

Black faces gaze skyward at the majestic flight of the small white baseball. Some lose sight of the sphere as it glides toward its destination. Jaws drop. A collective "aahhh" is audible from the grandstand. Young men just up from the South are speechless. Old grizzled fans who had seen Babe Ruth in his prime shake their heads in awe. The crisp sound of wood hammering balls continues as ball after ball hurtles over the fence and into the wooded field beyond. Children run out of the park and into the distant field in a vain search for the prized souvenirs.

Batting practice with Josh Gibson is a treat for all. No man, black or white, has hit more balls with more power than Gibson. The same scene was rerun everywhere he played: Pittsburgh; New York; Chicago; Kansas City; Lincoln, Nebraska; Birmingham, Alabama; Havana, Cuba; the Dominican Republic—anywhere black players were allowed to perform before a paying audience. Old black men who witnessed his power still mumble about "ol' Jarsh," the barrel-chested ballplayer who rocketed low line drives out of Negro League parks, minor league stadiums, barnstorming fields and ballparks south of the border.

The white dailies seldom covered Gibson's exploits. Radio broadcasts failed to describe his beautiful stance and his graceful stride. Statisticians were too busy following mediocre Major Leaguers to document his astonishing achievements. No tape measure was available to register his home-run distance, nor was his average memorized as those of Lou Gehrig, Babe Ruth and Ty Cobb were. White players of lesser caliber received more press in a weekend than Gibson received in a year.

Yet he kept on hammering. No one really knows how many homers Josh Gibson bashed. Some say 832, others say it was 898; we will never know, as his career was obscured by the mists of segregation. We may not know the numbers, but those who saw his blasts know his power. They tell us how his large black hands gripped the end of the wood and leapt out at pitches as his stride and strength broke yet another hapless pitcher's heart and confidence.

Those who called Josh Gibson "the black Babe Ruth" were corrected by those who knew him. The Babe, they maintained, was the white Josh Gibson. Whether in the uniform of the Homestead Grays; the Pittsburgh Crawfords; or the Cuban, Puerto Rican, Mexican, or Negro League All-Star teams; Josh brought thrill to the fans and drama to the game.

On January 20, 1947, two months before Jackie Robinson broke the color barrier in Major League Baseball, Gibson fell asleep and never woke up. Racism may have kept him off a Major League team, but he still played "major league" ball. Few Negro League players—and there are many great ones—gave so many fans as much pleasure as Josh Gibson. Each time he launched a home run, he told his black fans, in effect, "Don't let racism hold you back; you just keep on keeping on!"

Negro League player Josh Gibson died of a brain tumor in Pittsburgh, Pennsylvania, on January 20, 1947. He hit over 800 homeruns in his career.

≣ Fanny Jackson Coppin: A School for Black Women

Fanny Jackson Coppin rose from the degradation of slavery to become the first black woman to head a major educational institution for blacks in the United States. Born the property of a white family, she was freed from slavery's grip when her aunt purchased her from the plantation master. Intelligent and compassionate, Fanny Coppin attended Oberlin College in Ohio. Blacks, especially ex-slaves, attended Oberlin not for their own advancement but for the elevation of the race. Like other students at Oberlin, she studied during the day and tutored black children and adults at night.

After graduation, Coppin moved to Philadelphia to serve that city's relatively large black population. She walked around town for days, pondering how she could best help others. As she observed black women trying to hold their families, their communities and themselves together, she decided to teach home economics and nursing to help poor black women become more independent and stable.

At the same time, the Society of Friends—the Quakers—were starting the Institute for Colored Youth to provide quality education for black children. The Quakers and their black comrades wanted to build the most prestigious educational facility in the nation and, therefore, wanted America's best black teachers. They knew of Fanny Jackson Coppin's success and asked her to direct their Institute. Coppin agreed and became the head of the Women's Department of the Institute for Colored Youth. The good works she had already done were multiplied at the Institute, and black girls facing formidable odds now had a tireless advocate and friend in their leader. Fanny Coppin taught, counseled, cajoled and nurtured black girls to lead productive self-respecting lives. When her career ended, Coppin left a legacy of love and success that continues to this day.

Fanny Jackson Coppin, the first black woman to head a major education institution for blacks in the United States, died in Philadelphia on January 21, 1913. In addition to her illustrious teaching career, Fanny Coppin was an outspoken proponent of women's rights. Thousands attended her funeral, and memorial services were held in numerous cities on the East Coast.

≣ Amilcar Cabral: Roots and Revolution

Portuguese spies lurked everywhere in Guinea and Cape Verde in West Africa. Yet, one by one, six African men found their way to Amilcar Cabral's apartment, timing their arrival such that the authorities would suspect nothing. Because Cabral was known as an "agitator" and "dangerous influence," these African peasants and workers knew they could be arrested just for meeting with him, but they still came. Cabral, an agricultural engineer by day, would later lead the meeting to its historic conclusion. Before they left, those in attendance had created the *Partido Africano da Independencia da Guine e Cabo Verde* (PAIGC). No political party in other parts of colonial Africa united opposing tribes under the banner of national liberation as the PAIGC did. It was the most successful of the revolutionary formations that defeated European colonialism, and much of their achievement was rooted in Cabral's brilliance and passion. Few leaders were as beloved as Cabral; those who knew him say his devotion to Guinean and Cape Verdian peasants was unshakeable.

Cabral studied in Lisbon, Portugal, where he became an agricultural engineer before returning to Guinea. An educated man, he could have lived out his days in security and comfort. Instead, he chose revolution over the easy life. He later explained, "I saw folk die of hunger in Cape Verde, and I saw folk die from flogging in Guinea, you understand? This is the entire reason for my revolt."

Once he chose national liberation over personal comfort, Cabral never wavered. In his speeches, writings and policies, he urged peasants and workers to free themselves from mental bondage. His teachings on the role of party discipline, sacrifice and culture energized people's struggles in Guinea, Cape Verde and across the Third World, influencing black activism everywhere. Few radicals understood the role of culture in national liberation as did Amilcar Cabral. His love for all things African and his willingness to risk his life for others stands as a model that we would all do well to emulate.

On January 20, 1973, at 10:30 p.m., Amilcar Cabral was walking home with his wife when he was shot and killed in front of the headquarters of the PAICG by agents of the Portuguese secret police

≣ Paul Robeson: "I Have Made My Choice"

Paul Robeson was an immensely talented and remarkable human being. Whether on the football field, the courtroom, the stage, the concert hall or the podium, Robeson astonished viewers with his talent. Yet it was his deep love for humanity, his unquenchable search for justice and his lifetime fight for human solidarity that set him apart. Had he devoted his considerable skills to any one venue, he would be remembered with fondness. Yet Robeson gave us much more, sacrificing personal fame to stand by the oppressed, to fight for the outcast and to embrace the poor of the world.

It was in 1933, while performing in London, that he embraced his blackness. He wrote home, "I came to consider I was an African.... I am proud to be black, for no one respects a man who does not respect himself." Yet for Robeson, being black did not mean personal isolation and black superiority. Instead, black pride became the foundation from which he embraced all humanity. He was a friend of African anti-colonialists, the Spanish Republic, Chinese peasants, Jamaican dockworkers, U.S. autoworkers—anyone suffering the oppression caused by the excesses of multinational capitalism.

His stand for freedom brought him into direct and violent conflict with the power of the United States government. The greatness of Robeson is reflected in the powers that conspired to destroy him. His voice, his music, his passion, his love, his courage were all too much for America to bear. The United States, in all its hypocrisy, greed and inequality, could not stand the noble example of Paul Robeson. The White House, the Congress, the FBI, the State Department, the CIA, the Internal Revenue Service, Hollywood, the House Committee on Un-American Activities, the police—all sought to destroy him. His phone was wiretapped, his passport revoked, his singing career decimated, his acting curtailed, his mail opened, his movements watched.

Eventually, the great Robeson began to wear down. Yet even to the end his convictions never changed. He once wrote,

> Every artist...must decide now where he stands.... There are no impartial observers.... The artists must elect to fight for Freedom or Slavery. I have made my choice.

Robeson chose freedom over slavery and paid dearly for his commitment. His legacy remains whenever we fight for justice, democracy or international solidarity. He was convinced that the artist must side with the peasants, the workers and the marginalized, and he lived his conviction with passion and dignity.

Attorney, athlete and actor Paul Robeson died in Philadelphia, Pennsylvania, on January 23, 1976. He suffered years of persecution, investigation, blacklisting and harassment from federal and local authorities.

JAN 24   ≡ **Thurgood Marshall: "The Best He Could With What He Had"**

As he approached his elder years, Supreme Court Justice Thurgood Marshall was asked how he wanted to be remembered. He replied, "That he did the best he could with what he had." The man who rose from humble origins in Baltimore to become the first black Supreme Court Justice, the man who made school segregation illegal, not only did his best, he did his best for others.

Early in his life, Marshall knew that segregation and equality were mutually exclusive because he had seen the contrast between his black Baltimore high school—with no gym, library, cafeteria or auditorium—and the astonishing resources, buildings and books available in local wealthy white schools. When he later attended Howard Law School, Marshall met his teacher, mentor and friend, the great Charles Hamilton Houston. Professor Houston told his students that black lawyers were in fact "social engineers" who could bring justice to black people through the courts.

Taking this to heart, Marshall sought to transform America using the Constitution of the United States. As national counsel for the NAACP, he and his fellow attorneys filed anti-segregation lawsuits in twenty secondary-school cases and twelve higher-education cases. They also sued five real-estate companies, five bus companies and six golf courses. The NAACP lost these cases, but they never gave up. In 1954, Marshall's work resulted in the famous *Brown v. Board of Education* decision by the Supreme Court. This ruling, which declared school segregation unconstitutional and ordered all of America's public schools to integrate, helped energize the entire Civil Rights Movement.

Years later, when Thurgood Marshall became the first black to serve as a Supreme Court Justice, he brought to the land's highest court the same passion he had as a young NAACP attorney. Marshall's opinions, whether in the majority or the minority, always advocated the rights and dignity of all Americas. Through his life's work, Marshall brought justice, equality and security to the lives of millions. Indeed, he "did the best he could with what he had" for us all.

On January 24, 1993, Thurgood Marshall, the first black Justice of the Supreme Court, died in Bethesda, Maryland. His work resulted in the **Brown v. Board of Education** *decision that declared segregation in schools to be unconstitutional.*

≣ Dorie Miller: Hero of Pearl Harbor

It was another Sunday morning in the Navy, and Dorie Miller rose early to begin his unending list of duties. For Messman Miller, this day began like all the others: preparing the mess hall for breakfast, cleaning latrines and washing floors. As a black man in the United States Navy, Miller was relegated to the dirtiest jobs aboard ship. Hard work did not spare him abuse, though, and he heard the endless litany of name-calling: "nigger," "jungle bunny," "spear-chucker."

Yet his spirit was not broken. His father was a Texas sharecropper, and Miller knew that his lot, however hard, was easier than his father's. Dorie Miller was proud to be in the United States Navy and prouder still to be on the powerful battleship the *USS West Virginia*, stationed in Pearl Harbor.

This particular Sunday, as Miller was busy with his duties, the ship suddenly shook violently; explosions, smoke and fire seemed to arise from nowhere. They were under attack! Dorie Miller was never trained for combat and could have easily leapt overboard to safety. Instead, he ran to find the ship's captain under burning debris and metal and dragged him to a safer location. All around Miller were dead and dying men, whizzing machine gun bullets, torpedo explosions, rushing fire and billowing smoke. He ran to an unattended machine gun station, strapped himself in and began firing at the enemy planes circling the *West Virginia* like buzzards preparing for the kill. Though never trained on machine gun operations, he knew enough to load, point and shoot. And shoot he did.

Before the morning was over, Dorie Miller had shot down four Japanese planes. For his bravery, he was awarded the Navy Cross and promoted to Messman First Class. His exploits were told and retold across the nation. Years later, Cuba Gooding, Jr., played him in the movie *Pearl Harbor*.

For courage under fire and initiative beyond duty, few can match the great Dorie Miller. He was not yet twenty-one when he jumped into the machine gun platform on the *USS West Virginia* and into the pages of black history.

On January 24, 1943, Dorie Miller and several crew members were killed when a Japanese submarine sank the aircraft carrier **USS Liscome Bay** *off Makin Island.*

≣ Andrew Young: On Top of King's Mountain

When Andrew Young and the other members of his summer Bible study class decided to climb the summit of King's Mountain, their instructor asked them to ponder their spiritual journeys on their trek. Each was at a different stage in ministry: some were training to be pastors, while others were called to foreign missions. Andrew Young was among those who had yet to decide their future.

Young's spiritual memoir, *A Way Out of No Way*, recounts his climb:

I looked down on the valley and the beauty of it suddenly overwhelmed me. On that clear day in June I could see for miles in every direction. The North Carolina pines were blue-green. The valley was in full bloom. The sun shone brightly in a deep, blue sky. I saw the harmony of the valley as the harmony I longed to have in my inner being…. Suddenly, at the top of King's Mountain, my whole life began anew…. If I was ever born again, this was the moment. A heightened awareness enveloped me. The earth is the Lord's and I am God's child, I said to myself…. I felt one with the heavens and the earth…. I decided that purpose, meaning and order in nature emanated from God and the same must be true for me.

That day on King's Mountain led Young to the ministry, the Civil Rights Movement and a lifelong commitment to justice. His father had wanted Young to become a dentist, but on King's Mountain, Andrew Young felt God leading him elsewhere. Believing that his life was in God's hands, Young stepped into the future on faith. He became a leader in the Southern Christian Leadership Conference, led citizenship classes throughout the South and marched with Martin Luther King, Jr.

Long after King had died and the Movement had been extinguished by violence and apathy, Young continued to live God's purpose. He became the mayor of Atlanta, a congressmen from Georgia and the ambassador to the United Nations. In each role he remembered the poor and disinherited. Young never forgot his call on King's Mountain, and he stayed faithful to justice for the poor, equality for the outcast and democracy for black people. From King's Mountain in Tennessee to the balcony of the Lorraine Motel in Memphis to the United Nations in New York, Andrew Young followed God's plan to bring justice on earth.

In January of 1955, Andrew Young was called to pastor the Bethany Congregational Church in Thomasville, Georgia. He was a prominent figure in the Civil Rights Movement and close confidant of Dr. King. When elected to Congress in 1972, Young was the first black congressman from Georgia since Reconstruction.

JAN 27 ≣ **Mahalia Jackson: "Move On Up a Little Higher"**

Mahalia Jackson brought black church music into the homes, churches and consciousness of America. She grew up in New Orleans, where she lived next to a Holiness storefront church. In 1927, she migrated north to Chicago, where she worked as a maid and laundress. But her love was singing gospel music. She ironed and washed all week, but on Sunday she shook the rafters at Greater Salem Baptist Church. From these humble beginnings arose a great and incomparable gospel singer.

One Sunday in 1946, Mahalia Jackson sang at a tribute to Lucie Campbell, the music director of the Baptist Training Union. Gospel artists from across the Midwest had packed the Mt. Olivet Baptist church, taking turns singing tributes to the popular Ms. Campbell. When Jackson finished her song, "I Will Move On Up a Little Higher," the whole congregation stood up, shouting and waving their arms in joy. When she later recorded the song on the Apollo label, "Move On Up a Little Higher" became the first gospel song ever to sell over one million copies.

Within weeks of the recording, Mahalia Jackson was featured on radio programs, in churches and at other venues across the nation. Her powerful voice was everywhere, and she went on to record over thirty albums during her lifetime. But it was never just about "Mahalia"; God was always at the center of her life and music. Her faith was not a separate part of life; it was her whole life, infusing her relationships and her politics.

After civil rights marches, she sang "I've Been 'Buked and I've Been Scorned"; at Dr. King's funeral, she sang "Precious Lord"; and she often opened civil rights benefit dinners with "We Shall Overcome." Mahalia Jackson's sound, energy and voice were unmistakable. Once her sound penetrated people's souls, they could never forget it. Even today, as Christians hum gospel tunes, their mind's ear can hear the voice of Mahalia Jackson. She sang as though God were real, and her range of expression and depth of faith continues to encourage us all to "move on up a little higher."

Gospel singer Mahalia Jackson died from a heart attack at the age of 61 in Chicago, Illinois, on January 27, 1962. Her song, "Move On Up a Little Higher," was the first gospel recording to sell over one million copies.

JAN 28　　　　　　　≡ Zora Neale Hurston: Their Eyes Were Watching God

The life of Zora Neale Hurston is a dramatic example of how brilliant artists are often unappreciated in their own country and in their own time. When she published *Their Eyes Were Watching God* in 1938, some loved her work, but many, both black and white, criticized her for her portrayal of black life and language.

Hurston grew up in a self-sufficient Florida black community and consequently developed an unquenchable pride in self and blackness. Her work minimized the power of white racism and celebrated black strength. Despite persistent criticism, she published other works on black life and was a significant figure in the Harlem Renaissance. She also studied black folklore and became an accomplished anthropologist.

Hurston later moved back to the South in hopes of finding kindred spirits and quiet venues for writing. She spent years drafting manuscripts for publication, but no book company would touch her work. As years passed without her name appearing in print, she supported herself through menial labor. In 1960, Zora Neale Hurston died in a welfare home and was buried in an unmarked grave.

Despite her undignified death, Hurston's work lives on. Black women loved *Their Eyes Were Watching God* and kept the book alive by circulating copies among themselves. Recently, black women authors such as Alice Walker and Maya Angelou have helped lead a revival of interest in Zora Neale Hurston. *Their Eyes Were Watching God* has become standard reading in universities across the nation, and this black woman who died in obscurity is transforming young readers today. Zora Neale Hurston was just a little too far ahead of the rest of us; fortunately for us, we have a chance to catch up with her.

Zora Neale Hurston, the author of **Their Eyes Were Watching God***, died of a stroke on January 28, 1960, in Fort Pierce, Florida, at 69 years old.*

JAN 29 ≣ Doug Williams: Super Bowl Champ

Life for most of us is a long train of ordinary events interspersed with moments of great joy and terrible sorrow. Life for Doug Williams is no exception.

Though he was a star high school football quarterback of considerable athletic ability, he was recruited by only two schools: the black colleges Southern and Grambling. In the early years of football, it was implicit that blacks were mentally unfit for the challenge of quarterback. Further, many thought that white fans would not accept a black man leading their team, either college or pro. Nevertheless, Williams continued to play a position with no future, and he had an impressive career at Grambling under the tutelage of the great Eddie Robinson. When he was finally drafted by the expansion Tampa Bay Buccaneers, he was one of the first black regular starting quarterbacks in NFL history.

In 1982, his wife became seriously ill. Williams' world was shattered when she later died. Burdened with grief, he left the NFL and returned to Zachary, Louisiana. But when the fledgling United States Football League (USFL) started, Williams decided to resume his career as a quarterback with the Oklahoma Outlaws. Later, when the USFL folded for financial reasons, he quit to coach college football.

Then, in 1986, when Washington Redskins talked Williams out of retirement, he embarked on one of the most remarkable comebacks in sports history. By 1987-88, he was the starting quarterback and led the team to the 1988 Super Bowl. Not only was he the first African-American quarterback to start in a Super Bowl, but he also put on a classic performance. With the Redskins down 10-0 in the second quarter, Williams threw four touchdown passes and led a drive ending in a rushing touchdown, all in the space of a few minutes. The thirty-five points scored in the second quarter set a Super Bowl record as the Redskins went on to win, 42-10. Williams was named the Super Bowl's Most Valuable Player and set several perhaps unbreakable records. Football fans will forever remember the sight of his perfect spirals dropping into the hands of wide-open Redskin receivers that Sunday afternoon.

Doug Williams overcame barriers against black quarterbacks, carried on after his wife's death and came out of retirement twice to become a record-setting Super Bowl winner. Yet his legacy is much more than a Super Bowl ring or a name in the record book. Williams demonstrated that perseverance, faith and resilience can overcome racism, tragedy and personal circumstance.

On January 31, 1988, Doug Williams made Super Bowl history by becoming the first black quarterback to win the MVP.

JAN 30 ≡ **Thomas Andrew Dorsey: "Precious Lord, Take My Hand"**

Of all the musical giants who shaped black religious music, only Thomas Dorsey deserves the title "the father of gospel music." Growing up in the South, Dorsey was shaped by the shouts and moans of the black church. He forged those sounds into the music we now call "black gospel," borrowing freely from the blues and spirituals to create the moving rhythms of gospel. Dorsey composed over a thousand songs, which have laid the foundation of black church music. Every Sunday morning across America, black congregations praise God through his music.

Like most artists, Dorsey created his songs not as the abstract musings of a theoretician but from his own experience. He composed songs of joy and grief because he was acquainted with both. His lyrics were not borrowed; they were felt. His most popular song, "Precious Lord, Take My Hand," is arguably the most popular gospel song in history. Martin Luther King, Jr., Mahalia Jackson and countless other African Americans have said that "Precious Lord" reminds them of God's nearness in life's darkest hours. As well it should, for "Precious Lord" was born in Thomas Dorsey's darkest hour.

In 1932, a young Dorsey was in St. Louis promoting his new gospel sound to churches and radio stations. As was his custom, he called home one evening to speak to his beloved wife, Nettie. A friend answered the phone and told him the unbelievable: His wife had suddenly taken ill and was near death. Dorsey returned home at once.

After an agonizingly slow journey, Dorsey arrived to find his wife dead. Paralyzed with grief, he sat for several days in darkness and wondered why Nettie had to die so young. Had God abandoned him? Had the love he and Nettie felt in Christ been all in vain? Was his faith in God merely an illusion? Had all his faith, all his life, all his love been for nothing?

With tears still on his face, Thomas Dorsey wrote the lyrics for "Precious Lord, Take My Hand." When he put the words to a haunting melody, one of the greatest songs in history was born. Out of the depths of grief came a song of hope. Through all the pain, Dorsey held on to the belief that Jesus was still with him.

He wrote, "My love has been taken from me, I have lost all hope and have nowhere to turn. I reach out my hand into the darkness and pray, 'Take my hand, precious Lord.' I have almost lost my way, but you, Oh Lord, are still precious to me. I want to fall down and give up, but please, help me stand."

Dorsey's song of hope resonates with all who hurt. Somewhere, right now in America, a sorrowful soul is moaning the hopeful lyrics of "Precious Lord, Take My Hand."

Thomas Dorsey, "The Father of Gospel Music," died in Chicago on January 23, 1993, at the age of 94. He wrote "Precious Lord, Take My Hand."

≡ **Reverend Lott Carey: Missionary to Africa**

Lott Carey knew nothing of life but slavery. Born on a Virginia plantation around 1780, every black person he knew—family, friends, everyone—was a slave. They were slaves now, they had always been slaves, and for all he knew they would always be slaves. Yet when all seemed dark, a glimmer of light appeared.

His master decided to hire young Carey out to a tobacco warehouse, where he could earn money for his labors. Though he had to give some of his salary to his master, he was able to keep a portion. He soon realized that if he saved enough money, he could buy his freedom. Carey knew it might take years, but he believed he could do it. His days in the fields and in the warehouse were lighter because of his hopes for freedom.

As he slowly earned money toward liberation, Carey was freed in a manner he did not expect. One Sunday he dropped in on a slave religious service. The preacher said that Jesus Christ was reviled, beaten and crucified so that we might become the children of God. Carey was astonished that the Son of God had chosen to be humble, poor and broken for him, and he at once gave his heart to God. He tasted freedom as a child of God, freed from his own weaknesses, faults and fears.

Years later, Lott Carey saved enough to buy his physical freedom and that of his two children, and he then chose to become a servant of Christ. His gifts as a preacher were recognized when he was called to pastor the African Baptist Church in Richmond, Virginia. Carey's mission field soon expanded beyond his congregation. He remembered how his grandparents had spoken of Africa, and he wanted to preach Christ in the land of his people. Many scoffed at his idea: How could one born a slave conduct a missionary enterprise on another continent? Yet Carey worked to make his vision real.

Through prayer, preaching and fundraising, Carey was able to leave for Africa as a missionary on January 23, 1821. A mere eight years after buying his liberty, Carey, Colin Teague and twenty-eight other black Christians arrived in Monrovia, Liberia. These brave believers overcame many obstacles and built the First Baptist Church of Monrovia.

Rev. Lott Carey had found liberty in Christ, and he gave his life to enable others to taste that same freedom.

On January 23, 1821, Rev. Lott Carey and other Christians from the Richmond African Baptist Missionary Society landed in Monrovia to found that city's First Baptist Church. His legacy lives on in the Lott Carey Foreign Mission Convention, which sends Christian missionaries around the world. The work of this ex-slave resounds each time a member of that Convention preaches the gospel of Jesus Christ.

FEBRUARY

Malcolm X

≡ José Carlos do Patrocinio: Tiger of Abolitionism

Young José Carlos do Patrocinio knew something was drastically wrong: He was mulatto, a child of a white Catholic priest and a black fruit vendor. He was also free, a rarity for a black boy in a land of slaves. But his freedom on the family's plantation near Rio de Janeiro did not shield him from slavery's horrors. He shuddered in fright as he saw white and mulatto planters abusing, whipping and maiming African slaves. By the time he was a teenager, Patrocinio burned with anger at racism and slavery.

When he reached the age of twenty-three, Patrocinio found his voice in print, and by 1877 he was advocating for abolition of slavery in the pages of Rio de Janeiro's daily paper. He was both a journalist and a poet, and his verse was yet another weapon in his crusade for justice. Patrocinio later founded *A Cidade do Rio*, a journal committed to the abolition of slavery in Brazil. So unrelenting and aggressive were his words for freedom that people called Patrocinio "the tiger of abolitionism." He was also a powerful speaker, and listeners declared his speeches as spontaneous events, "acted out with extraordinary power."

José Carlos do Patrocinio poured his soul into the cause of black freedom, and his lifetime crusade culminated in a direct appeal to Princess Isabela to end slavery. On May 13, 1888, she signed the *Lei Aurea*, the "Golden Law," that forever freed the black slaves of Brazil. As the largest home to blacks in the new world, Brazil's liberation of its African slaves was one of the major achievements in history.

Though thousands were engaged in the abolitionist struggle in Brazil, few did more to end slavery than the great "tiger of abolitionism," José Carlos do Patrocinio. On February 1, 1905, he died in Rio de Janeiro at the age of 51.

≡ Reverend Absalom Jones: "God Came Down"

Absalom Jones was the first African American to be ordained a priest in the Episcopal Church. He and the great Richard Allen were among the black parishioners of St. George's Methodist Episcopal Church who were expelled in 1787 for praying in the white pews. Their expulsion laid the seeds of the African Methodist Episcopal (AME) Church.

For Absalom Jones, Christianity was not a philosophical abstraction. Like the Apostle Paul, he believed that Christ lived within us and transformed our whole way of being and acting. He further believed that God answered the cries of the oppressed, that God was not a passive witness to pain but rather came to earth as an active participant to save the lost. The same Christ born in a manger was to be found wherever people were excluded, shut out and enslaved. Therefore, when Jones and his fellow black Christians were forced off their knees at St. George's, they left to found a black church that reflected the liberating hand of God.

Jones' theology was nowhere more evident than in his January 1, 1808, sermon on the Congressional abolition of the African Slave Trade, effective that very day. For him, that Act of Congress was parallel to Israel's exodus from Egypt. Just as the Hebrew writer of Exodus described Israel's liberation as being from the very hand of God, likewise Jones proclaimed that "God came down" to free Africans in this act that legally ended slave trade. Jones' sermon urged those at St. Thomas African Methodist Episcopal Church to thank God continually for the work of liberation and to commit themselves to building God's kingdom.

Jones declared that the misery of black slaves was not in vain, that their apparent endless anguish was God's way of preparing them to be part of the proclamation of the gospel of salvation to the world. He quoted Scripture that "where sin increased, grace abounded all the more" (Romans 5:20). Despite persistent racism and the difficult struggles ahead, his message to the people was the empowering belief that God was above all, in all and through all. He concluded his sermon with the triumphant cry, "Holy, Holy, Holy, Lord God Almighty; the whole earth is full of thy glory. Amen."

Rev. Absalom Jones died on February 13, 1818, in Philadelphia, Pennsylvania. He and Richard Allen formed the Free African Society in 1787, probably the first independent black organization in the United States, and in 1791 he and Allen formed the African Church, one of the first black churches in North America, which later became the African Methodist Episcopal (AME) Church.

FEB 3   ≡ Jean Blackwell Hutson: Building on a Dream

Jean Blackwell Hutson had a dream. As she sat in her dimly lit, cramped office at the New York Public Library, she gazed into the future. Around her were sagging stairs, peeling reading tables and crumbling bricks. Worse, the black book collection under her charge had long been neglected. The valuable African-American collection created by the great bibliophile and curator Arthur A. Schomburg was languishing under dust and cobwebs.

For weeks, Hutson had been asking the white administrators of the library to fund improvements to the building and the collection. After suffering through the passive "we'll think about it" and "we'll get back to you," she finally decided not to wait for someone else to build her dream. One quiet afternoon in her office, she decided to make her own future. Jean Blackwell Hutson, trained in Library Science and head of New York's black collection, sketched her vision for the old Carnegie Library and the Schomburg collection. It was a bold dream. She envisioned a place in the heart of New York where books, art, music and photographs would be the premier black catalog in the world.

As Hutson shared her vision with friends, politicians and potential donors—whoever would listen—money dribbled in slowly. Initially, only a few private donors invested in her cause, yet she persisted, and her incessant lobbying of the public sector finally generated enough to build a new facility. But that was only half the struggle; the next task was to build the collection.

Hutson knew her own history. As the second black woman to graduate from Barnard College after the great Zora Neale Hurston, she knew the history of her family and race and understood the healing power of books. Possessed with love for black culture, Hutson diligently proceeded to develop New York's black library collection. The fifteen thousand books she had inherited grew to five million separately catalogued items. Every book, article and artifact represented a piece of black past intended to awaken the latent power of black readers. Today, Jean Blackwell Hutson's passion continues to open minds and change lives in New York City and beyond.

Librarian Jean Blackwell Huston died February 3, 1998, in New York City. She was 84 years old and left a behind a legacy of education and cultural enlightenment.

FEB 4 — Nicomedes Santa Cruz: Canto Negro

A sensitive young man growing up in Lima, Peru, Nicomedes Santa Cruz saw the curtains of race drawn slowly around him. Though his father was a gifted writer, racism had denied him both opportunity and fame. The publishing world was but one area where discrimination reigned. Africans in Lima had far fewer opportunities and far more misery than fairer-skinned Peruvians. Prejudice had penetrated even the Catholic Church, which balked at recognizing the sainthood of popular Afro-Peruvian friar Martin de Porres.

Like his father, Santa Cruz loved to write. He loved it so much that, despite his father's frustrations, he quit his ironworker job to pursue a literary career. His zeal for justice and passion for poetry combined to make Nicomedes Santa Cruz a significant Afro-Latin writer. In addition to being recognized for several published works, he was also known for his live performances and sound recordings. By utilizing so many venues, Santa Cruz became well known among the common people of Peru.

Heard on radio and television throughout Latin America, Cruz sang and performed his poetic works, sustaining the popular tradition of folk poetry in Peru, while demanding justice and celebrating romance with equal fervor. Of his three sound recordings, his most memorable was *Canto Negro (Black Song)*, a classic released in 1968 that became an anthem of black pride.

Cruz supported African anti-colonial revolutions, denounced racism in Peru and exposed the exploitation of lower-class blacks in violent sports, such as boxing. The net of his compassion was cast wide indeed. His poems also celebrated the struggles of Cuban peasants, indigenous tribes and other oppressed peoples. In works such as *Cumanana*, *Canto a mi Peru (Song to My Peru)* and *Ritmos negros de Peru (Black Rhythms of Peru)*, Nicomedes Santa Cruz boldly upheld the beauty and dignity of black Peruviansm, and his poems remain literary masterpieces on the black Latin American experience.

A poet with a great passion for justice, Nicomedes Santa Cruz died on February 4, 1992, in Madrid, Spain.

FEB 5 ≡ **Black Sanitation Workers of Memphis: "I Am a Man"**

Perhaps one of the most stirring images of the Civil Rights Movement is a photo of black garbage workers in Memphis, Tennessee, protesting their working conditions by carrying signs that read, simply, "I Am a Man."

These working conditions were tragically portrayed on February 1, 1968. On that rainy afternoon, Echol Cole and Robert Walker rode in the back of a putrid, aging garbage truck. The city of Memphis relegated blacks to the most dangerous and difficult jobs, and this was no exception. The workers rode in older trucks the city kept in service despite complaints of malfunction and failure. In addition, black workers were not provided with gloves, uniforms, showers or anything else to combat the garbage they hauled. They and their trucks smelled of rotting food, dead chickens, stale milk and rancid meats.

On that rainy afternoon, as the truck drove toward the Shelby Drive dump, the driver heard the hydraulic ram activate and immediately pulled over. It was too late: Cole, thirty-six, and Walker, thirty, had both been killed. To compound the tragedy, the city of Memphis had classified Cole and Walker as hourly employees, so they died without insurance or workers' compensation, leaving their families in poverty.

For the black sanitation workers of Memphis, this was the last disgrace. They had been fighting city officials for years for the same rights and working conditions afforded their white counterparts. Sanitation worker T.O. Jones, who had been organizing American Federal, State, County and Municipal Employees (AF-SCME's) Local 1733 on behalf of black garbage workers, and his assistant, Joe Warren, were determined to respond. Despite the local's low membership and the city's refusal to recognize them, they began a strike and protest movement that lasted for weeks. Black preachers, such as Rev. Ezekial Bell; black women activists, such as Maxine Smith, Cornelia Crenshaw and Tarlese Mathews; and many more from the black community marched with the garbage workers.

When Martin Luther King, Jr., heard of their struggle, he diverted time from his long-planned Poor People's March to come to Memphis. His help, however, ended abruptly on April 4, 1968, when he was assassinated. But the conditions that spawned the strike continued, and Local 1733 and their supporters did not rest until the city agreed to some of their demands. The black sanitation workers of Memphis did not get all they wanted, and their actions were overshadowed by the death of Dr. King. Yet they left us an inspiring legacy of courage and persistence.

On February 1, 1968, black sanitation workers Echol Cole and Robert Walker were killed by a malfunctioning compactor in an old sanitation truck. Black workers had been complaining to management about the older trucks for months, to no avail.

FEB 6   ≡ Arthur Robert Ashe, Jr.: Days of Grace

Arthur Robert Ashe, Jr., rose to the top of the tennis world. He was a handsome, articulate black man who used the tennis court as both sports arena and stage where his athletic talents and his social character were on display. In 1970, Ashe won the Australian Open; in 1975, the Wimbledon; and he went on to win forty-nine other tennis tournaments. His black skin in white tennis shoes and white shorts on a green court, his Afro and his smile, and his amazing moves on the court became known all over the world.

Ashe, however, was more than a great tennis player. As he mounted the pinnacle of his sport, he moved the spotlight away from himself and onto African and African-American suffering. When sports reporters asked questions about tennis, he would respond, "What about apartheid?" or "What about southern brutality?" Personal fame and private glory meant little to him as long as his brothers and sisters were excluded from equality.

Inadvertently infected with the AIDS virus, Ashe was also one of the first popular figures to fight that horrible syndrome. An interviewer from *People* magazine once asked Ashe about his struggle with AIDS.

"Mr. Ashe, I guess this must be the heaviest burden you have had to bear, isn't it?"

He paused a moment and answered firmly, "No."

"Oh," replied the shocked reporter, "then it must be your 1980 heart attack."

Ashe looked the reporter in the eye and said, "You're not going to believe this, but being black is the greatest burden I've had to bear."

Stunned, the reporter muttered, "You can't mean that."

When the interview was published, white Americans were shocked. Even some of Ashe's white friends, who thought they knew him, criticized him for his comment. Blacks, however, nodded knowingly. They understood him when he said that racism was a heavier burden, because racism was omnipresent and affected people of color everywhere. Heart attacks and cancer, deadly as they are, were random and sporadic. Racism on the other hand, was both deliberate and ever-present.

The glitter of tennis titles and headlines never blinded Ashe to the suffering of others. He could not forget Johannesburg, Soweto, Watts or Harlem. His fame and success, his heart attack and fight with AIDS were always secondary to the joys and burdens of being black for Arthur Ashe.

Arthur Robert Ashe, Jr., published a three-volume work, **Hard Road to Glory,** *on the history of African-American athletes. His autobiography,* **Days of Grace,** *details his life and struggles. He died of complications from AIDS on February 6, 1993, in New York City.*

FEB 7 ≡ Edward Wilmot Blyden: "Greatest Defender of the Negro Race"

Edward Wilmot Blyden was a pioneer in the Pan-African Movement. He came to the United States from the Virgin Islands around 1850 and was immediately confronted with the Fugitive Slave Law. This vile law made every free black person in the United States a potential slave, as white kidnappers required little "proof" to return an alleged "ex-slave" to the plantation. Blyden vigorously protested this despicable law, which led him to believe that blacks would never be respected in America.

For Blyden, the haven of black salvation was Africa. He believed that while Christ saved people from their sins, only Africa could save the black race from racism and disrespect. After famous Calvinist preacher John Knox encouraged him to become a Presbyterian minister, Blyden traveled to Monrovia, Liberia, to implement his vision of African self-determination. Over the years, he would make seven round trips in all, each time bringing ex-slaves eager to start life anew in their Motherland. He scoffed at those who told him to remain in America, noting that any slight progress blacks could make in America was "irrelevant." He preached, and his followers believed, that Christ and Africa were their only hope in the world.

In 1857, Blyden wrote the classic *A Vindication of the Negro Race*. This work refuted the widely prevalent pseudo-science of black inferiority that was so universally accepted by this country's economic, educational and religious institutions. Several years later, Blyden became disillusioned with Christian complicity with racism, and in 1887 he wrote *Christianity, Islam and the Negro Race*. Some seventy years before Elijah Muhammad's formation of the Nation of Islam, he wrote that Islam was "the religion of the lost black man."

All his life Blyden worked to overcome the onslaught of European colonialism, white supremacy and economic deprivation, and to elevate his race from the ravages of racism and the bondage of self-hate. West African activist J. E. Casely-Hayford described Blyden as "a god descended upon earth to teach Ethiopians anew the way of life…a John the Baptist among his brethren, preaching national salvation."

As the first great Pan-African activist, Edward Wilmot Blyden encouraged black men and women not to sacrifice their souls on the altar of submission and shame but to embrace their African roots.

Edward Wilmot Blyden died on February 7, 1912, in Freetown, Sierra Leone. Stained-glass windows in a large meeting hall in Lagos, Nigeria, memorialize his life. Beneath Blyden's photograph are the words, "Greatest Defender of the Negro Race."

FEB 8   ≣ Saint Josephine Bakhita: "The Black Mother"

Like other Sudanese girls, young Bakhita often played in the fields near her village. One afternoon, while chatting with imaginary friends and animals, little Bakhita was snatched away by slave traders. Her secure, comfortable world was immediately transformed into a vortex of trauma, abuse and misery. Of the five different owners she had during the next ten years as a slave, some were kind, but others were barbarous. Her last owner, Signora Michieli, an Italian hotel owner, grew fond of Bakhita and treated her like family.

After years in Genoa, Michieli and her daughter, Mimmina, planned to leave to manage one of their hotels on the shores of the Red Sea. Before moving, however, Michieli decided to introduce Bakhita to Catholicism. Michieli enrolled her in a convent, where she stayed for ten months, learning the Catholic faith. As nuns taught the love of God, the sacraments, the Blessed Virgin Mary, the need for prayer, the communion of saints and other essential Catholic traditions, Bakhita sat in rapt attention. She saw that despite humanity's cruelty God was always present and loved her deeply. When Signora Michieli came to take her home, Bakhita refused to leave. While she loved the Michieli's, she loved God even more. Bakhita told the nuns, and later wrote, "I love the Signora dearly, and to part from Mimmina cut me to the heart. But I shall not leave this place because I cannot risk losing God."

Reluctantly and with great sadness, Michieli agreed, and Bakhita stayed at the convent of the Daughters of Charity of Canossa. She became a nun in the order, and her prayerfulness, humility and faith were evident in all she did. Sister Josephine Bakhita became a pillar in the ministry of the Daughters of Charity, and her selfless service to orphans and the sick earned her the title *Madre Moretta* ("The Black Mother").

Whenever she was invited to speak, Bakhita stood before the crowd and said, "Be good, love the Lord, pray for those who do not know him still!" The Black Mother would then make the sign of the cross and walk off the stage. Her simple words resonated as those gathered felt her sincere adoration of Christ. People would go home inspired, feeling closer to God and more devoted to their life of prayer.

Sister Josephine Bakhita was canonized a saint by the Catholic Church on October 1, 2000. Her love for God still influences those in search of holiness. In the cathedral in Obeid, Sudan, Catholics light candles, kneel before the icon of Madre Moretta and ask her to lead them closer to Christ.

Josephine Bakhita, called "The Black Mother" by her people, died on February 8, 1947, in Obeid in the Sudan. She was canonized a saint by the Catholic Church on October 1, 2000.

FEB 9   ≡ Paul Laurence Dunbar: Poet Laureate of the Negro Race

What rhyme emerges from the children of slaves? What words, verse and meter seep from the pen of one whose roots are planted in the soil of exclusion? Scan the work of Paul Laurence Dunbar, and you will find the answer. Of all the things a black boy could pursue in the cauldron of white supremacy at the time, poetry was perhaps one of the most difficult.

Dunbar's classic poems, "Sympathy" and "We Wear the Mask," convey the black experience in ways volumes of statistics could never attain. Even a cursory reading of "Sympathy" insists that every reader feel the pain of degradation. The centerpiece verse of "Sympathy"—"I know why the caged bird sings"— is so compelling that years later poet Maya Angelou used it as the title of her signature work. The powerful message of "We Wear the Mask," a saga of how blacks survived in the early 1900s, sadly still applies to black life one hundred years later.

Dunbar's first two books of poetry, *Oak and Ivy* (1893) and *Majors and Minors* (1895), were published during a time historians consider an especially difficult period in black American life. Yet despite the agony, Dunbar wrote of hope and promise. His poems, "He Had His Dream" and "The Colored Soldiers," look realistically at life's sorrow but affirm that courage and perseverance will prevail.

Dunbar was criticized for his use of southern dialect, but he defended that technique, noting that he was reflecting the way ex-slaves talked. His response to critics was, essentially, "Why pretend the crippling legacy of illiteracy and racism does not exist?"

During his lifetime, Dunbar never received the acclaim his poetry was due, and he was broken by both a failed marriage and the scourge of alcoholism. His poetry mirrored not only the sorrows of the black experience in general but also his own misery in particular. Many of Dunbar's works—such as "Religion," "Ballad," "Keep A-Pluggin' Away" and "Not They Who Soar"—are windows to the universal human experience, beautifully expressing our deepest yearnings. More significantly, the power of Dunbar's work is pertinent not only for his time but for ours.

Paul Laurence Dunbar, the poet laureate of the Negro race, died of tuberculosis on February 9, 1906. He died peacefully, in his mother's arms, in Dayton, Ohio, the city where he was born.

FEB 10   ☰ Reverend James Cleveland: Crown Prince of Gospel

Leader of the Gospel Workshop of America, composer of hundreds of songs and a charismatic revival leader, Rev. James Cleveland was an influential gospel ambassador. At sixteen, he wrote the masterful "Grace Is Sufficient." Many say that Cleveland is the symbol, personification and icon of the modern gospel sound; his songs are the foundation for black choirs across America. Every gospel choir, in high school, on college campuses or in church, has been influenced by "The Crown Prince of Gospel."

It is impossible to calculate Cleveland's impact on the vitality of the black church. Millions of black Christians have been strengthened by the growls, chants and meditations of his music. Choir directors, soloists and arrangers have been transformed by lessons learned in his Gospel Workshop of America.

Similarly, who can measure the spiritual uplift his songs have brought to black believers. "God Has Smiled on Me," "I Don't Feel No Ways Tired," "Lord, Help Me to Hold Out" and "I'll Do His Will" are but a few of his gifts. Black folks hum and moan these songs daily; they are the psalms of lament and praise of the collective black body of Christ.

James Cleveland captured, as few have, the beauty of the black church. His music sang black theology: hope in the midst of crisis, faith instead of sorrow. His songs continue to resonate with all whose journeys are difficult, and his music injects weary souls with the jubilation of black faith.

Gospel music composer Rev. James Cleveland died at the age of 60 in Los Angeles, California, on February 9, 1991. He has been called "The Crown Prince of Gospel."

≡ National Association for the Advancement of Colored People
Courage in the Struggle

America in 1908 was a harsh place for black folk. Slavery, just a generation away, had been replaced by violence, sharecropping and segregation. In Springfield, Illinois, whites erupted in a six-day orgy of lynching, burnings and murder. Black homes and businesses were torched; men, women and children were beaten; dozens were killed. The home of Abraham Lincoln had become host to a brutal race riot. Any hope for black redemption in America seemed to have been left smoldering in the embers of burned-out black homes.

In the midst of this hopelessness and despair, the NAACP was born. Black and white civil rights leaders were outraged at the Springfield riot and issued a call for action. Sixty leaders convened in New York at the National Negro Conference on February 12, 1909, to respond to white brutality. From these discussions arose the National Association for the Advancement of Colored People, clearly among the most significant civil rights organizations in American history.

No injustice escaped notice and reaction from the NAACP. Wherever racist acts raised their ugly form, local chapters of the NAACP came out fighting. Members of the NAACP risked employment, family and security to challenge white supremacy. In South Carolina, schoolteachers were fired for admitting their membership, and in Mississippi white sheriffs beat anyone associated with the NAACP. Many members lived by the creed espoused in Claude McKay's classic poem, "If We Must Die." The poem's powerful ending, "pressed to the wall…but fighting back," became in many respects the motto of the NAACP. Fighting the world's most racist power structure, out-numbered and under-funded, the NAACP stood tall in its fight for justice. Gradually, school desegregation, voting rights and employment discrimination were transformed because of the legal challenges of the NAACP.

Our lives and livelihood have been changed by the glorious legacy of the black leaders nurtured in the bosom of the NAACP: W.E.B. DuBois, Mary Church Terrell, Ida Wells-Barnett, Walter White, James Weldon Johnson, Ella Baker, Roy Wilkins, Thurgood Marshall, Ben Chavis, Benjamin Hooks, Kweisi Mfume and thousands of anonymous black folks. May we never forget their courage.

The National Association for the Advancement of Colored People (NAACP) was founded out of the National Negro Conference held on February 12, 1909, in in New York City.

≡ Reverend Henry Highland Garnet: "Let Your Motto Be Resistance!"

It took only one speech for Rev. Henry Highland Garnet to transform the abolitionist movement forever. Before Garnet's speech, abolitionists talked about a slow, gradual end of slavery, one where slave owners would actually be financially compensated for their losses. After Garnet, the idea of black violent rebellion seized the imagination of many.

Rev. Henry Highland Garnet, a black, free-born Presbyterian minister, articulated the horrors of human captivity as few ever had. He declared that slavery was so brutal and dehumanizing that anything less than its violent overthrow was a sin. He preached that slaves should not wait for benevolent masters or compromising abolitionists but should strike the blow themselves. Abolitionists from across America stirred in their seats as Garnet urged blacks to take up arms and free themselves:

> Brethren, the time has come when you must act for yourselves.... Brethren, arise! Strike for your lives and liberties.... You act as though you were made for the special use of these devils. You act as though your daughters were born to pamper the lusts of your masters and overseers. And worse than all, you tamely submit while your lords tear your wives from your embraces and defile them before your eyes.... Let your motto be resistance! Resistance! No oppressed people have ever secured their liberty without resistance. Brethren, adieu! Trust in the living God. Labor for the peace of the human race, and remember that you are FOUR MILLIONS.

Rev. Garnet's speech that night did more than radicalize the abolitionist movement. His call for active resistance to oppression continues to influence every generation tired of oppression and injustice.

Rev. Henry Highland Garnet urged black rebellion in Buffalo, New York, at the 1843 National Negro Convention. His speech was so radical that many sought to prevent it from being reprinted. Garnet died on February 12, 1882, in Monrovia, Liberia.

≡ Blackball: Birth of the Negro National League

On a chilly February morning, several cars cruised slowly to the Kansas City YMCA. They parked, and men in coats and hats walked up the stairs and into the YMCA's unheated meeting room. They settled in their chairs and the meeting got underway. Rube Foster, owner of the American Giants, was the first to speak. The other men leaned forward to listen:

We are gathered here, gentlemen, to put our resources together and build a black professional baseball league. With commitment and organization, we can create a place where black teams and black players can perform for black fans.

In attendance at this historic gathering were the black and white owners of the existing professional black baseball teams: C.I. Taylor of the Indianapolis ABCs, John Mathews of the Dayton Marcos, "Tenny" Blount of the Detroit Stars, J.L. Wilkinson of the Kansas City Monarchs, Charlie Mills of the St. Louis Giants and Joe Green of the Chicago Giants. Rube Foster represented the American Giants and also had the proxy of the Cuban Stars.

These men knew that Major League Baseball was nowhere close to integrating the game. They also knew that as long as black squads played as independent teams, they would never be taken seriously. The owners agreed with Foster, pooled their collective resources and created the Negro National League.

Organized play began in 1921 and would eventually showcase Josh Gibson, Satchel Paige, Oscar Charleston, Martin Dihigo, Leon Day, Ray Dandridge, Turkey Stearnes, "Cool Papa" Bell, "Bullet Joe" Rogan and thousands of others. Black players, umpires, sports writers and business owners kept the Negro Leagues alive for over thirty years. Negro baseball produced dynasties that rivaled the Major Leagues, as the incomparable Kansas City Monarchs won seventeen pennants, and the great Homestead Grays won twelve, including nine in a row. The East-West All-Star game featured blackball's best talent, and those contests consistently outdrew white Major League all-star games. The bosom of the Negro Leagues produced the black stars that integrated, and in fact transformed, the heretofore white Major Leagues, including men such as Jackie Robinson, Roy Campanella, Hank Aaron, Willie Mays and Larry Doby.

White racism had excluded blacks from the "national pastime," but black folks had created an organization that became the pride of the black community.

On February 13, 1920, Rube Foster and others created the Negro National League. Organized blackball would continue to the 1960s. The black leagues were created by segregation and destroyed by integration; in between, they provided excitement, opportunity and pride.

≡ Diane Nash: From Student to Movement Leader

Diane Nash was a talented black college student at Fisk University in Nashville, Tennessee. In the 1960s, not many black children had the opportunity to attend a four-year college, so the Nash family was very proud of their girl.

One February night, however, Nash's soul was uneasy and her mind restless. The next day, she and other students planned to sit-in, in protest of segregated lunch counters in downtown Nashville. This was not an easy decision, for whites did not like their rigid social norms threatened. The students, however, had been attending classes taught by the great Rev. James Lawson on nonviolent protest, and they were inspired to take action against injustice. Through their workshops on nonviolence and peace, they came to believe nonviolent protest was the only way to defeat segregation.

But that night, in her dorm room, the excitement had faded. Nash looked at photos of her family, glanced over at her textbooks and upcoming assignments, and questioned whether she should risk her future on this perilous calling. She and her friends could be beaten, spat upon, arrested, jailed or even worse. Her health, security, education and safety were all at risk. Yet, despite her fears, she resolved to be sitting in her lunch counter seat at the appointed time.

The next afternoon Diane Nash resisted segregation, and her life was never the same. This protest was the first of many, and shortly thereafter she was elected chair of the student steering committee. Slowly, the fame of Diane Nash spread throughout the South. Though her internal doubts persisted, Nash nevertheless confronted jailers, sheriffs and mobs with a courage that amazed her peers.

Later that year, the quiet Nash faced the mayor of Nashville on the courthouse steps during a peaceful march. He tried to patronize and belittle her, calling her "little lady" and boasting of his commitment to equality. Nash was unmoved, and the eighteen-year-old faced down the mayor of Nashville until he agreed to end segregation of Nashville's lunch counters. This was no small feat, for each fissure in the wall of racism weakened the entire structure for eventual collapse.

Diane Nash was a determined battering ram, hammering away at segregation and bigotry. Moving from self-doubt to a vital role in a historic freedom movement, Nash transformed her doubts into a fearlessness that became legendary; she was indeed one of the many heroes of black history and democratic struggle.

February 14, 1960, several college students, influenced by James Lawson's classes on nonviolence, protested segregation of Nashville's lunch counters. Diane Nash became one of the key leaders in the Student Nonviolent Coordinating Committee (SNCC).

≣ The Dominican Republic: The Legacy of San Lorenzo de las Minas

The black liberation struggle in the Dominican Republic began with the arrival of the first African slaves on the island of Hispanola. "Discovered" by Christopher Columbus in 1492, Hispanola was divided by the French and Spanish into Haiti and the Dominican Republic in 1697. The presence of slaves started with the arrival of Columbus and continued until the 1800s. Yet even before the division of Hispanola, blacks on the island had challenged European slavery. In 1678, Africans who had escaped from servitude had founded the Maroon community at San Lorenzo de las Minas. Maroons took their name from the Spanish word *cimarron*, used to describe cattle that escaped their masters. Such communities were common in the Americas, particularly the West Indies, Florida and Brazil. As ex-slaves built a community with schools, jobs and homes, San Lorenzo symbolized black self-determination.

In 1822, the island was temporarily reunited, and Haitian president Jean-Pierre Boyer abolished slavery. He also did something even more remarkable. In 1824-25, he invited six thousand free African Americans to live in the Dominican Republic. They founded the communities of Samana and Puerto Plata, and even today visitors can see the vestiges of black American influence.

Through the history of the Dominican Republic, leaders and common folk have responded to oppression with courageous sacrifices for national self-determination. In 1865, black Dominicans opposed Spanish domination, and in 1919, they fought U.S. occupation. Their land may have been poor and destitute, but it was theirs, and the people resisted all attempts to reduce them to political pawns.

Afro-Dominican heroes include people such as Pablo Ali, a slave who won his freedom by fighting the Spanish; Blas Jimenez and Manuel de la Cabral, who wrote poems and prose in celebration of Dominican independence; the great Florinda Muñoz Soriano, who died fighting for peasant rights and dignity; and José Joaquin Pueblo, who fought bravely for national sovereignty.

Because these black Dominicans threatened the system of inequality and privilege that ravaged their nation, they suffered violence and repression. On December 28, 1962, the military converged on the Afro-Dominican community of Palma Sala and massacred every man, woman and child. From the founding of the Maroon community of San Lorenzo de las Minas to the massacre at Palma Sala, the history of the Dominican Republic is a marvelous saga of the unconquerable human spirit. Long live the people of the Dominican Republic!

The Dominican Republic has suffered from poverty and domination for centuries. Yet, a vibrant zest for life pervades the culture and dignity of the people. On February 27, 1844, the Dominican Republic achieved its independence from Spain. This date marked but one of the many milestones in the struggles of Afro-Dominicans.

≣ "Lift Every Voice and Sing": The Negro National Anthem

"Lift every voice and sing till earth and heaven ring, Ring with the harmonies of Liberty…." At the sound of the first note, the whole black throng in the auditorium rises from their seats. Standing proud as they sing, they feel the power of the words wash over them. The haunting melody lifts their hearts, and the words, those beautiful words, bring tears to some. The panoramic struggle for black dignity is summed up in the words of James Weldon Johnson's song.

On February 12, 1900, in honor of Abraham Lincoln's birthday, James Weldon Johnson led a children's chorus in singing lyrics that he had recently written and that his brother, John Rosamond Johnson, had set to music. Their song "Lift Every Voice and Sing" slowly crept into the canon of black music and within twenty years was considered the Negro National Anthem. The words resonated with black Americans, expressing their deepest sorrows and proudest moments.

A talented writer and devoted organizer, Johnson was deeply moved by the faith of the common folk. Though a child of the tiny Southern black middle class in the 1880s, he was rooted in the life of the whole race. At age twenty, he traveled the Georgia backwoods to teach the children of slaves. After several weeks of teaching, he wrote:

> They were me, and I was they…a force stronger than blood made us one. I discerned that the forces behind the slow but persistent movement forward of the race lie, ultimately, in them, that when the vanguard of the movement must fall back, it must fall back on them.

Johnson was stirred by the latent power of the black masses, and he caught the mood, essence and soul of the black experience in his lyrics. They are a testament to hope in the midst of despair, faith when all seems lost. They are a tribute to the past—"We have come, over a way that with tears have been watered"—and a promise for the future. "Lift Every Voice" is sustained as the children of the wounded continue to march on:

> Sing a song full of the faith that the dark past has taught us.
> Sing a song full of the hope that the present has brought us.
> Facing the rising sun of our new day begun,
> Let us march on till victory is won.

James Weldon Johnson wrote the lyrics to "Lift Every Voice and Sing" for a choir of school children in Florida. The song was first sung on February 12, 1900, for the anniversary of Abraham Lincoln's birthday.

≣ James Yates: The Abraham Lincoln Brigade

James Yates was one of eighty-three African Americans who fought in the Abraham Lincoln Brigade in the Spanish Civil War. These men—and at least one black woman, a nurse named Salaria Kee—believed that the fight against fascism in Spain was the same as their war against racism at home. They were true internationalists, devoted to black liberation in America and human solidarity in Spain.

Born in Mississippi, Yates often fled to the woods with his neighbors when rumors of approaching lynch mobs swept through town. He later moved to Chicago, where he met communists fighting for the right to eat, live and learn. During his years as a dining car waiter, he became a union organizer to combat the abuses heaped upon black workers. When Mussolini invaded Ethiopia, Yates and his friend Alonzo Watson applied for passports to Ethiopia to assist the fight against the Italians—but their requests for passports were refused. The State Department did not want black Americans coming to the aid of a beleaguered African nation.

Ten weeks later, Francisco Franco overthrew the recently elected People's Republic in Spain, and Adolph Hitler and Benito Mussolini began sending bombers, arms and troops to help him. Irish brigades, German anti-fascists and American radicals rushed to Spain to risk their lives in the showdown between the Republic and tyranny. This time, Yates and his comrades were among them.

Yates and others returned home after the fascist victory, but for them the struggle was not over. For the next five decades, survivors of the Abraham Lincoln Brigade worked for peace and liberation. Long after the Spanish Civil War had ended, they led anti-war rallies and other movements for democracy. James Yates symbolized their commitment as he remained faithful to progressive politics the rest of his life. The Abraham Lincoln Brigade motto, *"No pasaran"* ("They shall not pass") was not empty rhetoric. It was a rallying cry in the unending fight against the forces that conspire to crush humanity.

On February 20, 1937, James Yates and 300 others sailed from New York to France to begin their journey to fight in the Spanish Civil War. In all, about 83 black men and women fought in the Abraham Lincoln Brigade against the fascist troops of Franco, Hitler and Mussolini.

≣ Mary Smith Kelsick Peake: America's First Black Teacher

Booming cannons at Fort Sumter signaled the beginning of the Civil War, the re-unification of the United States of America and the beginning of the long march from black slavery to black freedom. Amid the smoke and carnage of the Civil War, black folk were determined to create a new world for themselves. A significant but unknown event at the war's beginning was the appointment of Mary Smith Kelsick Peake as a teacher at Fort Monroe, Virginia. When Peake was hired by the American Missionary Association to teach ex-slaves in Virginia, she became the first in a long and distinguished line of dedicated black teachers.

As the forerunner of many future black teachers, Peake believed that education would expand opportunity for black children. With a commitment her many successors would later emulate, Peake worked hours beyond the job description, encouraged her students to excel and conveyed to her children the self-respect necessary to survive in a cruel world.

Through her patient teaching, Peake planted seeds that flower even today. On September 17, 1861, she opened a day school for children in Hampton, Virginia, and soon afterward taught adult school in the evening. Several years later, the adult school evolved into the Hampton Institute, a popular, historically black college.

Like Peake, legions of black teachers have given of themselves so that black children can march into the world with both knowledge and self-confidence. (Author's note: I know; I'm one of them. As the beneficiary of the work of black teachers in Washington, D.C., public schools, I experienced firsthand the profound contributions of such dedicated black teachers.)

On February 22, 1862, Mary Smith Kelsick Peake died of tuberculosis. She is thought to be the first professional black teacher in the United States of America.

≣ The Nubian Christian Church: The Power of Faith

For over one thousand years after the death and resurrection of Christ, African Christians overcame massacres, desecration and bloodshed to hold tenaciously on to their faith. As the Western church flourished in Rome and the Eastern church grew in Byzantium, Christians in the ancient black kingdom of Nubia in Northeastern Africa built a church that withstood a sustained and ferocious assault. Over the sweep of centuries, various Christian sects, Muslims and other invaders tried to destroy the Nubian Christian church.

According to legend, the Nubian church began when Saint Philip the Apostle converted Candace of Nubia, and she returned home zealous about her new faith. That conversion grew into a flourishing Christian church in eastern Africa. The Nubian faith brought together holy sacraments, biblical stories and black icons in a unique way that sustained these believers throughout the ordeals of life. A popular Nubian icon was of Shadrach, Mesach and Abednego surviving the king's fire. The icon shows the three men braving the fire, their lives spared by the protection of God's messenger, Michael the Archangel. Nubian Christians loved that story because they believed God also protected their lives, faith and families, which were constantly under attack.

In response to God's mercy, the Nubians lived their faith without wavering. In testimony of their high virtues, the Prophet Muhammad once said of them, "The man who does not have a brother or sister should choose one from among the Nubians."

In 1275, after several hundred years of persecution, the Sultan Bibars sought to eliminate the Nubian Christian church forever. The King of Nubia was imprisoned and the famous Church of Jesus was burned and desecrated. All the icons, candles, altars and silver vessels in the church were taken away and destroyed. Many Nubian Christians were massacred and others exiled, and the Sultan boasted that the Nubian Christians would never be seen again.

Two hundred and fifty years later, however, a Portuguese priest went to Nubia to establish a mission outpost and preach the gospel to the "pagans." To his astonishment, he found over one hundred and fifty local Nubian Christian churches in isolated parts of the country. Unknown to much of the West, Nubian Christians had been baptizing, preaching and praying all these years.

Eventually, persecution and isolation did lead to the disappearance of the Nubian Christian church, but not before hundreds of anonymous black Christians had held fast to Christ as few believers have done before or since.

For over one thousand years, the Nubian Christian church withstood invasions from Egypt, persecutions from other faiths and geographic isolation. Their survival over those centuries is a testament to the steadfast power of black faith.

≡ Frederick Douglass: "A New World"

Frederick Douglass was born into slavery, but that foul institution could not stain him with its foul odor forever. Slavery had power—masters, overseers, night patrols, courts, law, the military and the Congress—while the slaves had nothing but a desire for freedom. So ingenious was Douglass' escape from slavery that his first autobiography, published during slavery, was silent on its details. He did not want other slaves to lose that avenue of escape. When Douglass stepped onto northern soil, he celebrated as if born again. He later proclaimed, "A new world opened up to me." Yet he did not want this new world to be his alone.

Frederick Douglass made himself into the foremost African-American leader of his time—and perhaps of all time. He founded and edited *The North Star*, a radical abolitionist paper. He quarreled with William Lloyd Garrison, the great abolitionist, when he felt Garrison was too moderate. Douglass met John Brown before his raid on Harper's Ferry, recruited thousands of black soldiers for the Civil War and urged President Lincoln to transform the war's aim from saving the Union to ending slavery. Douglass was one of the first men to demand women's suffrage, and his books, *My Bondage and My Freedom* and *Narrative of the Life of Frederick Douglass*, are classics in African-American literature. At the end of the Civil War, Douglass fought on for black liberation and never stopped. Even as an aging frail man, Douglass joined the great Ida B. Wells in her quest for anti-lynching laws.

Douglass once wrote, "I never ran away from anything, except the bondage of slavery." During one of the darkest periods in black history, Douglass rose from slavery to become a black leader working to build a "new world" for his people.

Writer, abolitionist and activist Frederick Douglass died on February 20, 1895, in Washington, D.C. His writings, speeches and political work helped shape future generations of black leaders.

≡ Malcolm X: Nobody but Malcolm

The epic saga of Malcolm X conveys the agony and beauty of blackness. His life was marked by pain, loss, growth and transformation. His father was murdered, his mother institutionalized and his life's dreams mangled by racism. In response, Malcolm became a burglar, a pimp and a gambler—a parasite who preyed on black and white alike. Like many black men before and since, Malcolm was locked away in prison. Impressed by the self-respect and dignity of incarcerated Muslims, Malcolm dedicated his life to Allah. He embraced Islam as taught by the Honorable Elijah Muhammad and read everything in the prison library to learn the cause and solution to black misery. Through the Nation of Islam, Malcolm X elevated himself from the depths of street life to the heights of black humanity. Prayer, fasting and dedication transformed him from a parasite into a liberator.

Once released from prison, Malcolm's speeches, insights, wit and courage captured the deepest aspirations of black Americans. He said what many wanted to but could not, and whites soon considered him their worst nightmare—a bold and fearless black man. Just the mention of his name conjured images of uncontrollable black rage unleashed on an "innocent" white America. In contrast, blacks found inspiration and solace in his boldness; no black man spoke that way to white folks and lived to talk about it. Nobody but Malcolm.

Perhaps the most salient traits of Malcolm X were his profound growth at every stage of life and his personal integrity. He spoke the truth as he saw it and never hesitated to act on his convictions. His move away from the Nation of Islam to form the Muslim Mosque, Inc., threatened his mentor and leader, Elijah Muhammad. His brilliant insights into the significance of Mecca, Vietnam and Kenya made him a danger to white world supremacy. Yet despite threats from black Muslims, hatred from white America and surveillance by the greatest governmental power on earth, Malcolm never wavered. All he wanted for himself and his race was the respect due all human beings. His commitment to black humanity was undaunted.

Malcolm X resonates with us not because he changed the world but because he changed himself. He demonstrated self-mastery and triumph over the life's most formidable obstacles. Malcolm Little the boy became Detroit Red the hustler; Detroit Red became Malcolm X the prophet; Malcolm X became El Hajj Malik El Shabazz, the universal human. Circumstances and fate did not dictate his life; Malcolm X climbed from the abyss to scale the heights of human dignity.

Malcolm X died in a hail of shotgun and pistol bullets in the Audubon Ballroom in Harlem on February 21, 1965. Though he was assassinated by members of the Nation of Islam, some believe his murder was part of a larger plot orchestrated by the highest law enforcement powers in the United States. Malcolm's book, **The Autobiography of Malcolm X,** *is considered by many a classic of African-American literature.*

Newcastle, Wilmington, Trenton, Philadelphia, New York, Norristown, Baltimore, Greensboro, Toronto, New Hope, Snow Hill, Frenchtown, Westchester, Buffalo, Albany and Oswego—she was there. Union Church, Asbury Church, Bethel Church, Old Methodist Church, Mother Bethel Church, Wesley Church, schoolhouses, private homes, camp meetings and tent revivals—she was there.

They yelled at her, "Women can't preach! Women are not called by God to preach the word! Women are unable to lead a revival!" People who saw her asked, "Who is she, and who gave her authority to preach?" In 1811, few could conceive of a woman preacher…and a black one at that!

Who was this woman? She was Jarena Lee.

Some, including her pastor, told her that women could not be in the pulpit. Others reminded her that her husband of six years was dead, that four of her six children were dead, and she ought to spend her life in mourning. But Jarena Lee listened to only one voice, the voice of God. At twenty-one, she described herself as "a wretched sinner before the Spirit of God entered my conscience" who was called to preach the good news of salvation.

When Rev. Richard Allen, founder of the AME Church, told her that women could not preach, Lee boldly reminded him that the first witness of the resurrection was Mary Magdalene. While the eleven male disciples were hiding in Jerusalem in a dark room, Mary Magdalene conversed with the risen Savior.

Lee was the new Mary Magdalene, and she went on to preach all over North America. Year after year, she traveled by foot, horse and boat, often covering two thousand miles and preaching over one hundred and seventy sermons a year. Hundreds were converted and strengthened by the power of her sermons. Her classic book, *Religious Experience and Journal of Mrs. Jarena Lee*, is a powerful testament to faith and love. At her sunset of life, broke and ailing, she wrote:

> *My health being very much impaired, I knew not but that I should be the next one called away, but the Lord spared me for some other purpose, and upon my recovery I commenced traveling again, feeling it better to wear out than to rust out—and so expect to do until death ends the struggle— knowing, if I lose my life for Christ's sake, I shall find it again.*

Jarena Lee found her life in Christ, and through her countless efforts others found life as well.

The bold gospel preacher Jarena Lee died in 1850; the actual date is unknown. She was the author of Religious Experience and Journal of Mrs. Jarena Lee.

Venture was a slave in America, given the ubiquitous last name of Smith by his white masters, but he had been born free in Africa. In 1729, a Guinean family in Dukandarra once rejoiced over the birth of a son, Broteer. Several years later, their joy collapsed into sorrow as their beloved son was kidnapped and sold for four gallons of rum and a snippet of calico cloth. His owner renamed him "Venture" because, to the owner, the boy was a financial risk, a venture. A human being had become a "thing"; a son, a monetary transaction; a brother, an entrepreneurial gamble. Nevertheless, Venture did not allow slavery to strip away his human dignity.

In his book, *A Narrative of the Life and Adventures of Venture, A Native of Africa*, Venture wrote of his helplessness, of knowing that his wife could be taken from him any moment. He wrote that she could be raped and abused or sold away at the master's whim, and his children would then "belong not to me but to the master." But above all, Venture remembered that he, at one time, had been free. No matter how many masters owned him, he never forgot the sweetness of liberty.

Venture had to do something. When his master allowed him to hire himself out and to keep part of the earnings, he painstakingly saved everything he could. By the time he was thirty-six, Venture had earned enough—seventy-one pounds and two shillings—to purchase his freedom.

With a broken heart, he left his wife and children in slavery and moved to New England. For the next four years, he worked feverishly to earn enough to buy his own family. He ate sparingly, wasted nothing and slowly watched his savings grow.

When Venture returned to his old plantation with cash in hand, he made the agonizing choice to purchase his eldest son's freedom first. He missed his wife fiercely, but Venture thought that he and his son could earn enough together to buy the entire family. Years later, he was able to purchase his wife and other son, but he never had enough for his daughter. The joy of deliverance was tempered with the fate of the daughter he was forced to leave behind.

Through it all, Venture never succumbed to despair. During a time when blacks in colonial America barely made enough to survive, he saved for his family's freedom. There were but two things he wanted in life: that his family would be free and that they would be free together.

This is a story of love's triumph over callous capitalism and a barbarian social order. When the system, the courts, the government and the military all said that Venture Smith and his family were property, Venture worked with all his heart and soul to make his family free.

Ex-slave and writer Venture Smith's death is not recorded, but his book, A Narrative of the Life and Adventures of Venture, a Native of Africa, *was one of the many that helped abolitionists understand the horrors of slavery.*

≣ Frances Ellen Watkins Harper: "Most Worthy of Imitation"

Frances Ellen Watkins Harper was a respected and talented black woman in the nineteenth century. She embodied black pride, lived personal integrity and reflected Christ's light on earth. Her passion for justice, her sacrifices for racial uplift and her courageous deeds made her the symbol of black womanhood. In 1845, Harper burst upon the literary scene with her book of poetry, *Forest Leaves*. As she became more aware of the misery around her, her verse shifted from nature's pleasures to human suffering. Her words followed her heart, and soon her works focused solely on black life and women's issues. She moved to Philadelphia where her home became a destination on the Underground Railroad. Many evenings she listened as escaped slaves told their horrific tales of brutality and violence.

Harper gave her all to the Abolition Movement, and she became a frequent speaker in America. As she proclaimed liberation from the podium, her audiences were stunned by her fire and passion. Her oratory transformed them from passive spectators into committed abolitionists. But black freedom was not the sum total of her work, for she also was an outspoken advocate for women's rights and temperance. Most organizations at the time devoted to black freedom, women's rights and temperance were graced by her presence. The titles granted her during that era spoke of her greatness: Some called her "Empress of Peace" and "Poet Laureate."

Despite her intense political work, Frances Harper still found time to write. In 1854, she wrote her classic, *Poems on Miscellaneous Subjects*. In 1892, she published her novel, *Iola Leroy*, on the implications of racism and sexism for black women. Her devotion to personal integrity, social equality and Christian service earned her the grandest of all compliments: She became known as the "Woman of Our Race Most Worthy of Imitation."

Poet and political activist Frances Ellen Watkins Harper died on February 20, 1911, in Philadelphia, Pennsylvania. She combined poetry and political action to make significant contributions to the struggle for freedom.

≣ The Honorable Elijah Muhammad: The Prophet

Few black leaders have been as mysterious, controversial and unlikely as Elijah Muhammad. To see him, smallish in stature, with almost a retiring demeanor, one might have dismissed him as weak and frail. Born in Georgia as Elijah Poole, he was often unemployed in his early years. Many nights found him face down and drunk in the gutter. When his life was going nowhere, Poole was exposed to the black nationalist teachings of Wallace Fard's Islamic movement. He converted to the new faith and later became Fard's top assistant. As a leader in the Islamic movement, he was later renamed Elijah Muhammad. He took Fard's teachings and movement and transformed them into his own creation: The Nation of Islam.

In black communities across America, folks spoke with pride about "The Nation." People would say phrases such as, "He joined The Nation" or "The Nation just opened another store." Criminals hardened by life on the street and time in jail would join "The Nation" and find a self-respect that changed them forever.

For many, it was hard to believe that Muhammad's teachings could transform incorrigible black ghetto lives. Many disagreed with his teachings, found fault with his rampant womanizing and condemned his use of violence as a substitute for dialogue. But it is impossible to dismiss the power of the Prophet. It is safe to say that, without Elijah Muhammad, there would have been no Malcolm X. Changed lives, renewed purpose and black pride are but a few of his legacies.

Muhammad may have had some strange ideas, such as Yakub the mad scientist, or the Mothership hovering to save black America. But focus instead on the criminals and addicts who were transformed into fathers and husbands, on the black men such as Malcolm X who were redeemed by "The Prophet." Elijah Muhammad himself was redeemed by the theology he espoused. Before becoming a Muslim, he had been a listless drunken vagrant. After his conversion, he became a savior to many in black America.

Elijah Muhammad died on February 25, 1975, in Chicago, Illinois. In the Nation of Islam in particular and in the black community in general, he is known as the Honorable Elijah Muhammad or simply "The Prophet."

FEB 26 ☰ Jimmy Lee Jackson: Martyr of the Civil Rights Movement

Jimmy Lee Jackson, his mother, Viola Jackson, and his grandfather, Cager Lee, squeezed into the back pew at the Mt. Zion Baptist Church in Marion, Alabama. Jimmy Lee had already had another hard day at the pulpwood mill, but he was not too tired for church—especially that night. It was not going to be just another church service but rather the launch of a protest march for black rights in Marion.

That night Rev. C.T. Vivian of the Southern Christian Leadership Conference (SCLC) preached on courage in the face of violence. Though Alabama state troopers and white mobs were gathering outside, Rev. Vivian asked the people to be brave, to look to Jesus for strength. Jimmy Lee Jackson, Viola Jackson and Cager Lee held hands during the sermon and pledged to stick together as they filed out of Mt. Zion at the front of the marchers. The march would not be a long one; the church was but a block away from the courthouse.

But before the marchers even reached the courthouse, they were stopped by Alabama state troopers, led by Police Chief T.O. Harris. Harris ordered the marchers to disperse, and when Rev. James Dobynes knelt down to pray, all hell broke loose. Dobynes was clubbed in the head, and troopers charged the protesters. Those in front scattered, and those in the rear tried to run back into the church. What followed was one of the most shameful moments in American history.

Fifty state troopers pounced on the unarmed marchers, and Cager Lee, Viola Jackson and Jimmy Lee Jackson ran for shelter in Mack's Café. Cager, already bleeding from a billy club blow across his face, ran into the kitchen, where more state troopers kicked and beat him. Viola tried to come to his aid, but she was beaten to the floor. Jimmy Lee tried to protect his mother, but two troopers slammed him against the cigarette machine. As Jimmy Lee struggled to regain his balance, a trooper shot him twice in the stomach. Chaos was everywhere, with people being beaten, clubbed and dragged off to jail. Reporters later said streetlights went out, but they could still hear the loud whacks and screams through the darkness.

One of those screaming was Viola Jackson. She watched helplessly as her son was brutally shot. One week later, Jimmy Lee Jackson died of gunshot wounds. This young man died not only for the right to vote but also for the right for blacks to be treated as human beings. When Rev. James Bevel later asked Cager Lee whether the marches should continue, the old man from Marion replied, "Oh, yeah."

Jimmy Lee Jackson died on February 26, 1965, in Marion, Alabama, of wounds inflicted by Alabama state troopers. He became a symbol of black courage in the face of violence, and future civil rights marches were held in his memory.

FEB 27   ≡ Anna Julia Cooper: "When and Where I Enter"

Anna Julia Cooper saw herself eternally bound to her people. For her, nothing was personal; it was all about her race. Whenever she was slighted, ignored, discriminated against, threatened or harmed, it was not just about her; it was about her race. In 1892, she gave a speech entitled "Womanhood: A Vital Element in the Regeneration and Progress of a Race," proclaiming:

> Only when black women can say "when and where I enter in the quiet undisputed dignity of my womanhood, without violence and without special privilege," then and there the whole Negro race enters with me.

Never had solidarity with a race been stated more clearly. Everything Cooper said, everything she stood for, everything for which she sacrificed, was not about personal privilege or family security; it was for racial elevation and pride. She carried every Georgia sharecropper, every laid-off factory worker, every maid—indeed, every single black person—in her soul, and her dignity became a living symbol for all her race.

When Cooper started the Black Women's Club Movement, when she taught at prestigious "M" Street School in Washington, D.C., when she spoke out for black women's liberation, she held her race close to her heart. She chose every public word, every action, to elevate black people in general and black women in particular.

Her life was full of firsts. Cooper was the only woman member of the American Negro Academy, founded by the great Alexander Crummell. She was also one of the first black women involved in the 1900 London Pan-African Congress. Whether teaching, tutoring, speaking or organizing, Anna Julia Cooper carried the burden and privilege of representing and elevating the entire black race, "when and where" she entered.

Anna Julia Cooper died peacefully in her sleep at the age of 105 on February 27, 1964, in Washington, D.C. Her work for black equality and women's rights inspired later generations of activists.

FEB 28   ≡ The Compromise of Black Humanity: The Election of a President

In 1877, America was a bitterly divided nation. The Civil War smoldered on in the national memory, northern whites were tired of black issues and the South despised Reconstruction. All this and more erupted in the election of 1876, in which Republican Rutherford Hayes and Democrat James Tilden fought a bitterly contested election for president. The Electoral College, much like the nation, was deadlocked and incapable of determining who had actually won. Weeks dragged on as political analysts, the courts, congressmen, senators and the College tried to determine the election outcome.

On February 26, 1877, four southern Democrats and five Ohio Republicans met at the Wormley Hotel in Washington, D.C., to determine the future of Reconstruction and the presidency. Those present struck a compromise with significant implications for the course of American history. If the North would end its "interference" in southern affairs, the South would support Hayes' bid for President. The South proclaimed, "We don't care who is in the White House as long as we have Home Rule." The deal was struck, with horrific consequences to black Americans.

As soon as the last northern soldier left southern soil, the South embarked on a brutal campaign of victimization and subjugation. Night riders, Klan rallies, segregation, Jim Crow laws and the entire apparatus of white supremacy was quickly installed in the South. Rights that blacks had enjoyed in 1877 were gone by 1878 and were not restored again until after the bitter struggles of the Civil Rights Movement, almost one hundred years later.

Once again, blacks had been sacrificed on the altar of political expediency. For decades, America had been eager to compromise black humanity. The "three-fifths compromise" of 1787 (declaring that a slave was to be counted as three-fifths of a person), the Compromise of 1820, the Compromise of 1850, the Missouri Compromise and now the compromise at the Wormley Hotel—all had abandoned blacks in exchange for white privilege. After the meeting at Wormley, the *Chicago Tribune* declared:

> The long controversy over the black man seems to have reached a finality. The Negro will disappear from the forefront of national policies. Henceforth, the nation, as a nation, will have nothing more to do with him.

These prophetic words about a country that talked much of democracy but treated its black citizens like subhumans stand as a lesson on the dire consequences of compromising the dignity of another human being.

On February 26, 1877, Democrats and Republicans met at the Wormley Hotel to elect a president at the expense of black freedom, security and citizenship. The consequences of subverting Reconstruction, which had brought significant changes to the lives of the poor in the South, are still unfathomable.

The Port Royal Experiment
"A Thing Which Has Never Happened Before"

FEB 29

In 1862, Union soldiers chased Confederate troops from the South Carolina Sea Islands. The retreating rebels left behind plantations and cotton crops—and some ten thousand black slaves. After this large-scale liberation, northern abolitionists sought to prove that blacks could learn academic and social skills and become contributing citizens. Several teachers, black and white, went to the South to teach the newly freed slaves in what became known as the Port Royal Experiment. White businessman and abolitionist Edward Phillbrick joined the teachers so he could create a black economic enterprise. But the blacks needed little outside help. Each ex-slave was paid by the bale and given part ownership in the plantations. Within two years, they had exceeded their goal, earning $80,000 in cotton sales. All the myths about black docility, laziness, ignorance and sullenness were shattered as the Sea Island blacks worked their way to security.

The northern abolitionists, however, got more than they had anticipated. "Ol' Grace," one of the elders in the community, led a contingent of ex-slaves into a meeting with Mr. Phillbrick. One witness, Harriet Ware, described the scene: "The women came up in a body to complain to Mr. Phillbrick about their pay...a thing which has never happened before this." These women, who were accustomed to following orders, who had been whipped and beaten with impunity, stood up and demanded their rights. Though their requests were not granted, their boldness marked the first time in the South that free blacks attempted to negotiate wages and working conditions.

The abolitionists who had sought to prove that blacks could work found much more. They found people who wanted to be more than workers, children of Africa who demanded the rights and privileges of basic humanity.

The Port Royal Experiment took place following the 1862 ouster of the Confederate troops from the Sea Islands of South Carolina. Black ex-slaves demonstrated they were not only fit for freedom but also worthy of human dignity. In many respects, the Port Royal Experiment continues to this day.

MARCH

Fannie Lou Hamer

For almost four hundred years, from 1451 to 1850, African peoples were victimized by one of the world's most sustained horrors in history: the African slave trade. No poem, novel, song or painting can convey the pain of this brutal commerce in human traffic. According to the great African-American historian W.E.B. DuBois, eleven million Africans—including over a million under the age of fourteen—were brought to the New World. Scholars estimate that between six and fifteen million more captured men and women never made it out of Africa or across the deadly waters.

One story contains but a fragment of the horror. While walking home one day, seventeen-year-old Mojinda was jumped, slapped and gagged. Bleeding and dazed, she was shackled to other African youth huddled in the bushes. None of them looked familiar, and all look haunted. Each day, their tattered band grew as more Africans were captured; each step took her further from her parents, grandparents and friends.

After thirty days, Mojinda heard and smelled the ocean. Within sight of the endless water, she watched in horror as her captors killed the weak and sick. At the coast, they were herded into "barracoons," fortresses along the shore for enslavement, where more people died of hunger, beatings and disease. Every night, the screams and moans of her cellmates pierced the air, as they begged their gods and ancestors for mercy. Mojinda's idyllic village life had not prepared her for such barbarism and cruelty.

Two months later, her captors branded her and dragged her onto a wooden ship, locking her and the others in the bottom of the boat in a space too small for their bodies. The journey across the seas took two months, and each day was unbearable. Sometimes they were dragged on deck to be watered down and ridiculed; the rest of the time they huddled in the dark bottom of the ship. As the boat rocked back and forth, blood, diarrhea, sweat and vomit sloshed around her.

Many people died from dehydration and dysentery, and their bodies were thrown into the seas without ceremony or dignity. Worse, many of the women, including her, were dragged into dark corners and raped by foul-smelling men. Mojinda could hardly believe any of this was real, its horror and ugliness so vile as to be inhuman. By the time they arrived at a strange land, she was numb.

There she was washed, scrubbed and chained together with the other women and then forced to stand nearly naked atop a wooden block. White men and women touched her arms, tugged at her clothes, looked into her mouth, gazed at her breasts and treated her like an animal. Mojinda watched silently as frenzied people raised their hands and shouted out words she didn't understand. Suddenly, the shouting stopped, and she was dragged away by two white people she had never seen before. Thus began her life as a slave.

The great African slave and writer Oladuh Equiano noted that after his capture "the next day proved a day of greater sorrow." A "greater sorrow" is the only means to describe the unparalleled brutality of life as a slave. The miracle of slavery is truly that African Americans and Afro-Brazilians and black Cubans and Afro-Peruvians and Haitians and other black people were somehow able to survive and produce generations of functioning, loving descendants.

Some historians estimate as many as fifty million Africans died during the slave trade, either in Africa, on the voyage across the seas or during "seasoning," an often brutal process in the West Indies used to prepare a person for servitude.

MAR 2   ≡ Askia Toure Muhammad: "Our King Is Dead"

A fictious journal entry as it might have been written by a citizen of Songhay in 1538:

> *The funeral procession stretches for miles through the streets of Timbuktu. Our beloved king is dead. Muhammad lived among us for ninety-seven years, but now he is gone. Woodcutters, farmers, soldiers, peasants and others are wondering aloud about a future without Askia Toure Muhammad. It seems as if he has always been here; my grandparents and parents have known no king but him. He gave us so much. He took our many tribes and villages and created the powerful Songhay Empire. We were once easily invaded and often paid tribute to our powerful opponents, but under our king, we became the undisputed power of West Africa.*

> *King Askia Muhammad's genius created our mighty empire. He gave us a strong government, peace in the provinces, material advancement and a cultural renaissance never before known in our region. Today, universities flourish in Gao, Jenne and Timbuktu because of him. Our children learn astronomy, medicine, logic, mathematics, rhetoric, hygiene and music. The University of Sankore in Timbuktu is but one of many places where our minds can soar and pierce the mysteries of the universe. How about Professor Ahmed Baba? He alone has written forty books on theology, astronomy and biography.*

> *We of the Songhay Empire have much to be proud of, and we owe it all to mighty King Askia Muhammad. Material progress, peace in the land, cultural richness; oh, how all will miss Muhammad!*

King Askia Toure Muhammad died on March 2, 1538, in Songhay, West Africa. He was heralded as one of the great early rulers of Africa, and his country of Songhay ranks with Mali and Ghana as the three major civilizations of pre-colonial West Africa.

≡ Gordon Parks: A Choice of Weapons

In the story of blacks' heroic struggle for equality, African Americans have wielded various weapons in their quest. Langston Hughes composed poetry, Harriet Tubman traveled the Underground Railroad, Robert Moses registered voters, the Black Panther Party picked up shotguns; indeed, the weapons have been as varied as the people who used them.

In 1937, a North Coast Starlight railway waiter named Gordon Parks had time during a layover to browse through a pawnshop. There he purchased his "weapon"—a camera—and began to teach himself photography. This was the first step in a brilliant career. Parks shot images of his black world: Unemployed men on tenement steps, school girls playing jump rope, old folks walking home from church—all were captured in his lens. Parks' photos brought the drama, passion and anguish of black life to many who knew nothing of the African-American experience. Parks called his camera his "weapon against poverty and racism."

His weapon of choice was a powerful one. Parks sought to abolish racism by raising awareness through lively images of black life. If he could illuminate the consequences of discrimination, if he could portray the beauty of black folk, Parks believed, he could end racism. He later created two of the most important works in black cinema: *Shaft* and *The Learning Tree*. In *Shaft*, a black hero shattered the Stepin Fetchit and Amos 'n' Andy stereotypes of black Americans. In *The Learning Tree*, black audiences were inspired by youthful courage. In both cases, the camera of Gordon Parks was a weapon in his quiet revolution.

Parks was unrelenting in his task. From the Great Depression through World War II and into the Black Power Movement, Gordon Parks raised his camera to smash hatred.

Gordon Parks was a photographer, film director and political activist. He wrote **The Learning Tree** ***and*** **A Choice of Weapons,** ***two autobiographical sketches of his life. He died on March 7, 2006.***

≡ Kwame Nkrumah: "Service, Sacrifice and Suffering"

It was a day Kwame Nkrumah thought would never happen. That warm spring morning, England lowered the Union Jack and granted independence to the African colony of Ghana, also known as "The Gold Coast." Home of former kingdoms, birthplace of many of America's slaves, Ghana became the first free nation in sub-Saharan Africa. It was not, however, because English rulers suddenly felt generous; Ghana's liberty was born from a lifetime of struggle by leaders such as Kwame Nkrumah.

As a student in England and the United States, Nkrumah had ample chance to work for his comfort and affluence instead of his national obligations. But his studies were not for himself; he was committed to his people. In England, he and other Africans formed "The Circle," a study group requiring monthly dues and a sincere dedication to Africa's liberation. Not a party network or social club, The Circle prepared West African students for future struggle back home, providing contacts, discipline and an ideology. The organization did not advertise itself, nor was its success determined by the size of its membership. The Circle was deliberately kept small, focusing on quality of commitment rather than the quantity of members.

Kwame Nkrumah served as the first chairman of The Circle, and he helped develop the group's motto of "Service, Sacrifice and Suffering." Kwame and his fellow students pledged to "maintain ourselves and The Circle as the Revolutionary Vanguard of the Struggle for West African unity and national independence."

Upon returning to Ghana, Nkrumah put the creed of "Service, Sacrifice and Suffering" into action. He helped found an anti-colonial organization called the Convention People's Party; he organized strikes, led boycotts and instructed the peasants; and he was arrested and jailed for his activity. Nkrumah was serious about helping his people, and he sacrificed much for their welfare. While historians note that Kwame Nkrumah later employed repressive policies as the President of Ghana, they also record, with equal accuracy, that Nkrumah's personal sacrifices helped Ghana emerge from the darkness of colonialism and moved Ghana down the hard road toward freedom.

On March 6, 1957, Ghana became the first sub-Saharan African colony to achieve freedom. Kwame Nkrumah, leader of the Convention People's Party, became the first Prime Minister of Ghana.

MAR 5   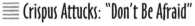 Crispus Attucks: "Don't Be Afraid"

The long day was near end, and none too soon, for tempers were short. Boston fishermen and common workers were antagonized by the British troops hovering around the local customs house. Their redcoats and loaded muskets were stark reminders of England's enforced economic strangulation.

Crispus Attucks, formerly a slave, saw his life as a seaman threatened by the stifling rules from London. That afternoon, Attucks was one of fifty men who gathered to protest continued British interference. The British troops, young and a long way from home, grew nervous and tried to scatter the crowd. As the jittery soldiers faced the angry civilians, Attucks stood tall in the front row and shouted to his fellow men, "Don't be afraid."

Then, without warning, shots rang through the streets, one volley followed by a second. Some men fell forward; others stumbled clumsily through the smoke and carnage. Within minutes, five Americans were killed or mortally wounded—Crispus Attucks and four white men.

This incident, later called "The Boston Massacre," fueled the American Revolution. But despite Attucks' courage, his race remained in slavery long after the Revolutionary War. Blacks would not be free for another one hundred years. Nevertheless, Attucks' death sowed the seeds for both the nation's freedom and the eventual liberation of the slaves.

Crispus Attucks, one of the first casualties of the American Revolution, was killed by British troops on March 5, 1770. For years afterward, blacks on the East Coast celebrated March 5th as Crispus Attucks Day.

☰ Dred "X" Scott: "We the People"

Most who are familiar with black history know the sordid story of the Dred Scott Decision. Many consider it the most racist decision ever rendered by the U.S. Supreme Court. Led by incorrigible racist Chief Justice Roger B. Taney, the Supreme Court stated unequivocally that "We the people" did not include black Americans. Further, the ruling declared slavery legal in all the remaining Western territories. Black Americans were appalled. Their struggle for human dignity in America had been completely demolished, and any continued work, tears, petitions, rebellions and resistance seemed useless. Every vestige of civil rights, human rights, equality and citizenship had been abrogated and denied by the Dred Scott Decision.

Yet forgotten in the agony of the Dred Scott Decision is Dred Scott the person. Ten years earlier, in 1847, this courageous slave had filed a suit in the Missouri court system for his freedom. He believed that since his master had taken him to places where slavery did not exist, such as the free soil of Illinois and the Wisconsin Territory, he could no longer be considered a slave. So illiterate that he marked his petition with an "X," Scott nevertheless sought his liberty in the courts.

Though his bid failed after a decade of appeals and court reversals, Dred "X" Scott still maintained his faith in justice despite all evidence to the contrary, a faith that allowed him to stand tall in the fight for his humanity. Scott laid down his own freedom to expose America for what it really was—a nation that held absolutely no regard for its citizens of color.

On March 6, 1857, Chief Justice Roger B. Taney handed down the infamous Dred Scott Decision declaring that the "We the people" phrase in the Constitution did not apply to slaves.

Bomber pilots scanned the skies, looking for signs of danger. They would soon be in enemy range, where German fighter pilots could cut their formation to pieces. Without fighter escorts, they were doomed. Suddenly, pulling up from below and taking position among the bombers, escorts appeared: silver P-51 Mustangs from the 332nd Fighter Group. Bomber crews broke out in cheers, for they all knew the 332nd never lost a bomber. Known as "The Red Tails" for the bright crimson markings on each plane's rear, the 332nd entered the bomber formations with flair. One bomber radio operator later said, "The Red Tails would roll that wing over and over and float through the formation like dancers…. When you saw them, you were happy. They were that hot, that good."

The flamboyant arrival of The Red Tails turned many white pilots into instant believers in black equality. Despite the racism, disrespect and injustice they endured, the 332nd left a legacy of military courage and excellence that may never be equaled. By the end of World War II, they had accomplished what no other escort unit could boast: They never lost a bomber to enemy fighters. The Red Tails flew 1,578 missions, destroyed 261 enemy aircraft and earned 95 Distinguished Flying Crosses. Their Captain, Roscoe Brown, was one of the first Americans to shoot down a German jet, and the Army used the film of his victory as combat training for new pilots. Their bravery was also evident in their own casualties: 66 members of the 332nd Fighter Group were killed in action.

The 332nd began on March 7, 1942, when the first class of the Tuskegee Army Air Field graduates completed their training. That day, Lieutenants Lemuel Custis, Charles DeBow, George "Spanky" Roberts and Mac Ross joined Captain Benjamin O. Davis, Jr., as the first black fighter pilots in the United States Army. They became the 99th Pursuit Squadron, later merging with other black units into the famous 332nd Fighter Group. These first Tuskegee Airmen were the idols of the black press and the darlings of black America. The very existence of black pilots and officers undermined the very foundations of white supremacy and brought hope to millions. Once people saw a black man in a pilot's uniform, it was impossible for them to go back to the prevailing image of black men as exclusively cooks, janitors and shoeshine boys.

On March 7, 1942, five black airmen completed training at the Tuskegee Army Air Field. By the end of the war, over 600 black Americans completed flight training and earned their wings as officers and pilots in the U.S. military.

If America were truly just, Harriet Jacobs would be recognized as one of the great women writers in United States history. Her book, *Incidents in the Life of a Slave Girl; Written by Herself*, was published in 1861 and remains a great work to this day. Although the smoke and carnage of the Civil War obscured her book for many years, readers who later discovered it were moved by her haunting account of slavery. Jacobs' writing was so good that literary critics assumed that *Incidents* must have been the work of a white woman; no slave woman could possibly have produced such writing!

Only recently has Harriet Jacobs been given her due. No book describes life for an enslaved African woman as *Incidents* does. "Incidents" is, indeed, a euphemism; "horrors" would be more accurate. In one passage Harriet said she would never forget how a field hand had cried, "O pray, don't, massa!" during a brutal whipping of over one hundred lashes. The following morning, when Jacobs walked by the barn, the floor was covered in blood and gore.

In the chapter, "The Slaves' New Year's Day," Jacobs described the southern custom of January first as "hiring day," a day of buying and selling slaves. While whites associated the day with celebration, blacks met it with fear: They knew their families could be torn apart. Jacobs recalled an "incident" where she encountered a slave woman stumbling back from the auction block, stammering, "Gone, all gone." Jacobs later discovered that all seven of the woman's children had been sold that morning.

In horrifying detail, Jacobs described what it meant to be a teenage slave girl, the property of lustful white men. She noted that the more beautiful the girl, the more lustful the master would be; that while beauty brought flattery and gifts for white girls, for blacks "beauty hastens degradation." At age fifteen, Jacobs herself resisted the sexual advances of her master, and she recounted how her master had scoffed at her desire to marry another field hand. Her lament—"Why does the slave love?"—speaks volumes about the despair of this young girl's life.

Harriet Jacobs' *Incidents* is a strong testament to what it means to be human, what it takes to carve out dignity and respect even in the most hopeless and degrading conditions.

Harriet Jacobs, author of Incidents in the Life of a Slave Girl, *died on March 7, 1897, in Washington, D.C.*

≣ Laura Adorkor Kofey: Mother Warrior of God

According to witnesses, Laura Kofey appeared in Atlanta in 1927 "out of nowhere." Within just two years of her arrival, disillusioned blacks living with unemployment, violence and poverty were finding hope in her message of positive living. A self-described "African princess," Kofey preached self-reliance, repatriation to Africa and worship of a loving black God. Early converts remember her message:

> My God showed me, it will come a time you will wish you were as black as the ace of spades. Negroes be proud of your woolly hair and the color of your skin. Go back to yourselves, that's back to Africa and that is back to God.

For black Southerners in the 1920s, just sixty years removed from slavery, life was grim: Blacks were murdered by lynch mobs, excluded from opportunity and smothered by sharecroppers' debt. Into such agony came the gospel according to Laura Adorkor Kofey, and her charisma left crowds gasping for more. To a despised people, she proclaimed God's love; to folks without self-respect, she urged looking within to find God. Often at her rallies she proclaimed, "Children, my hand is in Jesus' hand, Jesus' hand is in God's hand, and my other hand is in my children's hands." The message was clear: Hold on to Mother Kofey, believe in yourself, believe in Africa and believe in God. And hundreds did. Followers called her "Mother," "Savior," "Saint Kofey" and "Mother Warrior of God."

By creating black hope and self-respect, Mother Kofey undermined white supremacy. Then, one afternoon, as she was proclaiming the love of her black God, Kofey was assassinated in Miami's Liberty Hall with two shots to the head. She died instantly, but the African Universal Church she founded continued. For the church, March 8th became the Feast Day of Mother Kofey, a time to remember the message to "Find yourself, Find Africa, Find God."

On March 8, 1928, Laura Kofey, founder of the African Universal Church, was assassinated as she addressed a large crowd of followers at Liberty Hall in Miami, Florida. The denomination continues today with churches in Florida and Liberia, Africa.

≣ Harriet Ross Tubman: "Live North or Die Here"

The moon's absence was welcome; sky, trees and earth blended into an impenetrable shadow, swallowing up the silent group as they made their way north. No one made a sound, for any cough, gasp or murmur could bring armed night patrollers down upon them. The small column of shadowy figures followed their leader in a winding, single file through the woods, streams and trails. Walking along in darkness, the slaves did not know who to fear most: their masters in the South or this hardened black woman leading them to the North. But they followed this woman they called Black Moses. They knew she could lead them into the Promised Land.

Harriet Ross Tubman was the most revered conductor along the hazardous Underground Railroad. This serious black woman carried a pistol, in part for protection but also to ensure that her passengers listened carefully. Her work was serious, for one mistake could mean capture and execution for her and re-enslavement for them. Posters with her picture, announcing a reward for her death or capture, littered the slave states.

Loved by slaves, hated by whites across the South, Tubman persisted with courage and force of will. Fifteen times she made the journey South and returned with yet another group of brave ex-slaves. On one journey, she saved her own sister and daughter. Later, she fulfilled a long-standing dream and rescued her own parents.

Sometimes fear and fatigue would overwhelm the faint-hearted, and they would ask Tubman to take them back. She would stop the whole column and stare down the weak. Her answer was always the same: "Live North or die here." No pleading, no speech on racial equality, no treatise on the blessings of liberty—just a clear statement of their choice at the moment: They could keep going and live in the North or stay there and die; it was too late to return; going back meant death for them and everyone else in the group. Every single one of Tubman's passengers continued on with her. By 1860, over two hundred ex-slaves had tasted liberty because of her courage and perseverence.

Harriet Ross Tubman helped John Brown plan the raid on Harper's Ferry, led a raid on Confederate troops during the Civil War and converted her house into a home for the sick and poor. This black saint died on March 10, 1913, in Auburn, New York.

MAR 11   ≡ Frank Chikane: "This Is the Call"

Amidst the shouting and weeping, Frank Chikane knelt at the altar in hopes the Holy Spirit would fall upon his soul. As a member of South Africa's Apostolic Faith Mission, Chikane believed that after their salvation Christians received a second blessing from God—the anointing of the Holy Spirit. Chikane prayed and waited, and suddenly, like a flood, the Holy Spirit of God engulfed his being. Chikane rose, his knees wobbling but his soul revived, and walked out of church anxious to live in the power of the Spirit.

A devoted Pentecostal, Chikane led college-student Bible studies and prayer groups, preached at evangelical rallies and later pastored his own church. In his zeal to live as the Spirit guided, Chikane became increasingly opposed to South Africa's apartheid regime, which was dehumanizing black South Africans, robbing them of their dignity and denying them health care, education and employment. For no crime or reason, members of Chikane's church were being arrested, tortured, detained and harassed. Chikane knew his church frowned on political action, but what was he to do?

Believing that Jesus went to the cross in his fight against sin and evil, Chikane felt he could do no less. He entered the anti-apartheid struggle with vigor, preaching the gospel of liberation and demanding justice.

In 1977, Chikane was arrested and held for six weeks without charge. During his interrogation, police hung him upside down for hours and beat him with a stick. They later forced him to stand in one spot for fifty hours, beat him again and pulled out clumps of his hair. Despite this brutality, Chikane stood firm in his conviction that the Spirit of God was with him.

Years later, Chikane and his family were forced into exile, but the call to return to South Africa was too compelling. His friends tried to talk him out of it, citing dangers to his wife, Kagiso, and his sons, Obakeng and Otlile. In a "Letter to Those Who Care," Chikane wrote:

> Why have I moved against this tide of reason? The cries of my people at home, the call of those who are in distress, who live between life and death on a daily basis…who have no other option but to face the guns of the apartheid security forces…the call of the women, men and children of Soweto who believe that my presence…my ministry, will make a difference. This is the call that sends me back home.

And so Chikane and his family returned home to join Bishop Desmond Tutu, Rev. Allan Boesak and numerous others to lead the church's anti-apartheid movement. Their prayers, sermons and protests helped destroy the demonic powers of apartheid. From a Pentecostal church altar to the struggle for human dignity, Frank Chikane lived in the power of the Holy Spirit.

During the anti-apartheid movement, Frank Chikane followed Desmond Tutu as the General Secretary of the South African Council of Churches. He was also a leader in the Institute for Contextual Theology. His "Letter to Those Who Care," was written on March 12, 1987.

≡ Charlie Parker: "Bird Lives!"

Soon after the great Charlie Parker's death, graffiti started appearing in Harlem, Kansas City, Chicago's South Side and other black communities announcing, "Bird Lives!" These inscriptions bore more truth than fiction. Although Parker died in 1955, his music continues to live anywhere jazz is played. No jazz concert or album escapes the irrepressible Charlie Parker; his genius in measured by his omnipresence. His brilliant saxophone riffs and his inspired improvisations set the standard for the jazz world.

Charlie "Bird" Parker has been rightly named "The Father of Modern Jazz." Even his heroin addiction could not squelch his quest for pure music. Unfortunately, Bird was hooked at fifteen and remained so until his death twenty years later. Yet his genius transcended his weakness. In fact, some of his most significant music emerged during his addiction: "Moose the Mooche" was named after his drug dealer; "Relaxin' at Camarillo" recalled his hospitalization from a psychiatric breakdown.

Other Parker tunes are are the foundation of modern jazz. "Ornithology," "Lover Man," "Embraceable You," "Laura," "Lester Leaps In" and other Parker tunes are staggering in their brilliance. Parker the man may have succumbed to the ugliness of heroin, but Parker the musician lives on. Bird's music has a joy, creativity and beauty that lifts our spirits to face another day. His musical legacy contains a spiritual force, a celebration of life that transcends circumstance.

Bird's music sounds a continual reminder that beauty overwhelms ugliness, that redemption awaits us all. His music is a testament to the spiritual truth that life and love are stronger than death. Despite the tragedy of his life, Charlie Parker created beauty and affirmed the strength of the human spirit.

Charlie Parker, a prominent jazz musician, died of complications of heroin addiction on March 12, 1955. He is called "The Father of Modern Jazz."

MAR 13   ≡ John S. Rock: "True to Ourselves"

John S. Rock was a free black man from Boston who gave his all to abolition and equality, going beyond the cry for physical freedom to the demand for black pride and self-respect. His proclamations from the 1850s were equal in conviction to the black-power voices of the 1960s.

In 1858, Rock astounded the audience in Boston's Faneuil Hall with his pronouncements of black pride. That pre-Civil War period was one of the bleakest in black history. The Fugitive Slave Law had paved the way for free blacks to be enslaved with impunity. Judge Roger B. Taney had ruled in the Dred Scott Decision that black folks had no rights that whites were bound to respect. Every sector of society—sheriffs, judges, schools and churches—denied black humanity. Despite the odds, Rock proclaimed:

> *Judge Taney may outlaw us…and this wicked government may oppress us; but the black man will live when Judge Taney and this wicked government are no more. White men may despise…us; they may seek as they always have done to divide us, and make us feel degraded; but no man shall cause me to turn my back on my race. With it, I will sink or swim.*

As a dentist and a lawyer, Rock had opportunities few blacks could imagine. He could not, however, enjoy these benefits for himself while they were being denied to his race. He affirmed his solidarity with his people in these words:

My friends, we can never become elevated until we are true to ourselves.... Let us go to work—each...in his place, determined to do for himself and his race.... Whenever the colored man is elevated, it will be by his own exertions.... The colored man, who, by dint of perseverance, and industry, educates and elevates himself, prepares the way for others, gives character to the race, and hastens the day of general emancipation.

John Rock's rallying cry for blacks rings true even today.

John S. Rock gave a stirring speech, "True to Ourselves," in Boston's Faneuil Hall in March of 1858. It was reprinted in The Liberator *on March 12, 1858, rousing debate for many months and years to come on the relationship between blacks and whites.*

MAR 14   ≡ Fannie Lou Hamer: "I'm Gonna Let It Shine"

Voices raised the roof of the old Mississippi Baptist church as tired souls were lifted by the power of song. The energy in the room was contagious, and bodies swayed as the song leader sang, "This little light of mine, I'm gonna let it shine." Grandparents and babies; folks without assets, property, power or weapons; sharecroppers and servants—all sang until the church walls trembled. Unable to vote, go to school or see a doctor, these poor rural people nevertheless sang of spreading their light to others.

What light? What light did these poor blacks have to shine on others? Their song leader, Fannie Lou Hamer, had a ready answer for that question.

Fannie Lou Hamer was one of twenty children of poor farmers in Ruleville, Mississippi. She was poor, overweight and often sick. Yet her inner strength overcame the obstacles in her path. When Hamer was caught registering black voters, she was evicted from the plantation where she had worked for eighteen years. Unafraid and unbroken, she joined the Student Nonviolent Coordinating Committee (SNCC) and became a popular and effective Civil Rights Movement organizer.

Tired of continued racist treatment, Fannie helped found the Mississippi Freedom Democratic Party (MFDP). When she and her comrades descended on the 1964 Democratic Party Convention in Atlantic City to unseat the racist all-white delegation, Hamer's light shone for all to see: Her speech before the Credentials Committee stunned the nation. In broken English and with a heavy Southern accent, her voice crackling across television screens, she proclaimed that the MFDP was the only democratic and multi-racial party in Mississippi—and that the all-white delegation were imposters. If her party were not seated, then she would "question America."

Democratic Party officials, including those in the White House, watched in horror as this uneducated black woman publicly questioned the country's democracy. They frantically ordered the networks to bump her off the air, afraid her truth would undermine the government's credibility. When offered a compromise of two non-voting seats, Hamer responded, "We didn't come all this way for no two seats."

Senator Hubert Humphrey was dispatched to broker another compromise, but Hamer stood firm. She told Humphrey she was praying for him because he did not have the courage to do the right thing. When he protested and highlighted his civil rights record, she scolded him for asking them to sacrifice their democratic rights. By the end of the Convention, the Democratic Party refused the requests of Hamer and the MFDP, and many members returned to Mississippi disillusioned.

Despite this setback at Atlantic City, however, Fannie Lou Hamer's light continued to shine. She fought for the least and the lowest until her death in 1977. Through her words and deeds, she told us all, in effect, "My light might be small, it might only have a fourth-grade education, it might be poor and untrained; but no matter, I'm gonna let it shine."

Civil rights leader and activist Fannie Lou Hamer died March 14, 1977, in Ruleville, Mississippi. She challenged and eventually changed the rules of the national Democratic Party.

MAR 15   ≡ Bloody Sunday: The Selma to Montgomery March

Six hundred African Americans gathered quietly in Brown Chapel in Selma, Alabama. Though it was Sunday, they had not come to pray and sing. These black folks had had enough of white violence and discrimination; they were tired of separate and unequal schools, arbitrary literacy tests for voters and gun-toting mobs. Alabama's blacks planned to march from Selma to Montgomery, the state capitol, to show the state and the nation they would take abuse "no more."

As they filed out of the church and onto US 80, they approached the Edmund Pettis Bridge. On the other side of the river stood Alabama's blue-uniformed state troopers, lined across the road with bullhorns, nightsticks, tear gas and pistols. Despite the ominous scene, the marchers surged forward. Their fifty-four-mile march had hardly gone one mile before they heard Major John Cloud shout through a bullhorn, "This is an unlawful assembly. Your march is not conducive to public safety. You are ordered to disperse and go back to your church or your home."

Obviously, Cloud was unaware that it was their homes they sought to protect and their church that had urged them forward! The marchers filed slowly and bravely across the bridge. Suddenly, enraged troopers charged forward. A "flying V" formation of baton-wielding troopers pummeled the unarmed marchers, beating and bloodying dozens. Tear-gas canisters left the marchers dazed, and troopers took advantage of the choking mist to fracture ribs, break bones and crack skulls with their batons. Television cameras captured the state-sanctioned violence for the entire nation to watch. The marchers fled in confusion back to the church, while the injured were dragged away to local hospitals or friendly homes.

"Bloody Sunday," as it was called, demonstrated to a horrified country both the courage of black marchers and the violence of white racists. Violence won that day, but the ultimate triumph rests with the nonviolent marchers, whose courage eventually gave birth to black equality in this country.

On March 7, 1965, 600 peaceful black marchers were assaulted by Alabama State troopers. Several months later, those same marchers, plus many others, returned to complete their original march to Montgomery.

≣ Black Pentecostals: The Azusa Street Revival

The Rev. William J. Seymour, a Holiness preacher from Houston, Texas, led the famous 1907 Azusa Street Revival in Los Angeles that gave birth to the modern black Pentecostal movement. As was his custom, Seymour closed each sermon with an altar call; stepping back from the podium, he stretched forth his arms and invited forward anyone touched by the Holy Spirit. Every night, people of all races streamed down the aisles and committed themselves to Christ.

The Azusa Street Revival was in its third week, and thus far hundreds had accepted God's gift of salvation. That night, as Rev. Seymour called people forward, Charles Mason stood speechless. Although already a committed Christian and church elder, Mason had never heard about the richness Seymour described—the message that the Holy Spirit, the utter fullness of God, could fall down on him and live in him forever, that he could be saved, sanctified and filled with the Holy Spirit. Mason felt the inner tug of the Spirit and moved toward the altar. He later wrote,

The Spirit came upon the saints and upon me.... So there came a wave of glory unto me.... Oh! I was filled with the Glory of the Lord. My soul was then satisfied.

Elder Charles Mason received the Holy Spirit's anointing on Azusa Street that night and went on to found the Church of God in Christ (COGIC). Through him, the Spirit moved from Los Angeles to black neighborhoods across the nation, where storefronts, churches and temples still dot the urban landscape. Over the decades, the Church of God in Christ has transformed thousands, restored families and healed wrongs. Countless children, teenagers and adults have been changed by the preaching, music and prayers of the Church of God in Christ.

The Azusa Street Revival lasted from 1906 through 1909. There are today 3.5 million black members of the Church of God in Christ.

MAR 17   ≣ **The Last Poets: "I Understand That Time Is Running Out"**

At the height of the Black Power Movement, ghettos in Washington, D.C., Watts, Newark, Detroit and other cities were engulfed in flames. During this great upheaval, no one expressed black militancy like The Last Poets. Their poetry chronicled the traumas, agonies and contradictions of ghetto life, and they condemned racism, white folks and capitalism with scathing insights. Their most powerful lyrics were intended to shock black masses into self-elevation, transformation and revolution. Kim Green, author of *The Last Poets: On a Mission*, wrote, "The Last Poets' mission was to pull the people up out of the rubble of their lives."

The Last Poets' congas, djembes, bells, dashikis and staccato lyrics called the community to action. Their incisive clarity inspired the discouraged and energized the apathetic. Those who listened to The Last Poets, saw themselves, their families and their community with new eyes. The Poets asked people to decide whether they were contributing to destruction or to redemption.

Jalal Nilija, Umar Ben Hassan and Abiodun Oyewole combined words and music to preach a revolution in values. Their album *Niggers Are Scared of Revolution* analyzed and celebrated black culture. In the classic song, "Run Nigger," their chant, "I understand that time is running out," became a rallying cry in the ghetto. Another album, *This Is Madness*, critiqued America's ugliness and laid bare the fallacy of democracy. The Last Poets were indeed the voices of black revolution, redemption and salvation.

In the 1970s, Jalal Nilija, Umar bin Hassan and Abiodun Oyewole formed The Last Poets, a group that prepared the path for contemporary urban hip-hop.

☰ The University of Sankore at Timbuktu: Summit of African Learning

The young students sat in circles under the pleasant springtime sunlight. The campus grounds were full of students from Songhay, the Sudan, Benin, and cities and villages all across Africa. They had come to the great University of Sankore at Timbuktu to study from the most learned Africans on the continent. One of these students, Ahmed Baba, would later become one of the great scholars of Africa.

Baba and his fellow students considered themselves the luckiest people in Africa. Here they were, at a renowned university, blessed with the privilege of learning from masters such as Mohammed Abu Bekr, who promoted a love of learning and a sense of community. Babu once wrote that Bekr was:

> ...one of the best of God's virtuous creatures.... He was a working scholar, a man instinct with goodness. Calm and dignified...he captured all hearts. Everyone who knew him loved him.... His whole life was given in service to others. He taught his students to love science...to associate with scholars. He lavishly lent his most precious books, rare copies; and the copies he most valued he never asked for again.

Under the loving tutelage of professors such as Bekr, Baba and other African students flourished. Reading rare texts and engaging in lively debate, they learned mathematics, science, history and grammar. Timbuktu's students were truly among Africa's most gifted children. Towns and villages across Africa held joyous celebrations when one of their own returned from the great university in Timbuktu.

The University of Sankore reached its pinnacle in the sixteenth century. Its fame spread all over Africa, Europe and Asia, and for hundreds of years, professors and students converged on this center of science, literature and mathematics. At its peak, the library at Timbuktu was thought to be one of the greatest in the world. During that same era, the University of Sankore was considered one of Africa's most prestigious places of learning and study. Across the continent, villages and towns were renewed with knowledge brought home by students of Sankore.

On March 18, 1594, the Moorish troops sacked the University of Sankore, burned the library and books, and deported many of the scholars to Morocco. This was the beginning of the destruction of West African culture and the beginning of the African slave trade.

≡ Texas Western Miners vs. Kentucky Wildcats
The Transformation of College Basketball

Two teams gathered on the court at University of Maryland's Cole Field House for the 1966 NCAA championship game. On one side of the court, the all-white Kentucky team stood with their coach, Adolph Rupp. Winner of eight hundred and seventy-six NCAA games in his career, Rupp personified the paternalism, arrogance and segregation of college basketball. His was not an obvious segregation marked by signs and barriers but rather a more subtle and sinister exclusion: Rupp and his fellow coaches and athletic deans believed that blacks were too undisciplined to play college ball. Further, they believed that few blacks were capable of mastering the academic rigor of college. While they allowed some blacks on some teams in the North and West, if there were "too many" black players on one team, it hinted of recruiting violations, low academic standards and undisciplined basketball. Rupp and others like him talked of fairness and equal opportunity, but somehow their teams were always white.

On the other side of the court were the Texas Western Miners from El Paso, Texas. This small school did not have a basketball tradition and was considered too far away from places where recognized college basketball powers came from—places such as Indiana, Kentucky and North Carolina—to be a serious contender. Texas Western, however, had a more serious defect in the eyes of many: All five of their starting players were black. For the first time in college history, five white players would confront five black players on a championship basketball court with the entire nation watching.

No one gave Texas Western a chance. Rupp was heard to say that five blacks could never beat his Kentucky Wildcats (although he did not use the word "blacks"). Kentucky was favored to win and to win big. White coaches, players and the college establishment sat back and awaited confirmation of their racist views. They expected that Texas Western's undisciplined blacks would be demolished by Kentucky's basketball juggernaut, and the exclusion of blacks from college basketball would be justified and continued.

Willie Worsley, Bobby Joe Hill, Harry Flourny, Orsten Artis and David Lattin walked to center court that night playing for much more than an NCAA title: They were playing for the future of blacks in college ball. A crushing defeat would mean more of the same, while a victory would bring a championship to Texas Western and a revolution in college sports.

Forty game-minutes later, the final score was the Texas Western Miners, 72; the Kentucky Wildcats, 65. College basketball has not been the same since. Those five young black men raised the hopes of black high-school stars and opened doors formerly closed to hundreds of black athletes throughout the nation. In one of the great upsets in sports history, one game radically changed the dreams and expectations of black youth in America.

On March 19, 1966, the Texas Western Miners defeated the Kentucky Wildcats 72-65. In addition to the Miners starting five, the other two Texas Western players to see action that night, Willie Cager and Nevil Shed, were also black.

MAR 20 ≣ **Hubert Henry Harrison: Father of Harlem Radicalism**

Hubert Harrison was born in St. Croix and migrated, like many West Indians, to New York City. Harrison was an intelligent young black man who was shocked by America's bigotry and discrimination. Soon after his arrival in Harlem, he sought to uncover the origins of and solutions to America's persistent racism. He spent hours in New York's libraries studying history, literature and social sciences. His social observations and historical studies led him to conclude racism was rooted in class exploitation. Anxious to alleviate the suffering of his race, Harrison became a passionate socialist. Later, however, the racism of his white socialist comrades led Harrison to combine his socialism with black nationalism. For a brief period, he edited *Negro World*, the official newspaper of Marcus Garvey's United Negro Improvement Association.

A powerful orator, devoted to the black cause, Harrison became a popular and inspiring Harlem radical. He taught from Harlem street corners, stirring hundreds of Harlem's common folk with his teachings of equality and black pride. In 1912, he said:

> *Socialism…is right because any order of things in which those who work have least while those who work them have most, is wrong…. Therefore, if you want…to make this woeful world of ours a little better for your children…study Socialism—and think and work your way out.*

Whether preaching class struggle or racial pride, Hubert Harrison was one of the great black radicals in history. His work foreshadowed that of later greats, such as A. Philip Randolph, Adam Clayton Powell and Malcolm X.

Hubert Henry Harrison, "The Father of Harlem Radicalism," died in 1927.

Nella Larsen's prose was a reflection of her life. Born to a black father and a Danish mother, Larsen valiantly affirmed her wholeness in a culture that squeezed everyone into a racial box: You were either white or you were black; "biracial," "mixed" or "mulatto" were not accepted options; a single drop of black blood made a person black. There was no room in America to embrace both sides of one's heritage.

Nella Larsen was an upper-class, mixed-race woman who could have escaped such pain. She could have ignored her identity, focusing instead on foreign travels, spending binges and leisurely activities. Instead, Larsen confronted and embraced her dual identity. She claimed her Danish roots, studying in the University of Copenhagen and living in Denmark; and at the same time she held on to her black roots, embracing her African-American heritage and staying current on black affairs. She sought to live as black and white, and her writing chronicled this painful quest.

Nella Larsen was a significant female writer of the Harlem Renaissance, and she received the first Guggenheim Fellowship given to a black woman. Larsen's first book, *Passing*, was about two mixed-race friends, one "passing" for white and the other living as black and white.

Her next book, *Quicksand*, was the story of a biracial (Danish-black) woman who could not find a home in either world. Both books explored the anguish of the race, class and gender issues at the core of Larsen's life. *Passing* and *Quicksand* stand as powerful testimonies to the need for a complex yet unified identity in a world divided by race and class.

Nella Larsen was found dead in her New York City apartment on March 30, 1964. She was a significant contributor to the literature of the Harlem Renaissance.

MAR 22 ≣ Reverend Albert Cleage, Jr.: The Shrine of the Black Madonna

The assembled panel of prestigious clergy listened intently to the witnesses who paraded before them, bringing charges against Rev. Albert Cleage. The panel had convened to decide whether Cleage should be expelled from the fellowship of the United Church of Christ. The witnesses claimed, among other things, that Cleage preached hate and a heretical gospel of blackness. One by one, they stated their testimony to the panel: "Cleage says Jesus saves from racism and not sin;" "I've heard him preach that nonviolence will never work;" "At a conference he said Dr. King's tactics were a failure and Jesus called for revolution." The charges kept coming, including the allegation that Cleage had appeared on the same platform as Malcolm X.

When the witnesses were done, Rev. Cleage rose to defend himself. He did not waver from his convictions that Jesus was black, and he called his followers to destroy white supremacy. Confronting his accusers, Cleage declared that while nonviolence may have allowed blacks the right to eat a sandwich at a lunch counter, it was powerless for the task of bringing equality to the Senate, the corporate boardroom or the university.

Addressing the Malcolm X charge, Cleage quietly responded, "Yes, you'll hear in reports that I gave a Christian invocation [for Malcolm X], and you ought to have Malcolm out in your churches.... He could do you so much good."

Cleage successfully defended himself that day and was allowed to remain in the United Church of Christ. He continued to proclaim a black Christ from the pulpit of Central Congregational Church in Detroit, and the church became known for its Afro-centric ministries.

On Easter Sunday, 1967, Cleage unveiled an eighteen-foot painting of a Black Madonna—a dark-skinned, barefoot Mother of God embracing a black baby boy. His congregation was overwhelmed with pride, and blacks who for years had prayed to a white Jesus openly wept at a God depicted in their image. Cleage renamed the church "The Shrine of the Black Madonna." In this bold move, he laid the foundation for a black theology in which a black Jesus healed the spiritual, physical, mental, economic and communal needs of the black community.

March 26, 1967, Rev. Albert Cleage, Jr., stunned traditional Christian circles when he unveiled the beautiful painting of the Black Madonna at Central Congregational Church in Detroit. He became a proponent of picturing Jesus as a black man.

≡ Ida Bell Wells-Barnett: "I Have Only Begun to Live"

Ida Bell Wells-Barnett was a wife, mother, teacher, journalist, activist, crusader and organizer. She was also an evangelist for black rights, women's suffrage and economic justice. Her condemnation of lynch mobs and support for human rights was both bold and uncompromising. She also helped found the National Association for the Advancement of Colored People (NAACP) with W.E.B. DuBois, worked with Frederick Douglass and supported Marcus Garvey's United Negro Improvement Association.

Wells-Barnett's zeal for justice was rooted in her own anguish. She was not politicized by radical speeches or pamphlets; her sense of duty was born in grief and tears. When she was sixteen, both her parents died of yellow fever. She dropped out of school and taught in rural Mississippi to provide for herself and her siblings. Yet even as she struggled for economic stability, she stood up for the rights of others. Wells-Barnett boldly criticized preachers, presidents, legislators, sheriffs and businessmen—anyone who trampled the rights of her people. She wrote editorials about racism in schools and sued railroad companies for discrimination. In a journal entry on her twenty-fifth birthday, she expressed her life's calling:

Within the last ten [years] I have suffered more, learned more, and lost more than I ever expect to again. In the last decade, I have only begun to live—to know life as a whole with its joys and sorrows.

Though dead parents, persistent racism and lynch mobs shaped her world, Wells-Barnett held on to what it means to be human. Instead of retreating into hopelessness, she worked to change the world for others. She walked away from her painful past, looked boldly toward the future and proclaimed, "I have only begun to live!"

Ida Bell Wells-Barnett died in Chicago on March 25, 1931. Her courage and persistence are well-documented and remembered in black political history.

MAR 24 ≡ Father Laurean Rugumbwa: African Cardinal

Laurean Rugumbwa was born to a Catholic family of the Nsiba tribe in the town of Bukoba, Tanzania. As an eight-year-old, Laurean told his parents he wanted full communion in the Catholic faith. He was baptized in a beautiful Mass where dancing, drumming and singing preceded his immersion into the holy waters. Just as Christ arose from the grave in the power of God, so Laurean Rugumbwa was born anew.

Even as a boy, Rugumbwa showed an unusual dedication to the obligations and sacraments of the church. For him, the Eucharist was the real presence of Christ; he could almost feel Jesus giving himself for the salvation of humanity. The images of African saints and the dark Virgin Mary were not mere symbols to him; they modeled a deep communion with God. Young Rugumbwa would sit for hours in the town chapel, absorbing the meaning of the baptismal font, the altar, the cross and all the other gateways to God's grace.

This zeal led him to the Catholic priesthood in 1943. Each year, Fr. Rugumbwa came closer to God with ever-increasing devotion and renewed commitment. On March 28, 1960, he became the first black African Cardinal in the history of the modern Catholic Church. His elevation to the College of Cardinals gave him an influential position in the church.

When the Second Vatican Council was called in 1962, Cardinal Rugumbwa was a powerful voice for ecumenism. Though a devoted Catholic, he was nevertheless convinced that God was not fully expressed in any denomination. He believed God to be so immense, so gracious and so universal that God's image could not be exhausted by any one church.

Cardinal Rugumbwa's love for God and care for his flock was expressed in innumerable acts of service to the church. In 1968, he became the Archbishop of Dar es Salaam and the pastor of all priests and Catholics in urban Tanzania.

On March 28, 1960, Father Laurean Rugumbwa became the first black African Cardinal in the history of the modern Roman Catholic Church.

≡ Henry Dumas: "Man, Let's Just Tell It!"

Henry Dumas is almost a mythic figure in the annals of black literature. Though raised in Sweet Home, Arkansas, he spent his adult years in the black communities of Harlem and East St. Louis. His insights into black life were conveyed through a unique and creative writing style. Dumas believed that black culture inherently contained beauty and grace, and he viewed his task as a writer to tell and preserve that story. He once wrote, "I was born in the South and came quite definitely from the rural elements.… My interest in Gospel music coincides with my interest in folk poetry." He later added, "I am very much concerned about what is happening to my people and what we are doing to our precious tradition."

For Dumas, short stories became the way to carry on that precious tradition he so adored. He also considered stories as acts of resistance, transmitting the values of a people the rest of society considered inferior and unworthy. His stories—such as "Ark of Bones" (about an ark holding every black soul in America), "Goodbye, Sweetwater" and others—depict the humor and genius of black life. His insights, use of language and allegiance to blues and gospel music created almost a cult-like following among black Americans.

Dumas was not just a writer, he was a husband, father, activist, educator and organizer. He taught language to the young, organized civil rights actions, attended classes and gave his life to racial equality. When he was in East St. Louis organizing black writers, musicians and artists, he used to urge his comrades, "Man, let's just tell it!" Through his stories and his work in the community, Henry Dumas told a story that resonates with us still.

In a case of "mistaken identity," Henry Dumas was murdered by a New York City transit policeman on March 23, 1968. He was a well-known writer, educator and organizer in the black communities of Harlem and East St. Louis.

"If God created me in his image, why should I degrade myself and remain, excluded from others, in this balcony?"

That question haunted Richard Allen every time he attended St. George's Methodist Episcopal Church in Philadelphia. He thought of the day Christ had called him to new life; he recalled the purpose he felt, knowing God had touched him; and the more he recalled the dignity of conversion, the less he tolerated discrimination. How could he fulfill God's call if he allowed others to treat him as subhuman?

While white parishioners sat wherever they pleased, black Methodists were treated like unclean strangers and forced into the balcony. "Why should I," decried Allen, "as devoted a Methodist as anyone here, not be a full member of my own church?"

His friend Absalom Jones was tortured by the same thoughts, and one Sunday Jones decided to go downstairs to join the white congregation in prayer. Allen and other blacks watched from the balcony as two horrified white trustees removed Jones from the church. Disgusted with Christian racism, Allen and the others followed Jones out the front door, vowing never again to be victimized by white Christians.

Richard Allen, Absalom Jones and several others formed the Free African Society for religious instruction and mutual aid. The Society was not enough, however, for Allen; he was a devout Methodist and needed a church to express his faith. Two years after his exile from St. George's, Allen founded the Bethel African Church in Philadelphia, the pioneer congregation in the black freedom movement. Allen was ordained its first bishop, and black folks took responsibility for their own religious formation.

Out of Bethel's roots grew the African Methodist Episcopal (AME) Church, with its stations along the Underground Railroad and history of activism. Richard Allen had walked out of St. George's Church into the dignity of black independent churches.

Rev. Richard Allen died on March 26, 1831, in Philadelphia, Pennsylvania. After he and Absalom Allen were removed from St. George's Methodist Episcopal Church in 1792, they founded the Free African Society, the African Church of Philadelphia, the Bethel Benevolent Society and the African Society for the Education of Youth. The African Church of Philadelphia later became the Bethel African Church, and eventually, Mother Bethel African Methodist Episcopal Church, the original AME Church.

Hints to the Colored People of North America

Mary Ann Shadd Cary said exactly what she thought and was never intimidated by racism or sexism. Born free in Delaware, Cary wanted freedom for every member of her race. Her uncompromising fight for black liberation troubled white women suffragettes, and her insistence on women's rights agitated black male abolitionists. She criticized Susan B. Anthony for not confronting racism and condemned Henry Bibb's assertion that ex-slaves were already able to have equality in America. One of her biographers wrote:

> By nineteenth century norms, Shadd Cary's caustic jolting language seemed ill suited to a woman. She used phrases such as "gall and wormwood," "moral pest," "petty despot," "superannuated ministers," "nest of unclean birds"…in order to keep her ideas before the public.

When she was twenty-six years old, Mary Ann Shadd Cary published her book *Hints to the Colored People of North America*. The title is indicative of her brash courage and biting tongue. In *Hints*, she pre-dated the nationalism of future generations by arguing for a strict black self-reliance. Later she wrote *Notes on Canada West*, in which she argued that America was hopelessly racist and urged her people to migrate to Canada and start over.

Cary herself moved to Canada, but later returned to the United States to help the Union defeat the Confederacy. She served as a recruiter in Indiana and registered hundreds of black Union troops. After slavery's fall in 1865, Cary advocated for full and equal rights for blacks and women. In 1874, she and sixty-three other women marched on a Washington, D.C., voter registration office in a flagrant act of civil disobedience. To the end of her life, Cary fought for black rights and women's equality, giving her gifts of boldness and conviction to the world.

Mary Ann Shadd Cary spent her life in the fight for black liberation. She was the first black women reporter in America and the first black woman to attend Howard University Law School. Cary died in 1893 at the age of 70 in Washington, D.C.

☰ Dr. Benjamin Mays: Born to Rebel

Benjamin Mays grew up in the South as a child of the black church and a product of segregation. Segregation taught Mays and his peers that blacks were inferior, subhuman and unclean. However, the black church taught him that blacks were loved, protected and redeemed by Jesus Christ. His religion taught him to love others as himself and to struggle for his God-given dignity. So well did he learn these lessons that Mays refused to allow racism to denigrate his humanity. When southern custom demanded that blacks tip their hats in deference to every white person, Mays responded by "forgetting" to wear a hat.

But Mays' revolt against racism went much deeper than that: He believed that the black church could save black America—not of its own strength but because the black church was where the treasures of Jesus Christ were most accessible.

In 1921, Mays was ordained a minister in the Baptist Church and later earned a Ph.D. in Religion from the Chicago Divinity School. In 1934, he accepted the position of Dean of the School of Religion at Howard University. In 1938, he published his classic book, *The Negro's God as Reflected in His Literature*. Through sermon and the written word, Mays described how salvation resided in the bosom of the black church.

In 1940, Mays became the president of Morehouse College, where he molded hundreds of future African-American leaders. From 1944 to 1948, Mays befriended a young black Christian named Martin Luther King, Jr., and the two spent hours in dialogue about the political call of the gospel. King was profoundly influenced by his encounter with Mays and later wrote that Mays was "my spiritual mentor and intellectual father." Dr. Benjamin Mays helped shape Dr. King, along with several hundred other Morehouse men, teaching them what he himself had learned: that God created them, loved them and called them to give themselves for the common good.

Dr. Benjamin Mays died on March 28, 1984, in Atlanta, Georgia. Mays described his lifetime of Christian ministry in his book **Born to Rebel.**

☰ Jean Toomer: "To Seek and to Search"

The popular but enigmatic Jean Toomer was a talented writer and author. He is most renowned for his book, *Cane*, often considered the seminal work of the Harlem Renaissance. Published in 1923, *Cane* was hailed as a masterpiece and, in many respects, became a catalyst for later black publications.

Toomer began his literary career when he quit his job selling Ford cars and moved to Harlem to become a writer. Few of his poems were published and, like many poets, he could not make a living at his art. Seeking more steady income, he moved to Sparta, Georgia, as temporary head of Sparta's Industrial and Agricultural School for Negroes. He immersed himself in the culture of rural black folk and was never the same again. His students were mostly poor uneducated blacks, of whom he later wrote:

A visit to Georgia last fall was the starting point of everything of worth I have done.... A deep part of my nature, a part that I had repressed, sprang suddenly to life and responded to them.... Now I cannot conceive of myself as aloof or separated. My point of view has not changed; it has deepened and widened.

He expressed his transformation in *Cane*, and his poetic portrayals of race, gender and nature stunned the literary world. Critics and fans waited for him to produce another *Cane*, but it never happened. Toomer considered *Cane* not the beginning but the end. He believed *Cane* enabled him to find his race, and his work for the rest of his life was to find himself.

For the rest of his life, Jean Toomer searched for peace and harmony wherever he could find it, including psychoanalysis, East Indian religions and the Society of Friends. He sought an elusive universal bond with humanity, and he later described himself as "the first American of a new race"—a combination of black, white and red, which Toomer described as "blue." Though many were shocked by his transformations, Toomer was unfazed. His search for inner peace was not dependent upon outside approval. When he decided to become a Quaker in the 1940s, he wrote:

Perhaps our lot on this earth is to seek and to search. Now and again we find enough to enable us to carry on. I now doubt that any of us will completely find or be found in this life.

Jean Toomer, author of the book, Cane, which is considered a seminal work of the Harlem Renaissance, died on March 30, 1967. He never wrote a second book.

MAR 30   ≣ Sister Thea Bowman: "To Live Until I Die"

The Bowmans were horrified to learn that their young daughter could not yet read. Though they were but a working class family from Yazoo City, Mississippi, they knew that the only way to security and independence was education. Yet even after all their work and prayers, their little girl still could not read. They had heard of a Catholic school run by the Franciscan Sisters of Perpetual Adoration that welcomed blacks. Scraping together what little money they were able, they sent nine-year-old Thea Bowman to the Holy Child Jesus School.

An eager student, Bowman blossomed there, learning to read and to write, but her world changed far beyond academics. By the time Bowman was ten, she asked her parents if she could become a Catholic. Though they were devout Methodists, the Bowmans believed that God was larger than any denomination. They were also impressed with the spirituality of the nuns at the school, and they supported their daughter's decision.

Bowman later wrote:

> I had witnessed so many Catholic priests, brothers and sisters who made a difference that was far-reaching, I wanted to be part of the effort to help feed the hungry, find shelter for the homeless and teach the children.

Bowman became a Catholic to join in Christ's ministry of love and compassion on earth, and she went on to become a sister, nun and member of the Franciscan Sisters of Perpetual Adoration. For many years she taught children and worked to end racism, in the church in particular and in society in general. She was gifted in singing, storytelling and preaching and soon became a consultant on intercultural awareness. Her work took her all over the world, teaching black culture, African history, anti-discrimination and mutual respect in countries from Nigeria and Kenya to the Virgin Islands to Hawaii and throughout the United States. Bowman was known to move audiences of bishops and priests to tears as she told heart-wrenching stories of the consequences of intolerance and exclusion.

As an advocate for black pride, Bowman was often told that her message was divisive and that she should work harder to assimilate blacks into the church and into society. To this she replied:

> To heck with the melting pot. If you want to melt to fit into my mold, if you want to adapt to my values and way of life, go right ahead, but don't expect me to melt to fit into yours.

Even after Bowman was diagnosed with breast cancer, she continued to work for her people's full acceptance in the church and the nation. Sister Bowman prayed that she would "live until I die," and she pressed on despite a wheelchair, chemotherapy and pain. When she died in 1990, she left behind a legacy of love, faith and courage.

Sister Thea Bowman died of breast cancer complications on March 30, 1990. A member of the Franciscan Sisters of Perpetual Adoration, she was also the first black Catholic woman to receive a Doctorate in Theology. She was nationally recognized for her powerful stand for racial justice and understanding.

Father Norman Anthony DuKette: "He Endured with a Fine Elegance"

The black priest sat alone in the cathedral, his figure illuminated by burning votive candles. The smell of incense lingered, and carvings and paintings of the Virgin Mary and Sacred Heart of Jesus looked down on him. Alone at prayer in Detroit's cathedral, he asked God for wisdom in his mission in Flint, Michigan. He had been called by the Archdiocese to build a church among black Catholics in Flint, and now the task seemed impossible.

It was 1929, and the Great Depression ravaged American families. It was worse for blacks, for the thirty-percent unemployment among whites skyrocketed to sixty-percent among black workers. How could he build a church when the potential members were too busy surviving and those who joined were too poor to give?

After months of hard work and tears, Father Norman Anthony DuKette had gathered but five members who met for Mass in the basement of a parishioner's home. Given the obstacles, success appeared impossible. Yet when he arose from prayer in that Detroit cathedral, the black priest felt peace and power in his soul. With no assurance of success and beset by insurmountable challenges, Fr. DuKette knew God was with him. No matter how great the Depression, or how few the members, or how hard the road, he would continue. With the gospel message on his lips and the peace of Christ in his soul, DuKette walked out of the cathedral confident in his calling.

The small mission DuKette had begun in a basement later became Christ the King parish, a vibrant community of black Catholics. From 1929 to 1971, when he retired, Father DuKette served as parish priest at Christ the King. The church had grown from its humble, lonely years to over three hundred members. For over forty years, DuKette baptized, counseled, married, buried and served Flint's black Catholic community. He also was a member of the NAACP, the Urban League and many other political groups. As only the fourth black priest ordained in the United States, Father DuKette was a beloved and admired servant of Christ. Brother Cyprian Rowe wrote of him:

> He was the doyen of the Afro-American clergy—one of those cornerstones that God built.... He was great because he endured with a fine elegance. He was great because he had worked out in his flesh the words of Christ about love and faithfulness.

Father Norman Anthony DuKette was ordained into the priesthood on February 7, 1926, at Saints Peter and Paul Cathedral in Detroit. He founded and pastored Christ the King parish in Flint, Michigan. He died on March 31, 1980.

APRIL

Dr. Martin Luther King, Jr.

APR 1   ≣ Marvin Gaye: "What's Going On?"

When Marvin Gaye released his classic song "What's Going On?" in 1971, he transformed the relationship between music and politics. Before the song's release, protest had been divorced from mainstream music. Songs of heartbreak and romance dominated popular culture, while music about struggle was relegated to the margins. With Marvin Gaye, all that changed.

God, the Vietnam War, drug abuse, unemployment, children, ecology—everything was captured in the popular music of this Motown singer. It wasn't just that Gaye sang of politics and injustice; it was the way he did it. Listen again to "What's Going On?" and see for yourself. The insights and critique are contemporary; Gaye's genius has the ability to transcend its context and touch those living in other times and places.

The release of Gaye's *What's Going On* hit America as few albums ever have. People literally stopped where they were to listen as Gaye's soothing voice called for peace in Vietnam, love in the neighborhood and unity in the nation. His haunting lyrics and smooth tones called us to find a way to work for peace, equality and community wherever we are—and to do it not sometime in the abstract future but right now, today.

The album was a masterwork; its melodies, comforting; its lyrics, energizing. Even the album cover was unforgettable: Brother Marvin Gaye huddled in a raincoat, standing somewhere in the neighborhood. Other song titles tell it all: "Inner City Blues," "Mercy, Mercy Me" and "Save the Children" opened minds and hearts across America. Gaye went on to record other memorable albums, but none had the lasting impact and revolutionary impulse of *What's Going On.*

Marvin Gaye was shot to death by his father following a bitter argument on April 1, 1984, in Los Angeles, California. His album, **What's Going On,** *was ranked number six on* **Rolling Stone Magazine's** *list of the 500 greatest albums of all time.*

APR 2   ≣ Reverend George Liele: "Give Me a Work"

The shock ripped away young George Liele's breath: His master had just sold him! Liele was to be taken from his mother and family to be a slave in Savannah, Georgia, miles from all that was familiar. Yet God had plans for Liele that transcended servitude in Savannah. Years later, as a young man, he heard a preacher talk about Jesus, the cross and the resurrection, and he decided to give his life to God:

> I found no way I could escape the damnation of hell, only through the merits of my dying Lord and Savior Jesus Christ; which caused me to make intercessions with Christ, for the salvation of my poor immortal soul; and I full well recollect, I requested of my Lord and Master to give me a work, I did not care how mean it was, only to try and see how good I could do it.

From this humble request for "a work," Liele could not have grasped the magnitude of the mission God would give him. This ex-slave, whose family had been separated forever, was to become the founder of the first independent black church in the United States. American history was about to be changed by Rev. Liele's "work."

In 1773, Liele and his followers founded the First African Baptist Church of Savannah, Georgia. The church brought hope to slave and free alike, as Liele encouraged his flock with singing, prayers and sermons. Despite the lash and the auction block, blacks of Savannah could praise their God like free men and women.

But the church didn't stop there. The seeds Liele planted grew beyond Savannah. The Underground Railroad, the Civil Rights Movement, the Pentecostal revival, black theology—all had their origins in Savannah's First African Baptist Church. Harlem's Abyssinian Baptist Church, Atlanta's Ebenezer Baptist Church, Chicago's Pilgrim Baptist Church, Montgomery's Dexter Avenue Baptist Church, indeed it can be argued that all the great black churches in America sprouted from the bosom of Savannah's First African Baptist Church. Not only the large popular churches but every storefront, tabernacle and independent congregation in America can trace its roots back to Rev. George Liele and his followers.

In 1773, George Liele purchased his freedom and immediately gathered slaves and free blacks for Bible reading, singing and praying. Thus began the First African Baptist Church in Savannah, Georgia, and the independent black church movement.

APR 3   ≡ Carter Goodwin Woodson: The Father of Negro History

Carter G. Woodson was an important intellectual whose studies and writings promoted black history as a path to pride and racial uplift. His mother was a slave, his circumstances were grim and nothing indicated hope for the future. Yet young Carter loved to read, despite America's concerted institutional efforts to ensure that black education was a waste of time. He kept studying and went on to graduate from Berea College in 1903 and the University of Chicago in 1907, and to earn a Ph.D. from Harvard University in 1912. But his learning was not for his own gain; he did not study black history to build his estate or multiply his portfolio. For Carter Woodson, education was a means of uplifting his race from the grasp of poverty, racism and exclusion.

In 1915, Woodson founded the Association for the Study of Negro Life and History "to encourage research and writing of the Negro experience." In many respects, this was the beginning of black studies as a legitimate academic discipline, with its emphasis on research, cultural critique and intellectual analysis.

Woodson's book, *The Mis-Education of the Negro,* contained insights that shaped the debate about education for black youth. He contended that education in America was destroying black pride and preparing blacks only for servitude and debasement. Through analysis and critique, he noted that the education system diminished black potential and alienated blacks from their own community.

Perhaps Woodson's most notable contribution was the eventual establishment of Black History Month. In 1926, he proposed and implemented Negro History Week as a way to counter the omission of black culture from education. No longer would history be relegated to Greece, Rome and Western Europe. Black history would be taught alongside these world events to demonstrate Africa's significance. Eventually, Negro History Week evolved into Black History Month.

How many schoolchildren and adults have been inspired by speakers and programs during Black History Month? Woodson's annual homage to blackness exemplifies how intellectuals can change society. It is conceivable that Woodson influenced more people through Negro History Week than any one of his wonderful books.

Because of his recognition of black history, people called Carter G. Woodson "the father of Negro history." He died on April 3, 1950, in Washington, D.C.

APR 4 ≣ **Dr. Martin Luther King, Jr.: "I've Been to the Mountaintop"**

Thunder and lightning raged outside, and a long day of stressful meetings and confrontations had left Dr. Martin Luther King, Jr., exhausted. For the last fourteen years, Rev. King's body and soul had served at the altar of nonviolent struggle. He had prayed, preached, cried, marched, sang, argued and fought that the poor and outcast might be treated as human beings.

Though King lived by nonviolence, America had responded with hatred and violence. For fourteen years, kindness and mercy had been met with anger and force. King and his followers had been barraged with rocks, frequently jailed, threatened with death; their phones had been tapped, letters opened and hotel rooms bugged. So on this stormy night, turbulent with winds and heavy rain, Dr. King was tired. He lay comfortably on his bed, settling in for a quick nap before his friends returned from church.

King's fleeting tranquility was shattered when the phone rang next to his pillow. It was his friend and confidant Rev. Ralph David Abernathy.

"Hey, Doctor," Abernathy exclaimed, "I'm over here at the church, but they don't want to see me; they want to see you." Rev. Abernathy was at the Mason Temple Church of God in Christ, where hundreds had gathered to hear Dr. King. Abernathy was a good preacher, but he was no Martin Luther King, and he was begging his friend to come.

King agreed to leave the comfort of his hotel to address the gathering crowd. On the drive over, he pondered all that weighed him down. Black power advocates considered him, and nonviolence, a failure; racism remained steadfast; liberals opposed his anti-war stance; and the FBI hounded him wherever he went. Yet despite his burdens, King pushed himself into the pulpit that night.

In stirring words that continue to inspire every proponent of civil rights to this day, King admitted, "We've got some difficult days ahead," and with uncanny prescience, added, "I may not get there with you." But with a heartfelt joy, he told his people, "It really doesn't matter with me now, because I've been to the mountaintop....I've see-ee-ee-n the promised land." No one can forget his pledge: "I want you to know tonight that we, as a people, will get to the promised land."

King could hardly walk back to his seat, and the ministers on the podium helped him to his chair. Hours later, as he and Billy Kyles stood on the balcony of the Lorraine Motel, assassins horribly ensured that King would not travel further. Yet the ringing promise of his words live on, calling us to radical love. In the face of opposition, he stood up to hatred's glare and did not bend under pressure. May the vision and valor of Dr. Martin Luther King accompany our climb to the mountaintop.

Dr. Martin Luther King, Jr., was murdered on April 4, 1968, on the balcony of the Lorraine Motel, in Memphis, Tennessee. He is recognized internationally as one of modern history's greatest preachers of nonviolence and was awarded the Nobel Peace Prize in 1964.

≣ The Honorable Adam Clayton Powell, Jr.: Harlem Congressman

Few black leaders in history have been as controversial and flamboyant as the Honorable Adam Clayton Powell, Jr. It would take volumes to convey his contributions to equality and justice in America. Preacher, activist, city council member and congressman from Harlem—Rev. Powell stretched the boundaries of bravado and candor. He collaborated with anyone who stood for black rights, including Communists. He marched so Harlem blacks could work where they shopped. He agitated for equality, and he proclaimed black pride from the pulpit of the famous Abyssinian Baptist Church. Martin Luther King, Jr., considered Powell's book *Marching Blacks* the handbook of black revolution.

Yet it was in the House of Representatives that Adam Clayton Powell lifted black hopes—and generated white resentment. Early in his first term, the outspoken congressmen publicly condemned President Truman's wife for her membership in the racist Daughters of the American Revolution. That a young black man would berate a beloved First Lady sent shock waves through America.

Few causes promoting African-American dignity escaped the voice of this outspoken progressive and political wizard. His most lasting contribution, historians say, was his work as Chair of the House Committee on Education and Labor. Many of the social innovations Americans take for granted today were born in Powell's committee: the War on Poverty, increases to minimum wage, Medicare, Medicaid, Head Start and the denial of federal funds to organizations that discriminate.

Though Powell was a member of the most powerful legislative body in America, he never forgot the common black folk of America. His sense of justice arose from a deep connection with the poor black voters of Harlem. Even as he lived his passion on the national stage, he enhanced opportunities for all black people.

Congressman Adam Clayton Powell, Jr., of New York City died of cancer on April 4, 1972, in Miami, Florida. He was among the first modern black political leaders in the United States.

≣ Leopold Sedor Senghor: African Poet, African President

Leopold Sedor Senghor—scholar, poet, founder of the Negritude movement, President of Senegal—was a powerful voice for a united Africa. As a young man, he enrolled in a Roman Catholic seminary in Dakar but was soon expelled for his protests against racism. Senghor then turned to poetry and politics. While studying in Paris, he met the great Aimé Césaire from Martinique, as well as other West Indian and African émigrés. Senghor and his comrades founded the newspaper *L'Etudiant noir (The Black Student)* as a forum for Afro-centric poetry and anti-colonial agitation. Thus began the famous Negritude movement, the Harlem Renaissance on a global scale.

Negritude was an artistic and political revival of blackness, a proclamation of African dignity. Black writers from Martinique, Senegal, Trinidad, Ghana and elsewhere celebrated African cultural solidarity. (It is no coincidence that Negritude preceded the end of colonialism.) The great journal *Presence Africaine*, published by Alioune Diop and Senghor, became an important venue for the movement.

During World War II, Senghor was captured by the Germans and imprisoned for eighteen months. While interned in a Nazi prison, he wrote *Songs of the Shadow*, a powerful poetic collection. After the war, he returned to Senegal and became a leader of the independence struggle. In 1960, Senghor's work culminated in his election as Senegal's first president. Although Senghor was a Serer in a majority Wolof nation and a Christian in a Muslim land, he nevertheless was the choice of the people. For Senghor, to be African was more important than belonging to any particular tribe or faith.

For twenty years, Senghor faithfully led Senegal, not stepping down from office until 1980. In 1988, he described his life in his autobiography, *Ce que je crois (What I Believe)*, in which he recounted his lifetime of struggle on behalf of African people in general and the Senegalese people in particular. Senghor's book is a testament to his work for liberation, first as a poet, then as president.

Leopold Sedor Senegal helped create the Negritude movement and gave birth to the Senegal nation. The Mali Federation, of which Senegal was a part, achieved independence on April 4, 1960.

APRIL 7   ☰ Benedict the Moor: The Black Saint

Benedict was born in Messina, Italy, to a slave family. In 1544, when he was eighteen years old, he was freed as a reward for his parents' loyal service. Once out of bondage, he felt drawn to help the poor and destitute and began traveling from town to town helping others. In 1547, he discovered that his desire to serve could be fulfilled best by becoming a Christian. A few years later, he deepened his spiritual journey by joining the Order of Friars in Palermo as a Franciscan lay brother.

Benedict's first assignment in the monastery was to be the order's cook. But his culinary tasks did not diminish his desire to serve others. When he was not cooking, people lined up outside his kitchen for prayers, blessings, counsel and food. He became known throughout Palermo as *Il moro santo*, or "The Black Saint." Draped in his cook's apron, Benedict was so generous that crowds gathered to wait until he appeared outside the abbey's back door. He was so popular among the poor, the sick and the homeless that mention of his arrival brought crowds just to be near him. Those he touched, prayed for and blessed often remarked that they felt the hand of God in the embrace of Benedict, the Black Saint.

Benedict the Moor died in Palermo, Italy, on April 4, 1589. He was canonized a saint by the Catholic Church and has since become the patron saint of blacks in North America.

≡ Hank Aaron: Move Over, Babe

Babe Ruth smashed such prodigious home runs that later blasts were called "Ruthian." He was acclaimed as an American hero, an icon whose many short-comings were overlooked in a frenzied love fest. Hank Aaron, on the other hand, was a black pioneer in Major League Baseball, a quiet man who overcame major obstacles just to play a game.

Babe Ruth had set a seemingly untouchable record that was the joy and delight of all America; Aaron toiled in the obscurity of Negro League teams such as the Pritchett Athletics, Mobile Black Bears and the Indianapolis Clowns. Ruth had played before the adoring accolades of Yankee fans; Aaron played in Milwaukee and Atlanta, far from the media centers of New York and Los Angeles.

Yet with unbelievable grace Aaron achieved the impossible and smashed Ruth's record for most Major League home runs in a career. Even as hate mail poured in by the thousands, Aaron was unbowed. (The post office later reported that Aaron received more mail than anyone in history—more than the president, Hollywood stars, or Santa Claus.)

Though Hank Aaron was devoted to the game of baseball, he was even more serious about his obligations to his family and his race. He was a role model for other black players and used his baseball fame to speak out for civil rights. He catapulted from the sandlots of Mobile, Alabama, to national fame.

Hank Aaron is a treasure of black America. Still the all-time leader in runs batted in, holder of the career home run crown (until it was surpassed in 2007 by Barry Bonds), tireless advocate of black rights, family man and ambassador of the game of baseball, Aaron is one of the all-time great human beings—who just happened to hit more home runs than the Great Bambino himself.

On April 8, 1974, Hank Aaron hit a 385-foot home run to break Babe Ruth's previ-ous "unbreakable" record of 714 major league home runs. Aaron finished with 755 home runs. He was the model of consistency, playing for 23 years and never hitting more than 50 home runs in a single season.

≣ Dr. Charles Drew: Creator of the Blood Bank

During the years that Dr. Charles Drew taught Pathology at Howard University and did research at New York City's Columbia Medical Center, one particular problem of medicine caught his attention: Trauma victims often died because the medical profession was unable to preserve blood for transfusions. Many doctors had sought in vain to solve this problem, but despite this legacy of failure, Dr. Drew devoted himself to finding a solution. Remarkably, this brilliant doctor discovered that blood plasma, the liquid portion without the cells, could supplant whole blood in transfusions. Unlike whole blood, plasma could be preserved until needed in an emergency or a scheduled surgery.

Meeting resistance in America, Drew traveled to London to establish the British Blood Bank. During World War II, the British Blood Bank saved the lives of thousands of English troops and civilians. When Drew returned to the United States, he established the American Red Cross Blood Bank. However, the United States Army, blinded by racism, ordered the Red Cross to separate "black" blood from "white" blood. The War Department wrote, "It is not advisable to collect and mix Negro blood and Caucasian blood."

Drew protested vigorously, noting that the medical profession and common sense verified that blood differed only by type, not by race. Ironically, the Red Cross dropped Drew—the very founder of blood banks—because of his opposition to separating blood by race. Although his research saved thousands of lives, Drew was ousted for insisting black blood and white were the same. Yet despite his expulsion, Dr. Charles Drew continued to practice medicine for all, regardless of race. He literally brought life to thousands who otherwise would have died. His thesis, "Banked Blood: A Study in Blood Preservation," transformed the practice of medicine.

Dr. Charles Drew, the founder of the Red Cross Blood Bank, died on April 1, 1950, in Burlington, North Carolina, from an automobile accident. Some accounts note that he died because he was refused access to the closest hospital, a hospital alleged to have treated whites only.

≣ Howard Thurman: A Vision of Unity

Howard Thurman was truly an American spiritual giant. Considered by many to be one of the ten most important preachers in American history, he influenced world leaders such as Mahatma Gandhi and Martin Luther King, Jr. Rev. Thurman served as chaplain at Boston University, taught theology all over the world and conversed easily with Quakers, Hindus and Muslims. He was a mystic, author, pastor, preacher and servant of God whose ideas challenged the status quo.

At a time when American Christendom was marked by rigid racial separation, Thurman founded the Church of the Fellowship of All Peoples. This San Francisco congregation of African Americans, whites and Asians contrasted with the racial intolerance of much of Christianity. Thurman saw all categories, classifications and religions as human-made barriers that limited God and prevented spiritual growth, and he preached a new understanding of a God who was in all and above all, a God who transcended dogma, ritual and institutions. This fundamental concept of God accomplished a unity that even today few Christian denominations can duplicate. Thurman later wrote of his church:

> Here at last I could put to the test…the major concern of my life: Is the worship of God the central and most significant act of the human spirit? Is it really true that in the presence of God there is neither male nor female, child nor adult, rich nor poor?

Rev. Howard Thurman understood that humanity's great flaw is our propensity to mold God in our own image, to see God in our complexion, our politics and our flag. His challenge was to hear God's call beyond ourselves, to sit in silent awe at God's glory and to allow ourselves to be renewed by that compelling and transcendent vision.

For Thurman, God was not simply to be believed; God was to be experienced. And through that experience, he believed, we could understand our world, others and ourselves with a clarity that would change us forever.

Howard Thurman died April 10, 1981, in San Francisco. Martin Luther King, Jr., is said to have carried Thurman's book Jesus and the Disinherited *with him throughout the Civil Rights Movement.*

APR 11    Chris Hani: Spear of the Nation

Out of South Africa's oppressive history arose leaders whose courage is unmatched anywhere in the world: Nelson Mandela, Steve Biko, Oliver Tambo, Mary Moodley and others shine brightly among this constellation of heroes. South Africans, however, still say that the most courageous, the most charismatic, was Chris Hani. Mere mention of his name brings a smile to the disheartened.

Hani's dedication to black liberation inspired everyone in his presence. Every word, action and movement had but one aim: freedom for black South Africans. He graduated from Fort Harare University in 1962 as a classics scholar. Though a comfortable career as a teacher awaited him, Hani tied his future to the oppressed. He joined the African National Congress (ANC) Youth League and marched, petitioned and advocated for an end to apartheid.

Young Hani watched as his comrades were whisked away at night, exiled from their homes and murdered with impunity. Reluctantly, he concluded that his people would continue to die unless blacks took more revolutionary measures. He joined the armed wing of the ANC, *Umkhonto we Sizwe* ("Spear of the Nation"), and began a violent struggle against apartheid's infrastructure.

Hani was also active in the South African Congress of Trade Unions and the South African Communist Party. He sought the complete overthrow of any system that left black children, workers, elderly and others without healthcare, power or dignity. He was immensely popular among the poorest and most abused sectors of black South Africa. They knew that their cause was his, and that no sacrifice was too great for their emancipation.

In 1987, Hani served as Chief of Staff for *Umkhonto*, and four years later he was elected Secretary-General of the South African Communist Party. His energy and brilliance were such that many saw him as the successor to the great Nelson Mandela.

In 1993, however, black hopes ended when right-wing whites assassinated Hani outside his home. His death sparked riots and threatened to end the negotiations between the ANC and the apartheid regime. Mandela invoked Hani's legacy, urging both sides back to the table. Hani, he said, would have wanted nothing more than to end apartheid and see blacks treated as human beings. To turn away from negotiations would be to play into the hands of the right wing and further white supremacy.

Even in death, Chris Hani hastened the end of apartheid.

In the spring of 1993, while the ANC and the South African Communist Party were negotiating with the apartheid regime to end white rule in South Africa, white racists murdered Chris Hani in Boksburg, South Africa. He was widely mourned, and his death on April 10, 1993, almost destroyed the ongoing negotiations.

≡ Joe Louis: The Brown Bomber

One of America's great heroes was born Joseph Louis Barrow, son of poor Georgia sharecroppers. He later dropped "Barrow," so most of us know him as Joe Louis, the man who transformed the brutal sport of boxing into an epic struggle of right against wrong. During Louis' time, America was rigidly segregated, and there was no sphere of life in which blacks could be equal to whites. Whites ruled, blacks served and that was that. Blacks shined shoes, served dinners and swept streets, performing tasks particular to their role as "subhumans."

Boxing, however, was the one major sport where blacks could compete against whites, and in that arena Louis triumphed. In match after match, his defeat of white opponents earned him the title of "The Brown Bomber," and it seemed that he was unbeatable…until he met up with the great German boxer Max Schmeling. In the twelfth round, Schmeling knocked out Louis, to Adolph Hitler's exultation of Arayan supremacy.

Two years later, however, when Joe Louis and Max Schmeling met again, Louis climbed into the ring bearing the weight of his race, his nation, and indeed the entire free world. This time, the courageous young black man, just barely twenty-four years old, stunned the world in the first round. Even before the first bell sounded, the hope of the fascists, the symbol of the Nazis, lay prostrate on the canvas. The "subhuman" had won!

It was more than a boxing match; Louis' defeat of Schmeling was the first kink in the supposed impenetrable Nazi armor, exposing vulnerability in the purported Aryan supremacy. Even the hate preached by Hitler suffered a defeat that day in the friendship that grew between Schmeling and Louis.

Black children across the nation wanted to emulate Joe Louis, not just as a boxer but as someone who could compete against whites in other fields of life. After every Louis victory, black communities in Harlem, South Chicago, Detroit, Nashville and Washington, D.C., erupted in celebration. Before Muhammad Ali, Jackie Robinson and other sports figures brought pride to black America, Joe Louis inspired African Americans with his flat-foot shuffle and his compact punch.

Joe Louis died on April 12, 1981, in Las Vegas, Nevada. He completed his boxing career with a record of 68 victories and 3 losses; 54 of his victories were knockouts.

APR 13   ≡ Reconstruction: True Democracy

At the end of the Civil War, four million black Americans cast off their shackles, left their masters and marched into the shining light of freedom. No one knew what the future held. Blacks knew slavery was over, but few understood what it was to be free. Southern whites had nightmares of ex-slaves rampaging through their homes, exacting revenge for centuries of whippings, beatings and rapes. With thousands of Confederate white men lying in graves in battlefields such as Gettysburg, Antietam and Cold Harbor, Southern widows, elderly men and young children had visions of a black orgy of vengeance.

But the much-feared bloodshed never happened. Instead, slaves used their freedom to reunite families, build homes and live peacefully as citizens of the United States. They also participated in America's most significant attempt at true democracy: Reconstruction. During the brief span from 1865 to 1877, Reconstruction empowered ex-slaves to help rebuild the political and social infrastructure of the South.

The Reconstruction years reflect the unquenchable generosity and fairness of the human spirit. Black voters held the ballot as sacred and used that power to elect progressive black and white legislators. Black officials opened the public school system for blacks and poor white children who formerly had been excluded in the "Old South." In fact, Reconstruction legislation, written mostly by blacks, was the first in the nation to make public education both free and compulsory. Ex-slaves also created self-help organizations at a frantic pace. Black Americans formed Union Leagues all over the South, and by 1867 almost every black voter was a member of a local League. These organizations advocated social issues, collected dues for the poor and conducted political education classes.

Reconstruction also witnessed the dawn of black political power. Benjamin Turner, P.B.S. Pinchback, Blanche K. Bruce, Robert Elliot and others served in federal and state offices. When Reconstruction was betrayed by the Compromise of 1877, the nation lost its black progressive voice and political leadership, and the entire nation has since paid dearly the price of that duplicity.

The Reconstruction lasted from 1865 to 1877. In their excellent histories, Eric Foner and the brilliant W.E.B. DuBois have enumerated the social, educational, cultural and political advances of Reconstruction.

APR 14   ≡ Chinua Achebe: The Truth of Fiction

Perhaps no African work of fiction has been critiqued, discussed and analyzed more than Chinua Achebe's classic novel *Things Fall Apart*. In this retelling of the story of European domination from the viewpoint of the colonized, Achebe turned traditional storytelling on its end. While most writers described Africans as puppets in the hands of white masters, Achebe portrayed the dignity, complexity and contradiction of African people. His fiction brought Africans to life, portraying Africans as actors and creators, not pawns and victims. Yet Achebe did not blindly condemn Europe and glorify Africa. Instead, he wrote of humans trying to survive feudalism, conquest and subjugation:

> African people did not hear of culture the first time from Europe; their societies were not mindless but frequently had a philosophy of great depth and value and beauty; they had a poetry, and above all, they had a dignity.

Each of Achebe's major works described a phase in the transition from servitude to self-determination. *Things Fall Apart*, his most important novel, chronicled in stunning detail the implosion of post-colonial Africa. His later novels, *A Man of the People* and *No Longer at Ease*, continued the insights of *Things Fall Apart*. *No Longer at Ease* depicted the stranglehold that materialism and corruption had on young Africans, while *A Man of the People* exposed the contradictions of black leadership in post-colonial Africa.

He saw his fiction as a weapon, enabling the reader to better understand the social forces and personal weaknesses that hindered human progress. In his brilliant essay, "The Truth of Fiction," he wrote: "Art is man's constant effort to create for himself a different order of reality from that which is given to him."

Nigerian Chinua Achebe is an important African writer. **Things Fall Apart,** *published in 1958, is his most significant literary work.*

APR 15   ≡ Truth and Reconciliation Commission: To Heal a Nation

On April 15, 1996, Archbishop Desmond Tutu opened the proceedings for a remarkable event in human history. Though South Africa was freed from apartheid, past crimes threatened to tear the nation apart. Unmarked graves, missing persons, broken limbs and haunting nightmares were the legacy of that ghastly social system. Not all whites were guilty of crimes, but the horror permeated the nation. The world wondered what would happen to whites when liberated blacks were free to take their due vengeance. What tortures, kidnappings and murders awaited whites who had for years inflicted those same horrors on blacks? White South Africans, indeed the entire world, feared the reaction of black South Africans.

The world was stunned by the black reaction to the long history of abuse. Instead of building a Robben Island-type prison for whites and preparing the gallows for white torturers, black South Africans created the Truth and Reconciliation Commission. Chaired by Desmond Tutu, this sixty-person, multi-racial commission sought to heal the nation with a heart-wrenching quest for truth. The Commission heard testimonies of imprisonment, torture and murder so horrific that many, including Tutu, broke down and cried.

Tutu felt that truth was the first step toward forgiveness, reparations and reconciliation, and that punishment should be reserved for only the most sadistic crimes. Truth, however, was not easy to ascertain. Survivors and victims listened as officials, assassins and jailers described their "duties." Likewise, the perpetuators were forced to hear the consequences of their inhuman acts against mothers, fathers, sons and daughters. For many, confession was itself tortuous, as they faced the devastating losses they had inflicted.

While many might have thought the time was ripe for revenge and reprisal, the Truth and Reconciliation Commission exemplified the height of human capacity for forgiveness. South Africa arose from the ashes of despair to demonstrate just how wise and compassionate we human beings can really be.

The Truth and Reconciliation Commission of South Africa first met on April 15, 1996. The 60 people who comprised the commission investigated crimes committed against 10,000 victims between 1960 and 1993.

Ralph Ellison created a novel many consider a modern literary classic. The message of *Invisible Man* speaks to anyone whose identity has been swallowed by circumstances, to anyone who seeks to understand what it means to be human. For seven years, Ellison labored over what became *Invisible Man*, and it has since been called a moving and innovative literary work. He spent the next forty years on a sequel to *Invisible Man*, but it was never completed.

In Ellison's classic novel, the reader never learns the name of the protagonist, who is called "boy," "brother," "you" and "nigger" but is never named. Though often unseen, the hero's life is intimately woven with those he encounters. Whether on a southern black campus, in a Harlem factory, at a street protest or as a member of the revolutionary "Brotherhood," the invisible person symbolizes how African Americans were seen or, more accurately, not seen by white society.

Many have noted the link between the book's opening line, "I am invisible" and its ending, "Who knows that on the lower frequencies…I speak for you." By the close of the novel, the protagonist has come to the realization that he must become visible and take responsibility for himself. This in essence is Ellison's message to us all—not just to black Americans but to all who have struggled to understand their purpose in life. Ellison concludes by saying, "Life is to be lived, not controlled; humanity is won by continuing to play in spite of certain defeat." This echoes what oppressed people everywhere know: Life is not about the triumph; it is about the struggle. Our humanity is attained when we do not surrender to despair. For all of us, Ellison triumphantly claims:

> I'm coming out [of my hole].… And I suppose it's damn well time. Even hibernations can be overdone.… Perhaps that is my greatest social crime, I've overstayed my hibernation, since there's a possibility that even an invisible man has a socially responsible role to play.

Ralph Ellison's message is inescapable: We cannot sequester ourselves from death, loss and pain; our humanity requires that we become visible.

Novelist Ralph Ellison died on April 16, 1994, in New York City. His novel **The Invisible Man** *continues to be required reading at high schools and colleges across the nation.*

☰ Harold M. Washington: Mayor of Chicago

On April 12, 1983, Harold M. Washington rocked the nation with his stunning mayoral victory in Chicago. As the most segregated city in the United States, Chicago was considered by some the most racist urban area above the Mason-Dixon Line. In addition, Chicago had an Irish political machine that excluded anyone not in the "club." Even President John F. Kennedy and Dr. Martin Luther King, Jr., were forced to pay homage to the Chicago power structure. This machine had operated without upset for fifty years, dispensing privilege and service according to voting patterns, race and quid pro quo. Black Chicagoans resided on the margins, at best. Further, white demagogues such as then Alderman Ed Vrdolyak, recently indicted on corruption charges, exploited racial fears, urging voters to "keep the city the way it is."

In 1983, all that changed in a transformation so sudden that it resembled more a revolution than a mayoral election. Few cities have witnessed such rapid change in so short a time. Blacks astonished poll watchers as three out of every four cast their ballots, helping to elect Harold Washington, who assumed his mayoral role with a generosity that astonished observers.

Rather than unleashing a torrent of reprisals and payback, Washington pushed a progressive agenda that embraced all of Chicago. Infant mortality for Chicago's poor was an embarrassment for a civilized city, and Washington developed healthcare programs geared toward poor mothers. He also brought jobs to the South Side, housing to the West Side, and educational and judicial fairness throughout the city. Mexicans, Puerto Ricans, poor whites and others benefited from Washington's progressive policies.

Though his tenure was brief, cut short by a massive heart attack on November 25, 1987, Harold Washington left Chicago with a lasting legacy not only of tangible benefits for the poor but of justice and fairness for all.

Harold Washington defeated Republican Bernard Epton on April 12, 1983. Though Chicago had not had a Republican mayor in decades and though Epton was especially poorly qualified to be an urban executive, Washington won by only a narrow margin, a reflection of the city's long-standing history of opposition to real black leadership.

The Souls of Black Folk: Our Truer and Better Selves

At the beginning of the twentieth century, American blacks were but one generation removed from slavery. With very few exceptions, any African American over thirty-eight had been a slave. Yet the abolition of slavery had done little to change white supremacy and economic injustice. Lynchings left a trail of terror and fear, and black sharecroppers and tenant farmers lived with debt and despair that mimicked slavery itself. The Ku Klux Klan roamed dark nights with impunity, voting rights were completely restricted, white churches denounced black equality and white scientists justified white supremacy with distorted theories on race. Historian Rayford Logan considered the early 1900s the lowest point in black life, calling it the "nadir" of black history. The title of a popular book of 1900 encapsulated the terrible prejudice of this racist climate: *The Mystery Solved: The Negro a Beast.*

Into this cauldron of hate stepped the great black scholar W.E.B. DuBois. His brilliant mind surveyed the black condition and wondered aloud if his people would ever be treated as humans in America. In 1903, at the height of black agony, DuBois published his classic book, *The Souls of Black Folk.* Since its publication over a century ago, *Souls* remains an important commentary on black life and race relations. DuBois' biographer, David Levering Lewis, wrote:

> [The Souls of Black Folk] *redefined the terms of a three-hundred-year interaction between black and white people and influenced the cultural and political psychology of peoples of African descent throughout the western hemisphere.... It was an electrifying manifesto, mobilizing a people for bitter, prolonged struggle to win a place in history. Ironically, even its author was among the tens of thousands whose conceptions of themselves were to be forever altered by the book.*

Angela Davis, Cornel West, Manning Marable, Stokelely Carmichael, Malcolm X and many others have described how DuBois informed their search for authentic black identity. I, too, count myself as one of the thousands changed by *The Souls of Black Folk.* In a memorable verse, DuBois wrote:

> *One ever feels his two-ness—an American, a Negro; two souls, two thoughts, two unreconciled strivings; two warring ideals in one dark body, whose dogged strength alone keeps it from being torn asunder. The history of the American Negro is the history of this strife, this longing to attain self-conscious manhood, to merge his double self into a better and truer self.*

The Souls of Black Folk *by W.E.B. DuBois was published by the Chicago firm of A.C. McClurg and Company on April 18, 1903. It is considered one of the most influential books in black history.*

Charlotta Bass' dreams were slipping away. She had left the East Coast for the open spaces and opportunities of 1910 Los Angeles, hoping to succeed as a black female newspaper reporter. When she arrived, she signed on with the *California Owl*, but she was soon disillusioned by the paper's poor management. In addition, the editor's failing health exacerbated the company's fragile existence. Bass was in a quandary: She had traveled three thousand miles only to find fewer opportunities than where she left. After days of agonizing, she decided upon a drastic course. She would do something unheard of for black women in 1912—Charlotta Bass would purchase the paper.

The next several weeks, Bass worked feverishly toward her dream. She secured bank loans, borrowed money from friends and successfully negotiated the purchase of the failing *California Owl*.

Bass' first move was to change the name to *The California Eagle*. Intrigued by the great bird that "flies high and sees all," Bass advocated journalism that exposed white supremacy, buoyed black hopes and analyzed events from a black perspective. She exhibited a keen understanding of the power of the media. For example, when the racist 1915 movie *The Birth of a Nation* was hailed by white audiences and given a private showing in the White House, she courageously condemned this national icon, unafraid of the consequences.

The paper went on to expose military bigotry in World War I, covered the 1919 Pan-African Congress and encouraged the Scottsboro Boys. *The California Eagle* became the voice of black Los Angeles. Bass' activism continued unabated for decades, culminating in 1952 with her candidacy for vice-president on the Progressive Party ticket.

As the first black woman to own and publish a newspaper in America, Charlotta Bass cast aside limiting stereotypes and obstacles to become an advocate of justice and a model of perseverance.

Charlotta Bass died in Los Angeles on April 29, 1969. She described her life in her book, Forty Years: Memoirs from the Pages of a Newspaper.

Ann Lane Petry's father was a pharmacist at a time when few blacks could be professionals. She followed her father's steps but soon explored her more creative gifts. When she moved to Harlem to write for *The Amsterdam News*, her investigative reporting led her to Harlem tenements. It was here that the woman from Connecticut's small black middle class experienced the poverty, violence and economic exploitation of an emerging ghetto for the first time.

Observers have said that this exposure gave her later fiction a "compelling edge," a power expressed in her 1946 novel *The Street*. The novel portrays a single mother surviving the callousness and violence of the city. It was the first time any writer had shown black women coping with urban life, describing the fight for dignity amidst economic and racial degradation. *The Street* sold two million copies, the first book by a black woman to reach that milestone. Petry's works *A Country Place* and *The Narrows* explored similar themes. She later wrote:

> *Over and over again, I have said: These are people...look at them and remember them. Remember for what a long, long time black people have been in this country, have been part of America: a sturdy, indestructible, wonderful part of America; woven into its heart and into its soul.*

Ann Lane Petry's novels help us remember that, above all else, it is people who are sacred.

Gifted novelist Ann Lane Petry died in Old Saybrook, Connecticut, on April 28, 1997. Her novel The Street, about a single black mother in New York City, has sold over two million copies.

APR 21   ≡ Nina Simone: "Young, Gifted and Black"

Music was her life, and she sang of hurt, trauma and triumph. Nina Simone expressed, as few others could, the loneliness, romance and ecstasy of living. By 1963, she was a popular singer who defied category. Though Simone was not considered a blues singer, few could convey emotions like she could. Though not widely known, those who heard her adored her. Nina Simone was not a "political" artist, but many in the Civil Rights Movement held her albums as prized possessions.

In the fall of 1963, Nina Simone was changed forever. She recalls in her autobiography, *I Put a Spell on You*:

> *I was sitting there in my den on 15 September when news came over the radio that somebody had thrown dynamite into the 16th Street Baptist Church in Birmingham, Alabama, while black children were attending a Bible study class. Four of them...were killed. It was more than I could take, and I sat struck dumb in my den like St. Paul on the road to Damascus; all the truths that I had denied in myself for so long rose up and slapped my face. The bombing of the little girls in Alabama and the murder of Medgar Evers were like the final pieces of a jigsaw that made no sense until you had fitted the whole thing together. I suddenly realized what it was to be black in America...but it wasn't an intellectual connection...it came as a rush of fury, hatred, determination. In church language, the Truth entered into me and I "came through."*

That night, Nina Simone entered the Movement, and she worked for social equality the rest of her life. She performed benefits for civil rights groups, conferred with political leaders and loaned her talents to various struggles. Her music reflected her political transformation. The night she "came through," Simone wrote, "Mississippi Goddamn," a self-explanatory title that exemplified her radicalism.

A few months later, she wrote the anthem of black liberation, "Young, Gifted and Black," which reflected the "Black Is Beautiful" slogan sweeping the nation's ghettos at the time. Civil rights organizations passed resolutions that proclaimed the dignity of the song, black children woke up to her haunting voice on the radio and teenagers hummed the tune on street corners. Just as the Movement changed Simone, her music changed the Movement. While America told black youth that they were worthless and useless, she countered with a message that they were young, gifted and black.

Nina Simone died at her home in France on April 21, 2003. She was one of many black American artists who found a more just society in France than in America.

APR 22 ≣ Charles Hamilton Houston: "It All Started with Charlie"

In 1929, Howard University's Law School was slipping into oblivion. The American Bar Association had denied Howard's application for accreditation, and graduates from the Law School were being viewed with skepticism. The night school, which had been created to provide opportunities for full-time workers, was draining the school of resources and reducing the quality of its legal education. Graduates of Howard Law School were at a serious disadvantage—first, for being black and, second, for graduating from Howard…until Charles Hamilton Houston was appointed Vice-Dean.

At once things began to change. Houston set out to make Howard University Law School the "West Point of Negro Leadership," and he started by stocking his school with the best black students and best legal minds he could recruit. While academic quality was the goal, it was not an end in itself, for Houston believed that only the judicial system could rescue blacks from segregation and execution, and so he wanted good black lawyers and judges. He would visit each incoming class to impart his vision of their responsibility and role in the black struggle. He would tell future lawyers that litigation was the only way blacks' civil rights could be guaranteed. He told them they had a choice—either to be a lawyer who is "a parasite or a social engineer." They had a choice about whether they wanted to live off the misery of others or change injustice into fairness.

Houston not only transformed the Howard University Law School, but he also dramatically placed legal action at the center of the Civil Rights Movement. Putting his creed into action, he left Howard to become special counsel to the National Association for the Advancement of Colored People (NAACP). Further, many of his students went on to secure legal liberties for black Americans. The most notable of these, the great Thurgood Marshall, toppled school segregation and later became a Supreme Court Justice. Marshall, who understood Charles Hamilton Houston's role in the civil rights struggle, once remarked, "It all started with Charlie." Black legal activism began with Charles Hamilton Houston, and it continues each time a black attorney defends justice in America's courtrooms.

Attorney Charles Hamilton Houston died on April 22, 1950, of heart failure, at the age of 55. He transformed the Howard University Law School and made it a catalyst for social justice.

APR 23   ≡ June E. Johnson: "A Free Spirit"

In 1962, June E. Johnson was a young girl of only fourteen, but she saw how her people lived in her town of Greenwood, Mississippi, and she did not think it was right. While whites occupied nice homes and attended new schools, her people lived in dilapidated shacks, her friends were often sick and shoeless, and everyone she knew stayed poor no matter how hard they worked.

When the Student Nonviolent Coordinating Committee (SNCC) came to Greenwood in 1962 talking about change and empowerment, Johnson was excited. Despite her parent's admonition to stay away from that new organization, she found a way to attend some of the meetings. Listening to talk of how her people were kept powerless through violence, ballot restrictions and injustice, she vowed to become part of the movement to change Mississippi. This was daunting work, for white people were dominant in Greenwood. All those with power—sheriffs, judges, storeowners, plantation owners and the like—were white. Johnson learned through SNCC that any talk of black empowerment could be met with violence, threats and even death. But she was not deterred, and at age fifteen she became one of the original members of the SNCC chapter in Greenwood.

On June 11, 1963, June Johnson learned the cost of fighting for freedom. She and other activists were arrested in Winona, Mississippi, on the way back from a voter registration training course. In the booking room, white police officers—grown men trained in the arts of physical force—severely beat her, along with Annell Ponder and Fannie Lou Hamer. Blood streamed from Johnson's face and some with her reported that she had been beaten "within inches of her life." When Lawrence Guyot, former chair of the Mississippi Freedom Democratic Party, came to bail the women out of jail, he described the scene as "a horrifying experience for all of us."

Though she was still an impressionable teenager, Johnson was not deterred from her commitment to bring equality and justice to her family, friends and the black people of Mississippi. Once her wounds healed, she went right back to work in the freedom struggle. Not old enough to vote herself, she served as a witness for black residents attempting to register in Greenwood.

Johnson remained in the work for black rights and human dignity for the rest of her life, going on to become a paralegal investigator in lawsuits against racist practices in government and business. She later moved to Washington, D.C., where she worked as a daycare monitor for the city's Child and Family Services Agency. She never stopped helping those in need. People who knew her described her as "a free spirit who believed in the empowerment of people." More than most, June Johnson knew that empowerment came only through sacrifice and courage.

Activist June Johnson died of kidney failure on April 13, 2007, at Providence Hospital in Washington, D.C. As a teenager, she was a courageous leader in Mississippi for the Student Nonviolent Coordinating Committee (SNCC).

APR 24   ≣ George Moses Horton: Hope of Liberty

George Moses Horton's master allowed him to have paid employment outside the plantation and promised that, if he earned enough, he could eventually purchase his freedom. Horton seized the opportunity, and every day after his slave duties ended he hired himself out in nearby jobs. The University of North Carolina was close, and Horton washed laundry, cleaned rooms and painted doors on campus. Surrounded by books and students, Horton also learned to read and write.

Horton soon discovered that he had a gift for writing and began composing letters and poems for students. His expressions were so vivid and his words so powerful that many paid him for his works. Horton realized that if he could earn money writing, he might be able to publish a book and use the sales income toward purchasing his freedom. He was captivated by the idea and feverishly wrote whenever he was not working. Huddled with pen and paper, Horton scribbled by candlelight, often late into the evenings.

In 1829, after years of effort, Horton published *Hope of Liberty*, a poetry book some benevolent whites help him produce. Everywhere he went, Horton carried copies and sold them on campuses, at churches and down country roads. But his task was arduous, for whites were not inclined to buy a book about black freedom and blacks were generally slaves with no money to purchase books.

Though Horton's attempt failed, his hope for liberty did not. Thirty-six years after the publication of *Hope of Liberty,* Horton walked off the plantation when he heard the approach of Union soldiers. He died three years later in Philadelphia, but not before he tasted, at last, his precious hope of liberty:

Come Liberty, thou cheerful sound,
roll through my ravished ears!
Come, let my grief in joys be found
and drive away my fears….

Oh Liberty! thou golden prize,
So often sought by blood—
We crave thy sacred sun to rise,
The gift of nature's God!

In April of 1865, George Moses Horton escaped to freedom, 36 years after publication of his book of poems, Hope of Liberty.

APRL 25 ≡ **Reverend James Morris Lawson: "Don't Wait. Come Now!"**

Rev. James Lawson was a pacifist, a civil rights leader and a Methodist minister whose impact on African-American history is far greater than credited. He is less known that Malcolm X, Dr. Martin Luther King, Jr., Rev. Andrew Young, Fannie Lou Hamer and others, yet his influence on nonviolent struggle was remarkable.

Rev. Lawson's commitment to nonviolence preceded the teachings of Martin Luther King, Jr., and the strategies of the Civil Rights Movement. When Lawson was eighteen, he was drafted to serve in the Korean War. He had at least three legitimate deferment options, including pursuit of missionary service in Africa, but he also believed that war was morally wrong. He decided to take a stand as a conscientious objector, refusing to serve. Committed to his moral principles, he spurned his opportunities for deferment and chose jail instead.

This was but the beginning of his nonviolent struggle. He later traveled to India, where he spoke at length with the great Mohatma Gandhi. Inspired by the visit, Lawson returned to the United States anxious to participate in a nonviolent movement against racism and white supremacy.

Lawson intended to enroll in Yale Divinity School to study theology. Then, one fall day in 1956, he met Dr. King when King was visiting Oberlin College. King was so impressed with Lawson's insights and courage that when Lawson told King he was planning to come to the South after Yale, King exclaimed, "Don't wait. Come now!"

Lawson heeded King's request and within months was in Nashville as Field Secretary for the Fellowship of Reconciliation. Lawson recruited black college students for his popular classes on nonviolent resistance, and his gentle spirit drew many under his wing. Lawson transformed college students into a cadre of leaders who themselves would infuse the Movement with vigor. Diane Nash, John Lewis, James Bevel, Rodney Powell, Bernard Lafayette, Gloria Johnson and many more were empowered by the teachings of Rev. James Lawson. Heeding King's request to "Come now," Lawson changed Nashville, the South and all of America.

On April 25, 1951, James Morris Lawson entered a federal penitentiary for his refusal to serve in the United States armed forces. He declined the legitimate deferrals available and chose instead to stand on his convictions, regardless of the personal cost.

APR 26 ☰ **Black Monks of Skidaway Island: Self-Help and Prayers of Freedom**

Between 1877 and 1887, an extraordinary thing happened in South Carolina. Just a few years after the Civil War, with the South in ruins, blacks searching for life after the plantation and violence everywhere, a group of black men gathered as a monastic community of prayer, self-help and teaching. Imagine the scene: Black men seen only as slaves, pagans and brutes were now gathering for daily Mass, morning prayers, self-sufficient farming and teaching in the school they ran.

The Benedictine order founded the monastery on Skidaway Island, a few miles from Charleston, South Carolina, as a center of evangelization for the black community. For ten years, black monks taught children, farmed, fished and had full schedules of Mass, prayers and meditations. Who were these men who shattered the stereotypes of ignorance to form a disciplined monastic community in the South? How could black men fighting racism, poverty, violence and powerlessness find dignity and pride in a Catholic monastery? Somehow, the regime of prayers, the daily Sacraments, the service of teaching and the farming chores gave them a sense of respect and self-determination that they could not find anywhere else.

Brother Rhaban Canonge and Brother Albert Mason were but two of several black monks who spent time at Skidaway Island. Their community disbanded after ten years and the school closed, yet the seeds had been sown. Over the years, the prayers of these faithful black monks flourished and grew. The black children they taught, in turn, taught others. By their example of donning habits and living in a monastery, they had shown that black men could attain the heights of holiness in the midst of hatred, violence and racism. Their gifts of prayers for peace and healing continued to bless others years past the closure of the monastery and school.

When Canonge and Mason left Skidaway, they continued their commitment. Canonge went to another monastery where he served until his death in 1920, and Mason was one of the leaders of the first National Black Catholic Congress.

In April of 1868, Catholic bishops met to discuss the formation of black parishes and services. Out of their discussions came the formation of the black monastery at Skidaway Island, South Carolina. From 1877 to 1887, blacks were a significant part of the Benedictine monastery there, and their teaching and farming on the island stood as testaments to prayer, discipline and self-sufficiency.

APR 27   ≡ Haile Selassie I: The Roots of Rasta

In the spring of 1930, the Empress Zawditu of Abyssinia lay dying in her chambers. Anxious advisors and worried family gathered around, praying for her restoration. By late April, however, the great empress breathed her last and died. She was succeeded on November 2 by Haile Selassie I, the young Ethiopian who became Africa's newest king. At his coronation he was renamed King Negus Negusta, and he was also known as Ras Tafari. When the young Ras Tafari informed the world that he was taking his place among the community of leaders, this new king caught the imagination of black folk across the world, and parades were held in his honor—especially in Jamaica. Jamaica had long been a source of black nationalist teaching and Afro-centric ideology, as suffering peasants sought the return of Africa's glory.

Many Jamaicans believed that Haile Selassie was God incarnate, that this king of the black race, the Lion of Judah, had come to save his people. His supporters traced his roots to King Solomon of the Old Testament, making him the Son of David and the King of Kings. After Haile Selassie's crowning in Ethiopia, blacks in Kingston and the Jamaican countryside gathered to celebrate his reign. Calling themselves Rastafarians, Jah was their God; the Lion of Judah, Haile Selassie I, his incarnation; and Africa, their home. They developed a culture and religion of their own and preached love, peace and African pride.

In the 1950s, Jamaican newspapers printed photos of the great Field Marshall Mwariama of Kenya's Land and Freedom Army, also known as Mau Mau. Rastafarians loved his bold dreadlocks and took this style as their signature link to African resistance. Deep in the Jamaican jungle, their Nyabinghi drumming evolved into a new sound called "reggae" music. Within the next decade, reggae's polyrhythms, syncopated beats and lyrics of struggle, love, pride and triumph conquered the world. Burning Spear, Bob Marley and the Wailers, Culture, the Itals and several other reggae performers were nourished in the bosom of Rastafarian religion.

The great black scholar Walter Rodney described his encounter with the Rastas of Jamaica in his classic book, *Groundings with My Brothers*:

There are brothers who up to now are performing a miracle. They live and are physically fit. They have vitality of mind. They have a tremendous sense of humor. They live in depth.

That depth can still be heard today in the lyrics of reggae and in the Rastafarian emphasis on love and peace.

The coronation of Haile Selassie I of Ethiopia in 1930 also marks the origins of Rastafarian religion in Jamaica.

APR 28 ≡ Muhammad Ali: "I Am the Greatest"

There is no room in the sport of boxing for the frightened, the squeamish or the meek; it is one against one. The combatants circle each other, trapped in the ring by rope and desire. There are only two exits: either to be crumpled on the canvas in a defeated heap or to be bouncing victoriously in your corner. The men in the ring aren't Harvard or Yale or Stanford grads. Rich boys do not box. Future corporate CEOs have no need to don leather gloves. Boxers are men from the streets, brothers from the ghetto, home boys from the barrios, Puerto Ricans from the Bronx, white kids in poverty. They are survivors of poverty, hardship and danger.

Of all who ever graced the ring, none is greater than Muhammad Ali. He destroyed Liston with speed, beat Frazier with an iron will and defeated Foreman with guile. When he shouted, "I am the greatest," his claim was backed by stunning victories in the ring. Yet despite his stature in the boxing world, Ali's greatness transcended the ring. His most courageous fight was Ali vs. the United States, a classic heavyweight epic that took place on April 28, 1967, when he and twenty-five inductees were summoned to the U.S. Armed Forces Examining and Entrance station on San Jacinto Street in Houston, Texas.

A young lieutenant asked recruits to step forward as their names were called. One after another, boys responded as their names were announced. The officer finally called out, "Cassius Clay! Army!"

No one moved.

Again, only louder: "Cassius Clay! Army!"

Still, no movement.

Ali could have stepped forward, kept his boxing title and eased quietly into a pampered assignment. His Louisville boxing promoters had worked a deal for him so he could join the National Guard, not violate the draft and still maintain his title and boxing form.

Ali's hands and feet, lightning fast in the ring, did not move. By refusing to come forward, he risked everything—his freedom, his title, his career and his money. But by standing against the increasingly discredited war in Vietnam, he became an international hero.

A black athlete, whose fame rose from a sport born in slavery, stood against American power. Ali didn't just talk; he paid the price of his convictions. He said he could not kill Asians who "never called me nigger" on behalf of a country that degraded him and his people. His example resounded throughout the world, and Ali remains a figure beloved as much for his conviction as for his athletic prowess.

On April 28, 1967, famed boxer Muhammad Ali refused induction into the United States Army on the grounds he was a conscientious objector as a minister of the religion of Islam.

APR 29   ☰ Oliver Tambo: "There Is No Doubt We Will Win"

During the struggle against apartheid, South Africa produced some of the most courageous leaders in history. Nelson Mandela, Steve Biko, Walter Sisulu, J. B. Marks, Chris Hani and many others sacrificed family, comfort and life for their cause. Perhaps among these radiant stars, however, Oliver Tambo's star shines brightest. Nelson Mandela called him "the strongest political force in the country." First impressions of Tambo obscured his strength; his stature, demeanor and eyeglasses hardly conveyed fearlessness. Despite his outward appearance, Tambo stood tall against South Africa's pass laws, security police and random violence. Even as young man, Tambo threw himself body and soul into the fight against apartheid, helping to create the African National Congress (ANC) Youth League in 1944 and leading many of their early revolutionary actions.

Tambo's most enduring legacy was sustaining the movement during the twenty-seven years that Mandela and Sisulu were imprisoned on Robben Island. Tambo could easily have given up the cause. With those two giants in prison, white supremacists celebrated the death of the ANC. Steve Biko was murdered and countless other black leaders were banned, exiled or jailed. The movement, the cause, the hope of black liberation seemed lost forever. Yet Tambo refused to give up.

At a time when there was no basis for hope, he declared to his comrades, "Whatever the cost, there is no doubt we will win."

Tambo sustained the energy of the ANC, inspired the sanctions movement in Europe and America, and spoke out everywhere for the destruction of apartheid. Tambo built the ANC into a force capable of assuming power at the end of white rule.

Nelson Mandela once described Oliver Tambo as more potent than white supremacy because, when all seemed lost, Tambo held onto the dream of black liberation.

Oliver Tambo died on April 29, 1993, in his beloved South Africa, of complications from a stroke he had suffered years earlier. He never witnessed the inauguration of Nelson Mandela as President of the Republic of South Africa, but he knew with eyes of faith that the day was inevitable.

Olaudah Equiano accurately titled his life story "Interesting." He was born of the Ibo people in Nigeria, sold into slavery at eleven, transported to the West Indies, worked as a seaman in Canada and the Mediterranean, traveled with his master to England and was sold to an American seaman. He purchased his own freedom in 1766, sailed to the Artic, lived with the Moskito Indians in Nicaragua, moved to England, lived in Sierra Leone, and became an abolitionist and an official for the Expedition for Freed Slaves in West Africa.

Equiano was indeed a remarkable African man. Despite slavery, he made himself indispensable through his work and character. He learned hairdressing, seamanship, winemaking, arithmetic and English. Through discipline and hard work, he took control of his own life.

His autobiography, *The Interesting Life of Olaudah Equiano, or Gustavus Vassa, The African, Written by Himself,* is noteworthy on two accounts. First, the obstacles he overcame stand as a testament to his courage, will to survive, faith and persistence in the face of any obstacle life threw at him. Even more importantly, his book was the first slave narrative written solely by the author and as such foreshadowed later autobiographical works. Frederick Douglass, William Wells Brown, Harriet Jacobs, Sojourner Truth, Nat Turner and others followed the pathway opened by Olaudah Equiano.

Olaudah Equiano died in England on April 30, 1797, when he was 52 years old. His autobiography, The Interesting Life of Olaudah Equiano, or Gustavus Vassa, The African, Written by Himself, *has been reprinted often and is used in high schools and colleges as a basic black history text.*

MAY

Nelson Mandela

≡ **Eldridge Cleaver: Soul on Ice**

No matter how people view the various phases or incarnations of Eldridge Cleaver's life, the power of his insights cannot be ignored; his search for meaning in the midst of racism cannot be denied. His search at times led to hurt and brutality, and at other times it led to hope and generosity. Cleaver was a convicted rapist, a drug user, a follower of Malcolm X, the Minister of Information for the Black Panther Party, a refugee to Cuba and France, the presidential candidate on the 1968 Peace and Freedom ticket, a fundamentalist Christian, and the author of the revolutionary *Soul on Ice* and later the reactionary *Soul on Fire*.

Critics ask, "Who is the real Eldridge Cleaver? If we are to learn from his life, which part do we choose?" It is important to understand that Cleaver's changes emanated from one primary question: "How do I survive as a black man in America?" Every black man in America resonates with Cleaver's struggle.

In 1968, Cleaver published his classic *Soul on Ice*, an illuminating statement on the bitter fruits of racism and exclusion. His work analyzed the 1960s, Vietnam, Muhammad Ali, Harlem and prison life. His insights on capitalism and racism—as seen from the perspective of his crimes, prison term and self-education—are invaluable.

The final essay of *Soul on Ice* hauntingly articulates the devastation of black male identity in America and the horrific consequences of self-hate:

> *Oh, My Soul! I became a sniveling craven, a funky punk, a vile, groveling bootlicker, with my will to oppose petrified by a cosmic fear of the Slavemaster.... I, the black Eunuch, divested of my Balls, walked the earth with my mind locked in Cold Storage. I would kill a black man or woman quicker than I'd smash a fly, while for the white man I would pick a thousand pounds of cotton a day.*

Many disagree with Eldridge Cleaver's politics and perspectives, and all condemn his crime of rape, but it is impossible to deny the power of his expressions of pain and exclusion.

Eldridge Cleaver, author of* Soul on Ice, *died at age 62 in Pomona, California, on May 1, 1998. He is one of the most controversial of all black historical leaders.

≣ Lucy (Gonzales) Parsons: Black Anarchist

Lucy Parsons is unique among black women who fought for freedom and justice: She began her life as a slave, became an anarchist and ended as a communist. For her, Karl Marx's theories on exploitation had been confirmed by her slave experience in Waco, Texas. She used many surnames, including Gonzales to emphasize her Mexican heritage. After securing her freedom, she married a white anarchist and former Confederate soldier turned radical-Republican revolutionary named Albert Parsons. The two moved to Chicago in 1873, where their militant protests for the poor led to constant harassment and surveillance. Lucy Parsons was an electrifying speaker, and listeners often left her speeches believing they could change the world. Police and hired thugs responded with rage, often chasing her off the stage and clubbing her supporters.

Parsons was a member of the Knights of Labor and the Socialist Revolutionary Club, the only woman to speak at the founding of the International Workers of the World (IWW) and an organizer of marches demanding an eight-hour workday. She wrote for, or edited, radical journals such as *Freedom: A Revolutionary/Anarchist/Communist Monthly* and *The Alarm*. One of her most famous articles was an 1884 classic entitled "To Tramps: The Unemployed, the Disinherited, the Miserable," in which the ever-vigilant Parsons advised the outcast and marginalized to "learn the use of explosives" if they were ever to seek true justice.

Parsons had an unquenchable love for the poor and once wrote:

> *Within the shadow of the statue [of Liberty], hundreds of families have been dumped on the street because they could not pay the rent of their miserable tenements.*

Her passion for justice was never extinguished. At the age of eight-six, Lucy Parsons finally joined the Communist Party, USA. Many of the benefits enjoyed by workers today, such as health benefits, the forty-hour workweek and fair labor practices, are due to the work of dynamic radicals such as Lucy Parsons.

On May 1, 1886, Lucy Parsons helped organize a general strike in Chicago, demanding an eight-hour workday. Prior to that struggle, it had been common for workers to toil ten to fourteen hours per day, with uncompensated overtime, frequent industrial injuries and no job security. Parsons died in a Chicago fire on March 7, 1942. Her papers were seized by the police and have never been seen again.

≡ League of Revolutionary Black Workers: A United Front

In the 1960s, autoworkers were subjected to brutal working conditions. Bone-crushing assembly lines, arbitrary terminations and long hours were common, and Detroit's black autoworkers endured some of the worst. More than any other group, blacks at the Dodge Main plant experienced layoffs, speedups, wage cuts and safety compromises. Abused by management and neglected by the union, black autoworkers sought to remedy their conditions.

Then in May of 1968, an action taken by some Polish women, who walked off the job in protest of a planned speedup, erupted into a larger wildcat strike. Soon black workers joined them on the picket line. When the strike ended, black autoworkers were fired and disciplined in numbers far greater than other races. General Watson, Bennie Tate, Chuck Wooten and others bore the brunt of corporate vengeance and were fired on the spot. Black workers at Dodge Main were outraged, and by February of 1969, General Baker, Ken Cockrel, Mike Hamlin and others had formed the League of Revolutionary Black Workers.

The name declared the group's mission: "Revolutionary" portrayed their rejection of moderation, and "League" expressed their desire to link with others. Excluded by the United Auto Workers (UAW), the League allied with Detroit's black community. They met with students from Wayne State University, with workers from other trades and with community activists to build a united front against racism. The League confronted both management and the UAW over issues of race and fairness, and defended many mistreated black workers.

The League's appearance changed the Detroit political climate. Some of their members founded Detroit's Black Panther Party, while others were instrumental in creating the National Black Economic Development Conference and its militant "Black Manifesto." The impact of the League of Revolutionary Black Workers lasted far beyond its short-lived existence; the movement energized Detroit's black community for years to come.

On May 2, 1968, black workers participated in a wildcat strike at the Dodge Main plant, thereby planting the seeds of the League of Revolutionary Black Workers.

≡ The Black Manifesto: "I Hear My Brother"

On May 4, 1969, black activist James Forman interrupted Sunday worship at New York's famous Riverside Church to demand black reparations from white Christianity for centuries of oppression. His speech ignited a firestorm. Reparations talk is bold even today, but in 1969, it was shocking. Many white Americans were already frightened by the rage of people such as Malcolm X, H. Rap Brown and the Black Panther Party. Dr. Martin Luther King, Jr., was dead, the Vietnam War raged on and race riots had left ghettos in flames. Fear, mistrust and violence were palpable.

James Forman and the National Black Economic Development Conference (NBEDC) believed white Christians bore some responsibility for black misery. At a gathering in Detroit the year before, they had calculated that white Christians, corporations and the government owed America's thirty million blacks repayment for hundreds of years of unpaid slavery, employment discrimination, lynch mobs, segregated schools and other sins. Unregulated white supremacy had left black business, black self-image, black health and black housing in shambles. And, ironically, the white church was the perfect target. During slavery days and beyond, Christianity had often made itself subservient to white supremacy and American nationalism, and Forman and his comrades believed that the white church should set the example on reparations.

Shortly after Forman disrupted Riverside Church, members of the NBEDC made demands of white Christians across America. The "Black Manifesto" called Episcopalians, Catholics, Presbyterians, the United Church of Christ, the Church of the Brethren, Southern Baptists and others to justice.

The reaction from one particular group portrayed in miniature the core of the struggle. When a young man named Muhammad Kenyatta rose at a meeting of the Society of Friends (Quakers) to demand reparations for black Americans, some asked him to quiet down so they could continue with worship. But he refused to sit, noting that the demands of Christian love cried out for redemption and justice. He was once again asked to be silent. Then a nun, Sister Mary Simon of the Society of the Holy Child, stood up and said, "I hear my brother; his words are right and true. I ask that we listen to him." She was quite alone in her embrace of the "Black Manifesto," however.

White churches were paternalistic, defensive, reactionary and plodding in their response to the issue of reparations. Nevertheless, the Black Manifesto lives on in the continuing debate and controversy about reparations for black Americans.

On May 4, 1969, James Forman of the National Black Economic Development Conference halted the service at New York's Riverside Church to demand economic justice and reparations. Most of the congregation walked out. Thirteen months earlier, this church had been the scene of Dr. Martin Luther King's anti-war classic sermon, "Beyond Vietnam," in which he linked racism, militarism and poverty.

MAY 5 ≡ Walter Sisulu: "Peace Among Peoples"

Walter Sisulu, as much as anyone else, was responsible for the end of apartheid and the beginning of a free and democratic South Africa. Some who know the history of the African National Congress (ANC) and the struggle for black freedom believe Sisulu's courage, conviction and perseverance resulted in their ultimate victory. Without Sisulu, there would have been no Nelson Mandela, no Oliver Tambo, no ANC Youth League.

Like most South African blacks, Sisulu grew up poor and destitute. After suffering months of abuse as a gold miner, he joined the ANC when he was twenty-eight years old. In 1941, Sisulu met and befriended Tambo and Mandela, helped them finish law school and encouraged them to join the ANC. From then on, this beautiful triumvirate of dedicated warriors transformed South Africa from a racist dictatorship to a multi-racial democracy. Their victory was won not with guns or bombs but through the patience of exile, the suffering of imprisonment and brutality, and the steadfast belief in a different future.

From 1940 to 1964, Walter Sisulu led the ANC through brutal repression, directing that organization through its difficult early years. In 1964, Sisulu, Mandela and others were charged with attempting to overthrow the government and sentenced to imprisonment for life. For the next twenty-six years, Sisulu and his freedom fighters lived through the darkness of the prison called Robben Island.

When he was released in 1989, one year before Mandela, Sisulu was seventy-seven years old. Still unbroken, he picked up the struggle where he had left off. He served as Mandela's Deputy President in 1991 and worked tirelessly for democracy and justice in the new South Africa.

When he finally retired, Sisulu was asked how he wanted to be remembered. He replied, "As one who did all he could to allow us all to live a full human life, and who worked to bring peace among peoples." Persevering through twenty-four years of repression and twenty-six years of prison, this great freedom fighter lived to see his dream of freedom become a reality.

Walter Sisulu, one of the great leaders of the African National Congress (ANC), died on May 5, 2003, in South Africa.

  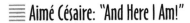 Aimé Césaire: "And Here I Am!"

Aimé Césaire is an important French-speaking black writer whose writing flourished at the beginning of Africa's anti-colonial movements. Césaire, along with other black artists such as Leopold Senghor, created Negritude, an Afro-centric artistic celebration in Africa, the Caribbean and the United States. Attracting young talent, Negritude produced some of the brightest stars in black art, fusing art and blackness with a progressive demand for human rights.

Born in the French colony of Martinique, Césaire left as a young man to study in Europe, where he discovered that he had a talent for poetry and literature. When he returned to Martinique, it was not as a distant intellectual or irrelevant poet, but as a speaker for the impoverished of his country.

Césaire was devoted to his people's freedom, and history records that he kept his commitment. As the first communist member of the French Parliament from Martinique, Césaire was a militant supporter of the poor. When the Communist Party reduced its commitment to France's black citizens, he resigned from the Party. For Césaire, literature and political action had but one aim: the liberation of his people from all forms of oppression. He believed that "philosophies and movements must serve the people, not the people the doctrine and the movement," and he used his art as a tool in the liberation struggle.

In one of his most powerful works, *Notes of a Return to the Native Land*, Césaire wrote:

> I would come to this country of mine and say to it, "Embrace me without fear.... And if all I know how to do is speak, it is for you that I shall speak." And I would say more. My lips shall speak for miseries that have no mouth, my voice shall be the liberty of those who languish in the dungeon of despair.... And above all, my body, as well as my soul, beware of crossing your arms in the sterile attitude of a spectator, for life is not a spectacle, a sea of pain is no proscenium, a man who cries out is not a dancing bear.... And here I am!

Though Martinique is a tiny and forgotten island halfway between Puerto Rico and Trinidad, Césaire's writing burst across the Atlantic and reverberated in Europe, Africa and the United States.

Author Aimé Césaire of Martinique has used his writing to speak for his people and to rebel against injustice. He wrote, "Philosophies and movements must serve the people, not the people the doctrine and the movement. A doctrine is of value only if it is conceived by us and for us."

Henry Walton Bibb: "Lighting Up the Path"

To read slave narratives is to plunge into the dark recesses of human degradation. Henry Walton Bibb's book, *Narrative of the Life of Henry Bibb*, is no exception. His work has much in common with today's hip-hop artists: Just as rappers take us on uncomfortable excursions into ghetto life, so too Bibb's narrative walks us through the treacherous paths of slavery.

Bibb described his love for his wife, Malinda, and for their only daughter, the beautiful Mary Frances. Like families around the world, the three of them loved one another with an intense bond of affection. But they were the property of a white plantation owner—property to be worked, abused and sold away if necessary.

Henry Bibb recounted how he and his wife stood by in horror while the master whipped their daughter, Mary Frances. He also wrote, "On this same plantation I was compelled to stand and see my wife shamefully scourged and abused by her master." For Bibb, the love that gives most of us pleasure and fulfillment was a source of utter despair.

> I could never look upon the dear child without being filled with sorrow…of being separated by slaveholders…. And unfortunately for me, I am the father of a slave…. If ever there was any one act of my life while a slave that I have to lament over, it is that of being a father and a husband of slaves.

Yet, despite slavery's brutality, Bibb did not lose heart. Rather than succumb to hatred and cynicism, he demanded that we strive for a better world, and he concluded his *Narrative* with this message of hope:

> Prayerfully and earnestly relying on the power of truth, and with the aid of divine providence, I trust that this little volume will bear some humble part in lighting up the path and freedom. And I here pledge myself, God being my helper, ever to contend for the natural equality of the human family, without regard to color which is but fading matter, while mind makes the man.

Henry Bibb died in 1854 at the age of 39. His Narrative of the Life of Henry Bibb was published on May 1, 1849.

MAY 8 ≣ **Bishop Henry McNeal Turner: God's Thundering Prophet**

Young Henry McNeal Turner was speechless, a rare condition for this black teenager from Abbeville, South Carolina. Even as a child, he had been outspoken, and the African pride imprinted onto him by his grandmother was obvious. For Turner, blackness and Africa were not emblems of shame but sources of strength. Now, at the Sharon Camp Ground church meeting, the preacher had left him breathless. Turner felt as if Christ himself was calling him forward out of his seat. When he heard that Jesus came to earth, lived among wounded humanity, died and rose in triumphant victory over sin, Turner thought he could follow this Jesus anywhere. This Jesus was a perfect symbol of black America: abused, humiliated, oppressed—and yet ultimately victorious. Turner's grandmother had taught him that black folks could not afford to look out only for themselves; they also had to uplift their entire race. In Christ, Turner found the answer to both struggles: a savior from both personal sin and social oppression.

After several years of study, Turner felt called to the ministry in the African Methodist Episcopal (AME) Church, and he eventually came to lead a growing church in Georgia. He rose quickly through the ranks, becoming an AME bishop by 1880. But he did not confine his ministry to the church; by 1867, he was a leader in the Republican Party's platform on black equality. His voice was heard from pulpits and political rallies all over the South as he spoke out for spiritual salvation and political equality.

In 1868, the Georgia legislature illegally expelled Turner and twenty-six other black Americans from their elected seats. Turner addressed his white tormentors with dignity:

> Mr. Speaker.... It is extraordinary that a race such as yours, professing gallantry, and chivalry and education and superiority, living in a land where ringing chimes call child and sire to the Church of God—a land were Bibles are read and Gospel truths are spoken…it is extraordinary to say that, with all these advantages on your side, you can make war upon the poor defenseless black man....

> You may expel us, gentlemen, by your votes today; but while you do it, remember that there is a just God in Heaven, whose All-Seeing Eye beholds alike the acts of the oppressor and the oppressed, and who, despite the machinations of the wicked, never fails to vindicate the cause of Justice, and the sanctity of his own Handiwork.

For Turner, Christianity was no empty faith; his embrace of Christ fueled his passion to uplift the dignity of black folks everywhere. Bishop Henry McNeal Turner was indeed God's thundering prophet.

Bishop Henry McNeal Turner died on May 8, 1915, at 81 years of age, while attending a church conference in Windsor, Canada. He was a leader of the African Methodist Episcopal (AME) Church in Georgia after the Civil War.

≣ Reverend Florence Spearing Randolph
"A Real Telling Work for God and Humanity"

Looking at the life of Florence Spearing Randolph, it's hard to imagine how she mustered the energy to do what she did—especially considering that she was active from the 1880s through the 1950s, very difficult times for both blacks and women in the United States. But for Florence Randolph, obstacles only seemed to urge her on to greater action.

At the foundation of her commitment was her faith in God and service to Jesus Christ. Randolph's mission in life was formed and shaped by her church, the African Methodist Episcopal Zion (AME Zion) denomination. There she learned not only of God's love for all people but of Christ's example to empower and serve those at the margins of society. For young Randolph, this was not just book knowledge; she accompanied her blind grandmother on visits to homes of the sick and poor to deliver food and pray for their needs.

Imbued with this activist theology, Randolph lived a life of Christian service. In 1886 she joined the Monmouth Street AME Zion Church in New Jersey, where she taught the younger members. She studied under George Biddle, an AME Zion biblical scholar, and later took correspondence courses from the Moody Bible Institute in Chicago. In 1898, she was admitted to the New Jersey AME Zion Conference and became a Conference Evangelist.

Randolph believed that she was called to fulltime ministry, however, and at the May 1900 AME Zion Church Conference, she was ordained a deacon. This was the beginning of her formal pastoral ministry, but it was not an easy calling. Often during her career, male ministers protested her role and position. For over four decades, Rev. Randolph pastored several churches, with her last assignment as pastor of Wallace Chapel, AME Zion, in Summit, New Jersey, where she served from 1925 to 1946.

At Wallace Chapel, Randolph was much more than a church pastor. She often preached on and fought against racism, colonialism, sexism and alcohol abuse. She was inspired to become an activist in the New Jersey chapter of the Women's Christian Temperance Union (WCTU). She was one of the chapter's key leaders and became an outspoken advocate for prohibition and sober living.

Rev. Randolph was a member of the Negro History Movement and the Association for the Study of Life and History of the Negro, founded by historian Carter G. Woodson. Through these organizations, she and others fought to get black culture and history taught respectfully in schools, and their work laid the foundation for the black studies movement of the 1960s. This tireless minister also brought together the black women's clubs of New Jersey by helping to found the State Federation of Colored Women's Clubs. In this role, she led the fight for equal housing opportunities, just employment practices, anti-lynching laws, and women's suffrage, as well as an end to colonial oppression overseas.

As she looked back upon her life and ministry, Randolph said, "I developed into a Bible student, discovering one can do a real telling work for God and humanity." This work included evangelism, preaching and standing up against all indignities against women, black people and the poor.

In May of 1900, Florence Spearing Randolph was ordained a deacon in the AME Zion church. She pastored Wallace Chapel in Summit, New Jersey for over twenty years and died in New Jersey in 1951.

MAY 10

Nelson Mandela: Walking Tall

The courage of Nelson Mandela shines as a beacon for the world. He overcame repression, exile and jail with his single-minded devotion to freedom. If anyone embodies the triumph of life over death, love over hate and light over darkness, it is Nelson Mandela. When he was twenty-five years old, Mandela joined the emerging African National Congress (ANC). With his friends Oliver Tambo and Walter Sisulu, Mandela transformed the ANC Youth League and the ANC into powerful forces of apartheid resistance. In 1952, he was banned for his leadership in the Defiance Campaign, yet even under a ban Mandela remained a threat to South Africa's racist regime.

In 1964, Mandela was sentenced to life imprisonment with no possibility of parole and sent to notorious Robben Island, a prison known to break the spirit of the proudest of black men. For twenty-seven years, Nelson Mandela was a prisoner at the Robben Island hell-hole. Confined to a seven-by-seven-foot cell, restricted to one letter every six months, forced to break rocks every day, Mandela somehow sustained his passion for racial justice. He did not recant, lapse into self-destruction or self-pity, or succumb to bitterness. Despite nearly three decades in prison, he held both himself and his cause together with a simple but unshakable faith. He became the living symbol of human freedom as signs across the world proclaimed "Free Nelson Mandela."

In 1990, Mandela was released from prison, and after months of tense negotiations and political violence, the government of South Africa agreed to its first free election. On April 26, 1994, the polls opened and blacks stood in line for hours to cast their first ballot. The ANC received 62.6% of the vote, electing Mandela the first black president of South Africa. May 10, 1994, the day Mandela was inaugurated, is considered the greatest day in the history of South Africa. Millions sang and danced in the streets. One hundred and seventy nations sent representatives to the occasion. And Mandela, in a stunning act of reconciliation, invited his jailer to sit on the dais with him. While many predicted black retribution, Mandela astonished the world with his overwhelming generosity:

> Out of the experience of extraordinary human disaster that lasted too long must be born a society of which all human society will be proud. We enter into a covenant that we will build the society in which all South Africa, both black and white, will be able to walk tall, without fear in their heart, assured of their unalienable right to human dignity.

Mandela's presidency was a fulfillment of his promise to advocate for racial reconciliation, economic advancement and equitable social services. The courageous journey of Nelson Mandela from political activism to brutal confinement to the presidency of his country is a testament to love, courage and faith.

On May 10, 1994, Nelson Mandela was inaugurated as the first president of a free South Africa. That day marked the culmination of 51 years of struggle and the beginning of the hard work of national reconstruction.

MAY 11 ≡ Bob Marley: "Lively Up Yourself"

Bob Marley was the first global Third World megastar. He brought his reggae beat and sounds from Trenchtown, a Jamaican ghetto, to concerts, clubs and homes around the globe. Before Marley, reggae music—with its driving bass and drums and unforgettable polyrhythms—was virtually unknown. After Marley, people all over the world, from Zimbabwe to San Diego to El Salvador, recognized both Marley and the music he popularized.

In 1967, Bob Marley converted from Christianity to the Ras Tafari religion, and became an ardent believer in Jah, the almighty Creator who sides with the weak and the oppressed in their struggle for dignity, peace and freedom. Songs such as "One Love" and "Redemption Song" point to the universal truth of love. Marley's music became a banquet of spiritual sustenance, urging praise to Jah, fighting injustice, and calling people to live right and work for peace.

Bob Marley constantly called upon our higher selves to work for love, unity and peace. "Lively Up Yourself," "Natural Mystic," "Rebel Music," "Wake Up and Live," "Africa Unite," "Get Up Stand Up," "Walk the Proud Land," "Sun Is Shining," "So Much Things To Say" and many other of his songs elevate and transform us.

For Marley, the greatest moment of his career was an invitation from Edgar Tekere, noted freedom fighter of Zimbabwe's liberation movement, to appear at that country's independence ceremony. On April 17, 1980, Marley performed before forty thousand joyous Zimbabweans as they celebrated their transformation from the colony of Rhodesia to the free nation of Zimbabwe. At the ceremony, black activist Dick Gregory introduced Marley as:

> *A young man who understands racism, understands poverty, who understands all the hurts, and didn't let it defeat him. He set out to share his joy, his love, his great respect, his religion, his spiritual power, with the whole world.*

This memorable concert fulfilled Bob Marley's vision and music; many of his later compositions, such as "Zimbabwe," spoke of a glorious future for an independent Africa. The joy and love Marley shared live on in his musical call to peace and unity.

Reggae artist Robert Nesta (Bob) Marley died on May 11, 1981, in Miami, Florida from cancer of the toe. He is widely considered the first global Third World megastar.

MAY 12   ≡ Samuel Morris: Jesus Is Mine

Few have loved God as Samuel Morris, a man without religious title or office, did. Born Prince Kaboo of the Kru people in Liberia, Morris fell from the privilege of royalty into a cauldron of torture. As a teenager, Prince Kaboo was captured by the neighboring Grebo people, who tortured and whipped him constantly, using his pain to leverage payments from Kaboo's father. They flayed open his back with poisonous vines, often leaving him unconscious. One particularly brutal day, Kaboo felt himself slipping toward death. Inexplicably, when he awoke from his semi-coma, he found himself freed from his captors and their perpetual torment. He could not remember how he had escaped; all he knew was that he was free.

Months later, Kaboo met white missionaries who told him of Jesus Christ. Kaboo was amazed that God would die for his salvation and soon committed his life to God. Following the practice of the times, upon conversion, his name was changed to Samuel Morris. The convert eagerly began learning as much as he could about his new faith. One day a missionary named Miss McNeil told him how the very Spirit of God lives within and provides comfort, guidance and strength.

"Tell me more about this Holy Spirit!" Morris exclaimed.

McNeil replied that she had taught him all she knew, and that if he wanted to know more he should go to New York and see Stephen Merritt, the New York City evangelist.

"Then I will go see him," replied Morris. He was soon on his way to America.

Morris found Merritt and launched wholeheartedly into studying and working with Merritt in his street mission and in St. James Street Church. Despite Morris' lack of formal theological training, he often testified in churches and revivals about what God had done for him. After he spoke, hundreds would come forward to seek redemption.

When he was just twenty years old, Samuel Morris died from illness. Before his death, however, almost ten thousand people in New York City missions and the St. James Street Church had found Christ in his message. As Morris lay dying in the hospital, a hymnbook spread on his lap was open to this song:

> Fade, fade, each earthly joy
> Jesus is mine.
> Break, every tender tie,
> Jesus is mine.

Though Morris died prematurely, without money and thousands of miles from home, his love for Jesus was contagious and gave hope to the thousands who heard him preach "Jesus Is Mine."

Evangelist Samuel Morris died on May 12, 1893. He was born Prince Kaboo of the Dru people in Liberia, Africa.

MAY 13   ≣ Sara G. Stanley: "A Glorious Destiny"

In March of 1864, Sara G. Stanley wondered where her life was headed. As a twenty-eight-year-old free black woman in a nation fighting a bitter war over slavery, she wanted to help any way she could. One afternoon she came across an ad from the American Missionary Association (AMA) requesting teachers for newly freed slaves. She saw this as her vocation and headed to the AMA office for an application. She later said:

> My reasons for seeking to engage in the work of instructing the Freed people of the South are few and simple. I am myself a colored woman, bound to that ignorant, degraded, long enslaved race by the ties of love and consanguinity; they are socially and politically my people.

Stanley added that she would endure "any suffering and privation, even death, for this great work." Believing that dedicated Christian teachers could unleash the spiritual and intellectual energy that lay dormant among the ex-slaves, she left her home and moved to the South to teach black children survival skills and basic education.

Though Stanley did encounter the suffering she had predicted, she did not shrink from her duties. She confronted the racism and paternalism of the AMA, and often challenged her white peers and superiors when they fell short of Christian ideals, contrasting their intolerance and discrimination with the example of Christ's love. Once, after a white missionary had treated southern blacks with contempt, she wrote AMA offices, noting, "He needs to learn the ABCs of Christianity." In an argument articulated by black theologians one hundred years later, she told her Society that their message must be, "God is man, Christ clothed in...the flesh, the Son of God in the person of a Negro."

Whether teaching ex-slaves or challenging racist missionaries, Sara Stanley was fearless and unwavering. She believed that God called her to bring "a glorious destiny" to her black brothers and sisters, and nothing would stand in her way.

Sara G. Stanley was a missionary with the American Missionary Association (AMA) from 1864 to 1868. She not only taught hundreds of children during her ministry, but she also forced the AMA to examine the motives and actions of many of their white missionaries.

MAY 14　　　　　　　　　　　　≣ Georgia Douglas Johnson: Heart of a Woman

Georgia Douglas Johnson, a significant voice of the Harlem Renaissance, did not even live in Harlem. And, unlike many other artists during that period, she did not always write about race. Such was the uniqueness of this enigmatic black woman.

Her home in Washington, D.C., became a salon, school and restaurant for the luminaries of the Harlem Renaissance. Langston Hughes, Jean Toomer, Zora Neale Hurston and other black artists gathered at her home for mutual support, engaging conversation and political analysis. Their collective artistic conversations nurtured the birth of countless theater themes, book subjects and song lyrics.

Johnson was more than a hostess, however. In 1918, she published a book of her poetry—the first to be published by an African-American woman in the U.S.—entitled *Heart of a Woman*. Johnson's poems, such as "Heart of a Woman" and "My Little Dreams," viewed the soul of black women through the lens of romance, love and family. Her later works *Bronze: A Book of Verse* and *An Autumn Love Cycle* continued that theme.

As a poet and matron of the arts, Georgia Douglas Johnson was one of the great figures in black literature.

Georgia Douglas Johnson, a poet of the Harlem Renaissance, died of a stroke on May 14, 1966, in Washington, D.C. She published the first book of poetry by a black woman in the United States.

≡ Black Baseball Writers: Beyond Runs, Hits and Errors

There are few alive today who realize that a core of black sportswriters kept black baseball alive at a time when the white press was ignoring the stars in the Negro Leagues. The baseball exploits of Josh Gibson, Buck Leonard, Cool Papa Bell, Leon Day, Satchel Paige and many others would have faded into the mists of history without the written record of black sportswriters.

They were, however, much more than sports reporters. Sam Lacy of the *Baltimore Afro-American*, Wendell Smith of the *Pittsburgh Courier*, Frank A. Young of the *Chicago Defender*, Joe Bostic of the *People's Voice*, Chester L. Washington of the *Pittsburgh Courier*, Dr. W. Rollo Wilson of the *Philadelphia Tribune*, Dan Burley of the *Amsterdam News* and Ed Harris of the *Philadelphia Tribune* were also trumpets for justice and integration.

Their crisp writing gave life and substance to the black game and challenged the exclusion of black players from the all-white Major League Baseball. Almost weekly, their columns bristled with open letters to big league owners, politicians and the baseball commissioner. Often these black writers would quickly cover yesterday's runs, hits and errors, and then fire a full broadside at hypocritical owners who mouthed platitudes about equality in America's pastime. In efforts to break the color barrier, these writers challenged white owners and general managers to look at some Negro League players. Sam Lacy and Wendell Smith arranged tryouts for Negro League stars, and Bostic and others met with politicians and the baseball commissioner to agitate for an integrated national game. Some writers polled white managers and players on the issue of allowing blacks in Major League Baseball and published the results to make their case.

Though they knew that integration of baseball could mean an end to the Negro Leagues and perhaps even their jobs, these men continued their relentless pursuit of justice. For them, sports reporting was a means to an end. It was a way to promote justice for black ballplayers, raise the tough questions of race and challenge America to live up to its promises.

When Jackie Robinson finally walked onto a major league field in 1947, it was not talent alone that brought him there. It was years of agitation, protest and action by these brave and selfless black sportswriters.

In May of 1942, Chester Washington wrote an open letter to baseball commissioner Judge Landis stating that if blacks were brave enough to fight at Pearl Harbor they surely should be allowed to play Major League Baseball. Such articles were typical fare for the black sportswriters of that era.

A. Philip Randolph: A Cloak for the Shivering

Although their memories fade with the passage of time, old warriors in the strug-gle still marvel at the life of Asa Philip Randolph. Gracious, humble, caring, re-fined, austere, polite, serious—all these words describe a man who was devoted to anyone who suffered discrimination because of race, gender or class. As a young man in 1914, Randolph moved to Harlem from Florida and soon met the militant and irreverent organizer Chandler Owen.

The two began a friendship based on mutual affection and a common zeal for justice. In the City College of New York, they "read Marx like children read Alice in Wonderland" and followed with interest the politics of Socialist Party leader Eugene Debs. Seeking an outlet for their activism, Randolph and Owen started the radi-cal newspaper *The Messenger*. Revolutionary articles blazing from *The Messenger's* pages attracted the attention of the U.S. government, and Attorney General Palmer called Randolph and Owen "the most dangerous Negroes in America."

By 1925, Randolph and others organized the Brotherhood of Sleeping Car Porters, which eventually became the first successful black trade union in America. Randolph's work for the Porters improved life for thousands of black families, and the influence of the Brotherhood expanded throughout organized labor.

As black arts and literature flourished in the Harlem Renaissance, Randolph and others were the political complement to that cultural revival. The culture of the Renaissance merged with political activism to form what many called the "New Negro Movement" in Harlem.

As President of the National Negro Labor Congress, Randolph brought blacks into the labor movement and challenged the racism of traditional union leader-ship. In 1941, tired of President Roosevelt's empty promises to desegregate the military and open industry to blacks, Randolph called for a March on Washington to demand the right to fight and the right to work. Roosevelt, afraid the March would unravel the New Deal, agreed to concessions if Randolph would call off his protest. The March was finally cancelled, but only after Roosevelt created the Fair Employment Practices Commission. Randolph's planned March is considered forerunner to the massive Civil Rights March on Washington in 1963.

From 1955 to 1968, Randolph served as Vice-President of the AFL-CIO. Throughout his career, whether organizing socialists in Harlem in the 1920s, building a black labor union in the 1930s, negotiating with the president in the 1940s or integrating the labor movement in the 1950s and 1960s, Randolph was devoted to human dignity. His work was not ephemeral, abstract or intellectual; he was on the picket lines, in the streets and in the boardrooms.

At Randolph's funeral in 1979, the great Bayard Rustin affirmed, "No individual did more to help the poor, the dispossessed and the working class…than A. Philip Randolph." On another occasion, writer Murray Kempton said, "As always, when the cold wind blows upon a sinner in Harlem, there is no cloak for him but Mr. Randolph's." There is no black worker in America who has not benefited from the efforts of A. Philip Randolph.

Champion of black labor A. Philip Randolph died on May 16, 1979, in New York City, at age 65. He founded the Brotherhood of Sleeping Car Porters, the first black trade union in the United States.

≣ Brown v. Board of Education
Common Folk in Quest of Black Equality

MAY 17

Few legal actions in American history can match the significance of the Supreme Court's decision, *Brown v. Board of Education*, which outlawed school segregation as unconstitutional. On May 17, 1954, at 12:52 p.m., America held its collective breath as Supreme Court Justice Earl Warren read the unanimous decision. Much was at stake: For whites, schooling would deprive them of a race of servants, janitors and maids; for blacks, education held the keys to the Promised Land.

No one could predict the deluge of reaction unleashed by this decision. Exposed and rooted out, white racism responded with new levels of violence and more devious forms of discrimination. It was truly a watershed event, and many consider it the beginnings of the Civil Rights Movement.

What is often forgotten, however, are the thousands of heroic black men and women who sacrificed and struggled to force the issue to the courts in the first place. Many have studied the actions of the judges, politicians and attorneys, but without the black litigants who were willing to risk retribution and physical danger to plead their case, white America would never have confronted its failings. From 1909 to 1954, the NAACP had fought and lost case after case, seeking to undo rigid color barriers. Black families across America had risked their children's immediate futures in hopes of achieving equality in the long term. Without these earlier struggles, *Brown v. Board of Education* would never have happened.

We know that the "Board of Education" was that of Topeka, Kansas. But who was "Brown"? Oliver Brown, the thirty-two-year-old father who brought the challenge, epitomized the heroic black people who changed America. Brown was a World War II veteran, a welder and an associate pastor of his local Methodist Church; he was not an activist or civil rights leader. Few in Topeka's political circles even knew who he was. Yet Oliver Brown's love for his children and his race lead him to challenge the evils of segregation.

Brown was not alone: The testimony of Kenneth and Mamie Clark on the psychological effects of segregation and the brilliant work of lawyers such as Thurgood Marshall, George C. Hayes and James Nabrit, Jr., hastened the fall of segregation. Hundreds of courageous black children and parents fought discrimination by enrolling in all-white schools. They faced rocks, taunts, isolation, hostility and violence in search of equality for themselves and others. Fifteen-year-old Dorothy Counts of Charlotte, six-year-old Ruby Bridges of New Orleans, Autherine Lucy at the University of Alabama, Elizabeth Eckford and the Little Rock Nine—the roll call of their courage is stunning. Real equality was born not in the court's decision but in the selfless acts of courage and grace of ordinary black folk.

On May 17, 1954, the Supreme Court rendered a unanimous decision for which blacks had worked for years—Brown v. Board of Education—that ended legal segregation in schools. Oliver Brown was the plaintiff in the case.

MAY 18   ≡ Mary McCloud Bethune: Last Will and Testament

As Mary McCloud Bethune neared the end of her life, she wondered what would become of her work. Would her efforts be forgotten? Bethune had worked a lifetime for her race, and in the twilight of her life she sought to empower others to follow. She had founded the National Council of Negro Women, started Bethune-Cookman College, steered Roosevelt's New Deal toward black concerns and served as Director of Negro Affairs for the National Youth Administration. As if that were not enough, this elderly black woman wanted more. She wrote:

> *Sometimes as I sit communing in my study, I feel that death is not far off. I am aware that it will overtake me before the greatest of my dreams—full equality for the Negro in our time—is realized. Yet, I face that reality without tears or regrets…the knowledge that my work has been helpful to many fills me with joy…. My possessions…are few…but my experiences have been rich. So as my life draws to a close, I will pass them to Negroes everywhere in the hope that an old woman's philosophy may give them inspiration.*

Bethune's last will and testament was reprinted in a classic September 1963 special edition of *Ebony* magazine. In a beautiful expression of devotion, Bethune left words of wisdom for future generations, telling us about the gifts of love, hope, self-confidence, thirst for education, respect for the uses of power, faith, racial dignity and responsibility. Bethune concluded:

The freedom gates are half ajar. We must pry them fully apart. If I have a legacy to leave my people, it is my philosophy of living and serving. I pray now my philosophy may be helpful to those who share my vision of a world of peace, progress, brotherhood and love.

Mary McCloud Bethune died on May 18, 1955, in Daytona Beach, Florida. When she was a young girl, a woman named Emma Jane Wilson mentored her and taught her to serve her race. Ms. Wilson's lessons for Bethune have now become Bethune's for ours. It lives on in all who fight for black progess.

MAY 19 Julia A.J. Foote: "A Brand Plucked from the Fire"

Julia Foote took her religion seriously. Born the fourth child of former slaves, she experienced both the evil of humanity and the grace of God. In later years, as she reflected on her journey, Foote described her life as "a brand plucked from the fire." That image was so real for her that it became the title of her autobiography. Julia believed the "fire" was both America's collective racism and her individual sins conspiring to destroy her body and soul.

In 1838, at the age of fifteen, Foote devoted her life to Christ. Little could she have imagined where that commitment would lead. By her twenties, she was preaching the gospel in places she would not have thought possible. Despite the many prohibitions against women preachers, she forced her way into gospel ministry. Whenever a camp meeting, tent revival or church program needed an evangelist, Julia Foote was there. Her God-given talent for preaching soon became evident to others as she was invited to preach across America.

On May 20, 1894, Foote became the first woman ordained a deacon in the AME Zion Church. Six years later, she was ordained an elder in the church. Despite the sexist misgivings of many clergy, Foote's eloquent sermons and theological insights compelled the church to ordain her a deacon. Julia Foote was, indeed, "a brand plucked from the fire," and she spent her life telling the story of her salvation.

On May 20, 1894, Julia A.J. Foote made history as the first woman ordained a deacon in the AME Zion Church.

≣ Nannie Helen Burroughs: "We Specialize in the Wholly Impossible"

Twenty-one-year-old Nannie Helen Burroughs had seen just about enough. She had listened to black ministers talk about organizing the church, ministering in the community and building up the congregation. There was just one problem— every conversation, every speaker and every solution was exclusively male. The role and importance of black women was never deemed worthy of acknowledgment. Burroughs thought to herself, "It is 1900, thirty-five years after slavery, and it is high time we stopped this nonsense."

At a National Baptist Convention (NBC) in 1900, Burroughs requested and gained the opportunity to speak. Her speech, "How the Women Are Hindered from Helping," accused the black clergy of not doing what they should be doing while at the same time hindering others from doing the good they needed to do. She argued that black women were bursting at the seams to contribute to the moral and political transformation of the black community. Men, not lack of desire, hindered them from service.

The speech shook the foundations of the National Baptist Convention. Reluctantly, the male ministers allowed her and others to create a women's auxiliary in the NBC. The Women's Convention (WC) was born, and Nannie Helen Burroughs became its leader and secretary. In the first year, she gave two hundred speeches and wrote nine thousand letters. By 1903, she had helped draw one million women into the WC.

Burroughs and her sisters took on much more than church business: They advocated for anti-lynching laws, employment opportunities and desegregation. They created the National Training School for Women (NTSW), which attracted women from all over the United States and the Caribbean. The motto of the NTSW was the slogan by which Nannie Helen Burroughs and the other black women lived their lives: "We specialize in the wholly impossible."

During the sixty-one years from 1900 to 1961 that Nannie Helen Burroughs served as secretary, then president, of the WC, she empowered women to take responsibility for their lives, their families and their race. She saw impossible odds not as an excuse for inaction but as an avenue for black women to demonstrate their strength and capability.

Nannie Helen Burroughs died of natural causes on May 20, 1961. The Nannie Helen Burroughs School in Washington, D.C., continues to train young black people in skills to improve their lives and the lives of their communities.

≡ John Robert Lewis: "Stand Together, Don't Run!"

The Greyhound bus arrived in the Montgomery station early Saturday morning. John Lewis, leader of the integrated Freedom Riders, was aboard, and he peered out the front window to see what awaited them at the station. Unlike other Saturday mornings, the sidewalks near the bus terminal were deserted. The quiet was almost eerie, and Lewis felt his stomach tighten as they pulled into the bus bay.

A poor southern youth with a thick "country" accent, Lewis was a veteran of civil rights protests from his courageous work in Nashville, Tennessee. But no prior sit-ins could have prepared Lewis for what happened next. As the Freedom Riders, carefully trained in nonviolent protest, disembarked from the bus, two hundred angry whites appeared from nowhere and surrounded them. Like a pack of savage wolves, the whites set upon them with fists, bats and chains. Some of the riders screamed in fright, others tried to run, but Lewis cried out above the shouting and cursing, "Stand together, don't run!" He knew that a protestor running solo could be overtaken, seriously wounded or even killed; at least in a group, they had a chance of surviving. At his urging, the riders stayed close together.

The racists pounced on John Lewis and Jim Zwerg, a white student. Both were punched, kicked and bashed with bricks, and there was so much blood that each thought the other was dead. Finally, as they lay within seconds of being beaten to death, state troopers arrived to break up the melee.

After the Montgomery beatings, John Lewis did not despair. He continued in the human rights struggle with a fervor matched by only the most stalwart. Arrested forty times, beaten on several other occasions and threatened with death, Lewis never gave up. From 1963 to 1965, he chaired the Student Nonviolent Coordinating Committee (SNCC), and in 1964, he participated in the Mississippi Freedom Summer project. John Lewis was at the forefront of almost every major battle for dignity in the South, and his command to "Stand together, don't run!" would come to signify the theme of his life commitment. For years he continued his fight for human dignity, equality and justice as director of the Voter Education Project (VEP), a member of the Atlanta City Council and a member of the U.S. House of Representatives.

On May 20, 1961, the Freedom Riders arrived in Montgomery, Alabama. Apparently, the local police conspired with the Ku Klux Klan to allow racists several minutes of uninterrupted time to pummel the defenseless Freedom Riders. John Robert Lewis' command to stand together most likely saved several lives that Saturday morning.

Langston Hughes left an amazing body of work in black America's literary canon. Hughes' works include poetry, plays, short stories, autobiographies, history, anthologies and fiction. From the 1921 publication of his classic poem, "The Negro Speaks of Rivers," to his poetry readings at UCLA in 1967, Hughes' work covers many aspects of the black experience in America.

During the radical 1930s, when Hughes was associated with the Communist Party, his writings spoke of justice and revolution. "Goodbye Christ," "Good Morning, Revolution" and other poems inspired activists around the world. His classic "Let America Be American Again" was a favorite of black Communists in Harlem seeking radical change in the United States. Years later, black radicals recalled, with tears in their eyes, how that poem described their deepest yearnings for justice.

It has been said that Langston Hughes strolled the byways of Harlem, listening to black folk talk about the rent, love, racism, jazz, presidents and God. His works are windows into the soul of black people, and his poetic utterances have crept into the sinews of black culture. For example, in the exemplary "Mother to Son," a black mother talks of her harsh life: It had not been a "crystal stair," but she was still climbing upward and she urged her son not to fall. In 1951, Hughes wrote the powerful poem ,"Harlem," that asks what happens when the dreams of a race, a community and a human being are cast aside. He said that the dreams shrivel like "a raisin in the sun." References to the "crystal stair" and the "raisin in the sun" are now embedded in the black lexicon.

Hughes' genius was his ability to depict the fullness of black life in the written word. It is impossible to talk about any genre of black writing without paying homage to Langston Hughes.

Poet Langston Hughes died on May 22, 1967, in New York City. One of his last public acts was a speech condemning the Vietnam War.

Claude McKay: "If We Must Die"

Claude McKay's life was a beautiful confluence of literary excellence and passion for justice. His travels, writings and causes reflected his zealous quest for black salvation. Born of peasant parents in Jamaica, McKay won a literary prize and used the financial award to sail to the United States. He went to Tuskegee Institute and then to Harlem. He later lived in Russia and North Africa before returning to the United States. Everywhere he traveled, McKay searched for the solution to black misery.

The 1922 publication of his book *Harlem Shadow* is considered by most scholars to mark the beginning of the famous Harlem Renaissance. But for McKay, publishing was not enough; his real aim was to help set his people free from bigotry and poverty. Disenchanted with mainstream politics, he was attracted to the militant stand of the Communist Party, USA. Though he joined the Party, McKay never became a blind follower of communist theory. In 1922, when he was a delegate to the Fourth Congress of the Communist International (Comintern), he proclaimed to the gathering that black liberation was central to any revolutionary movement. When he later realized that the Comintern cared more for Stalin than the poor, he resigned from the Party.

The life of Claude McKay is summarized in what many believe to be his greatest creation, the poem, "If We Must Die." Some say this poem is the single most powerful work from the Harlem Renaissance. The year was 1919, a pivotal year in American race relations. As black soldiers returned from fighting for democracy in World War I, their hopes and aspirations were brutally crushed. Race riots broke out in Chicago, East St. Louis and other cities across America, and dozens of blacks were killed as ravaging white mobs lynched, burned and murdered at will. In response to the "Red Summer" of 1919, McKay wrote to the hurting black community:

> If we must die, let it not be like hogs
> Hunted and penned in an inglorious spot….
> Like men we'll face the murderous cowardly pack,
> Pressed to the wall, dying, but fighting back!

Boldly summoning black courage, "If We Must Die" signaled a militancy that racism could not crush. Future generations would cite McKay's words as they sought the courage to do battle with the demons of racism. Claude McKay's search for black liberation was fulfilled in his poetry, and his words resound throughout the ages.

Jamaican-born poet Claude McKay died in Chicago on May 22, 1948. The publication of his book Harlem Shadow marks the beginning of the Harlem Renaissance.

≡ Edward Kennedy Ellington: The Duke

Edward Kennedy Ellington emerged onto the music scene in 1924 as leader of a dance band aptly named "Duke Ellington and His Washingtonians." For the next fifty years, Duke Ellington produced some of the world's most memorable music. There is hardly a corner of the musical world Ellington has not touched. No single adjective can define the power, influence, creativity and magnificence of his music. He was able to attract excellent and selfless musicians, artists willing to subordinate their talents for the good of the band. Kay Davis, Billy Strayhorn, Johnny Hodges, Paul Gonsalves, Jimmy Hamilton, Cat Anderson, Sam Woodyard, Harry Carney, Joe Nanton and many others were central to the band's success.

Ellington may have gained his fame in Harlem, but it would eventually spread around the world. He and his orchestra played before packed crowds in the Cathedral of St. John the Divine in New York, Southampton in England, Dakar in Senegal, the Gran Rex in Buenos Aires, Cteisphon in Iraq, the Roman amphitheater in Jordan, as well as in Calcutta, Bombay, New Delhi, Mexico City, Montevideo, Uruguay, Goutelas in France, Leningrad, Belgrade and many other places.

Ellington performed literally thousands of live concerts, and his recordings reached tens of millions. Today, his music is hummed, sung and played around the world. "Don't Get Around Much Anymore," "East St. Louis Toodle-Oo," "Creole Love Call," "Come Sunday" and many other classics continue to enrich the lives of millions.

Duke Ellington carried himself with the air of royalty yet was familiar with the ordinary in life. His aim was to bring joy through music, and he succeeded beyond his wildest dreams. He gave the world the gift of his music, which inspired minds and uplifted hearts to the beautiful things in life. At this very moment, someone somewhere is probably experiencing the joy of Duke Ellington's music.

Duke Ellington died on May 24, 1974, in New York City. Four nations have made postage stamps of his image, and he received the Presidential Medal of Freedom, France's highest honor in the Legion of Honor, and hundreds of other awards in tribute to his music.

≡ Captain Diagne Mbaye: "He Was the Bravest of Us All"

It seemed the end of the world was near; chaos, betrayal and murder were everywhere. In 1994, the Rwandan government, military, militia, youth gangs—even radio stations—conspired to perpetrate genocide. Frenzied by alcohol and facilitated by the machetes they had been given, Hutu mobs set out to massacre every Tutsi in the nation.

The story of how it happened is a sordid tale of colonialism, tribalism, government manipulation, hate-filled rhetoric and scapegoating. It culminated in one hundred days of rampaging mobs slashing and killing over eight hundred thousand Rwandan men, women and children. The agony, butchery and horror defy belief.

At the height of the murderous frenzy, a tiny force of United Nations observers courageously tried to save lives and stop the killing. One of these was Captain Diagne Mbaye from Senegal. In United Nations lingo he was a "MILOB," an unarmed military observer, stationed in Rwanda to keep the peace.

When the killings broke out, Mbaye left his headquarters in a jeep to do what he could to save lives. One of his first stops was the home of Prime Minister Agathe Uwilinigiyimanu, a moderate Hutu and supporter of national unity. Though he knew she would be one of the first persons targeted, he hoped to be able to save her. But by the time he arrived, the doors were splintered from grenade explosions, and blood was all over the walls. Knowing the killers were close, he quickly searched the compound and miraculously found the Prime Minister's children, in shock but still alive. He hid them in his jeep and drove through roadblocks and mobs to safety behind UN lines. UN staff were stunned to see Mbaye drive up with the children of the Prime Minister.

This was one of many times Mbaye risked his life to save others. Lt. General Romeo Dallaire, the Canadian commander of the UN forces, once wrote of Mbaye, "He personally saved the lives of dozens upon dozens of Rwandans. Braving direct and indirect fire, mines, mobs, disease, and other threats, he eagerly accepted any mission that would save lives."

Within two weeks, Mbaye's courageous struggle was brought to an abrupt end when a grenade exploded at a roadblock and killed him instantly. The UN mission was stunned, and one of his peers noted, "He was the bravest of us all." One reporter from the British Broadcasting Company noted that a dead British or American officer who had displayed Mbaye's courage would have been blanketed with hero status around the world, yet Captain Diagne Mbaye "got almost none."

While unknown to most of us, Mbaye's courage and sacrifice will never be forgotten by those who served with him. He lives with them, and in the lives of the Rwandan men, women and children he saved.

On May 31, 1994, Captain Diagne Mbaye of Senegal, part of the United Nation's observer force during the genocide in Rwanda, was killed by a grenade at a roadblock in Kigali, Rwanda.

≣ Dorothy Cotton: "Find Out What She Wants"

Dorothy Cotton scanned the maps in her office, pondering the next move for the Citizenship Schools. She had been director for three years, and slowly, almost imperceptibly, her schools had begun to make a difference. The South had devised ingenious tools for denying blacks full citizenship rights. Mayors were white, sheriffs were white, juries were white, judges were white—everybody who made decisions about black lives was white. Black citizens had no voice in any political component of their lives, but Dorothy Cotton was part of a movement to change that.

During her years as director of the Southern Christian Leadership Conference's Citizenship Schools, from 1962 to 1967, Cotton and her teachers taught thousands of southern blacks how local government worked, how to pass the ridiculous literacy tests aimed at black voters and how to be active, productive citizens. For many, these classes were their salvation. Cotton remembered a Georgia woman exclaiming after one class, "I feel like I been born again."

Cotton believed in the power of common folk to shape their destiny. One incident that she liked to recall was the story of a young radical from New York who complained to her that her methods were too slow and that the system needed to be incinerated and rebuilt. Cotton told the young man to take what she called a "trust walk" with Miss Lucy from Alabama, an old woman who had seen many years of turmoil and struggle in the South. When the radical returned, he reported to Cotton all that he had told Miss Lucy. Cotton responded,

> Did you listen to what she said? If you want change, if change is to mean anything, the people whom change is intended for have to want it and have to be part of the decision. Now, go with Miss Lucy again, and find out what she wants.

As Cotton sat poring over maps of Alabama, considering the future of her schools, she realized that this statement symbolized her life's work: Find out what the people want and empower them to get it themselves. Such was the mission of Dorothy Cotton and the Citizenship Schools of the SCLC.

Dorothy Cotton is a political activist who spent years in the Civil Rights Movement. From 1962 to 1967, when she was director of the Citizenship Program, over 6,000 people learned to take political power for themselves. Her work planted the seeds for grassroots political movements across the South.

The afternoon sun was glorious. There is nothing like spring in Kentucky: clear sky, crisp air and, above all, the thunder of horse races. Since colonial times, Kentucky had been home to the greatest amateur races in the country, and on this day of May 17, 1875, that tradition blossomed into the running of the first Kentucky Derby. Ten thousand fans poured into what later would become Churchill Downs. The glamour of the crowds, the singing of "My Old Kentucky Home," the drama of great horseracing—it all began in 1875.

As the jockeys rode their horses into the gate, few of the ten thousand bettors even noticed what would stun the nation that day: Thirteen of the fifteen jockeys in that first Kentucky Derby were black! The winning jockey, Oliver Lewis, was decked in orange and white silks as he rode Aristides to victory. The next five horses to cross the finish line were also ridden by black jockeys. Howard Williams, Dick Chambers, William Walker, Moen Kelso and James Carter rode their horses into history that day. This was a custom carried on from the days of slavery, when white owners left the care and feeding of their horses to their black slaves, never dreaming that blacks would transform their servitude into glory.

Horseracing was soon to become the nation's most popular sport, and black jockeys became the first American sports heroes, basking in national adulation. However, Oliver Lewis and the jockeys of the Kentucky Derby were not the first black jockeys. In the 1770s, black jockey Austin Curtis consistently defeated his competition. Three brothers—Jesse, Cato and Charles Stewart—were well-regarded colonial jockeys, and George "Spider" Anderson was the first black jockey to win the Preakness. In 1890, Isaac Murphy won one of the great races of all time when he rode Salvator to victory over Tenny. In another stunning race, the great Tony Hamilton, outfitted in his blue cap with red stars, ran to victory aboard Pickpocket.

By 1908, the greatness of black jockeys was reduced to memory as racial discrimination excluded them from racing for many decades. Nevertheless, we can never forget that America's first sports heroes—and definitely the most flamboyant—were the great black jockeys of the late nineteenth century.

May 17, 1875, was the first running of the Kentucky Derby. That afternoon, 13 of the 15 jockeys aboard were black.

☰ Billy Strayhorn: A Beautiful Human Being

Billy Strayhorn merged personal pain and artistic genius into many memorable musical compositions. Like many other musical geniuses, Strayhorn lived a life of complex paradox. A teenage concert pianist from working-class Pittsburgh, a gay black in a society in which both homosexuality and black skin were discriminated against, the son of a witty but abusive father, Strayhorn channeled personal struggle into his music. Eventually, his artistic talent was recognized by the great Duke Ellington. As Ellington's songwriter and composer for thirty years, Strayhorn was part of the most prolific band in the history of the world.

Through the Duke, Strayhorn's world expanded. He jammed with Bud Powell, had a deep friendship with Lena Horne and consorted with Martin Luther King, Jr. Caring and sensitive, Strayhorn enjoyed the friendships that had eluded him as a child. Lena Horne said of him, "Billy was the source of my consciousness-raising, not about being black but about being me…. He was there as my backbone." As a result of Strayhorn's help, Horne took risky political stands as an artist, and she became a staunch supporter of civil rights and black equality.

Acquainted with pain, rejection, love and triumph, Strayhorn used his music to mirror his reality. His life and compositions covered the range of human emotion: "Take the 'A' Train," "Lush Life" and hundreds of other songs conveyed the loneliness, joy and mystery of his life. Billy Strayhorn was a wonderful composer, a good friend to many and a beautiful human being.

Billy Strayhorn, best known for his song, "Take the 'A' Train," died of esophageal cancer on May 31, 1967, in East Harlem, New York.

☰ Geronimo Pratt: B-40319

For twenty-seven years, Geronimo Pratt was known only as B-40319, his prison identification number. As a leader of the Los Angeles Black Panther Party, Pratt was targeted by the FBI and local police. Despite lack of evidence and eyewitnesses, he was convicted of the brutal slaying of Caroline Olsen at a Santa Monica tennis court. Witnesses who placed him in Oakland at the time of the slaying were ignored, and Pratt was convicted to a life term.

Pratt's time in prison was marked by callousness, brutality and mistreatment. Guards laughed as he was beaten and subjected to "BAAC"—"Bare-Assed And Concrete," a procedure where prisoners were left naked on the concrete floor. On another occasion, smirking guards informed Pratt his pregnant common-law wife, Saundra Lee, was found murdered in a street gutter. For eight years, Pratt lingered in the darkness of solitary confinement.

Many were convinced of Pratt's innocence and believed that his only "crime" was his complexion and his politics. Faith United Methodist Church held the first of many "Free Geronimo Pratt" rallies, and the meetings started a legal defense team that eventually appealed his conviction. Months of legal battles ended with a decision by a judge who ruled that "The petitioner's conviction is reversed."

In May of 1997, B-40319 emerged unbroken from prison. Despite almost three decades of illegal detention, Geronimo Pratt held firm to his dignity. He came out of prison as he had gone in—a proud black man advocating change and a better life for his people.

On May 29, 1997, a judge acknowledged persistent lack of evidence, witnesses and motive in the original trial of Geronimo Pratt and reversed his conviction for murder. He spent over 25 years in prison for a crime he did not commit.

MAY 30 — Henry "Box" Brown: "I Waited Patiently for the Lord"

A large, heavy wooden box appeared at the offices of the Philadelphia Anti-Slavery Society. Moments later, the contents began to move. When the lid was opened, Henry Brown stepped out into freedom. Brown, who had once been thought dead, was alive. Like the Christ he worshipped, he had come back from the grave, miraculously resurrected from beatings, the auction block and slavery.

Months before his redemption, Brown had watched helplessly as his wife and child were sold to work the North Carolina swamps. His groans and cries could not halt their disappearance over the horizon, and Brown knew he would never again embrace his beloved family. Twelve years of marriage ended as the master stuffed the proceeds of the sale into his bulging purse.

Brown was stricken with grief and resolved to get free no matter the cost. A three-by-two-foot wooden crate to Philadelphia became his wings of salvation, and the Adams Express Shipping Company was the agent of his resurrection. With the aid of sympathetic southern whites, Brown climbed into a box to be shipped across the Mason-Dixon Line. He spent twenty-seven hours sideways, upside down, right-side up, without ventilation, bathrooms or water. He waited in constant fear that his box would be forgotten, dropped or accidentally opened.

The box arrived at the home of abolitionist William Johnson on Philadelphia's Arch Street and then was rushed to the Anti-Slavery Society's office. There, the crate was forced open with iron bars and knives, and up from darkness arose Henry "Box" Brown. Brown came forth singing the praises of Psalm 40, beginning with these words: "I waited patiently for the Lord; he inclined to me and heard my cry."

Henry Brown had waited on God, and God had answered his prayer. The lips that had quivered at the sight of his wife's torment were now opened in praise of God's liberation. He had a new song, the song of a freeman.

On May 30, 1849, Henry Brown arrived by crate in Philadelphia. His story gave momentum to the abolitionist movement and hope to millions still in slavery. Henry "Box" Brown fell from public view while in Europe, and the place and date of his death are unknown.

≣ C.L.R. James: Was It Worth It?

Sunset sprinkled a pink glow across the old Trinidadian's face. As he watched people hurrying home from their day's labor, he pondered whether his eighty-eight years of work for black liberation had been in vain. All his life James had cared about the miner, the farmer, the common daily worker—especially if they were black. As darkness enveloped his room, James wondered, "Did I make a difference? Have I, with all my education, my Marxist theory and insights, given any hope and life to working people?"

We may not know his conclusion that night, but we can draw our own today. We who enjoy the legacy of Cyril Lionel Robert James can testify to his contribution. The old black man who pondered his last days in a London apartment fundamentally shaped how we view the world. His book *The Black Jacobins*, published in 1938, changed the discourse of black activists all over the world. After this monumental work about the Haitian revolution, no act or history of black rebellion would be complete without reference to self-determination as a moving force in history. One can rightly say that *The Black Jacobins* fueled the future of black revolt. Armed with James' wisdom, black people in England, Africa and the United States began to assault the bastions of white supremacy and colonialism.

But C.L.R. James' contribution didn't end there. He went on to organize black sharecroppers and autoworkers in the U.S. and to help build the Socialist Workers Party. Above all, James articulated what the dispossessed and forgotten could not. He was not duped by tokens tossed to the black middle class. He did not spend his academic career weaving harmless theories that comforted the powerful and advanced his personal standing. James always looked to the bottom of society to determine whether a system worked or not, and he taught us to judge a system by its victims. Such compassion for the poor ensured James' expulsion from the United States in 1952. James once wrote:

We must not be afraid, we must not think because we are small and insignificant that we are not able to take part in all that is taking place. The first thing is to know. Anyone who tries to prevent you from knowing, from learning anything, is an enemy, an enemy of freedom, of equality, of democracy.

Today, we can answer his question: "Yes, C.L.R., your life and work were worth it." His vision for a just world informs our struggles for liberation; whenever we work for the common good, we honor his legacy.

Organizer C.L.R. James died in London on May 31, 1989, at the age of 88. He was the author of the seminal book The Black Jacobins. *The marks of his work are found in Africa, Trinidad, England and the United States.*

JUNE

John Hope Franklin

≣ Naomi Williams: The Southern Tenant Farmers' Union

It is difficult for us today to imagine the life of a tenant farmer in the South in the last century. Farmers used countless schemes to exploit their tenants: charging for tools, adjusting the rent, dropping the price, rigging the scales—all were used with impunity. As a result, tenant farmers were condemned to a life of dependency, poverty and perpetual debt.

Then, in 1933, Congress passed the Agricultural Adjustment Act to aid farmers during the Depression. The Act lowered prices for farm products by paying planters to reduce crop production. Though the law required that tenant farmers be paid a share of the benefits, few ever saw this money. Even worse, fewer crops meant a need for fewer tenant farmers. And black women were among the most abused: The earnings for a black woman tenant farmer at the time averaged $41.67 per year.

In 1934, the Socialist Party formed the Southern Tenant Farmers' Union (STFU) in Tyronza, Arkansas. The STFU was one of the first labor organizations in which whites and blacks, men and women were accepted equally as members. Scholars of STFU history note that black women "were active in the union; including speaking out and making decisions." Black women were seeing their friends evicted and starving in the Arkansas backcountry, and they saw no hope except through radical change.

Naomi Williams was typical of the rural black women who formed the backbone of the STFU. Williams, who lived as a tenant farmer in Gould, Arkansas, once said, "I done worked myself to death." During harvest season, she would pick three hundred pounds per day of her landowner's crop. When that backbreaking labor was done, she tended a vegetable garden, cultivated her own cotton patch, taught school for her neighbor's children and organized for the STFU.

Naomi Williams embraced the Southern Tenant Farmers' Union work with undying devotion. She was not just a union member; she was a vital part of the leadership. She saw that others, too, were working themselves "to death" just to survive. She therefore concluded she would somehow find the energy to work for justice, not only for herself but also for her fellow farmers.

The Southern Tenant Farmers' Union (STFU) was formed in 1934. In addition to Naomi Williams, other important organizers included Carrie Dilworth and Henrietta McGee.

It's a close game, with a few seconds left. Magic Johnson drops a pass to Kareem Abdul-Jabbar, and everyone in the building knows what is coming: the skyhook. Everyone knows, but no one can stop it. He fakes one way and turns the other, then makes a fluid motion across the paint. A second later the basketball drops gently through the net. Two points, or rather two more points.

His teammates called him "Money," "Big Fella" or just "Kareem." His skyhook was devastating, particularly in the clutch. He had learned the move in the fourth grade on the playgrounds of New York City, and years later he rained it down on opponents with relentless consistency.

Kareem Abdul-Jabbar redefined the role of a National Basketball Association (NBA) center. The center, the "big man" on the court, was usually there for rebounding and blocking shots. With Kareem, there was a new dimension: graceful moves, shooting and scoring. He ended his career with 38,387 points, six NBA championships and six Most Valuable Player awards. In addition to his skill on the court, Abdul-Jabbar was much more than a basketball player. His life was a struggle for identity in a world that abuses anyone who stands out. And at seven-feet tall he definitely stood out. He also stood up for what he believed and often paid a price for that conviction. Many would not let him forget his boycott of the 1968 Olympics in protest of America's racial injustice.

During the years that Abdul-Jabbar played center for UCLA, from 1965 to 1969, college officials changed the rules to try to prevent his dominance. But dominate he did anyway, leading UCLA to an 88-2 record during his career.

Here was a tall, proud black man who spoke out against injustices and racism. He became a Muslim in a Christian nation, and as a public figure he was often misunderstood and maligned for his beliefs. In his autobiography, *Giant Steps*, Kareem Abdul-Jabbar writes of the struggles and traumas of his life. Despite public criticism, he never wavered or apologized. He lived his convictions, and his clutch skyhooks symbolized his transcendence over obstacles. His chosen Muslim name says it all: Kareem (noble and generous) Abdul (serves Allah) Jabbar (powerfully). His nobility, service and power were visible both on the court and in his convictions.

Kareem Abdul-Jabbar was good all season, but he was particularly good when a championship was at stake. He still holds the record for the most points scored in a career in the National Basketball Association (NBA).

White men in black suits shuffled papers and whispered among themselves. A serious tone hovered over the meeting.

"Her speeches are inflammatory; she urges labor unrest and plants dissatisfaction among the blacks," one man said. Heads nodded vigorously.

Another joined in: "She undermines national security with talk of solidarity with poor nations and Communists." Eyes rolled in disbelief.

"At the City College and in labor rallies, she says she is a Marxist," added a third. Groans all around.

The man in charge spoke firmly: "I think we have all we need. For the good of America, she must be deported." They all agreed, and the meeting was adjourned.

The target of this investigation was Claudia Jones. Born in Trinidad and raised in Harlem, she was an eloquent, poised and powerful opponent of injustice. Devoted to ending poverty and racism, at age eighteen Jones joined the Young Communist League in Harlem. The Communist Party was so impressed with her work that, after seven years, she became the League's national chair.

Jones was a brilliant orator and writer who urged the Party to put black women's struggles at the forefront of their mission. She believed that black women were the most nascent revolutionary force in America: As workers, nurturers of children and repositories of values, they had the most potential to impact their communities. With relentless fervor, Claudia Jones advocated for labor rights, gender equality and civil rights. Blacks all over Harlem talked about Claudia Jones, the firebrand sister who told it like it was, who stood up to police, the banks, the companies and other manifestations of the white power structure.

By 1951, the U.S. government had had enough of Jones. As the men adjourned their meeting, their feelings were clear: "Here we let this Trinidadian woman into our country and all she does is complain. Who does she think she is anyway? She is a danger to us all. We need to get her the hell out of our country."

Jones was arrested, charged and found guilty of violating the Smith Act, which essentially declared it illegal to advocate Marxism and just about anything else that inhibited free enterprise. Decreeing that Jones' talk of gender and racial equality was too dangerous, the government deported her in 1951. However, expulsion did not destroy her zeal, and she continued her struggle in London.

Angela Davis and others attributed their political enlightenment to Claudia Jones. Whether organizing chapters of the Young Communist League, demanding fair wages for black workers or staring down her accusers, Jones worked tirelessly for her beliefs. No matter the cost to herself, her devotion to human progress outweighed her fears. Like so many others, she sacrificed herself for the oppressed.

Communist leader and political activist Claudia Jones, born in Trinidad and raised in Harlem, died in exile in London in 1964.

With his subtle and unassuming manner, black historian John Hope Franklin has changed race relations in the United States. While many think of history as just a list of obscure names and complicated dates—and the historian as an irrelevant figure safely ensconced in an ivory tower—Dr. Franklin has taught us that African-American history is the best tool we have to understand our past and transform our future.

Franklin is known primarily as the author of one of the first major surveys of black history, *From Slavery to Freedom*. When it was first published in 1947, *From Slavery to Freedom* stood in sharp contrast to the popular historical works about black folk. This definitive history of African Americans destroyed the myths of black docility and irresponsibility and replaced them with the saga of black self-determination. Now in its eighth edition, *From Slavery to Freedom* has sold over three million copies.

Because of Franklin, generations of black students have emerged from school with a sense of dignity and pride. For many—myself included—Franklin has opened our eyes to the astonishing history of our people. His sense of black history enlightened the liberation struggle in many arenas. He provided much of the historical research for the NAACP in the *Brown v. Board of Education* desegregation lawsuit. He participated in civil rights marches with other history professors, walking under a handwritten cardboard sign that read "U.S. Historians." They were often led to the front of the march so they could record, for future generations, the truth of the struggle. Rather than seeing history as something that is "over," they became history in motion.

Through the eyes of John Hope Franklin, we have seen that history offers us a great challenge and a great gift: We are both the products and the producers of history and through history we can learn what is needed to transform our society and ourselves.

In June of 1997, President Bill Clinton selected historian John Hope Franklin to chair a panel to advise the President on resolving racial conflict in America. His book From Slavery to Freedom *has sold more than three million copies.*

≡ Rafer Lewis Johnson: That Others Might Win

In the 1960 Olympics, Rafer Lewis Johnson made history. Improving on his 1956 Silver Medal for the Decathlon, Johnson walked away with a Gold Medal in 1960. Even more impressive, he set a new Olympic record by amassing 8,001 points for the decathlon. When he returned to the States, Johnson found that his Olympic accomplishments provided a status few other events could duplicate. However, rather than milking his name recognition for personal advantage, he devoted himself to community service, using his newfound popularity to bring dignity, equality and opportunity to others.

In 1968, Johnson was inspired by what he saw at a Special Olympics event, and he and a small group of volunteers founded California Special Olympics the following year. As one of the original members of the Board of Directors of Special Olympics Southern California, he served as its President from 1983 until 1992, when he was named Chairman of the Board of Governors, a position he still holds. The same man who shattered world records in Olympic competition continues to help thousand of disabled citizens find dignity and honor through sports.

Johnson also became a leader in progressive causes and the Civil Rights Movement. He supported Robert F. Kennedy's presidential bid because he believed deeply in Kennedy's platform of peace, civil rights and economic equality. When Robert Kennedy was assassinated on June 5, 1968, Johnson witnessed the murder firsthand, assisted in capturing the assassin and retrieved the murder weapon. He was a pallbearer at the funeral and testified at the murder trial of Sirhan Sirhan.

Like the rest of the nation, Johnson was devastated by the murder. Still, he maintained his commitment to a just political and social order in America, turning his athletic abilities and celebrity status into a forum from which he could help others achieve self-respect and justice.

Olympic athlete Rafer Johnson shared the podium with Senator Robert F. Kennedy minutes before the presidential candidate was murdered on June 5, 1968.

≡ James Meredith: March Against Fear

In 1962, James Meredith became the first black student to enroll in the University of Mississippi. Though the governor had sworn that "Ole Miss" would never be contaminated with blackness, Meredith's court-ordered admission changed that.

What followed was unreal, as three thousand whites rioted in protest. Twenty-three thousand federal troops—a virtual division—were required to quell the rampage. Two people died and one hundred and sixty were injured in the melee before troops arrived. Despite these violent beginnings, Meredith did graduate from the University in 1963.

In 1966, the courageous Meredith returned to Mississippi and was saddened by how little progress he saw. Suddenly, Meredith seized upon an idea. In a vivid display of fearlessness, he would march—alone—from Memphis, Tennessee, to Jackson, Mississippi. His lonely trek across the hateful landscape of the South would spur blacks to vote, en masse. His March Against Fear would demonstrate that racism could be defeated, that courage could overcome fear, hatred and violence.

Walking two hundred and twenty-five miles anywhere is hard; but for a black man walking alone in the South in 1966, it was potentially fatal. Everyone told him he was crazy, that he would be killed before nightfall. Despite the danger, Meredith started out on his lonely trek. On the second day, a sniper shot him as he walked by. A famous photo shows Meredith dragging himself along the highway, leaving a trail of blood behind. He did not finish his march, but he did inspire others as he had hoped. Shortly afterward, the Student Nonviolent Coordinating Committee (SNCC) and the Southern Christian Leadership Conference (SCLC) completed Meredith's March Against Fear. In both his enrollment in Ole Miss and his lonely March Against Fear, James Meredith helped topple segregation.

On June 6, 1966, James Meredith, the first black person to enroll in the University of Mississippi, began his March Against Fear in Memphis, Tennessee.

JUN 7   ≣ Reverend Andrew Bryan: Black Saint of Savannah

When Rev. George Liele purchased his freedom in 1773 and founded the First African Baptist Church in Savannah, Georgia, a slave named Andrew Bryan was one of the first to be baptized. Years later, Bryan felt called to preach the gospel. He eventually purchased his freedom, and when Rev. Liele moved on, Bryan returned to serve the congregation as an ordained Baptist minister.

At the time, whites were particularly fearful that black churches were merely places to plot rebellion and mayhem. One day they seized Rev. Bryan and fifty of his parishioners and "beat them so severely that their blood ran down and puddled on the ground about them." Yet Bryan, with uplifted hands, cried out to his persecutors, "If you would stop me from preaching, cut off my head, for I am willing not only to be whipped but would freely suffer death for the cause of the Lord Jesus!" Stunned by his faith, Bryan's tormentors sheepishly walked away.

On another occasion, white authorities eavesdropped on a prayer meeting that Rev. Bryan was leading in a local barn. Pressing their ears against the walls, they overhead him praying for those who had beaten him and his church members. One spy heard Bryan call the man's own name, asking that God forgive him and save his soul for heaven. The tormentor fled the scene in shock, amazed that the minister's faith could be so genuine. Rev. Andrew Bryan followed Jesus with such conviction that even his tormentors marveled. He showed his congregation how to live as Christ lived, despite hatred, violence and persecution. His name should be listed among those saints whose courage built the foundation of the Christian faith in America.

On June 6, 1790, Rev. Andrew Bryan bought a 95' x 100' lot from Tom Gibbons for 27 pounds sterling. The site later became home to the first church ever owned by blacks in Savannah, Georgia. Bryan died in 1812 at the age of 96.

JUN 8   ☰ **Fannie B. Beck: The Housewives League of Detroit**

The Great Depression had wrought great devastation in Detroit's black neighborhoods. Even before the Depression, many of these folk, just up from the South, were familiar with poverty and despair. Now, with thirty percent of the entire population without work, the black community was in agony. In some communities, over half of working-age blacks were unemployed. Even those who had jobs held the lowest, dirtiest and most dangerous jobs in Detroit, earning a fraction of white salaries. The Great Depression was threatening to destroy black families.

On June 10, 1930, Fannie B. Beck of the Bethel African Methodist Episcopal (AME) Church of Detroit convened a gathering of fifty women from the church to seek a solution. Rather than petitioning the federal government for help or begging for crumbs at the table of Detroit's white elite, they created the Housewives League of Detroit. Fannie Beck knew that black women controlled the family budget, educated the children and organized the household. If that power could be harnessed, she felt, they could transform the black community.

Almost immediately, the League's commitment to self-help made an impact. Though the Depression had reduced spending power, there was still enough left to make a difference. The League initiated a concerted effort to promote black businesses, black projects and black professionals. Fannie Beck and the women of the League visited stores to inquire about fairness in hiring and the distribution of black products. Any storeowner who failed to respond was subject to an immediate black boycott. Businesses who agreed with the League's modest demands were given lists of qualified black adults and teenagers to select from when hiring for open positions.

The Housewives League of Detroit was a phenomenal success. Historian Jacqueline Jones notes that their chapters, organized in America's ghettos, were second only to the powerful Congress of Industrial Organizations (CIO) in local influence. By 1934, just four years after its founding, the Housewives League boasted ten thousand dues-paying members.

Clearly ahead of their time, the Housewives League is a beautiful example of local women taking initiative to transform and enhance their communities.

The Housewives League of Detroit was founded on June 10, 1930, by Fannie B. Beck and the women of the Bethel AME Church of Detroit.

JUN 9   ≣ Alain Locke: The New Negro

Alain Locke unselfishly placed his personal gifts in the hands of the collective. Locke was the first African-American Rhodes Scholar, and he continued his graduate education at the University of Berlin. He returned to America with credentials that could have opened doors of academic prestige and personal security. Instead, Locke cast aside private gain and immersed himself in the black struggle for dignity. His intelligence, art and energy were not for himself but for his race.

Intrigued by the artistic talent assembled in New York City, Locke became the definitive interpreter and promoter of the Harlem Renaissance. His most notable anthology, *The New Negro*, announced to the world that black culture had arrived. Locke's insightful celebration of the emerging artists of that time included the names of W.E.B. DuBois, James Weldon Johnson, Jean Toomer, Anne Spencer, Claude McKay, Zora Hurston Neale and J.A. Rogers.

Locke was an unparalleled scholar, philosopher and intellectual. He looked at black artists not as separate phenomena but as reflections of the broader struggle. In his 1925 essay, also titled "The New Negro," Locke wrote:

> *If in our lifetime the Negro should not be able to celebrate the full initiation into American democracy, he can at least, on the warrant of these things [the art of the Renaissance], celebrate the attainment of a significant and satisfying new phase of group development, and with it a spiritual Coming of Age.*

Locke understood that flourishing arts in the Harlem Renaissance did not alone bring political empowerment and economic equality. But he recognized that the spiritual revival expressed by the arts was a significant phase in black self-identity and progress.

Locke also believed that visual art was a tangible link between Africa and America. He wrote *Negro Art: Past and Present* and other books to show the African roots of Negro art. His passion for black elevation through art lasted his entire life. When he died in 1954, Locke left on his desk an unfinished work titled *The Negro in America Culture*. Much of our understanding of the Harlem Renaissance, black art and political literature comes from the work of Alain Locke.

Rhodes Scholar Alain Locke died of complications from lung disease on June 9, 1954, in Washington, D.C. He was the definitive interpreter and promoter of the Harlem Renaissance.

JUN 10　　　　　　　≣ **Marcus Mosiah Garvey: African Fundamentalism**

He was an immigrant with no credentials, a newcomer shunned by established organizations, but in just a few short years Marcus Mosiah Garvey came to embody black aspirations and created a movement rarely seen in world history. On July 2, 1918, the Universal Negro Improvement Association (UNIA) filed articles of incorporation, and black life would never be the same again. The UNIA began when Garvey called the First International Convention of the Negro Peoples of the World to meet at Madison Square Garden. Fifteen thousand delegates came from Harlem, Chicago, Kansas City, Jamaica, Sierra Leone, the Gold Coast, Trinidad and any place able to afford a delegation.

One could argue that all future black struggle was shaped by the agenda set that summer. The Convention demanded a capital "N" in the word "Negro"; mandatory black history courses in school; an end to lynching and European colonialism; and equal employment, education and justice. It proclaimed "red, black and green to be the colors of the Negro race."

Through the UNIA, Marcus Garvey preached a message black folks desperately needed to hear:

You have a history! You are an important human being! You have a culture! You have a continent! You come from a race of kings, queens, warriors, inventors, griots, and leaders! Black is not ugly and ignorant and enslaved, black is beautiful, intelligent and free! Africa for Africans, at home and abroad! Up You Mighty Race, and do what you will! One God, One Aim, One Destiny!

The rise of Garvey and the UNIA is even more significant considering the many opponents scheming to destroy his movement. The United States government, European governments, the FBI, black intellectuals and black civil rights organizations all conspired to undermine the UNIA. Despite virulent opposition, however, by 1921 the UNIA boasted millions of members in eight hundred and fifty-nine chapters across the world. Garvey's message overcame negative press and hostile governments, and reached the anxious ears of black listeners around the world. His work titled *African Fundamentalism* summarized his convictions:

> The time has come for the Negro to forget and cast behind him his hero worship and adoration of other races, and to start out immediately to create and emulate heroes of his own. We must canonize our own saints, create our own martyrs, and elevate to positions of fame and honor black men and women who have made their distinct contributions to our racial history.... Africa has produced countless numbers of men and women, in war and peace, whose luster and bravery outshine that of any other people. Then why not see good and perfection in ourselves?

Marcus Garvey's movement flourished because deep in the hearts of all who are oppressed is the yearning to be fully human, the desire to be respected and the urge to create a world that reflects each person's inner beauty—a message Garvey took to the black world, and no power on earth could prevent it from being heard.

Marcus Mosiah Garvey was arrested on mail fraud charges, jailed and eventually deported from the United States. He died of a brain hemorrhage on June 10, 1940, in London, England. His teachings live on in the actions of self-reliant black people across the globe.

JUN 11   ☰ Jack Johnson: Great Black Champion

Long before television and media hype created icons of athletes, Jack Johnson toiled away at the sport of boxing. Yet his charisma and boldness extended his fame beyond sports. How did he leap into the nation's consciousness without benefit of satellites, cable television and 24/7 sports shows? The answer is that Jack Johnson challenged white supremacy, and racist America wanted him destroyed.

America in the 1900s was immersed in the mythology that whites were stronger, smarter, purer and better than "niggers." Within this racial climate, Johnson devastated white opponents in the boxing ring—and doing it with such strength and confidence that white America could not bear to see it. While blacks saw Johnson as their ultimate champion, whites believed he kept company with the devil. For Johnson did not just whip his white opponents, he taunted, sneered and laughed as he knocked them to the mat, crushing the myth of the weak, docile and inferior black man. White America hated Jack Johnson.

Then, in 1910, writer Jack London coaxed World Heavyweight Champion Jim Jeffries out of retirement and challenged him to "wipe that smile off Jack Johnson's face." In a July 4th match, Johnson defeated the man the white press had hailed as the "Great White Hope." As the white messiah lay crumpled on the canvas, Johnson's post-fight stare cheered black folks across America, but white folks went crazy. Race riots erupted across the nation as gangs of whites beat, burned and sometimes killed any black in their path. They could not allow any hint of black superiority. Yet white mob violence could not extinguish the black pride that had been engendered by Jack Johnson.

In this harsh and racially-charged climate, Johnson foreshadowed the career of the great Muhammad Ali. Never before had a sports figure generated such hate and loathing from whites—and such love and adoration from blacks.

Jack Johnson, first black World Heavyweight Champion, was killed in an automobile accident in Raleigh, North Carolina on June 10, 1946.

≣ J.A. Rogers: Great Man of Color

Young Joel Augustus Rogers was astonished at what he saw and heard in the United States. Fresh off the boat from Jamaica, he sought to understand why African Americans endured such difficult conditions. To his amazement, Rogers soon realized that white Americans believed the descendants of Africa to be inferior and subhuman. Law, custom, films, jobs, schools, books, jokes—all reinforced the notion of black subordination. Worst of all, America's dominant religion, Christianity, taught that blacks were eternally cursed by God in the book of Genesis because their forebear—the "black" Ham—had looked upon his father's nakedness.

J.A. Rogers wanted desperately to correct this horrible myth and its devastating implications, and he spent the next fifty years conducting his own research into history, politics, languages and geographies of human development. He taught himself French, German and Spanish, studied ancient civilizations, and spent months in museums, libraries and bookstores. He attended lectures, took copious notes, cross-referenced and verified facts, and meticulously compiled what he learned on note cards. Long before computers and the Internet, Rogers educated himself with astonishing diligence. As he learned of black accomplishments, African kingdoms and the powerful influence of Africa upon the world, Rogers began a crusade to destroy the myth of white supremacy.

In 1931, Rogers self-published a small paperback book that described the great black men and women of history. The work was privately printed and circulated underground in the black communities of Harlem, South Chicago and other places. Passed among friends and discussed on street corners, Rogers' book gave life and hope to a burdened people. While his first book was being circulated, Rogers continued his diligent research, which culminated in the publication of his classic, *World's Great Men of Color*. This two-volume work, depicting the lives of great black men and women in history, transformed black self-understanding.

In an era long before the emergence of black studies and black power, J.A. Rogers celebrated the humanity and value of black people. At a time when the dominant image of blacks was embodied in the stereotypes of Stepin Fetchit, housemaids and buggy-eyed buffoons, Rogers wrote about Makeda, Queen of Sheba; Hannibal of Carthage; Al-Jahiz; Kafur the Magnificent; Menelik II and many other heroes of black history. Rogers was the forerunner of later Afro-centric scholars who would continue to energize black self-understanding. His work burst open the floodgates of truth about African history, and many followed in Rogers' footsteps, enlightening the black laborer, teacher, janitor and shoe-shine boy of their dignity and honor as a race. The far-reaching benefits of the self-determined research of J.A. Rogers are almost unfathomable.

Author and black history scholar J.A. Rogers died in New York City on March 26, 1965. He was the among first to document the great heroes of black history.

≡ Walter Rodney: Groundings with My People

Walter Rodney was an intellectual and scholar who challenged the common idea that academic study was a pursuit outside the struggles of common people. His studies, analyses and conclusions were remarkable for their clarity and power. At age twenty-four, he earned a Ph.D. in history from London's prestigious School of Oriental and African Studies, and he went on to teach in London, Dar es Salaam (Tanzania), Jamaica and Guyana. His books, *How Europe Underdeveloped Africa* and *History of the Guyanese Working People*, describe the impact of imperialism and the power of people's struggle.

But Rodney did not stop with academic study; direct political work informed his writings. Most significantly, Rodney co-founded the Working People's Alliance (WPA) in Guyana, a multi-racial formation that fought for equality and democracy.

Though Rodney had studied at the world's finest institutions and broke bread with leading intellectuals of his day, including great black scholars such as C.L.R. James and Eric Williams, his political commitment was forged on the streets. His energy, wisdom and strength emerged from his contact with the poor. In his classic, *Groundings with My Brothers*, Rodney wrote that he often visited Jamaica's "gulleys" after completing his academic duties. These gulleys were rubbish dumps where the poorest Jamaicans lived, where "criminals, hooligans, failures" were left to rot along with the garbage. Among the common black folk of the gulleys, Rodney found hope, humor and a heroic struggle for dignity. Their fight for humanity became his.

Rodney often said that working people taught him how to be a true Marxist. His years of study and activism led him to believe that socialism was the only means to equality and self-determination. However, he wrote that it was not enough to study Marx and reshape his analysis into our context. Rodney argued that we needed to study current conditions and develop our own unique liberation strategy. No outsider, no matter how brilliant, could solve our oppression.

For Walter Rodney, the black intellectual was not found in the comfort of the library or the campus but in the ghettos, gulleys and prisons of the world. He believed—and lived—the principle that the intellectual must live with the oppressed, learn what they know and build a movement alongside them.

On June 13, 1980, agents of the government of Linden Forbes Burnham of Guyana assassinated Walter Rodney, a black intellectual and founder of the Working People's Alliance. A bomb exploded in Rodney's car outside the headquarters of the Working People's Alliance.

≣ Jacob Armstead Lawrence: "I Paint the Things I Know"

Jacob Lawrence is one of the more recent talents in a long tradition of black visual artists. His greatness, however, stands in sharp contrast to his humility, gentleness and wholehearted devotion to his craft. For sixty years, Jacob Lawrence painted figurative narrations of black life with unmistakable clarity and passion.

Growing up in Harlem during the flowering of black culture, Lawrence learned from the best: Claude McKay, Alain Locke, Katherine Dunham, Countee Cullen, Langston Hughes and many others. He also spent many hours in the Schaumburg Library studying African culture, black art and American history. Jacob Lawrence painted what he learned and created an art form unique in intensity and expression. He combined cubism, impressionistic influences and African tradition into his own unique style. His bright colors and abstract lines made the black experience come alive.

In 1940, Lawrence completed the classic series of paintings in tribute to Frederick Douglass and Harriet Tubman. Immediately following the paintings' release, Lawrence said simply, "I paint the things I know." His other works were no less significant. Some say his "Migration" series depicts the trauma and glory of the African-American move to the North like few other mediums. He also painted the "Toussaint L'Ouverture" series in tribute to this leader of the Haitian revolution, paintings about the Harlem Renaissance and other scenes of black life. In the 1970s, Lawrence created "The Builders" series, a set of panels depicting carpenters and workers. "The Builders" was both a tribute to labor and a symbol of the work required to construct a just society.

Perhaps Jacob Lawrence's mission is best summed up in his own words. As he told his biographer:

> We don't have a physical slavery, but an economic slavery. If those people, who were so much worse off than people today, could conquer their slavery, we certainly can do the same thing…I am not a politician. I'm an artist, just trying to do my part to bring this thing about.

Artist Jacob Lawrence died of cancer on June 9, 2000, in Seattle, Washington. His paintings are owned and exhibited throughout the world.

≡ Ella Fitzgerald: First Lady of Song

For over sixty years, Ella Fitzgerald reigned, almost without dispute, as "The First Lady of Song." Others may have had more range, better voices and sharper pitch, yet none put it all together like Ella Fitzgerald. From gutbucket clubs to concert halls, Fitzgerald gave life to songs like no one else. Ira Gershwin said it all after hearing her perform songs that he and his brother George had composed: "I never knew how good our songs were until I heard Ella sing them."

When Fitzgerald was a teenager, she entered Amateur Night at the Apollo Theater in Harlem as a dancer. At the last minute, she decided to sing instead of dance, and music became her life.

Listening to Fitzgerald with a tight trio or an orchestra is like making a visit to paradise: Her sound is so clear, it is hard to contain the joy. Life becomes good and problems diminish when her music hits our souls. It's all about the song—not about Ella or the place or the audience—it's the song that gives life. Fitzgerald lifted us up when she was seventeen, and at seventy-seven, she still brought life to the weary. Wherever she is now, whatever seventh heaven or paradise she inhabits, it is made richer by her unmistakable voice. Ella Fitzgerald, the first lady of song!

The most popular female jazz singer in the United States for more than half a century, Ella Fitzgerald died on June 15, 1996, in Beverly Hills, California.

≡ Bishop Smallwood Edmund Williams: The Bible Way

In 1919, Smallwood Edmund Williams was a twelve-year-old black boy growing up in Columbus, Ohio. He went to church with his parents one Sunday morning and experienced what he called "the greatest event of my life." He responded to the altar call and later wrote, "I was so 'drunk' by the power of the Spirit, two deacons had to hold me down." From that moment on, nothing or no one could hold him down from God's call.

Williams became a minister in the Church of God in Christ and was soon one of that denomination's most powerful young preachers. The Pentecostal faith at that time was characterized by vibrant singing, preaching and prayer, and by a focus on the spiritual needs of life. The faithful considered politics, economics, social justice and the physical needs of people "worldly concerns," secondary to the "things of the Spirit." However, Williams was influenced at Howard University's School of Religion by Howard Thurman and Benjamin Mays. Under their teachings, and following the lead of the Spirit, Williams realized that God called his church to redeem the whole of life.

In 1957, Smallwood Williams founded the Bible Way Church of Our Lord Jesus Christ World Wide, Inc. Unlike most Pentecostal organizations, his denomination fused powerful gospel preaching and prayer meetings with political action and economic justice. He wrote in his book, *This Is My Story*, "Members of Bible Way were pretty involved in places that didn't make us particularly popular with Pentecostals." Sunday after Sunday, Williams urged his congregation to be advocates for the poor and downtrodden. He believed that God's love extended to all of life, and he implored the Bible Way Church to feed the hungry, find shelter for the poor, register voters, advocate for healthcare, teach the young, provide jobs—and preach the gospel. He taught all of us that Christians must work to make the kingdom of God a reality on earth, and that when God's redemption, peace, justice and love rule, we will experience the power of God in this life.

When Bishop Smallwood Williams died in 1991, Judge Eleanor Holmes Norton praised his commitment to justice and credited him with bringing religious zeal and commitment to political and social issues.

Bishop Smallwood Edmund Williams, founder of the Bible Way Church, died on June 28, 1991. He was one of the first Pentecostal preachers who encouraged his congregation to work for social justice.

JUN 17   ≡ **Reverend Fred Shuttlesworth: "God Is on Your Side"**

The black church produced innumerable saints during the Civil Rights Movement. None was more energetic, courageous and uncompromising than the Rev. Fred Shuttlesworth. He arrived at Birmingham's Bethel Baptist Church in search of a church that matched his radical understanding of the gospel, of a people who followed the Christ who criticized injustice and uplifted the downtrodden.

Rev. Shuttlesworth pursued his beliefs with a passion that racism could not deter. Despite hateful and violent mobs, he led nonviolent marches and protests for the right to learn, vote and work. Despite numerous bombings, beatings, arrests and threats, Shuttlesworth never wavered.

On Christmas Day 1956, terrorists planted a bomb in his bedroom that injured his beloved children and almost killed his entire family. A year later, a knife-wielding mob viciously beat him to the ground in front of his children and wounded his wife. Following this brutal attack, Shuttlesworth climbed the podium at Bethel Baptist Church and, still bruised and bandaged, preached these words of encouragement: "If you can endure and continue to do right, then God is on your side and you can't lose."

To all in the congregation, his sermon was more than abstract theological musings. His scars, wounds and bandages testified of his courage. Shuttlesworth stayed the course and fought the good fight, always believing that God was present in every struggle. While most Americans sought a faith that brought comfort and solace, Rev. Fred Shuttlesworth followed Jesus to the suffering of the cross.

Rev. Fred Shuttlesworth was a principal figure in the Civil Rights Movement in Birmingham, Alabama, and across the Deep South. His courage in the face of harm has brought hope to black activists everywhere.

JUN 18   ≡ Larry Doby: Following Jackie

Eleven weeks after Jackie Robinson stunned America with his National League debut, Larry Doby played his first game as a Cleveland Indian. Doby's breakthrough came on July 4, 1947. It was significant that the national day of celebration of America's freedom also marked the American League's desegregation. In some ways, Doby's road was harder than Jackie Robinson's. Since Jackie was the first to break the color barrier, he received more support and more press. Doby suffered the same abuse that Jackie did, but without the media coverage. His game suffered as he batted an anemic .156 in his first year.

With such a horrendous beginning, Doby could have forgotten about his quest to integrate the American League. He could have left the struggle up to Jackie and anyone else brave enough to follow him. Jackie had enjoyed a great first year, with no choice but to continue. Doby had suffered a horrible year and easily could have quit. Yet he did not. Quitting would have upheld segregation and set integration back several more years. (The Boston Red Sox did not sign their first black player until 1959, twelve years after Jackie Robinson integrated Major League Baseball.)

Doby returned for a second year, and for his act of courage, all black America is grateful. He rebounded from his disastrous first year with a flair few could match. He hit .301 and led the Indians to a rare World Series title. Doby and white pitcher Steve Gromek were photographed hugging each other in jubilation. The photo shocked the nation, and many protested the sight of a black man and a white man celebrating together. Their image displayed, for all to see, that teamwork made everyone equal.

Larry Doby led the American League in home runs twice, was selected to the All-Star team seven times and stirred Cleveland fans with his defensive play. In 1998, Doby was elected to Baseball's Hall of Fame. More important than the home runs and the honors, Larry Doby did for the American League what Jackie Robinson did for the National. No longer could owners say blacks couldn't play America's national pastime. All excuses and arguments vanished each time Doby drove a game-winning homer or slid safely into second with a double. Above all, Doby showed extraordinary grace and courage when he came back from his dismal beginning, when fans looked at his .156 average and smugly nodded, "I told you so."

The first African-American player in the American League, Larry Doby, died on June 18, 2003, in Montclair, New Jersey. He helped lead the Cleveland Indians to a World Series championship in 1948.

JUNE 19   ≡ **Medgar Evers: Martyr of Mississippi**

There were countless black casualties in the cause of freedom, and many came before Medgar Evers. Yet many consider Evers one of the most significant martyrs of the Civil Rights Movement. Perhaps it was because he was the Field Secretary for the National Association for the Advancement of Colored People (NAACP) in Jackson, Mississippi. Some believe Ever's death was magnified because it occurred right after President John Kennedy's extemporaneous civil rights address to the nation. Or it could have been the sheer horrific and cowardly nature of his assassination. Whatever the reasons, Medgar Evers' assassination became a symbol of the cost of freedom, a chilling example of the extent white racists would go to deny blacks the most fundamental human rights.

On the night of June 12, 1963, Evers wife, Myrlie, had allowed the three Evers children to stay up late to watch President Kennedy's address and to wait for their father to come home. When they heard the car door close, they jumped up and ran to greet him. But before they reached the front door they heard another sound—a loud crackle that sent them all diving to the floor. They quickly got up and ran outside to find Evers lying face down with a bullet wound in his back. Myrlie went to call an ambulance, and the children cried, "Please, Daddy, get up." Medgar Evers could not and did not get up. An assassin had been waiting for him in the bushes near his home. Those who investigated the scene realized that his white dress shirt had made a perfect target for the killer on that dark night.

Evers had known that Mississippi was violent, and he had had no illusions about how dangerous his work was as Field Secretary for the NAACP. From the beginning, when he took the position in 1954, he had often been threatened, mocked, followed and beaten. Though he and his colleagues were fighting simply for the right to vote, work and live in peace, in the eyes of white supremacists they represented a danger to the existing "way of life." Evers and hundreds of other black Americans were martyred to protect a society that subjugated its black citizens to misery and poverty. Despite the danger to himself, he had organized, protested, written and struggled. For his courage, he is often remembered, along with Martin Luther King, Jr., and Malcolm X, as one of the significant martyrs in the struggle for black freedom in the United States.

NAACP Field Secretary Medgar Evers was murdered on the night of June 12, 1963, by Byron de la Beckwith, a member of the local Ku Klux Klan. Beckwith was not arrested and brought to trial until over thirty years later, even though many people knew who had committed the crime.

JUN 20   ≣ John Jasper: "I'se Got Religion to Give Away"

The morning was unusually hot, even for Virginia, and the congregation waited uncomfortably in the humidity. This was the last day of a week-long revival, and hundreds were gathered to hear black preacher John Jasper. Some in the crowd knew him only by reputation, others were already converted by his sermons and more than a few came to scoff at this illiterate preacher. Regardless of the motives, the meeting hall was full; people crowded in the back, along the walls, and many more were gathered outside the open windows. It was 1884, and Jasper had been preaching in America for forty years. Wherever he preached, large crowds followed.

Once the songs and prayers concluded, Jasper rose and stood boldly behind the pulpit. The audience was immediately caught up in his first words:

I stand before you today on legs of iron and none can stay me from preaching the Gospel of the Lord God. I know well enough that the old devil is mad as a tempest about my being here; he knows that my call to preach comes from God; for he knows that the people is going to hear a message from heaven. I don't get my sermons out of grammars and rhetorics, but the Spirit of the Lord puts them in my mind and makes them burn in my soul.

Captivated from the outset, the crowd hung on his every word. Those outside stood still so no sound could compete with his voice. Every eye was riveted on this old black preacher. It was 1884, and Jasper was now seventy-two years old. Yet his love of preaching gave him persevering energy. He concluded:

Bless God, I'se got religion to give away. The Lord has filled my hands with the Gospel, and I stand here to offer free salvation to any that will come. If in this big crowd there is one lost sinner that has not felt the cleansing touch of my Saviour's blood, I ask him to come today and he shall never die.

Jasper took his seat and bowed his head, as people from all over the hall came forward to be healed. Amazingly, some of those who had come to ridicule were among the converted. John Jasper stood on the platform and quietly offered thanks for the privilege of helping lead God's children back home.

John Jasper was born a slave in Fluvanna County, Virginia. In 1837, at the age of 25, he converted to Christianity, and after the Civil War ended in 1865, he was freed from slavery. On June 20, 1884, he delivered one of his most famous sermons, "The Stone Cut Out of the Mountain." Hundreds of people gave their hearts to God once they heard the gospel preaching of John Jasper.

JUN 21 ≡ **James Edward Chaney: Martyr of Neshoba County**

James Chaney wanted desperately to improve life for his people in the South. He was from Mississippi, he knew Mississippi, and he sought to transform the poverty and fear he saw into equality and dignity. Freedom Summer gave him a chance to do that. During the summer of 1964, he and hundreds of black and white young people worked to register voters and teach citizenship classes. Chaney and the others knew, however, that white racists would kill to maintain their privileges. Death haunted every move of these young people; danger lurked whenever a white mob gathered or headlights appeared in the rearview mirror.

James Edward Chaney and white students Andrew Goodman and Mickey Schwerner were arrested for "speeding" in Neshoba County, Mississippi. The sheriff held them for a few hours, then ordered them out of town. The three were unaware that the delay was a ruse to gather a mob of racists. Once released, the three turned on Highway 19 toward home. Shortly, headlights appeared in their rearview mirror—not just two lights, but a trail of cars. Angry white men overtook them and ordered them out of the car. Chaney, Goodman and Schwerner were cursed, beaten and executed. Their bodies were buried in an earthen dam, and their car was burned and pushed into a lake. No one was convicted for the murders, and injustice reigned in Mississippi.

Yet, as with all martyrs for righteousness, their cause was not lost. Chaney and his white comrades inspired untold future acts of courage, love and faith. James Chaney died when he was but twenty-one-years old, his future destroyed by blind hate. Yet this young man will now and forever remain a beacon of hope for those who walk the narrow path of justice.

On June 21, 1964, a gang of white men executed James Edward Chaney and his two white companions in Neshoba County for their work in registering black voters. Their murder horrified the nation and energized the entire Civil Rights Movement.

JUN 22   ≣ Henry Winston: "My Vision Remains"

On June 30, 1961, Communist Party leader Henry Winston was freed from the federal penitentiary at Terre Haute, Indiana. President Kennedy had ordered his release, following appeals by Eleanor Roosevelt, A. Philip Randolph, Reinhold Neibuhr and many others. Winston had served nearly eight years in federal prison for violating the Smith Act, which made it a criminal act to "teach, advise or encourage" anything that advocated the "overthrow the Government." Winston had been found guilty on two accounts: being a Marxist and advocating economic equality.

As Winston walked out of his cell into that sunlit afternoon, he could see nothing. He could not see the sun, the clouds or the crowd that welcomed him back, for Henry Winston was blind. While in prison, he had developed a brain tumor that had gone untreated. Prison officials, believing a traitor like Winston deserved whatever he got, had ignored his pains and complaints, and his untreated tumor eventually blinded him.

Yet imprisonment and blindness did not quench Winston's quest for justice. A few days after his release, he wrote:

> *Despite my handicap, I intend to resume my part in the fight for an America and a world of peace and security, free of poverty, disease and race discrimination…. I return from prison with an unshaken conviction that the people of our great land, Negro and white, need a Communist Party fighting for the unity of the people for peace, democracy, security and socialism. I take my place in it again with deep pride. My sight is gone, but my vision remains.*

Over the next several years, Winston's vision guided his life. He backed Angela Davis' fight against persecution, mobilized against the Vietnam War and walked with Amilcar Cabral and other Africans fighting to overthrow brutal colonial regimes. Inequality, racism and war were everywhere, yet Winston had a dream of economic equality and true democracy, and he worked countless hours in darkness to turn that dream into a reality. Winston may have been robbed of his eyesight, but his vision remained and is with us still.

Political activist Henry Winston died in Moscow in 1986. He was buried there along with other famous American Communists and radicals.

≣ **Maynard Holbrook Jackson, Jr.: Politician Beloved by the People**

Elected officials often experience ridicule, apathy or hostility from disgruntled voters. Corruption, empty promises, self-serving legislation and scandal sometimes make cynics of the most avid citizen. Yet in this cynical political context, there arise a few genuine public servants who are beloved by the people. Maynard Holbrook Jackson, Jr., was one of those politicians.

At age thirty-four, Maynard Jackson became the youngest mayor in Atlanta's history; he was also that city's first black mayor. Jackson and his colleagues transformed Atlanta from stagnation into the South's prosperous urban center. He demanded that white businesses cater to, hire and develop black people, and he helped black businesses flourish. Most importantly, Jackson built programs that benefited the most marginalized, least educated and poorest segments of Atlanta.

When Jackson stepped down from his office in 1994, he left behind a city able to host the Olympic Games, the Democratic National Convention and several other signposts of progress. More importantly, he left a legacy that said the common folk were important.

When Jackson died on June 23, 2003, I met a woman by chance who worked for the City of Atlanta. She told me that when people spoke of Jackson, it was with a reverence and respect granted very few politicians. She said they spoke in hushed tones of how "Maynard changed this," and "Maynard built that." At his funeral, he received the kind of grief and honor that is not demanded but earned. The words of the people made clear how dear, how special and how significant Maynard Jackson was to the common folk of Atlanta.

Former Atlanta Mayor Maynard Jackson died at age 65 of a massive heart attack on June 23, 2003, in Atlanta, Georgia. He is remembered as one of the truly great mayors of any U.S. city.

≣ **Martin Robison Delany: A Better Life for His People**

Few in history lived with the vigor of Martin Robison Delany. Delaney was a proud black man who transformed himself from the son of a slave into a doctor, publisher, judge, explorer and military man. He, like every black person of his generation, had reason to lapse into despair, apathy and self-pity. Growing up "free" in Kerrstown, Pennsylvania, he had been taught that Africans were filthy savages without culture or arts.

Delaney cast aside such rubbish to commit his own talents to black liberation. Through independent study and apprenticeship, he became a practicing medical doctor in Pittsburgh. He published one of the first black newspapers in the United States and later joined with the great Frederick Douglass to create *The North Star*, a powerful abolitionist paper.

Before the Civil War, Delaney risked his liberty and traveled South to document the misery of slaves. In 1850, when the Fugitive Slave Law was passed, putting every free black at risk of being taken off the streets as a "runaway," Delaney despaired for his people. He rented a room in New York to be alone and consider the future of his race. Weeks later, he emerged with his manuscript, *The Condition, Elevation, Emigration and Destiny of the Colored People of the United States, Politically Considered*. He concluded that blacks would never be accepted as human in America, and their only solution—in fact, their destiny—lay in the creation of a black nation in Mexico or South America. Many faulted his conclusion, but none questioned his commitment. To his critics, Delany responded, "If I'm wrong, show me another way for my people to be free!" Delany's interest in Africa was not just theoretical, for in 1859 he became the first American child of a slave to explore Africa.

During the Civil War, he recruited hundreds of black troops and was promoted to the highest field grade rank of any black person during that struggle. President Lincoln appointed him a major in the 104th US Colored Troops Regiment. After the war, Delany was appointed to be an official of the Freedman's Bureau and later became a judge.

Delany was always ahead of his time. He promoted women's right to vote in the 1850s, wore dashikis in the 1860s, and promoted black pride and black nationalism long before the Black Power Movement. For Martin Robison Delany, it was never just about himself; everything he embarked upon was to further the progress of his race. All that mattered to him was whether his work, deeds and vocation could make life better for his fellow black people. Such was his stature that at various times Frederick Douglass, John Brown, Abraham Lincoln and other notables sought his advice.

Martin Robison Delany died on June 24, 1885, in Wilberforce, Ohio. He was a doctor, publisher, military officer, explorer and judge who promoted the establishment of a separate black nation in Mexico or South America.

JUN 25   ≡ Roy Campanella: It's Good to Be Alive

Segregation kept Roy Campanella out of Major League Baseball during his most productive athletic years, injuries curtailed his career as a Brooklyn Dodger power hitter and a traffic accident left him paralyzed. When he was injured, Campanella had been about to begin the second phase of his career, moving from being a popular Dodger in Brooklyn to being a popular Dodger in Los Angeles. His car careened out of control on an icy street, and the accident shattered his neck, leaving him a paraplegic for life.

Roy Campanella faced his obstacles with faith in himself and confidence in the beauty of life. Whether dealing with racism, injury or paralysis, he held on to his infectious joy and undying optimism. He was confined to a wheelchair, his baseball career was over, and he had to learn to eat from a straw and relieve himself without use of arms or legs; yet he was not broken.

Campanella coached young Dodger catching prospects and brought his talents and contagious smile to spring training for years after his career ended. A year after he was paralyzed, he published his autobiography in 1958. The title summarized his attitude and continues to give hope to all who read it: *It's Good to Be Alive*. This was not just a catchy phrase to sell the book; it was the creed by which Roy Campanella chose to live his life.

Roy Campanella died on June 26, 1993, in Los Angeles, California at the age of 71. When he died, hundreds of Dodger organization minor and major league players recalled how he had inspired them. His autobiography is titled It's Good to Be Alive.

JUN 26 ≡ James Weldon Johnson: "He Lifted Us with Him"

James Weldon Johnson was an immensely talented man who utilized his gifts for black progress. In the words of the black encyclopedia *Africana*, "Poetry, song lyrics, fiction, history and editorials flowed from his pen and made him one of the great men of African-American letters."

Johnson's pen had but one goal: the elevation and liberation of black people. He once wrote, "The world does not know that a race is great until that race produces great literature." Johnson was determined that the world learn the literary accomplishments of his race. His works include *Autobiography of an Ex-Colored Man*, *Thirty Years of Lynching*, *The Book of Negro American Poetry*, *God's Trombones*, *Black Manhattan*, *Along This Way* and many others.

This prolific writer was also a political titan, for he saw art and politics as two sides of the same struggle: Art inspired political action and involvement fueled further creativity. Much of what Johnson did laid the groundwork for the Civil Rights Movement. He was instrumental in the growth of the NAACP, and his tenure in the organization was marked by intense legal and organizational activity. He also led the anti-lynching movement, walking the halls of Congress, writing editorials and leading marches to end the atrocity of lynching.

Throughout Johnson's life, black Americans were subjected to segregation, random violence, political disenfranchisement and inferior education. During this time of crisis, he wrote:

I will not allow one prejudiced person or one million or one hundred million to blight my life. I will not let prejudice…beat me down to spiritual defeat. My inner life is mine, and I shall defend and maintain its integrity against all the powers of Hell.

Johnson protected the dignity of his inner life and vowed to work until every black person in America could taste the sweetness of freedom. As one person remarked at his funeral, "Mr. Johnson climbed very high and lifted us with him."

James Weldon Johnson, considered "one of the great men of American letters," was killed in an automobile accident while on vacation in Wiscasset, Maine, on June 26, 1938. His funeral was led by Rev. Frederick Cullen, father of black poet Countee Cullen.

JUN 27 ☰ **Archbishop James P. Lyke: Lead Me, Guide Me**

The housing projects were trouble enough, so James P. Lyke's mother was not about to send him to the decrepit public school down the street. No way would her children be subjected to taunts, violence and low expectations. She had enough cousins, uncles and brothers in jail, on drugs or out of work to know what awaited uneducated black boys. Lyke's mother scraped and saved enough to send her son to the local Catholic school. There she believed he would learn the discipline that would lift him beyond his circumstances.

She got more than schooling for her son. Young Lyke was so impressed with the Catholic faith that he entered seminary and became a Franciscan priest, taking a lifetime vow of poverty and humility in service to Christ.

Fr. Lyke's contributions to the Catholic Church extended beyond his priestly duties. He helped create the African-American Catholic hymnal, *Lead Me, Guide Me*. Soon after publication, the hymnal gave black Catholics a Mass with songs from their own rich spiritual heritage. No longer were European rhythms and Caucasian music the only Catholic liturgical fare; after Lyke's work, black gospel and spirituals were interwoven with the Word and Eucharist.

Lyke's mother had sent him to Catholic school to escape the projects, but he did much more than that. In recognition of his contributions to the Catholic Church, Fr. James P. Lyke was installed as Archbishop of Atlanta in 1991.

Archbishop James P. Lyke was ordained a Franciscan priest in 1966, and on June 24, 1991, was installed as Archbishop of Atlanta. He died of cancer the next year.

"Did you hear about that tract from Boston?" whispered the old black slave. "Course I can't read, but I hear tell its about slaves rising up 'ginst masters."

"No tell!" exclaimed the younger slave.

Such conversations were repeated across the South after the publication of the incendiary "David Walker's Appeal." Its call to revolution was so powerful that slaves were hung for simply mentioning its name.

Published in 1829, "David Walker's Appeal: to the Colored Citizens of the World, but in particular, and very expressly, to those of the United States of America" had an audacious mission: to convince every black person in the world to participate in their own liberation. Walker argued that there were four causes of black wretchedness—slavery, ignorance, preachers of Jesus Christ and the colonizing "scheme"—and that only violence would end it. He believed God would surely bring judgment on the foul, brutal and murderous nation that had degraded Africa's "colored citizens."

Walker also condemned white preachers for flagrantly distorting the gospel, and he called for black self-help organizations and independence for Africa. He demanded that blacks free themselves and whites repent:

Will the Lord suffer this people to go on much longer, taking his holy name in vain? Will he not stop them, preachers and all? O Americans! Americans! I call God—I call angels—I call men, to witness, that your destruction is at hand, and will be speedily consummated unless you REPENT.

Walker did not call for moderate change. He insisted on a radical repentance, a complete break from the culture that had treated Africans no better than cattle; anything less would result in the destruction of America. This was radical talk in 1830, and even the most liberal abolitionists were astounded at Walker's position. He was hated across the South, and the Georgia legislature wanted him captured dead or alive, but many American blacks loved him for being willing to stand up and tell the truth about America.

Walker's tract changed the whole debate on slavery. Before Walker, folks talked of gradual emancipation and slave-owner compensation. After Walker, the entire tenor of the abolitionist movement shifted, and some began demanding immediate and total emancipation. Even after the fall of slavery, Walker's "Appeal" inspired subsequent generations of militants. He truly was the first black revolutionary in the United States.

Nine months after publication of David Walker's Appeal, the author was found dead on the doorstep of his shop in Boston on June 28, 1830. Though it was never proven, many believe he was assassinated.

≡ Eric Allan Dolphy, Jr.: "So Long, Eric"

Eric Dolphy was both an excellent musician and a special human being. Whether on flute, alto saxophone or bass clarinet, he created a sound that was elegant beyond description. The serenity of "God Bless the Child," the beauty of "Spiritual" with John Coltrane, and the energy of "Wednesday Night Prayer Meeting" with Charles Mingus symbolize the power and diversity of his sound. Anyone who listens to Dolphy feels what he's playing. His sounds and tones are so intense, haunting and joyful that his music resonates in our souls.

Who was Eric Dolphy? How could he so faithfully convey the trauma and drama of life through music? Listen to those who knew him:

Fellow musician Charles Mingus said, "Eric Dolphy was a saint—in every way, not just his playing."

Gunther Schuller once said, "Eric belonged to that select gallery of geniuses who know that the more we learn, the more there is left to learn…. He was, in short, one of the most beautiful men that one could, in a lifetime, be privileged to meet, and I consider it a privilege to have loved him."

The great John Coltrane once commented, "Whatever I'd say would be an understatement. I can only say my life was made much better by knowing him. He was one of the greatest people I've ever known, as a man, a friend, a musician."

"So Long, Eric" is a Charles Mingus composition in tribute to black musician extra-ordinaire Eric Dolphy. (The song also goes by the title, "Meditation for a pair of wire cutters.") Dolphy died of a heart attack on June 29, 1964, while on tour in Berlin, Germany.

≡ Venerable Pierre Toussaint: The Gift of My Life

Pierre Toussaint knelt in his pew while the priest performed the ancient rite of the Holy Eucharist. Toussaint lifted his head slightly to gaze on the beautiful scene. There upon the altar was the bread and wine, revealing the stunning presence of Christ on earth. "This bread," Toussaint thought, "is the body of my Savior, Jesus, broken so that I could be whole." His throat tightened and tears pooled in his eyes. Next came the cup. As the priest blessed the cup, the blood of Christ, Toussaint wept. That God would choose the humiliation of the cross so that he could be forgiven was too much to bear.

"How can I respond to such mercy? Can I possibly live as my Savior wants? Surely I am too weak, too frail, and too sinful to follow my Savior," Touissaint said. Soothed by Catholic incense and candles, he prayed for the courage and humility to follow Jesus without reservation.

Pierre Toussaint loved being Catholic. He could know and see and touch his God through the beautiful sacraments. He was not alone; there were saints, angels and the Blessed Virgin Mary to aid his journey. The Mass was his time to sense the power of Jesus coursing through his soul, and he attended daily, praying quietly at St. Peter's Church on Barclay Street in Lower Manhattan.

Born a slave in Haiti, Toussaint was freed by his mistress in 1807 in New York City. He left servitude to a human owner to enter a life of gracious service to his Divine Master. He worked as a hairdresser, raised funds for orphaned children, founded New York's first school for black children, and gathered food and clothing for his fellow black Haitians. For Toussaint, his life was a gift given by God, and a gift to be given away.

During his ministry, a frightening yellow fever epidemic struck New York City. While political leaders fled for their lives, Toussaint followed the footsteps of Jesus and served his dying fellow citizens. For these acts and innumerable others, Pierre Toussaint was considered a black angel, a saint trudging along New York City's streets and alleys to help the afflicted.

Toussaint's name became synonymous with giving, love and service. If any crossed his path in need or want, he did whatever he was able. If someone needed money or food or clothes, he would reach out, giving what he could and praying for them. As this humble man walked by, crowds gathered on the sidewalk and whispered, "There goes Pierre, a man who gives to any in need." When Pierre Toussaint died in 1853, hundreds of New Yorkers—Catholics and Protestants, blacks and whites—gathered to see him off to his Savior.

Pierre Toussaint died on June 30, 1853. He was buried in New York's St. Patrick's Cathedral, the only layperson to be buried there. He was declared "Venerable" by the Catholic Church in 1996, which is the first step on the church's road to canonization.

JULY

John William
Coltrane

≣ Confraternities: Black Catholic Communities

During the sixteenth and seventeenth centuries, black free and slave Catholics in Brazil often joined *cofradias*, confraternities of people pledged to support one another through life and death. These confraternities met for Mass and religious instruction on Sundays and gathered during the week to feed the poor and bury their dead. During Brazilian slavery, confraternity members worked for the freedom of all its members. Once a member became free, he or she helped free another member. Sometimes they raised money to buy the slave from the slave's master; other times, they plotted the slave's escape. Liberation was only the beginning of their service to one another. Members of the confraternities pooled their resources to ensure that no member would go hungry or die alone. Many black Catholics felt God's love for them through the work of their comrades.

The oldest group was the famous Confraternity of the Most Holy Sacrament. Founded by black Catholics in Brazil in 1540, this organization was the model others followed. As Christ was poured out for the life of the world in the Most Holy Sacrament of the Eucharist, so too did confraternity members give of themselves for their fellow members.

In Bahia, Brazil, the most powerful brotherhood was the Confraternity of Our Lady of the Rosary. Its members called on the Virgin Mary for deliverance, shelter and mercy. Legends of miraculous healings drew members to confraternities across Bahia. On the feast of *Corpus Christi* (Body of Christ), the confraternities would hold elaborate public dances. Their processions symbolized self-reliance, mutual love and group unity. The colorful customs, ornate dances and haunting chants represented the new life they found in Christ and in each other. Through their faith in God and sacrifices for each member, the confraternities offered salvation and community to its members.

Brazil and Peru claimed the most active black Catholic confraternities. In 1619, there were 15 confraternities in Lima, Peru, alone. Brazil was home to the most dynamic and active organizations. Future research is needed to plumb the riches of these groups in other parts of South America.

The courtroom fell silent as the white judge cleared his throat to speak. The defendant, if that term could apply to a black man in antebellum South, stood up to hear his sentence. The judge began, "Denmark Vesey, the court on mature consideration, has pronounced you guilty." He continued:

> It is difficult to imagine what infatuation could have prompted you to attempt an enterprise so wild and visionary. You were a free man, you were comparatively wealthy; and you enjoyed every comfort compatible with your situation. You had, therefore, much to risk and little to gain. From your age and experience, you ought to have known success was impractible.

From his privileged and lofty perch on the bench, the judge could not fathom why Vesey had risked his security for the freedom of his race. Vesey had been caught "plotting" to lead the largest slave rebellion in the history of the United States. The judge simply could not comprehend why this self-employed carpenter of upstanding reputation would sacrifice his home, business and twenty-two years freedom to try to free his people.

"What infatuation could have prompted you?" asked the judge.

Denmark must have thought to himself, "Look around you, white judge. While your people sip tea in the parlors of Charleston, mine are whipped, raped, sold like cattle and bred like pets. 'What infatuation,' you ask? I am infatuated with my black brothers and sisters! My freedom, my house, my business are but painful reminders of what my people lack. How could I enjoy security when all over Charleston and all over the South I hear my people scream? I hear tales of children sold from mothers, I know of women raped by masters. 'What infatuation,' you ask?"

Denmark Vesey was sentenced to death, and July 2, 1822, he and thirty-four other black men, including Peter Poyas, Gullah Jack and Ned Bennett, were hung on Blake's Lands outside Charleston.

What infatuated you, Denmark? May we be empowered by the selfless infatuation of Denmark Vesey.

In 1799, slave Denmark Vesey purchased a lottery ticket from the East Bay Street lottery in Charleston, South Carolina. In early 1800, the winning numbers were called and Vesey won $150—and his freedom. Denmark Vesey then helped to organize a slave rebellion and was hanged from the Ashley Avenue Oak tree on July 2, 1822, outside of Charleston, South Carolina.

≡ Michelle Wallace: Fight the World

When Michelle Wallace joined the Black Power Movement of the late 1960s, she was energized by the upsurge of black pride and power. Her joy, however, was crushed when she experienced black male sexism that rivaled white racism. To her astonishment, she came to know two enemies: a white world that negated anything black, and black men who degraded black women. At the risk of causing controversy and backlash, Wallace exposed this contradiction in her classic, *Black Macho and the Myth of the Superwomen*, published in 1978.

Wallace clashed with black male leaders over the scope and extent of misogyny in the Black Power Movement. They felt she should focus her energy on racism. She did not retreat from her views, however, which were confirmed as many black men continued to demand that women do domestic things such as iron, cook, sew, have babies and leave the politics to them.

In 1975, Wallace wrote the article "Anger in Isolation: Black Feminist Search for Sisterhood," which appeared in *The Village Voice*. She restated her commitment to full humanity both as an African American and a woman, and she encouraged black women to keep the faith. She wrote to her sisters that even without a black women's movement there was still hope:

> [We are] stranded for the moment, working independently because there is not yet an environment in this society remotely congenial to our struggle…because being on the bottom we would have to do what no one else has done, we would have to fight the world.

In the great tradition of other black women radicals, Michelle Wallace tenaciously fought the twin evils of white racism and male sexism.

In July 1975, Michelle Wallace published the essay, "Anger in Isolation," a stirring call to black feminist struggle. She was opposed by many male leaders of the Black Power Movement.

≡ Frederick Douglass: "The Fourth Is Yours, Not Mine"

The indomitable Frederick Douglass mounted the podium in Rochester, New York, on July 4, 1852, and delivered a stirring call for justice and democracy. He began with America's revolution, the ascent of human rights and the freedoms of the Constitution, but soon he shifted from the glories of America to its unholy underside. Using the occasion of the anniversary of the nation's freedom, Douglass contrasted black suppression with the celebrations of liberty. He declared:

The sunlight that has brought life and healing to you, has brought stripes and death to me. The 4th is yours, not mine…. To drag a man in fetters into the grand illuminated temple of liberty, and call upon him to join in joyous anthem, [is] human misery and sacrilegious idolatry…. Fellow-citizen, above your national tumultuous joy, I hear the mournful wail of millions! Whose chains, heavy and grievous yesterday, are today rendered more intolerable by the jubilee shouts that reach them. What, to the American slave, is your 4th of July? I answer: a day that reveals to him, more than all other days in the year, the gross injustice and cruelty to which he is the constant victim. To him, your celebration is a sham; your boasted liberty, an unholy license; your national greatness, swelling vanity; your sounds of rejoicing, empty and heartless; your denunciation of tyrants, brass fronted impudence; your shouts of liberty and equality; hollow mockery; your prayers and hymns, your sermons and thanksgivings, with all your religious parade and solemnity, are, to him, mere bombast, fraud, deception, impiety and hypocrisy—a thin veil to cover up crimes that would disgrace a nation of savages.

Yet Douglass did not end his speech in despair. In triumph, he asked God to "speed the year of jubilee." Douglass then proclaimed his commitment to fight for freedom to the end. He closed with a poem declaring that he would "never from my chosen post, whatev'er the peril or the cost be driven." His "chosen post," that of advocate for his race, was the platform from which he delivered this Fourth of July speech and other orations for black equality.

Frederick Douglass' 4th of July speech in 1852 in Rochester, New York, articulated the vast difference between the white and black experience with American democracy. It called on both whites and blacks to work for freedom and justice.

JUL 5 ≣ **Saint Elesbaan: From Kingdom to Monastery**

Elesbaan governed Ethiopia in the sixth century. Unlike most rulers of his day, he was not feared for his power but was loved for his piety. He was the leader of Ethiopian society and the pillar of the Coptic Church.

During the time of his reign, Christians in neighboring Yemen were being persecuted, and they begged Rome for help. The Roman emperor, in turn, sent an ambassador to Elesbaan to ask for his assistance. When the ambassador, named Julian, reported back to Rome, he described Elesbaan as a king who was both regal and pious, a king who "wore golden bracelets on his arms and on his head a turban of linen embroidered with gold…and around his neck a golden collar. He stood on a four-wheeled chariot drawn by four elephants…. His council stood around…and played flutes."

Elesbaan agreed to assist his neighbors, and over the next several years, his intervention saved hundreds of Christian men, women and children.

Like other kings during his time, Elesbaan could have continued to reign until his death. He came to believe, however, that the trappings of power hindered his spiritual growth, and he resigned his throne to pursue a deeper union with Christ. King Elesbaan gave his jewelry to the Holy Sepulcher in Jerusalem, took a mat, a few clothes and a cup, and went to live in an Ethiopian monastery, where he spent the rest of his life in prayer, fasting and scripture reading. He is revered as a saint by the Catholic Church.

Elesbaan, the sixth century king of Ethiopia who became a Christian monk, is the patron saint of blacks in Spain and Portugal.

JUL 6 ≡ Ibrahaima Abdul Rahman: Islamic Prince of the Fulani

Ibrahaima Abdul Rahman lived an extraordinary life and overcame unbelievable obstacles. Born a Fulani prince in Africa, Rahman was kidnapped, sold into slavery and shipped to America. The boy, born in royalty, had become mere property, but he never abandoned his Islamic faith. When Rahman was fifty-six, his Mississippi master took him out of the fields to let him work in the plantation house, and there Rahman used his extra time to write down Koran verses from memory. He also would hide and pray, kneeling east, as required by his faith, several times a day.

Although four decades had passed since his youthful Islamic training, Rahman never forgot his faith, his Fulani people and his home in Fouta Djallon, in what is now Guinea in West Africa. Whenever he was free from the rigors of fieldwork, Rahman looked for someone to help him find his people in West Africa. After months of fruitless searching, he met a white newspaper editor who agreed to assist. Thrilled with hope, Rahman ran home that night to craft a letter to send to Fouta Djallon, letting his people know he was still alive. He wrote that he would try to return home someday.

What was most remarkable about this letter, however, was Rahman's expression of abiding faith in Allah. He began the letter with the Islamic Fatiha, one of the great prayers of the Muslim faith, found in the opening chapter of the Koran:

In the name of God, the Most Gracious, Most Merciful, Praise be to God, the Cherisher and Sustainer of the Worlds; Most Gracious, Most Merciful.... Thee do we worship, and Thine aid we seek. Show us the straight way, the way of those on whom Thou hast bestowed Thy Grace, those whose portions is not wrath, and who go not astray. Amen.

Rahman's prayers, and his faith in Allah, enabled him to do more than merely survive. His letter eventually made its way, via the Sultan of Morocco, into the hands of John Quincy Adams, who was able to secure Rahman's freedom. Freed at age sixty, Rahman promptly raised money to purchase his wife's freedom, and together they conducted a speaking tour in America until they could afford to return to Africa.

Few slaves in the New World were ever freed until after the Civil War, and even fewer were able to return to their homeland in Africa. Ibrahaima Abdul Rahman did both, and his Islamic faith enabled him not only to survive the horrors of slavery but also to return to his people.

Muslim Ibrahaima Abdul Rahman died on July 6, 1829, in Liberia, Africa. He lived only five months after his return to Africa, but he was able to see his homeland as a free man—the vision that had kept him alive as a slave for the greater part of his life.

JUL 7   ≣ Mother Elizabeth Dabney: Garden of Prayer

Elizabeth Dabney often heard the voice of God, sometimes in the silence of her quiet moments and other times in the midst of adversity, turmoil and confusion. In good times and in bad, Jesus spoke to Elizabeth Dabney, and she listened. Dabney and her husband founded the Garden of Prayer Church of God in Christ in Philadelphia, Pennsylvania, because she heard the constant whispers of Christ to do so.

Once, suffering from tuberculosis and pained in body and spirit, Dabney dragged herself to a revival led by Bishop O.T. Jones. At the end of his impassioned sermon, she was saturated with the presence of God, the Holy Spirit filling every corner of her soul. A warm sensation flowed through her, and moments later she was healed and her illness wiped away.

Years later, during her morning prayers, Dabney heard Christ again. God asked that she perform a special devotion for the next three years. During that period, she was to pray for one hour, at nine o'clock every morning. She was also to fast and pray three days each week, to empty herself of material comforts and to open herself to the loving presence of God. Dabney obeyed, and every morning she walked several blocks to the Garden of Prayer Church for her devotions.

Weeks passed, and despite persistent prayer and fasting, nothing seemed to change. Slowly, however, she began to see the fruits of her diligence. Friends and church members began following her to church every morning, and many were healed of spiritual and physical illnesses. God's blessings showered down upon the faithful.

One Sunday morning, Mother Elizabeth Dabney preached that all Christians needed a deeper understanding of Jesus. It was good to know church doctrine, to come to church every Sunday and to memorize the scripture, she proclaimed, but all that was useless without knowing Jesus. "Know Jesus and He will speak to you! Know Jesus and He will see you through! Know Jesus and He will open the gates of blessing to those who pray, fast and wait."

The devotional life of Mother Dabney would impact many lives for years to come. Stories were passed down about her early morning devotions, her fastings and her gospel preaching, and African-American Pentecostals in Philadelphia found blessing and strength in her example.

Mother Elizabeth Dabney, founder with her husband of the Garden of Prayer Church of God in Christ in Philadelphia, Pennsylvania, heard the voice of Jesus Christ directly and often in her life. She died in 1967.

JUL 8   ≡ Sister Maria Becraft: Not Just for Me

At dawn, just as the sun glimpsed over the horizon, Maria Becraft gathered her coat and walked to Mass. She and other Catholics from Washington's Georgetown area met weekly at Holy Trinity Church. Though just fifteen, Becraft had a vibrant faith and loved the Mass. She loved to gaze upon statutes of the Sacred Heart of Jesus and Our Lady of Perpetual Help, and she visualized them as present in all her struggles.

Fortunate enough to be educated at local private schools, Becraft discovered that knowledge was a giant leap toward black liberation. Reading, math and history opened her world to possibilities unknown to many blacks in Washington, D.C., in 1820. Not content to keep knowledge to herself, young Becraft believed Jesus wanted her to teach those around her.

Public education was still in the future, so learning was the privilege of the wealthy at the time. Becraft decided to open a day school in her home for the poor children in her neighborhood, and for eight years she taught faithfully, gaining a reputation for compassion, toughness and excellence. Then Holy Trinity Church asked her to lead a school for poor black and white children at their parish. Maria agreed, and in 1827 Holy Trinity, with Becraft as Head Teacher, opened its doors to neighborhood children. Becraft followed Jesus' call to teach, and eventually the institutional church followed her lead. Years later, she heard Jesus' call once again, this time to a life of prayer, contemplation and community. In 1831, she joined the convent of the Oblate Sisters of Providence in Baltimore.

After Maria Becraft left Holy Trinity, others followed in her steps, and the school transformed hundreds of lives. Becraft's work in Washington, D.C. left its mark on the hearts and minds of black young people for many years to come. The children she taught grew up to become productive adults, and many benefited from her call to live her faith through teaching and service.

Sister Maria Becraft, founder of a free school for black children in Washington, D.C., died in Baltimore in 1833, only two years after joining the Oblate Sisters of Providence.

JUL 9   ≣ **Father Augustus Tolton: First African-American Catholic Priest**

Augustus Tolton was a remarkable man who struggled against odds many of us cannot even imagine. He was born a slave in Ralls County, Missouri, and after the Civil War his mother moved their family to Illinois. She was a devout Catholic and enrolled her son in Catholic schools, but she was not about to let racist parents and teachers deter her son from learning the Catholic faith.

Young Tolton was not welcomed in the parochial school, and he faced much abuse and neglect. Yet despite constant rejection, the boy was drawn to the Catholic faith. He was so attracted to the sacraments, prayers and traditions of the church that even as a teenager, he expressed his desire to become a priest. Though many mocked and ridiculed this desire, Tolton persisted, and eventually he found two priests to tutor him in Latin and in Catholic tradition.

Many Baptist and African Methodist Episcopal young men of the time felt the call to preach. Few, however, heard God call them to a white institution that had yet to ordain a black priest—the Roman Catholic Church in the United States. Yet those obstacles did not intimidate Augustus Tolton. He believed in his call so deeply that he was convinced God would remove any obstacles in his path.

After years of schooling, Tolton was ordained in Rome on Holy Saturday in 1886. In just twenty-five years, he had gone from being the property of a white Missouri farmer to being recognized by pope, cardinals and bishops as Father Augustus Tolton.

Tolton's first assignment, a Catholic Church in Quincy, Illinois, brought many hardships. When some parishioners preferred to receive the sacraments from him rather than the white priests, his fellow priests became jealous and responded by ignoring him. He was also largely excluded from public life in the town, and his life was very lonely. Nevertheless, when he was later assigned to a Chicago parish, nineteen black Catholic converts moved with him to the new city.

When he arrived in Chicago, Father Tolton found that black Catholics in his new parish were meeting in the basement of another church, St. Mary's. He began raising money, primarily through his friendship with Blessed Katherine Drexel, and succeeded in building a black parish named St. Monica's, which was to become Chicago's center of black Catholic life for more than thirty years.

Midwestern African Americans were blessed to have Tolton in their midst. He wrote about one "colored" woman whom he visited on her deathbed. She had been insulted, cursed and, in her own words, "hurled out" by white Irish Catholics. As a result, she had been away from her beloved church for nine years. As she lay dying in the hospital, she begged the nurses for a priest. Expecting, at best, some insensitive Irish priest, the woman was shocked to see a black man in a priest's robe walk into her room. Tolton wrote that she thanked the Lord for sending her a black man with whom she could pray her last prayers.

Black Catholics to this day celebrate the life of Father Augustus Tolton, a man whose vision of God overcame the follies of humans, a man whose rise from slavery to priesthood gave black parishioners a dignity that could not be taken away from them.

Father Augustus Tolton, the first black ordained in the Catholic Church in the United States, died in Chicago on July 9, 1897, at the age of 43.

JUL 10   ≣ Mamie Garvin Fields: "Do What You Can"

If there had been a black aristocracy in South Carolina, Mamie Garvin Fields would have been a charter member. Though slavery was merely a generation away, Mamie's family and her husband's family were descended from free blacks. Both families were hardworking and had a rare level of financial security. Mamie Fields herself was a respected schoolteacher and successful dressmaker. When not teaching children in the South Carolina Sea Islands, she was home in Charleston making dresses for eager customers, and she used both vocations to improve life for her people. She chose to teach on the Sea Islands, for the poorest blacks in South Carolina lived there, and she often did far more than she was paid to do, working with children at night to help them survive. As a dressmaker, Fields recruited her customers to become members of the City Federation of Colored Women's Clubs, which she helped start in 1916.

Affiliated with the National Association of Colored Women, the Federation was comprised of women dedicated to racial advancement. Fields and other women of the Federation chose as their motto "Do What You Can"—a constant reminder that, while they could not do it all, they could do something. And Mamie Fields lived that motto her entire life.

She began working with Charleston's homeless young black girls. Burdened with the legacies of slavery, domestic abuse and racism, these girls were among the most vulnerable in Charleston. As Fields sought to find homes for the girls, she often was met by white apathy and outright resistance, but she never faltered or despaired. Clinging to the motto "Do What You Can," she helped children, girls and women of South Carolina work together to counteract segregation and poverty.

Mamie Garvin Fields, born in Charleston in 1888, was a schoolteacher, dressmaker and one of the founders of the City Federation of Colored Women's Clubs in Charleston, South Carolina. She told her story to her granddaughter in an oral history titled Lemon Swamp and Other Places *in 1983.*

JUL 11 ≡ Angelo Herndon: "I Am with You with All My Heart"

Angelo Herndon was acquainted with harsh labor; in fact, that was all he really knew. From the time he was a thirteen-year-old in Kentucky, he had worked in fields, mines and factories. He had seen the vacant stares, calloused hands and broken spirits of men much older and stronger than he. He had seen people laid off work and left without shelter, food or medicine. Although he had also seen the misery of white workers, he knew blacks received a double portion. Poor whites, seeking to ease their own pain, would find solace in knowing that, no matter what, "at least I ain't no nigger."

Years later, as Herndon walked through downtown Birmingham, Alabama, one afternoon, a white man handed him a leaflet. He scanned the print and could hardly believe his eyes: "Workers of Birmingham, White and Negro: Would you rather fight or starve?" The only fighting Herndon had seen was black against white; the idea that black and white workers would work together was unthinkable. He had to find out more.

That evening, Herndon went to the union hall for the meeting advertised on the flyer. Despite the rough-looking white men who were watching all who entered, he walked in anyway. Herndon's disbelief about the leaflet was reversed when he saw the hall full of both black and white men, sitting next to one another. They all bore the unmistakable signs of manual work: factory grime, injured limbs and fatigued countenance. Herndon listened in astonishment as two speakers, one black and one white, talked of the worker's struggle for dignity. At the end of the meeting, Herndon walked to the front of the room and told the leaders, "I am with you with all my heart, and I would like you to put me down as a member."

Angelo Herndon's political conversion was as deep as any religious transformation; that night was the beginning of a lifetime of sacrifice. He plunged himself into the work of the Communist Party. He headed up Unemployment Councils, led chapters of the League of Struggle for Negro Rights (LSNR), and organized black and white workers. He later wrote, "All of a sudden I had found myself in an organization which fought selflessly and tirelessly to undo all the wrongs perpetuated on my race."

In 1932, Herndon was arrested for "inciting insurrection," which meant having the audacity to suggest that unemployed black and white workers demand relief, food and medicine. Georgia authorities used an outdated 1861 law outlawing slave insurrections to sentence Herndon to prison. His case went all the way to the Supreme Court, where his conviction was eventually overturned.

Angelo Herndon's conversion to socialist principles, worker unity and class revolution fueled a lifetime of commitment to racial equality and justice.

On July 16, 1932, Angelo Herndon was arrested in Atlanta, Georgia, for leading an interracial march of unemployed black and white workers in search of food, medicine and rent money. The case against him for "inciting insurrection" went all the way to the Supreme Court, where his conviction was overturned.

JUL 12   ≡ **Mansa Musa I: Muslim King of Mali**

It was a typical bustling afternoon in the city of Niani, Mali, just south of the Saraha Desert in Africa. Mansa Musa I, King of Mali, arrived to conduct the typical duties of a busy monarch. He strode into town amidst fanfare and commotion to render judgments in business disputes, oversee land deals and grant titles to city officials. An Egyptian visitor observed the proceedings from the courtyard in wonder. He had never seen such devotion and reverence for a king. The visitor also heard murmurings in the crowd—not the complaints about rulers he usually heard in his travels but a genuine outpouring of affection.

The visitor was amazed and turned to ask the Moroccan next to him, "Is it true, as they say, that Mansa Musa is a generous and virtuous prince?"

The Moroccan answered, "I have come to Mali often. Mansa Musa is indeed a good ruler and a devout Muslim."

Typical of other rulers of the time, Mansa Musa was king by right of birth, not by merit. Yet it was his merit and faith that made him a generous and virtuous ruler for the twenty-five years he reigned as King of Mali.

For many, power creates corruption, arrogance and a belief that those with power are smarter or better than common human beings. Not so with Musa. He believed Allah was the Merciful Beneficent One upon whom all humans depend.

For many, religion consists of the externalities, such as mosque attendance and adherence to ritual and doctrine. Not so with Musa. He believed there was no distinction between life and faith. The citizens of Mali knew that Mansa Musa lived his faith. He was not a king who happened to be a Muslim; Musa was a Muslim whose faith shaped his reign.

Few kings were as beloved and revered as was King Mansa Musa I. His people did not fear him but gave him their true love and genuine respect.

In July of 1324, King Mansa Musa I made a religious pilgrimage to Mecca. The journey took months to prepare and included thousands of pilgrims. When the group stopped in Cairo, Egypt, the Sultan of Egypt hosted a celebration in honor of Mansa Musa's pilgrimage. His faith and fame were known throughout Africa.

JUL 13   ≡ **Black Seamen: Heroes of Port Chicago**

On July 17, 1944, America suffered the worst home-front disaster of World War II. That night two ships, the *USS E.A. Bryan* and the *USS Quinalt Victory*, were docked at Port Chicago while crews were loading them with munitions. Black seamen hauled forty-millimeter shells, fragmentation cluster bombs, thousand-pound bombs and six-hundred-fifty-pound incendiary shells onto both ships. The bombs were packed tightly in boxcars, and sailors had great difficulty transferring this "hot cargo" from the dock to the ships. Loading bombs and high explosives was very dangerous work, and the United States Navy often reserved such duty for their black servicemen. At 10:18 p.m., two huge explosions rocked the loading station of Port Chicago. A column of smoke and debris rose twelve thousand feet into the night sky, and a consuming ring of fire moved three miles in every direction. Both vessels were destroyed, three hundred of Port Chicago's homes were damaged and the naval base was in shambles.

Worst of all, three hundred and twenty U.S. sailors were killed, including two hundred and two African Americans. Most of the black seamen were mere teenagers: For example, John Dunn was seventeen; Charles Widemon, nineteen; Martin Bordenave, eighteen. Black teenagers from Georgia farms and Harlem tenements were consumed instantly or burned to death slowly in this horrible conflagration.

For the black seamen, however, the explosion was but the first disaster. The U.S. Navy granted thirty-days leave, with pay, for each white survivor, but the black survivors were relocated to another working base. Just days later, they were ordered to load the same dangerous bombs, under the same hazardous circumstances. While whites were given a month to heal, blacks were marched by the Navy right back into harm's way.

Two hundred and fifty-eight of the black survivors refused to do as they were instructed. Despite direct orders from their commanding officers (all of whom were white and would not be loading any bombs), despite facing mutiny charges and potential death penalties, these young black teens from across America stood their ground. They were hauled off to the brig, and fifty were charged with mutiny, court-martialed and sentenced to fifteen-year terms.

Black civilians and white progressives protested this gross injustice. Thurgood Marshall and the NAACP defended the accused, and forty-seven of the protestors were released two years later.

The black seamen of Port Chicago are now recognized among the heroes of the war, and their stand for justice—even in the midst of a military crisis—is seen as a shining example of human courage and perseverance.

On July 17, 1944, 320 sailors, including 202 blacks, were killed in explosions at Port Chicago in the worst home-front accident of World War II. Black survivors of the initial blast were later court-martialed for refusing to obey orders to load the same dangerous bombs onto ships just days later.

JUL 14   ≡ The Bambara People: Bonds of Love

For the Bambara people of West Africa, the family was a temple where the spirits of each member lived. When an elder died, they believed the elder's spirit was reborn in the youngest member of the family. Consequently, the family was an eternal formation, with each death merely strengthening and renewing the bonds of love.

The Bambara were an unconquerable people, a people with no fear of external power and authority. It did not matter who owned the land or who held political or military power. For the Bambara people, their kingdom traveled with them. They carried within their breasts their own dignity and their own nation. With them, there were no individual family members, because each person and each family contained the memories and spirits of generations past.

The Bambara people were almost impossible to enslave because their family bond fueled repeated revolts and acts of rebellion against would-be oppressors. Yet, like millions of other black African people, the Bambarans were eventually captured, transported across the seas and forced to work as slaves.

Despite that trauma, their autonomous and rebellious spirit remained unbroken. Hundreds of Bambara were involved in a 1731 slave rebellion that frightened white southerners for generations to come. Just the mention of the name "Bambara" caused white plantation owners to reach for their guns, ropes and clubs.

Like the Bambara, may each of us call upon our ancestors for strength, hope and faith. May we carry within ourselves the courage and love of those who struggled before us, those who brought us this far. Long live the descendants of the Bambara—in their culture of memory, community and hope!

The Bambara were one of the Senegambian peoples of West Africa who were enslaved in Louisiana to work on rice plantations. They often joined with other African tribes, Native Americans and even poor whites to fight their French slaveholders.

JUL 15 ≡ **John Henrik Clarke: "Run the Race, and Run It by Faith"**

The old black woman, the one they called Mom Mary, sat shivering in her dilapidated shack. Her grandchildren and great-grandchildren were gathered at her feet in rapt attention. She told stories of Africa and slavery, about how their family had survived what seemed like impossible circumstances. The oldest of her great-grandchildren, John Henrik Clarke, hung on her every word. She ended her story this day as she always did: "Run the race, and run it by faith." Those words stayed with Clarke for the rest of his life.

Mom Mary's admonition fueled an unquenchable yearning in this young man to understand and change the world around him. As a young student in poor rural schools in Georgia and Alabama, John Clarke went to the public library every week and checked out a dozen books at a time. He would read those twelve, go back a week later and take out another twelve. White supremacy and black subjugation anguished his soul, and he wondered why the church walls were filled with pictures of a white Jesus, a white Moses and a white Abraham. Those images made John Henrik Clarke ask, "Who painted the whole world white?"

Years later, when Clarke moved to Harlem, he searched out Arthur Schomburg and begged the great librarian to teach him black history. Schomburg admonished Clarke to "study your oppressor, for that is why you don't know your history." Clarke followed Schomburg's lesson and devoured European history. Having mastered white culture, Clarke then embarked upon a lifetime of African studies. His devotion to truth and scholarship made him the intellectual dean of black nationalism and liberation for sixty years.

Through lectures, writings and articles, Clarke informed an entire generation of black radicals. Countless intellectuals and activists credit Clarke with their enlightenment and liberation. Though he was entirely self-taught following high school, his immersion into black truths earned him a professorship of African Studies at Hunter College. Mom Mary would truly have been proud, for John Clarke did indeed run the race!

Professor John Henrik Clarke, the initiator of early black studies, died on July 16, 1998, in New York City.

Nicholas Guillen is a literary giant whose poems were beloved in his Cuban homeland and by activists and artists all over the world. Few have combined black awareness with poetic musings with as much verve as Guillen. A close friend of the great Langston Hughes, a member of the Communist Party, a courageous advocate for world peace, Guillen was an extraordinary human being.

His father was assassinated by government soldiers in 1917, and thereafter Guillen faced poverty and discrimination. Rather than turning his bitterness inward, however, Guillen became a rebel and noncomformist who sought to change the world. By 1920, he was composing poems on the pain of black life in Cuba.

Guillen later became part of the Negritude movement in America and the Caribbean in the struggle for artists to define a black cultural motif independent of European influence. On the strength of his verse, Guillen became a poet of the Cuban people, and his work was an uncompromising call for justice. By the 1930s, he sought to do more than write about reality; Guillen wanted to change it. He joined the Communist Party and became part of the organization's work to improve life for working people.

After the Cuban Revolution in 1959, Guillen infused Cuban culture with his progressive writings. Always and forever a poet of the people, he wrote works that common folk could recite. His works were memorable primarily because they reflected the life of working people.

In his classic 1958 collection *Elegias (Elegies)*, he wrote the poem *"El Apellido"* ("The Last Name"), which articulated his quest for black meaning in the New World. He described his sense of alienation from Africa and how that loss diminished his identity as a Cuban. In a sense, his search for his *"El Apellido,"* his "last name," was a search for who he was. Finding our own humanity, Guillen believed, is the first step to creating a more humane world for all. He calls each of us to find our own *"El Apellido"* and to use that identity to create a better world.

The beloved black Cuban poet Nicholas Guillen, author of* Elegies, *died at age 87 in Havana, Cuba, on July 16, 1989.

≣ John William Coltrane: "Chasin' the Trane"

John William Coltrane. Coltrane. 'Trane! The name evokes images of beauty, passion and blues spilling from the cusp of a silver tenor sax. Who else has captured humanity and divinity through music as Coltrane has? 'Trane's life is our life, his blues are our blues. He has been with us, and he has been places we have not. 'Trane "walked the bar" in juke joints, honking and screaming for tips in his cap. He spent years in New York, succumbing, like many of his peers, to the demon of heroin. Though he was addicted and often strung out, 'Trane still mesmerized audiences with his solos—though Miles Davis once fired him for missing rehearsals and gigs.

John Coltrane eventually overcame his addiction, but not before he had full acquaintance with the misery and destruction of drugs. This foray into the dark abyss of life helped shape his unique sound. Legends abound about the power of Coltrane's music. It is said that he walked around the house, his saxophone always with him, trying new techniques, constantly working to explore, improve and take his music to ever deeper levels. His continual search for truth in life formed his musical explorations. He studied not only African and Eastern music but also philosophy and physics.

The growth and evolution of John Coltrane, the person, is evident in the sounds of John Coltrane, the tenor saxophonist. At each stage of his life, he created beautiful music that only got richer and more complex with time. On the Prestige label, and with Miles Davis, Coltrane recorded excellent jazz. When he signed with Atlantic, he recorded many classics, including "Giant Steps," "My Favorite Things," "Equinox," "Liberia," "Cousin Mary," "Dahomey Dance," the eternally beautiful "Naima" and many others.

Many regard Coltrane's recordings with Impulse, from 1962 to 1967, as his most challenging, profound and deeply spiritual recordings. For haunting lyricism, beautiful tones and sheer power, the Impulse label has it all. The titles reflect Coltrane's love for Africa, his global connections, his universal longings and his spiritual quest: "Spiritual," "Dear Lord," "A Love Supreme," "Afro-Blue," "India," "Impressions," "Ascension," "After the Rain," "Compassion," The Father, the Son and the Holy Ghost," and "Chasin' the Trane."

Words alone cannot express the power of John Coltrane's music; it must be experienced. Spend an evening listening closely to his recordings. Listen to "Alabama" and remember the four black girls killed in the September 1963 church bombing in Birmingham; think of the black experience when you hear "Afro-Blue," and let the albums *Meditations, Crescent, Kulu Se Mama, Transition, Live in Japan, Sun Ship, Live at the Village Vanguard, Interstellar Space* and others take you on a profound spiritual journey. Listen with open heart and mind, and his music will literally strip away your assumptions about music, art and life. 'Trane's sounds—particularly his later works—will take you deep within yourself, push away all the trivial things that weigh you down and open you to exciting possibilities.

Tenor saxophonist John Coltrane died of liver cancer on Long Island on July 17, 1967. Many of his recordings are still available and enjoyed to this day.

JUL 18 ≣ **Billie Holiday: God Bless the Child**

Who is the seminal blues vocalist in American history? Who helped set the standard for Ella Fitzgerald, Sarah Vaughn, Frank Sinatra and many others? Who emerged from life's harsh underbelly to present the world the gift of her voice?

The answer is none other than Billie Holiday. Holiday was abused as a child and became a teenage prostitute and a heroin addict. Yet through sheer force of talent she climbed to the top of the jazz world. Her songs "I Cried for You," "I'll Get By" and others chronicled her pain and became classics. Familiar with hurt, Billie Holiday sang to heal herself, and in so doing she soothed her listeners as well. In a time of lynch mobs and white violence, Holiday stirred our conscience with the song, "Strange Fruit." Many who had never seen a lynch mob could visualize the horror through her profound lyrics. For many, Holiday's signature piece is "God Bless the Child," a poignant song embracing pain, hope and redemption.

Billie Holiday never escaped her demons. Abusive men and heroin tracks were forever near. Nevertheless, she lived enough to share her gifts of romance and hope, despite life's anguish, with all of us.

Blues singer Billie Holiday died on July 17, 1959, in New York City at 44. She is widely considered the seminal black female jazz singer. Diana Ross was nominated for an Academy Award for best actress for her portrayal of Billie Holiday in the movie, Lady Sings the Blues.

The Africans locked together in the rancid hull shuddered in horror. Already several were dead, and the living were covered in bloody gashes, vomit and excrement. Few of them spoke the same language, so communication was almost impossible. Since none of them had ever been so far out to sea, they did not know where they were. Yet Cinque sought answers. In Africa, Cinque's village had often looked to him for advice, wisdom and courage. When times had been hard or food low or enemies had lurked nearby, villagers had come to Cinque's home for inspiration.

Now, somewhere in the middle of the Atlantic Ocean, surrounded by well-armed whites, Cinque gathered like-minded Africans for resistance. As the ship sailed from Havana to Puerto Principe, Cinque gave the signal. Immediately, would-be slaves fought desperately for their freedom. Whites frantic to save their lives and blacks seeking liberty fought a brutal hand-to-hand combat. When it was over, several blacks and whites lay dead, but Cinque's Africans held the ship.

They left enough whites alive so they could sail back to Africa, but the sailors tricked the blacks, landing them in Long Island, New York. There, the Africans were arrested, and what ensued was an incredible legal battle. Abolitionists, missionaries and progressives rallied to assist the Africans, while the United States government and local authorities sought to extradite them to Spain to be charged with mutiny and murder.

During the trial, Cinque wrote, in very broken English, a letter to his attorney, ex-President John Quincy Adams, who was representing them with a vigorous defense. Cinque begged Adams to "give us free!"

Almost miraculously, they were acquitted, and on November 27, 1841, Cinque and thirty-four Africans set sail for home. Cinque of Mani, Nazahulu the blacksmith, Kagne the peasant, Gilabaru from Eulu, Teme the young girl and others returned home from their journey into hell. Their struggle aboard *The Amistad* and their legal fight for freedom stands as stirring testimony to the cost—and the value—of the struggle for dignity, self-respect and liberation.

On July 2, 1839, African leader Cinque led a successful rebellion and took control of the slave ship The Amistad. *Later tried for mutiny, the black prisoners were acquitted and thirty-five of them returned to their homelands in Africa as the free people they were before their ordeal began.*

The setting sun draws a curtain of darkness over the South Carolina sky. Rows of black soldiers in blue uniforms stand silently on the beach. In the distance, outlined against the horizon, lies the fortress of Battery Wagner. Confederate gunners hide behind brick, metal and wood. The 54th Massachusetts Volunteer Infantry awaits the signal from their white regimental leader, Colonel Robert Gould Shaw. Suddenly, his sword sweeps upward, he orders the bugle to call the charge, and columns of black soldiers move forward. They know that, directly ahead, certain death awaits. As they move forward across the beach, explosions erupt in the sand around them. Huge holes appear in the ranks where comrades and friends used to be. Confederate musket fire joins the artillery to devastate the ranks of the colored soldiers. Black troops fall broken and bloodied into the sand.

The ranks squeeze inward as the forward path becomes pinched where the marsh and the ocean converge. This only magnifies the horror, for when the troops close ranks, they become an easier target for Confederate gunners. Still, the black troops keep coming. Nothing stops them—not smoke, fire, mangled bodies, blood-soaked sand or cries of comrades.

Their courage propels them forward. They know the rebels will give no quarter. They know also that they stand for four million slaves. They know that if they falter the word will spread that Africans have no courage and are not deserving of freedom. No bombs, bullets or rebel yells deter them. On and on they come.

Those black troops in blue uniforms displayed a heroism that Massachusetts would talk about long after the war. But the odds against them were too much: bayonets trying to take a fort, men in an open field valiantly marching against an entrenched enemy. That evening, the 54th Massachusetts lost the battle to take Battery Wagner, but struck a mortal blow against slavery, racism and injustice: They marched into history under the banner of black courage. No longer would Union officers question the valor of black troops. or doubt that black soldiers could hasten a Union victory and slavery's defeat.The black troops that lay in heaps in the sand live forever as monuments to black sacrifice for equality and justice.

On July 18, 1863, the all-black 54th Massachusetts Volunteer Infantry launched a courageous assault on Battery Wagner in South Carolina. Companies A through K suffered 54 dead, 52 missing and 149 wounded. Among the many killed, wounded or missing in the battle were First Sergeant Andrew Benton, waiter from New York; Private George Dugan, farmer from Connecticut; Private Sanford Jackson, teamster from Massachusetts; Private David Bailey, laborer from Philadelphia; Private Morris Brown, wagoner from West Chester; Private George Price, farmer from Pennsylvania; Private Eli Franklin, laborer from Pittsfield. Their story was told in the movie Glory, which starred Denzel Washington, who won an Academy Award for Best Supporting Actor for his portrayal of Private Trip, a former slave.

≣ Juan Francisco Manzano: Black Cuban Poet

Juan Francisco Manzano was just another black Cuban destined to a life of slavery. But somehow, despite dehumanizing forces, Manzano learned to read and write. Discovering the magic of the pen, Manzano composed poems and stories of the misery that surrounded him. After working all day in the fields, he would often sit alone in the darkness and by candlelight and moonlight write of the physical and mental aches of injustice. Europeans mocked his effort, fellow slaves wished him well (but they were sure his work was in vain) and none believed he would succeed. Undeterred, Manzano continued to write.

In 1821, the unimaginable happened. With help from progressive Cubans, Manzano published *Cantos a Lesbia (Song of Lesbia)*, Cuba's first book of black poetry. In the 1830s, Manzano stunned audiences across Cuba with his famous sonnet, *"Mis Triente Anos,"* a brilliant account of his thirty years as a Cuban slave.

Manzano was not only a great poet, but his prose recreated reality and forced the reader to feel the suffering of injustice. He published the first and only known autobiographical account of black slavery in Latin America—an amazing feat, considering that most slaves could not read, let alone get published. His classic, *Autobiografía de un esclavo (Autobiography of a Slave)*, was the only source for those who sought to understand and abolish the horrors of slavery. When slavery was finally abolished in Cuba, it was in no small part due to the collective consciousness raised by Manzano's poetry and prose.

*Black Cuban poet Juan Fransisco Manzano died on July 19, 1853. Although a slave, his remarkable creativity was unleashed a mere three years after he learned to read and write. His **Autobiography of a Slave** is the only autobiographical account of black slavery in Latin America.*

JUL 22   ≣ Charlotte L. Forten Grimke: "Words of Truth and Deeds of Love"

Charlotte L. Forten was born into a wealthy black family that had been free from slavery for generations. In terms of prosperity, security and opportunity, the Fortens experienced affluence unimaginable to most black families. Nevertheless, their relative good fortune did not separate them from their people. At seventeen, young Charlotte was radicalized forever as she watched a black man, Anthony Burns, dragged away from the streets of Boston and taken South into slavery.

From that moment forward, Charlotte Forten dedicated her life to black liberation. She was an educator, writer, proponent of immediate abolition and the first teacher of the Port Royal Experiment, a project of the U.S. government to educate slaves. She traveled to the South Carolina Sea Islands to set up a school at the Central Baptist Church on St. Helena's Island and spent the next several years teaching children by day and adults after they returned from the fields in the evenings. On November 13, 1862, Charlotte Forten wrote in her diary:

> *Talked to the children a little while today about the noble Toussaint [L'Overture].... It is well that they sh'ld know what one of their own color c'ld do for his race. I long to inspire them with courage and ambition and high purpose.*

When Forten returned home and married Francis Grimke, their home became a gathering place for black intellectuals seeking refuge from a hostile world. There, writers, leaders and activists could discuss—in private—how to advance racial equality. With the end of the Civil War, Charlotte Forten Grimke worked to secure full human rights for all black Americans. At the turn of the century, she was involved in organizations such as the National Association for the Advancement of Colored People (NAACP) and the National Association of Colored Women (NACW).

Despite her lifetime of activism, Charlotte Forten Grimke is most known for the wisdom of her journals. Written between 1854 and 1892, her journals are windows into the past. Her descriptions of slavery, the abolitionist movement, early black schools and life as a black woman are unparalleled. Each entry reveals the heart of one striving to make sense of inequality and injustice. She once wrote a poem, "A Parting Hymn," in honor of her students from South Carolina:

> *Forth to noble work they go.*
> *O, May their hearts keep pure,*
> *And hopeful zeal and strength be theirs*
> *To labor and endure.*
> *That they an earnest faith may prove*
> *By words of truth and deeds of love.*

Charlotte Forten Grimke spent her life giving to others. She taught the young, wrote of freedom, founded civil rights groups, hosted intellectual gatherings and lived by "words of truth and deeds of love."

Charlotte L. Forten Grimke, the first teacher in the Port Royal Experiment in South Carolina after the Civil War, died in Washington, D.C., on July 22, 1914, at the age of 76. Her journals provide insights into slavery, the abolitionist and civil rights movements, early black school and the lives of black women.

≡ James H. Cone: Black Theology and Black Power

Ghettos were ablaze from Newark to Watts to Washington, D.C. Nonviolent marches seemed superfluous niceties, a form of expression rendered obsolete by the assassinations of Martin Luther King, Jr., Medgar Evers, Fred Hampton and Malcolm X. Black nationalists' calls for separation and revolutionaries' calls for armed resistance seemed justified in light of intransigent white supremacy. Black churches were searching the scriptures for answers to this time of turmoil at the same time black intellectuals and college students were abandoning the church in droves. For them, the Jesus upheld up by the church appeared to be an effeminate sustainer of white privilege and the status quo.

Suddenly, onto this canvas of social dislocation appeared the revolutionary theology of Dr. James H. Cone. The 1969 publication of his book *Black Theology and Black Power* sent shock waves through white Christianity. The message was compelling: Cone argued that Jesus Christ identified with and liberated the most marginalized of society; that new life in the gospel and the indwelling Holy Spirit had profound political implications; that God is present to and working for the full liberation of all humans, particularly the afflicted.

Dr. Cone's message that God does not side with the privileged and the powerful but rather with the hungry and the destitute went one step further. Cone believed that Jesus Christ advocated black power to the extent that power elevated and redeemed the poor:

> For white people, God's reconciliation in Jesus Christ means that God has made black people a beautiful people; and if they are going to be in relationship with God, they must enter by means of their black brothers, who are a manifestation of God's presence on earth. The assumption that one can know God without knowing blackness is the basic heresy of the white churches. They want God without blackness, Christ without obedience, love without death…. Reconciliation makes us all black. Through this radical change we become identified totally with the suffering of the black masses. It is this fact that makes all white churches anti-Christian in their essence. To be Christian is to be on the side of those whom God has chosen. God has chosen black people…. Being black in America has little to do with skin color. To be black means that your heart, your soul, your mind, and your body are where the dispossessed are.

Cone's idea that black peoples' very salvation could be found in their blackness, not in white evangelical rallies and prestigious seminaries, turned the theological world upside down. But the essential truth of Cone's message—that Christ lives in us to the extent that we are present in the anguish of the wretched and the damned—gave hope to all that God gives power and life life to the weak, the forgotten and the black.

Dr. James H. Cone has written several books on black theology, including, **Black Theology and Black Power God of the Oppressed; For My People: Black Theology and the Black Church;** *and* **Black Theology of Liberation.**

JUL 24 ≡ **Mary Church Terrell: A Colored Woman in a White World**

For a black woman in post-slavery America, Mary Church had an unusually privileged life. Her father had emerged from slavery to become one of the richest blacks in the South. Therefore, his daughter had benefits normally reserved for well-off whites. Mary Church earned a master's degree from Oberlin College and traveled through Europe for two years after graduation. When she returned to the States, she married Robert Terrell. Some months later, however, Mary Church Terrell heard that a lifelong black friend, Tom Moss, had been lynched by a white mob in Memphis, and the news shattered her world. Here she was enjoying the fruits of America's education and wealth, while a dear friend had been brutally murdered by a crazed mob.

Mary Church Terrell responded with a fury, embarking on a commitment to black equality. This was not a temporary cause; for the next six decades Terrell was a force in the black freedom movement. In 1896, she became the president of the National Association of Colored Women (NACW), an organization devoted to black self-help. The Association grew rapidly as hundreds of women worked for better housing, healthcare and employment. Later, Terrell helped W.E.B. DuBois found the National Association for the Advancement of Colored People (NAACP).

Unlike many activists, Mary Church Terrell became more militant with age. She publicly criticized America's abuse of black rights and became increasingly intolerant of injustice. The activism that had begun with a friend's murder grew stronger as time passed. Terrell was a fair-skinned, affluent black woman who could have melted away into the anonymity of privilege. Instead, the image of Tom Moss' lynching led to a lifetime of struggle to make America more just and compassionate.

In 1940, Mary Church Terrell wrote her autobiography, **A Colored Woman in a White World,** *describing her journey from privilege to activism. She died on July 24, 1954, in Washington, D.C.*

Maurice was an enigma—a black African serving as a general in the Roman army. Even more of a contradiction, he is now remembered as an apostle of non-violence.

Maurice's legion was stationed for years in North Africa, where the African Catholic Church was particularly strong. Hundreds of soldiers converted to Christianity, including Maurice. He became a devout believer, attending church meetings regularly and practicing the essentials of the Catholic faith.

A few years later, when Germanic tribesmen in Aguanaum (Switzerland) revolted against Roman rule, Maurice's legion was sent to crush the uprising. Many, including General Maurice, questioned whether war was consistent with their faith. Maurice contemplated disobeying orders, an almost unthinkable act in the military chain of command. To further complicate his moral dilemma, he soon discovered that the rebellious Bagaudae tribe was Christian. He could be forced to kill his Christian brothers in a war he did not believe in.

After several days of prayer and reflection, Maurice decided to disobey orders. When he told his soldiers of his decision, all the Christians and many of the others also decided not to fight. The Roman high command was livid, and Augustus Maximian ordered Maurice and the African legion to renounce their faith and sacrifice to Roman gods. Rome could not have both a rebellious tribe and a mutinous army.

When Maurice and his troops refused to betray their faith in Christ, Maximian decreed that every tenth man in the African legion be executed until they obeyed. Even after ten percent of the African legion had been slaughtered, Maurice and his legion stood by their Christian conviction that war was contrary to the gospel. Enraged, Maximian ordered the entire legion executed. Maurice, bold in faith as well as in battle, refused to give in and was executed along with the rest of his legion.

Maurice's unwavering conviction in the face of death is honored to this day. His image and name adorns monasteries in Switzerland, Savoy, Sardina and Poland. The Pinakothet chapel in Munich and the St. Maurice-en-Valais monastery bear his relics and paintings of his courageous act of peace.

Maurice and his African legion embraced the Christian faith around 287, while stationed in North Africa. Today he is considered an apostle of nonviolence. He was martyred by the Romans for refusing to fight fellow Christians and is considered a saint by the Catholic Church.

≡ James Ford: Black Communist in Harlem

When James Ford graduated from Fisk University in 1920, his classmates believed he was bound for success. Ford had all the tools: He was a model student, a football and baseball star, and an articulate communicator. Teachers and peers expected him to squeeze into the tiny black middle class as a doctor, lawyer or teacher. Upon graduation, however, Ford joined the Army Signal Corps. After serving in World War I, his reward for a college degree and military service was a low-level post office job. Sorting mail next to white high-school dropouts, Ford seethed. He joined the postal union where he met communists who were dedicated to ending racism and poverty. Their zeal intrigued Ford, and he attended study cells to learn how Marx's theories empowered workers to build a new world.

James Ford joined the Communist Party to change America. He poured his energies into his new faith and soon became the most significant African American in the Party. He spent countless hours trying to improve the living and working conditions for both black and white workers. Any place a voice was needed to shout for justice, democracy or peace, James Ford could be heard.

In 1933, he was sent to Harlem to be Party chief in that critical community. Soon after his arrival, the Harlem Communist Party grew in number and clout, and Ford presided over the heyday of black influence in the Party. During his time as chief, the Party was respected in the black community for its tangible support for racial and economic equality.

James Ford also was the first African American in a presidential campaign when he ran for vice-president on the Communist Party ticket. His Fisk classmates would not have been surprised that Ford had been chosen for a presidential ticket, but few had expected it would be as a communist. It turned out, however, that James Ford was more serious about transforming the world than he was about achieving individual wealth and success.

James Ford died in 1957 at the age of 64. When he presided over the Harlem Communist Party, membership grew from 560 to 1000. As vice-presidential candidate, he and presidential candidate William Foster received 103,000 votes.

≣ Reverend C.L. Franklin: "The Black Prince"

Rising from the poverty, violence and racism of Mississippi, Clarence LaVaughan Franklin became a popular and nationally recognized black preacher in the United States from the 1940s through the 1970s. So powerful were his sermons that he was known as "The Black Prince" in African-American Christian circles. The title was no idle flattery. During the height of his ministry, Franklin was as well-known among black Christians—and heard just as often—as evangelist Billy Graham was among white churches.

Rev. Franklin was the first to discover the power of radio in spreading the gospel. When he was sixteen years old at St. Peter's Rock Missionary Baptist Church in Cleveland, Mississippi, he heard a voice telling him to "go preach the gospel to each and every nation." Years later, he would fulfill this call on WLAC, a radio station out of Nashville, Tennessee. His Sunday sermons were carried on the air several times over the weekend, and aspiring young black preachers within a thousand-mile radius huddled by their radios to learn from the master.

Franklin was also among the first to record sermons and gospel singing on albums, and his classic recordings on the Chess Label could be heard in black communities across America. During the 1950s and 1960s, black preachers modeled their sermons, styles and ministry on the sermons of Rev. C.L. Franklin. Even well into the 1970s, he was still recording his sermons, always remaining a consistent voice for racial justice and economic equality. Though he was regularly the pastor of New Bethel Baptist in Detroit, Michigan, Franklin likely was heard by more people than any other black preacher in American history.

His classic sermon, "The Eagle Stirreth Its Nest," is studied in seminaries today for its depth and clarity. In it, Franklin depicted God as an eagle, occasionally stirring the nest, firmly but gently, so we can become better humans. When we need to learn to fly, he proposed, God exposes us to harsher material in the nest, forcing us to leap skyward. Franklin noted that suffering makes us stronger, that "history is one big nest God stirs to make man better and to help us achieve world brotherhood. Pain is not random, but a universal, redemptive experience."

During the upheaval of the 1960s, black militants were urging African Americans to find salvation in Africa, Islam and other venues. Franklin countered this, challenging his congregation to answer the essential question, "What think ye of Christ?"

If you get straight on Christ, my brothers and sisters, you believe in equality and you believe in the justice of all men…. To follow Christ is to set out upon the highway of justice, the highway of peace, the highway of brotherhood, for Jesus does not trod any other highway.

Such was the power of the "The Black Prince," a man whose voice and ministry shaped much of the black church as we know it today.

Just a few days after his 33rd anniversary celebration as pastor of New Bethel Baptist Church in Detroit, Michigan, burglars shot Rev. C.L. Franklin in his home. He never recovered. The famed Baptist preacher died on July 27, 1984, after spending five years in a coma.

JUL 28 ≡ Harry Haywood: "I Began to See I Had to Fight"

By age twenty-one, Harry Haywood recoiled under the destructive impact of racism. Hatred reached back generations in his family: His grandfather had fled Tennessee after killing a Klansman in self-defense; his father had been beaten by a gang of whites in Nebraska, forcing his family to move. Haywood remembered how it had shattered his father, leaving him "with a frightened, hunted look in his eyes." Racism had followed them to their next home in Minneapolis. On the first day of school, white classmates had greeted Haywood by singing plantation songs. Years later, when he served in the United States Army, despite his heroic service in the 8th Regiment of Illinois, Haywood and his black colleagues were humiliated and abused by their white officers.

When he returned home, Haywood worked as a waiter on the Michigan Central Railroad in Chicago. On July 28, 1919, he and his family watched in anger as whites rampaged through the city. White gangs roved the streets in search of victims, hunting down and beating blacks, burning homes and businesses. When things finally subsided, thirty-eight were dead, five hundred and thirty-seven were injured and thousands were left homeless. During that "Red Summer," anti-black riots erupted in Chicago and twenty-five other American cities. For Haywood, that was enough. In his classic autobiography, *Black Bolshevik*, he wrote:

> The Chicago rebellion of 1919 was a pivotal point in my life.… My experiences abroad with the Army and at home with the police left me totally disillusioned about being able to find any solution to the racial problem through the help of the government; for I had seen that official agencies of the country were among the most racist and most dangerous to me and my people. I began to see I had to fight; I had to commit myself to struggle against whatever it was that made racism possible.

Looking for a place to channel his energies, Haywood noticed that many activists on the frontline of struggle were communists. He joined the Communist Party, USA, and quickly became one of their most devoted comrades. Haywood developed the famous "Black Nation" thesis, arguing that Negroes in America constituted a distinct nationality, thereby affording them the right to self-determination. He also helped build the League of Struggle of Negro Rights, went to Spain to fight against Franco's fascists, organized maritime workers and sharecroppers, and was prominent in nearly every struggle involving black liberation during his lifetime.

Haywood's tireless work between the 1920s and the 1950s laid some of the groundwork for the later Civil Rights and Black Power Movements. He never tired of struggle, and he remained an active radical until his death in 1985.

Black activist Harry Haywood's life direction changed on July 28, 1919, during the "Red Summer" of anti-black rioting in Chicago. In addition to his organizing, he wrote the classics Negro Liberation *and* Black Bolshevik: Autobiography of an American Communist. *He died in 1985. In Richard Wright's novel* Black Boy, *the character of Buddy Nealson is supposed to represent Harry Haywood.*

≡ Catherine Devereaux: Invisible Teacher

In 1834, slavery and white supremacy ruled the South. Blacks were either enslaved or, if free, victims of discrimination and arbitrary violence. Free blacks could not vote, teach or act like normal human beings. For example, free blacks had to be careful not to offend any white person, from the wealthiest to the poorest, lest they be publicly abused.

Catherine Devereaux was one of the free blacks living in Savannah, Georgia. She worked as a house-servant for a wealthy white family, but she was not a slave. She had a home, her privacy and, above all, her freedom. She did not consider her freedom, however, hers alone. She often wondered, "What can I do with this freedom?" One day as she watched black children playing near her home, she was saddened to think it was illegal for them to learn, read or even appear intelligent. She knew that education was key to success and that without it these children did not have a chance.

Without telling anyone, Devereaux began inviting children into her home for cookies, a gathering that soon evolved into an improtpu school. Often after work, she arrived home to find a waiting group at her door. They never spoke of their visits, for she warned them no one must ever find out about their school. She taught math, reading, history and science, and this went on, day after day, for twenty-seven years. When her students grew up, they had their own children and sent them secretly to "Ms. Catherine." Though she could have been punished and jailed, Catherine Devereaux risked her own freedom to free the minds of black children.

Catherine Devereaux held school for black children in her home in Savannah, Georgia, from 1834 until the beginning of the Civil War in 1861. White authorities never knew she undermined the foundation of white supremacy by teaching black children that they were fully human and equal to white people.

JUL 30   ≣ Louis G. Gregory: "Pure Gold"

Louis G. Gregory was a young, intelligent African-American male searching for answers to the persistent riddle of racism and black misery. This task, difficult at any time, was almost impossible in 1909. Gregory looked to politics, Christianity and other ways to change human hearts. One evening, he attended a meeting where he heard members of the Baha'i faith describe their belief in the oneness of humankind. Gregory could hardly believe his ears: Here was a group of whites and blacks talking seriously of interracial unity at a time when white supremacy was at its peak!

Gregory converted to the Baha'i faith and was soon devoted to their principles of racial unity. For the next forty years, he carried the message of unity across the nation. During the "Red Summer" riots of 1919, mobs of whites chased, beat and killed defenseless blacks, and drunken hordes looted homes, but Gregory was not discouraged. Despite hatred raging all around him, he continued to teach, write and live his creed of unity. He was later elected to the National Spiritual Assembly of the Baha'i faith and from that platform proclaimed the uncompromising word of racial oneness.

We cannot, in retrospect, imagine how revolutionary Gregory's ideas were. At the time, whites considered themselves genetically different from blacks. Whites believed they were better, smarter and more human, while blacks were lesser, less intelligent and subhuman. Most whites believed in segregation, and even those who were not segregationists still felt that blacks were somehow inferior to whites. Gregory tossed aside such rubbish and boldly proclaimed that whites and blacks were created to live in unity. When he became a Baha'i, Louis G. Gregory wrote that his new faith gave him "an entirely new conception of religion," and that with it, "my whole nature seems changed for the better." The change in his nature was manifest in a bold and uncompromising commitment to interracial unity.

Baha'i member Louis G. Gregory died on July 30, 1951. Abdul Baha, one of the pillars of the Baha'i faith, once wrote of Gregory, "He is like unto pure gold. That is why he is accepted in any market and current in every country."

JUL 31   ☰ **The Prayers of the Black Church: Cries to God**

Church is scheduled to begin at 11:00 a.m., but before the choir procession, the opening prayer and outpouring of religious energy, the old folks gather. One at a time, they wander in—people who have been Christians for years, elders whose wrinkles and hobble reveal years of the good fight. They have seen it all. They have survived what would break many. They've seen lynch mobs, "White Only" signs, unemployment and brutality. They have also lived through traumatic black self-destruction, self-hate, black-on-black crime and drug use. Some have seen their children overcome, while others still mourn their family's acquaintance with drugs, jail, teenage pregnancy and homicide. Yet still they press on. These old folks still come to church. They have leaned on God through it all, and despite the wear and tear on their souls and bodies their faith in Christ lives on.

This Sunday, like all others, they come early to pray. They come to pray for children, to pray for grandchildren, to pray with groans and utterings unknown to the affluent and comfortable. First, all are silent. Then comes the moan that reaches all the way back to West Africa, a Georgia plantation or a Mississippi hamlet. Neither the lyrics nor the melody is written down, but the old folks know when to start and what to sing. Some elder lady in the front starts the moan:

ahh, ahh, ahhh
Lo--o---v---v-----e
Thu -uh---uh---uh
Lo---o----o---rd.

The words roll out slowly, almost too slow to sing. Everybody present sings along in a unity and depth no choir director could orchestrate. It is spontaneous, unrehearsed and real. They continue to sing for several minutes, each verse as slow as the first. The words are based on Psalm 116, but the prayer comes from their acquaintance with God's grace:

I love the Lord, He heard my cry,
and pitied every groan,
While I live and troubles rise,
I'll hasten to his throne.

Such a prayer cannot be read and analyzed; it must be lived and sung. I remember the first time I ever heard that prayer. It was an unforgettable scene of people carrying their burdens to the God they loved. Despite all the traumas of life, these elders feel God's hand in their world. They know that God is real and God's love endures forever.

Many black churches still have spontaneous prayer time before the scheduled service begins. For many, it is their most important time with God.

AUGUST

W.E.B. DuBois

≡ Bilal: The First Muezzin

The second pillar of Islam is to give praise, honor and glory to God, the compassionate Allah. Therefore, five times a day, at dawn, noon, mid-afternoon, sunset and nighttime, the faithful kneel toward Mecca for prayer. In Muslim countries the faithful are called together by a *muezzin*. Where Christians use church bells and Jewish believers have rams' horns, Islam calls people to prayer with a human voice. This voice is a holy voice, a solemn call to communion with God. Not anyone can be a *muezzin*; the appointed one must be someone who has demonstrated devotion to Islam and its five pillars of the faith. Only the most holy are selected.

The first *muezzin* in Islam was Bilal, a black Abyssinian slave, selected by Muhammad the Prophet himself—quite an honor for a late convert to the faith. Shortly after Bilal's conversion, however, Muhammad's enemies captured him. Once they learned of Bilal's status, they tortured him and sentenced him to death. But before the sentence could be executed, Abu Bakr, one of Islam's early leaders, rescued Bilal.

Bilal returned to Medina and the next morning called the faithful to prayer once again. Torture and imprisonment had done nothing to diminish his faithfulness. Muslims in Medina responded to the familiar and melodious voice of Bilal. Each dawn brought both the rising sun and the call to prayer. Bilal cried four times, "God is most great." He continued, "Come alive to the prayer. Come alive to flourishing. There is no god but God." Quickened by the voice of Bilal, dozens of Muslims left their homes, with prayer rugs tucked under their arms, and came boldly to the place of prayer.

Bilal, an Abyssinian black man, was Islam's first muezzin, *the person who calls others to prayer. In Medina he was one of the Prophet's close companions and helped establish prayer as a foundation of Islam.*

≡ Pan-Africanism: The Glory of African People

Pan-Africanism emerged from the hellhole of slave ships even as the first abducted slaves began to long for home. Through the slave trade, western colonization and European domination conspired to cripple Africa and dehumanize African people, blacks in Africa and abroad have long sought to build a continent by Africans and for Africans. Though Africa and blackness became to some synonymous with ignorance, savagery, subhumanity and paganism, for the Pan-African, Africa evokes community, culture, equality, love and pride.

Pan-African vision has enriched black freedom struggles everywhere. Harlem, London, Kingston, Barbados, Paris, Martinique—indeed, anywhere descendents of Africa live—all host a vibrant Pan-African movement where activists seek a place to raise children, create culture and participate in civic life without the fouling stain of racism. In Africa itself, Pan-Africans toil to transform their continent from dependency to self-determination.

Pan-African advocates and organizations have illuminated black history since slavery. The greatness of Pan-Africanist thinkers is best understood in the context of the prevailing climate of their time. When *Africa* and *black* denoted *ugly* and *backward*, Pan-Africanists preached the glory of African history and the dignity of black people. After early pioneers such as Prince Hall in 1781, Paul Cuffee in 1808 and Rev. Lott Carey in 1819, such greats as Edward Wilmot Blyden, Benito Sylvain of Haiti, Rev. James Theodore Holly and many others followed. The 1893 Chicago Congress on Africa planted the seeds for the famous Pan-African Congresses: London in 1900, Paris in 1911, and London again in 1921 and 1923. Their Pan-African vision culminated in the great 1945 Manchester Congress, which birthed African freedom fighters such as Kwame Nkrumah and others.

Hear the roll call of some of those who have loved Africa: Marcus Garvey and the Universal Negro Improvement Association, C.L.R James and George Padmore of Trinidad, Duse Muhammad Ali of Egypt, Jomo Kenyatta of Kenya, Albert Marryshaw of Grenada, Harold Moody and the League of Colored Peoples, Ibidanni M. Obadende of Nigeria and the founder of the League of the Negroes of the World, Kweggyir Aggrey of the West African Student Union.

Their devotion to Africa is captured in a story told by the great Kweggyir Aggrey. He used to tell people that if he went to heaven and God told him he could return to earth he would reply, "Send me back as a black…. I have work to do that no white…could do. Please send me back as black as you can make me."

The Pan-African movement lives today in the Organization of African Unity, in solidarity agreements between African nations, and in the hearts of Jamaicans, African Americans, Brazilian blacks and others who long to journey back to mother Africa.

AUG 3   ☰ Fela Kuti: Movement of the People

Fela Kuti's music shook the walls and roof of the nightclub. The horn section, the dancers, the drummers and Kuti's unique voice energized the crowded dance floor. His nightclub in Lagos, Nigeria's biggest city, was known to thousands of party-goers as "The Shrine." But Fela's music was more than music for dancing; his lyrics left no social reality untouched. His albums and performances broadcast the sins of the Nigerian government, America's CIA, global corporations and corrupt police so that millions would think critically of their world.

Kuti constantly mingled his pulsating beat with militant politics, and Nigeria's undemocratic and militaristic police met his accusations with state repression. They burned down his home in Lagos and beat his mother, who later died of injuries sustained that night. Fela was grieved but not broken. He went on to form his own political party, Movement of the People, urging young Nigerians to take charge of their lives and their political circumstances.

Fela's music and movement inspired millions around the world. For almost thirty years his music exposed the injustices of globalization, colonialism, police brutality and U.S. intervention in African affairs. Songs such as "Sorrow Tears and Blood," "I.T.T." (International Thief Thief) and others have helped educate, inspire and agitate. Progressives throughout the world continue to be inspired by the life and struggle of Fela Kuti.

Musician and political organizer Fela Kuti died of AIDS on August 3, 1997, in Lagos Nigeria. In a nation where AIDS deaths are largely ignored, Fela insisted that people know how he died so they would learn more about the disease.

AUG 4   ≡ The Ritual of Baptism: Healing Waters

African slaves had nothing of their own. Their past, present and future were determined by the economic fortunes of white planters. Their fathers, mothers, wives, husbands, children or grandparents could be punished or humiliated at whim. Worse, their loved ones could be sold away, never to be seen again, should their masters need cash. Their bodies were owned in full by others. Even their names were not their own, but merely reflected the genealogies of their masters.

It was within the Christian ritual of baptism that slaves found a way to claim their identity. When the slave church would gather near the water's edge, the preacher would call each person by his or her given name. The slave's name, which had been a label given by another, would thus become the designation by which he or she was to be called by God. The preacher's call symbolized the slave's addition to the church's book of life. Though these people were poor, enslaved, illiterate and despairing, they knew God now understood their pain and called them by their name.

As each "traveler" walked toward the water, all eyes of the church rested on him or her. Once in the water, the preacher would lay hands on each person's head and pray for forgiveness, salvation and new life. The sinner would then be plunged into the waters and come up a person made new. The slave church would break out in song:

Oh Lord, I've jes come from the fountain,
I'm jes from the fountain, Lord,
I've jes come from the fountain,
His name so sweet.

Oh Sinner, do you love Jesus?
Yes, yes, I do love my Jesus.
Sinner, do you love Jesus?
His name so sweet.

The song would go on and on, each time substituting the name of the person being baptized for the word "sinner," and the newly baptized person would sing in response, "Yes, yes, I do love my Jesus."

Those southern mudholes were transformed into fountains of new life, the waters made holy by the prayers of the slave church, and the sinner made whole by immersion. Though the lives of the slaves were not fundamentally changed—they remained slaves—they were transformed inside. God loved them, called them by name and granted them eternal life, regardless of their status. Through the healing waters of baptism, they gained a dignity, self-respect and self-love that could never be taken away.

The ritual of Christian baptism by immersion, so important to black people during the years of slavery, remains a key component of the African-American church today.

AUG 5 ≣ Lucie Campbell Williams: "Something Within"

Lucie Campbell Williams emerged from the poverty of Duck Hill, Mississippi, to become a demanding teacher, talented gospel composer and powerful preacher. As a teacher in the rural South, she demanded excellence from her students. Even from her early days of teaching in Memphis in 1911, she did not tolerate excuses for failure. Yet there was a nurturing side to her; she constantly prayed for her students and provided them whatever they needed.

A devout Christian, Williams lived by the verses in Matthew 28 that urge believers to go everywhere and preach the good news of salvation. As music director of the National Baptist Sunday School and Baptist Training Union Congress, she proclaimed the gospel with power. Her songs, especially, described her experience with God. Drawing upon difficult times and painful moments, she recalled God's faithfulness in songs such as "Something Within."

Though the male Baptist clergy often denied Williams opportunities to preach, she nevertheless was in demand as a Woman's Day speaker. Her sermons energized the congregation and left them questioning the wisdom of limiting woman's access to the pulpit. In her sermon "A Call to Arms," she proclaimed:

Women have always been pioneers in the Great Call to Christianity. Lydia was the first European convert.... Lydia didn't have money, but she gave what she had: free room and board. I'm happy to say that the first evangel was a woman—the Samaritan woman at the well. She brought the town to Jesus.... Oh yes, sisters, we were the first at the tomb on the morning of the resurrection, and the first to see the risen Lord, and greatest of all, the first to hear the words, "Mary."

William's sermon that day stirred controversy and motivated many women to pursue a deeper Christian life. As a teacher, composer and preacher, she preached the gospel wherever she went. She proclaimed that "something within" changed her life, and she wanted everyone to know just what it was. In 1960, she married her lifelong companion and business partner, Reverend C.R. Williams.

In 1962, while preparing to attend a banquet held in her honor given by the National Sunday School and the Baptist Training Union Congress of the National Baptist Convention, U.S.A., teacher, preacher, composer and music director Lucie Campbell Williams, affectionately known as "Miss Lucie," became gravely ill. She died six months later in 1963 in Nashville, Tennesee.

AUG 6   ≡ Mississippi Freedom Democratic Party: A Stand for Justice

August in Mississippi is brutal; heat and humidity drain away any initiative. Even those born and raised in the Delta find August unbearable. Yet despite the heat, black folks crammed into the auditorium of the Masonic Temple in Jackson, Mississippi. Mechanics, sharecroppers, ministers, maids, schoolteachers and small landowners gathered to make history. Black Mississippians were among the poorest, unhealthiest, least educated and most abused population in America, and had little impact on politics and government. Since the overthrow of Reconstruction, the state had sent all-white delegates to the Democratic Party convention every four years. In 1964, only about one thousand black people were registered to vote in the entire state.

Despite the heat and the hopelessness, local blacks came that day for the first convention of the Mississippi Freedom Democratic Party (MFDP). Amidst several caucuses, debates and platforms, they crafted an agenda and a list of delegates to send to the 1964 Democratic Convention in Atlantic City. Their aim was high: to unseat the all-white Mississippi delegation and bring democracy to their state.

Upon arrival in Atlantic City, the MFDP walked onto the convention floor, a black stream in a sea of whiteness. They sought to make the Democratic Party honor its claims and to highlight the aspirations of poor black folk on a national stage. Winston Hudson, Henry Silas, Hazel Palmer, Fannie Lou Hamer, Lawrence Guyot, Annie Devine, E.W. Steptoe and others courageously challenged one hundred years of black exclusion and white privilege. Their demands generated attention from the highest levels of the Democratic Party, including Lyndon Johnson himself. The Democrats, however, were afraid of the consequences of seating the MFDP.

Worried that whites would flee if blacks were included, Democratic leaders conspired to marginalize the MFDP. After several closed-door sessions, they offered the MDFP a compromise wherein they were to have two seats in the "regular" (i.e., all-white) delegation. In angry response, the MFDP accused Hubert Humphrey and others of sacrificing justice on the altar of expediency. This was the occasion of Fannie Lou Hamer's infamous challenge, "We didn't come all this way for no two seats."

The MFDP challenged America to live up to its promises. Blacks in the South had been beaten by sheriffs, bombed by the Ku Klux Klan, neglected by schools and hounded by judges, and they were not about to satisfy white liberal consciences by accepting crumbs. They refused to allow their dignity to be trampled upon, and their stand has left a permanent mark on the American political scene. Ironically, to this day neither political party has approached the progressive and inclusive platform of the Mississippi Freedom Democratic Party.

On August 6, 1964, the Mississippi Freedom Democratic Party (MFDP) held its first convention in Jackson, Mississippi. It was, and remains, a shining example of empowerment and representative democracy for the poor.

≣ Robert Moses: Outside Agitator

It was another typical southern summer evening. Crickets, lightning bugs and other nocturnal critters added familiar sights and sounds to the darkness. Humidity and heat lingered long after sundown, so there was little relief for the weary. Nevertheless, twenty-five black Mississippi farmers, laborers and students gathered in the Masonic Lodge in McComb, Mississippi. Their numbers were modest, but their cause was revolutionary.

Robert Moses stood in front of the class and began to speak. This was a very different venue from the classrooms he had occupied the last few years. Just two years prior, he had been studying in the prestigious halls of Harvard University, obtaining a master's degree in philosophy. Then he had moved on to the Horace Mann School to teach equations and fractions to New York teenagers. Now he was teaching illiterate Mississippi farmers how to complete voter registration forms and how to respond to the irrelevant questions that white registrants used to disqualify black voters.

The black farmers left that evening wiser, stronger and capable of confronting white political power. Over the next several days, new potential black voters filed into the McComb courthouse to register. Because they challenged the system, Moses and his students became an immediate threat to this systemic exploitation. Any blacks who stood up for themselves were subject to brutality and violence. In this context, it is hard to overestimate the profoundness of the political transformation fueled by Robert Moses and others like him.

Robert Moses later became a legend in the Civil Rights Movement; stories abounded of his courage. Many recalled how angry whites beat him as he walked to a Delta courthouse, yet he refused to stop. His followers were threatened, his offices bombed and he was often beaten and jailed. Yet this philosophy student and mathematics teacher was undeterred. When someone needed help, Robert Moses was there, risking his life for their cause, teaching, marching and organizing for a better Mississippi. Folks such as Dr. King and Rosa Parks might be better known, but to black Mississippi Delta farmers, no one was more courageous, committed and devoted than Robert Moses.

On August 7, 1961, Robert Moses and Amzie Moore, a Mississippi postal worker, held the first voter registration class at the Masonic Temple in McComb. It was the beginning of a voter registration drive that reshaped voting laws and patterns in the South and across America.

AUG 8   ☰ **Amanda Berry Devine Smith: "Old-Time Spirituality"**

Amanda Berry Devine Smith was devastated, and her sobs were uncontrollable. Two of her children had died suddenly from sickness, and shortly thereafter her loving husband had also died. Even before she could wipe the tears away, her last child died of a rare disease. She who once had a husband and three children was now alone. Deafening silence had replaced the sounds of children's laughter, and family dinners were to be no more. Amanda Smith had nowhere to go. In her deepest agony, she called on God.

In God, Smith found solace for her burden and comfort for her troubles. But she soon found something else: God began to speak to her, quietly at first, then louder: "Be ye holy, as I am holy."

Smith was stunned. Here she was, crushed by the weight of grief, and God was asking that she be holy! All her life she had tried to be a good Christian, a devoted member of the Holiness Church, but she would not have described herself as "holy." Yet, despite her incredulity, she obeyed. She listened because she knew that God loved her, and that God would ask only what was good for her. Pushing aside her hurt, Smith sought the holiness of God through prayer, fasting and Bible reading. She asked God's Spirit for help in her journey and soon felt the Holy Spirit of God living in the deepest recesses of her soul. Praying fervently, testifying of the Lord's goodness and serving others became her life.

By 1878, she was a sought-after preacher on the Holiness circuit. She spoke to crowds in New York City and New Jersey; she preached at camp meetings in Maine and Tennessee; and she eventually traveled to Great Britain, India, Liberia and Sierra Leone to preach the gospel. Wherever Evangelist Smith preached, hundreds felt compelled to seek a deeper walk with Christ. Many gave their lives to God; many more were healed or rededicated themselves to God.

Amanda Smith continually called herself and her followers back to God. Her life and her work bore fruit beyond her imagination. Out of the depths of her personal tragedy came preaching that transformed hundreds, including Charles Mason, who would later become the founder of the Church of God in Christ. Smith summed up her mission in these words she wrote in 1893: "May God in his mercy save us from the formalism of the day; and bring us back to the old-time spirituality and power of the fathers and mothers."

Amanda Smith, evangelist in the Holiness Movement, died in 1915. In 1893, she had published her autobiography, **The Story of the Lord's Dealings with Mrs. Amanda Smith, the Colored Evangelist.**

AUG 9 ≡ Blessed Victoria Rasomanarivo: Shining with the Radiance of God

Victoria Rasomanarivo was born in Malagasy (also known as Madagascar) to a wealthy and powerful family. Her grandfather was minister to the queen for twenty years, and her parents held high positions in the royal government. There were few Catholics in Malagasy, but Rasomanarivo wanted to be one of them. When she was thirteen, she asked her parents if she could be baptized into the Catholic Church. They were horrified and said conversion would exclude her from burial in the family tomb—which meant not only exclusion from the tomb but also exile from the family memory and name.

Yet young Rasomanarivo chose baptism and life with God, and her parents later changed their minds when they saw how serious she was about her faith. She attended daily Mass, often said the rosary and the Angelus prayer, and demonstrated her interior devotion by exterior good works. She gave much of her wealth to the poor, the sick and the imprisoned, welcoming even lepers, who were trapped in their melting skin and excluded from social contact.

Often after attending Mass and receiving the sacrament of the Eucharist, Rasomanarivo would begin her ministry. She would leave the altar and go immediately to the sick, poor and destitute, where she gave herself as Christ gave himself to her in the Eucharist and the cross. It was said that her face "shone with radiance," and friends believed her interior light was the glory of God. Another contemporary said of her, "She made herself servant of others and it is for this above all that we had such veneration for her." Victoria Rasomanarivo was united with Christ at baptism and spent the rest of her life living that divine union.

Victoria Rasomanarivo of Madagascar died on August 21, 1894, at the age of 46. She has been declared "Blessed" by the Catholic Church, the final step before being declared a saint.

AUG 10   ☰ Matilda: "Time to Be Up and Doing"

The year 1827 was not a good time to be black, nor a good time to be a woman. Slavery ruled in the South, and the North vacillated between abolition and white supremacy. Women could not vote and were often seen as no better than property. The common black woman in these dire times survived only through grace, courage and resilience.

So it was all the more astounding that *Freedom's Journal* published an editorial written by a woman identified only as "Matilda," an editorial which remains to this day a manifesto of gender equality. In it the author boldly addressed the commonly held view that women, especially black women, needed no education beyond domestic duties:

> *I hope you are not to be classed with those who think that our mathematical knowledge should be limited to "fathoming the dish-kettle," and that we have acquired enough history if we know that our grandfather's father lived and died…. The diffusion of knowledge has destroyed those degraded opinions…and…we are capable and deserving of culture. There are difficulties and great difficulties in the way of our advancement; but that should only stir us to great efforts…. Ignorant ourselves, how can we be expected to form the minds of our youth and conduct them in the paths of knowledge? There is a great responsibility resting somewhere, and it is time for us to be up and doing.*

This single anonymous black woman, not often listed among the heroes of African-American history, eloquently demanded that the halls of education be opened to black women. She told white folks and black men that black women were ready to build community and family. She made no request for charity or handouts—just a plea for the means for women to achieve their liberation, a plea not to stand in the way or to keep women from what was rightfully theirs, a plea to let women use their talents to shape their destiny.

Matilda is one of the hundreds of anonymous women upon whom the survival of the black race rests; her call to be "up and doing" is a call that continues to echo through into the twenty-first century.

On August 10, 1827, **Freedom's Journal** *published an editorial written by a woman simply known as "Matilda." It was the first letter the* **Journal** *had ever published demanding woman's rights.*

AUG 11 ≡ Pauline Elizabeth Hopkins: Contending Forces

Those who shine during the darkest hours illuminate the way for those who follow. Pauline Elizabeth Hopkins was one of those early torchbearers. After the Civil War and Reconstruction, America settled into the business of neglecting, ignoring and abusing black Americans. The early twentieth century was a hard time for black Americans.

Yet during this time of lynchings, cross-burnings and "white-only" exclusions, Pauline Hopkins had the courage and dignity to write about her life as a black woman. She did not write about politics or religion or history; she wrote about romance. Her most famous work, *Contending Forces: A Romance of Negro Life North and South*, depicted love as a statement of resistance. She proclaimed that black life was not just about racism and white supremacy, and she portrayed her people as loving humans carving decency and romance out of despair.

At that time, science taught that blacks were kin to chimpanzees, religion preached that blacks were the "cursed children of Ham" and politicians decreed that blacks were second-class citizens. Pauline Hopkins rejected all that as nonsense and proclaimed to the world that black people were human beings.

Since black authors seldom made a decent living, Hopkins worked many years as a stenographer. Yet she continued to write, and in her later works she branched out from romance to explore other subjects. In 1905, she wrote *A Primer of Facts Pertaining to the Early Greatness of the African Race and the Possibility of Restoration by Its Descendants*. Her book declared that despite all the negative stereotypes African greatness awaited those willing to work for redemption. Other black activists and writers paid homage to Hopkins in their words and deeds. She scattered the darkness with her light, so that those in later times could continue to live the full humanity of their blackness.

Pauline Elizabeth Hopkins was a prolific African-American writer at the turn of the twentieth century, who wrote both Romance novels and non-fiction books. She died on August 13, 1930, from injuries sustained in a fire.

AUG 12   ≣ Helen Caldwell Day (Riley): A Home for Others

Who are the kind, generous people among us? Are they those who have never tasted the bitterness of misfortune? Or are they those who serve the poor and destitute and have felt the agonies of hardship themselves? Helen Caldwell Day is a model of the latter.

During World War II, she left Memphis, Tennessee, to study nursing in Harlem. While in Harlem, she converted to the Catholic faith and was transformed by her relationship with Jesus Christ. After reading the Gospels, she became convinced that her ministry lay with the poor and helpless. Yet before she could begin her Christian service, Day tasted life's bitterness: Her marriage fell apart, she contracted tuberculosis and her infant son was stricken with polio.

Helen Day's newfound faith was shattered. What once had seemed a hopeful future was now permanently scarred. She was down, but she was not destroyed. Day never lost faith that God was with her, and she slowly regained her physical strength.

Despite her traumas, she returned to her commitment to the poor. Though weighted down with grief and ill health, Day moved to Memphis, Tennessee, and opened a house of hospitality for the poor. She set aside her own hurt, recognizing that others suffered even more than she did. With the help of white and black Catholics, she established one of the few interracial ministries in the South. They started a home called the Blessed Martin House, a haven that served the destitute of Memphis for many years. When in need of a place of welcome, comfort, food or prayer, many men and women found their way to the Blessed Martin House. One of the volunteers was a man named Jesse Riley, whom Day married in 1955.

Helen Caldwell Day was one of those amazing individuals who transcend their own pain to touch and heal the hurts of others.

Helen Caldwell Day wrote an autobiography called Color, Ebony, *in which she described her conversion to Catholicism and her humble commitment to the poor and distressed.*

AUG 13   ≣ Jacques Roumain: Masters of the Dew

Jacques Roumain was a rarity in Haiti, a young black man formed in the fortunate bosom of Haiti's upper class. Wealth on the impoverished island of Haiti, as in most poor countries, was concentrated in the grasping hands of a minority, and Roumain was among those few. He experienced the privilege of upper-class life, European education, world travel and material comfort. Yet he was not satisfied. At the age of twenty—a time when many youth delay commitments and careers—Roumain left his carefree life in Europe and returned to Haiti, where he immersed himself in the misery of the lives of the Haitian peasants.

Pen and paper were his weapons; justice, his war. Jacques Roumain's early poems and novellas humanized Haiti's peasants and condemned the opulence of the rich. The more injustice Roumain saw, the more he wanted to change it. By 1934, he was elected secretary general of the Haitian Communist Party and emerged as a strong advocate of class struggle and economic justice. He also was head of the Haitian Patriotic Youth League, which helped end the United States occupation of Haiti. Roumain was rapidly becoming a serious threat to Haiti's power structure, and the government harassed, persecuted and eventually arrested him.

After his release, Roumain was exiled to France, where his voice was not muted. His poem "Madrid" exposed the fascists in the Spanish Civil War. Later, his article "The Grievances of the Black Man" angered many French for its condemnation of their complicity in racism and colonialism.

Roumain's lasting work and enduring legacy is the novel *Masters of the Dew*. Published in 1944, *Masters of the Dew* stunned the public with its humane depiction of Haitian peasants. The impact of this story of a Haitian peasant who united warring factions in a village to struggle for their liberation continues to this day. This powerful novel also celebrates the peasant *voudon* religion, noting how it explains their world to them and empowers them to transcend it.

Jacques Roumain's solidarity with the poor and oppressed was expressed both in his writing and his political work. He is the model of an activist for whom art, politics and compassion are inseparable.

The author of Masters of the Dew, *Jacques Roumain, died in Port-au-Prince, Haiti, on August 18, 1944. He was raised in wealth but became an advocate of class struggle and economic justice for the peasants of Haiti.*

Susan Baker loved her grandmother. She missed her parents back on the plantation, but the second best place for her to be was with her grandmother in Savannah.

Though technically a slave, Baker's grandma, Dolly Reed, had a mutually beneficial arrangement with her owner. She was allowed to live and work in Savannah, away from the plantation, in exchange for giving her owner most of her earnings. Though Reed was legally a slave, owned and controlled by a white man, she had carved liberty out of bondage, and she wanted to pass her sense of dignity and self-respect on to her granddaughter.

When little Susie Baker arrived in Savannah, the first thing Dolly Reed did was to find a black woman to teach her granddaughter to read. This was no easy task, for teaching black boys and girls to read was punishable by fines and imprisonment. The child, the parents and the teacher could all be severely punished by the sheriff. Nevertheless, despite the risk, seven-year-old Baker attended secret classes in a local home. She later wrote, "We went every day about nine o'clock, with our books wrapped in paper to prevent the police or white persons from seeing them."

In 1862, black gatherings were viewed with alarm, and the master's overseer caught Reed and Baker attending a "suspicious" meeting in a black church. Furious, the master had Baker taken away. We don't know if she ever saw her grandmother again. We do know, however, that Dolly Reed had changed Susan Baker's life.

Shortly thereafter, Baker escaped to a Union encampment on St. Catherine in the Sea Islands. When she arrived, her ability to read made the fourteen-year-old very valuable to the Union army, and the commander asked her to teach ex-slaves in camp to read and write. When the 33rd U.S. Colored Regiment was formed, Susan Taylor became the nurse for Company E. Though not trained as a nurse, she learned her skill under fire. Taylor and other nurses would go with the 33rd into battle and wait in the rear until the wounded arrived. She described how "our boys" were carried in with legs missing, arms gone and wounds unimaginable. Baker saved many black troops who would have otherwise died in the Civil War. Suffering soldiers thanked her for being there, for holding their hands and for doing the bloody work of a Civil War nurse.

Susan Baker survived slavery and the Civil War to marry twice, first to a Mr. King and, following a divorce, to a Mr. Taylor. The legacy of grandmother Dolly Reed lived on in her granddaughter's bravery and compassion. Susan Baker is but one example of an African-American girl who grew into a strong woman because of a black grandmother's guiding vision.

Susan Baker King Taylor was the author of **A Black Woman's Civil War Memoirs: Reminiscences of My Life in Camp with the 33rd U.S. Colored Troops, Late 1st S.C. Volunteers.** *Though she lived in the North for a time, she moved to the South to care for her dying son. She died somewhere in the South in 1912.*

≣ Lucy Stanton: "Slavery Is War"

Lucy Stanton grew up in a home where racial solidarity and activism were the norm. Her father was a barber in Cleveland, Ohio. His home was a school; his shop, a station on the Underground Railroad. Lucy Stanton did not disappoint her parents; she devoted herself to racial progress and uplift. The first African-American woman in the United States to complete a four-year college education, Stanton used her degree to help her people rise above segregation and discrimination. Her dedication was clear in her 1850 commencement address to the graduating class at Oberlin College in Ohio:

> Mother, sister, by thy own deep sorrow of heart; by the sympathy of thy woman's nature, plead for the downtrodden of thy own, of every land.... Slavery is the combination of all crime. It is war. Those who rob fellow-man of home, of liberty, of life, are really at war with them as though they cleft them down on the bloody field.

Yet despite the harsh portrayal of slavery, Lucy Stanton closed her talk with a pronouncement of hope. She urged her audience to "go to war" and work until they heard the sounds of freedom. Those would be the sounds, Stanton proclaimed, that inspired them forward. She concluded her address:

> How sweet, how majestic, from those starry isles float those deep inspiring sounds over the ocean of space! Softened and mellowed they reach earth, filing the soul with harmony, and breathing of God—of love—and of universal freedom.

On August 27, 1850, a few weeks before passage of the horrific Fugitive Slave Law, Lucy Stanton gave the commencement address at Oberlin College, urging resistance to slavery. She was the first black woman to give a college commencement address in U.S. history.

≣ Mary V. Cook: "A Long, Loud No!"

In the late 1880s, just a few years removed from slavery, the independent black Baptist Church flourished among ex-slaves. The message of the preacher and the mission of the church brought hope and healing to many African Americans. Yet some black women were disturbed that black preachers and deacons excluded women from leadership in the church. Virginia Broughton, Lucy Wilmot Smith and Mary V. Cook were among the most outspoken of these dedicated Baptist women. But none was as eloquent as Mary Cook. Cook and her colleagues often worked their way onto the agenda of Baptist conventions to demand full inclusion of women in the work of the church. In 1887, Cook delivered a powerful address to the American National Baptist Convention, proclaiming:

Emancipate women from the chains that now restrain her and who can es-
timate the part she will play in the work of the denomination. In the Baptist
denomination women have more freedom than in any other denomina-
tion on the face of the earth.... All women who are truly Christians are can-
didates in this broad field of labor. None whose soul is not overflowing with
love for Christ and whose chief aim is not to save souls need apply. Success
need not necessarily depend on learning, genius...but it is the earnestness
of the soul, the simplicity of the Word accompanied by the Spirit of the
living God.

Mary Cook's message was for both women and men. To men, she convinc-
ingly argued that the work of God belonged to everyone. To women, she urged
that they reflect the holiness and love of God in their lives. Cook concluded her
message with this challenge:

Should woman be silent in this busy, restless world of mission and vast
church enterprise? No! A long, loud no! Give place to her, brethren. Be ready
to accept her praying heart...her willing hands.

As a result of Cook's relentless call for the inclusion of women in mission
and leadership, the Baptist church slowly began to open its doors. Her message
helped bring women by the hundreds into leadership positions. Today, women
preachers, ministers and leaders in the Baptist Church owe their calling and position to the work of Mary Cook and her sisters.

On August 26, 1887, Mary V. Cook addressed the American National Baptist Con-
vention in Mobile, Alabama. Her speech highlighted the power of women and
urged men to open the church to that power.

AUG 17   ≣ Harriet E. Wilson: Our Nig

Harriet E. Wilson was a free black woman in Boston during the 1850s. Her life, like
that of most black women in America, was vulnerable, disrespected and painful. Also, like many of her sisters, Wilson was not a passive observer to her pre-
dicament. She captured the painful contours of her life in her novel, *Our Nig: or,*
Sketches from the Life of a Free Black. Published in 1859, this was the first novel
published by an African-American woman in the United States. Her work, however, was more than just another first. It was, in many respects, far ahead of its time;
it was a groundbreaking story that personalized the black struggle for equality.

In the mid-nineteenth century, slave narratives were becoming increasingly powerful hammers against the institution of slavery. Frederick Douglass, Olauduh Equiano, William Wells Brown, Harriet Jacobs and others had reconstructed tales of their servitude that had energized the abolitionist movement. Harriet Wilson, however, looked beyond slavery to the future of black America. She was already free, but racism prevented her from living a full and self-determined life. In essence, she told America that while slavery was bad and must be destroyed the more sinister and persistent enemy was racism. In her novel, the slave driver was not the enemy; it was the white women of northern households. Frado, the mulatto indentured servant and main character of her novel, was victimized and tortured by racism. Through Frado's life, Wilson emphasized to both blacks and whites that racism, not slavery, was the real opponent.

Since most whites at the time considered blacks incapable of self-expression, they assumed that *Our Nig* was the work of a white female. No one could believe that a black woman could develop and sustain such a moving story or tell that story with such literary acumen. Critics did not understand that Frado's story was Harriet's recollection of her own and that her eloquence rose from her experience. She did not care about offending sensibilities; she cared only for telling the truth.

Harriet Wilson was truly a woman ahead of her time. She told a story that was hard to tell and even more difficult to hear.

On August 18, 1859, Harriet E. Wilson registered her novel for copyright. She was the first African-American woman to publish a novel in the United States. Ironically, her preface declares the book "an experiment which shall aid me and my child in sustaining this feeble life." Wilson wrote to raise money to care for her sick child, but six months after publication her seven-year-old son died of "the fever."

     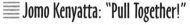 Jomo Kenyatta: "Pull Together!"

Many know that Jomo Kenyatta was the first Prime Minister and President of independent Kenya. What many do not know is that he gave a lifetime of sacrificial service to his nation and his people. By 1922, the young Kenyatta was involved in the East African Association and the Kikuyu Central Association (KCA). By 1928, Jomo Kenyatta was elected General Secretary of the KCA and led protests to return stolen lands to the Kikuyu people. He also worked tirelessly to improve British social services for the common folk of Kenya. Through dedication and compassion, Kenyatta became a hero to the Kikuyu and all the peoples of Kenya.

When he traveled abroad to further his education, Kenyatta maintained intimate bonds with his people. His thesis at the prestigious London School of Economics, *Facing Mount Kenya*, was a study of traditional Kikuyu customs and remains an anthropological classic. Kenyatta was also one of the prime movers in the 1945 Pan-African Congress. He returned home, and in 1952 was arrested by colonial authorities for his progressive activities. Once released from prison, he helped negotiate an end to colonial rule, and by December of 1960, he was elected President of the Kenya African National Union (KANU). He was later elected the first Prime Minister and President of independent Kenya.

As a student, organizer, party president and, ultimately, prime minister, Jomo Kenyatta gave fifty-six years of his life for the uplift and elevation of his nation. For fifty-six years he kept his eyes on freedom and sacrificed much for his beloved Kenya. Even today, Jomo Kenyatta is revered both in Kenya and in all of Africa.

On August 22, 1978, Jomo Kenyatta died in Mobassa, Kenya. He was a beloved leader in African history and was critical in Kenya's transition from colonial rule to self-determination. Kenyatta's motto was "Harambee!" (Swahili for "pull together").

AUG 19 ≡ Saint Moses the Black: "Everything Has Become New"

Egypt in the fourth century was a harsh and brutal place. Lawlessness, violence, war and poverty stalked the land, and Moses—also called Moses the Black—was a perfect fit for the times. He survived by preying on others and was a bully, thief and villain. Not content to steal and plunder alone, he soon gathered around him a crowd of hard-core thieves as callous and violent as himself.

Moses and his band of hoodlums often sought refuge in the vastness of the Egyptian desert. One day, however, something happened to Moses the Black. Whether it was a vision, the solitude or the witness of a hermit, no one knows. What we do know is that Moses the Black renounced his former ways and committed his life to Jesus Christ. From thenceforth he did not come to the desert to hide; he stayed for solitude and prayer.

Many Christians of the Egyptian desert believed that the sinfulness of urban life drowned the voice of God. Moses was no exception. He became a monk and lived in the Petra monastery at Skete. Not long after his arrival, Moses the Black emerged as one of several leaders in the community. Some were leaders by title, others by tenure, but Moses was a leader by his spiritual devotion. His prayerfulness and acts of mercy earned him the title "*Abba*," (Aramaic for "Father"). Moses the thief became *Abba* Moses; a Christian leader to whom others looked for leadership, prayer and counsel. He who had been feared for his violence was now followed for his holiness.

Moses the Black was the forerunner of many who would follow in his footsteps, lifted from self-destructiveness to a life of prayer. His conversion exemplified the scripture "So if anyone is in Christ, there is a new creation: everything old has passed away; see, everything has become new!" (2 Corinthians 5:17). Moses the Black believed that his old life of selfishness, violence and hatred was transformed by Christ into generosity, prayer and love.

Moses the Black died on August 28, 405, when a band of marauding desert nomads attacked the monastery, killing him and many other monks. Before he died, however, Moses was able to save some of his fellow monks by urging them to escape while he faced the attackers. He is revered as a saint by the Catholic Church.

AUG 20   ≡ Antony, Isabella and Pedro: The First Africans in America

On a hot day in August 1619, twenty Africans were unloaded at Jamestown from a Dutch man o' war. What did they think as they disembarked? Had the men been beaten and the women raped? Or had the slave trade not yet degenerated into those demonic dimensions? They certainly could not have known that centuries of pain awaited their descendants. Separated from their homes and consumed by their own agony, they had little inkling that they were but the first of millions of slaves in the New World. They could not have known that those chains would remain clamped and locked for two hundred and forty-six more years. By the end of slavery, the twenty who had come to Virginia had mushroomed to four million.

Who were these twenty? Historian Lerone Bennett records three of their names—Antony, Isabella and Pedro—in his classic, *Before the Mayflower: A History of Black America*. Bennett tells us that two of the slaves, Antony and Isabella, married and gave birth to the first African-American child born in what is now the United States. In 1624, their son, William Tucker, was the first of thousands conceived and delivered into the foul hands of slavery.

Whatever were hopes and dreams of these African slaves, centuries would pass before those dreams would be fulfilled. For the more than two centuries, enslaved people would battle to achieve human dignity and respect. Their struggle continues to this day in the ongoing work for justice, fairness and democracy.

On August 20, 1619, twenty "Negars" were unloaded off a Dutch man o' war into Jamestown harbor. They were the first African slaves brought to what later would become the United States. They arrived long before the Mayflower, the Constitution, the Bill of Rights and the Declaration of Independence.

George Lester Jackson was dead before his twenty-eighth birthday. Born in the ghetto and surrounded by despair, failure and crime, Jackson was already committing petty crimes against people and property by the time he was ten. At nineteen, he robbed a gas station of seventy-one dollars, a crime that earned him an indeterminate sentence of one year to life.

Jackson was the symbol of black failure and white fear: a violent, destructive black man locked down for the good of society. Yet while in prison, Jackson was transformed from criminal to revolutionary. He thought of the broken lives in his neighborhood—the poor schools, the scarce jobs—and wondered why there was so much black misery. In search of answers, he read voraciously and found hope in some of his reading and in the lives of some inmates:

> I met Marx, Lenin, Trotsky, Engels and Mao when I entered prison and they redeemed me…. I met black guerillas George "Big Jake" Lewis and James Carr…. We attempted to transform the black criminal mentality into a black revolutionary mentality.

In the study groups that Jackson formed, and in the prison chapter of the Black Panther Party he helped organize, Jackson taught that criminal behavior and society's response were the inevitable consequences of the supremacy of private wealth over public equality. Seeing himself as a victim of monopoly capitalism and white supremacy, he became the voice of revolutionary change. His book, *Soledad Brother: The Prison Letters of George Jackson*, was a powerful political manifesto and call for profound change. All talk of moderation, patience and compromise wilted before his scathing critique of America. In a 1967 letter to his father, he wrote:

> Chew on this a few moments: a colonizer, a usurer, the original thief, a murderer for personal gain, a kidnapper-slaver, a maker of cannon, bombs and poison gas, an egocentric parasite, the original fork tongue, the odd man trying to convey to us that we must adjust ourselves to his warp, that we must learn to be more like him, that because we're not we're backward, underdeveloped, unsophisticated! This is strange and contradictory.

Born in the ghetto, radicalized in prison, Jackson became America's nightmare: an articulate black man immune to compromise or purchase. The stories of his death vary, from the "official" version, which claims that he was shot rushing the fence during a prison riot, to witnesses who say that he was separated from the rest of the prisoners and murdered by white guards. In his death, George Jackson shared the fate of many other revolutionary prophets whose existence challenged wealth and power.

*On August 21, 1971, at age 28, George Lester Jackson was murdered at San Quentin prison. He was the author of the influential book, **Soledad Brother.***

≣ Huey P. Newton: Two Souls, One Body

Decked in black leather, a black beret atop his Afro, a rifle by his side, Huey P. Newton was the black man's black man. No one personified a "bad ass nigger"—a black man without fear of white power, unwilling to bow, scrape or shuffle—as did Huey P. Newton.

Co-founder of the Black Panther Party and an advocate for black self-determination, Newton was a role model for thousands of black youth across America. Instrumental in creating community patrols to watch the Oakland Police, organizing free breakfasts for poor children and spreading revolutionary theory to inspire the souls of black folks, Huey Newton was a larger-than-life hero to the black community. For a people subjected to police brutality and harassment for years, Newton's bold and visible confrontation with police officers inspired a generation of activists. He spoke, and people listened. The aura, the power, the mystique of Huey Newton was palpable. No one who lived through the 1960s was untouched by the outward ripples of his revolutionary life.

But there was another Huey P. Newton, a different and separate soul in one black body. This person was violent, abusive and addicted; he lived alongside the revolutionary. This man pistol-whipped black cab drivers over petty arguments, shot a black prostitute in the face and brutally beat comrades in the Black Panther Party. Paranoid, strung out and violent, this Newton destroyed many unfortunate enough to have crossed his path.

How could one so brilliant, so powerful, so unforgettably courageous be at the same time so deformed? Could it be that his love for his race could not bear the crushing pain? Could it be that he succumbed to self-destruction because the struggle was too great for one body? Great scholar W.E.B. DuBois taught that black Americans lived as divided persons. He said that the tension of being black and American was a powerful, almost fatal, force that could rip asunder a black soul.

Drugs and guns left Huey Newton, the black revolutionary prince, lying dead on an Oakland sidewalk. The man who spoke of black revolution, whose ten-point Black Panther program revitalized the ghetto, was gunned down over a drug deal. Yet his contributions remain untouched. He opened America's mind to police brutality, protected the black community, provided book knowledge and breakfast to children, and instilled a self-respect and pride that lasts even today. Huey P. Newton is truly one of the great black revolutionaries of our time.

Tyrone Robinson murdered Huey P. Newton, co-founder of the Black Panther Party, on August 22, 1989, on 9th and Center in Oakland, California. He shot Newton three times in the head over a long-standing dispute about drug deals.

≡ Saint Monica: Mother at Prayer

If any woman in history exemplifies the image of a prayerful mother, it is Saint Monica, the mother of the great Saint Augustine of Hippo. Monica's husband, Patricius, was unfaithful and verbally abusive; her eldest son, Augustine, was a wayward sinner most of his life; and her own life was filled with traumas and disappointments. As a faithful Christian, however, this persevering woman called on God through every trial. When life seemed hopeless, Monica never gave up. The more difficult her life became, the more time she spent in prayer.

Monica prayed that God would speak to the heart of her husband and son and also give her strength to continue. Her son abandoned his faith in pursuit of instant gratification; the allures and attractions of the world were too much for him. Even after he settled down, it was not in marriage. Instead, he and his girlfriend lived together for fifteen years, had a son, but never married. Augustine was intrigued with various pagan philosophies, disputed obscure cosmic concepts and argued rhetorical abstractions. He would often visit his mother in Tagaste (modern-day Algeria) and openly ridicule her beloved faith.

Yet Monica persisted. She gently shared her convictions with Augustine and prayed constantly for his salvation. After fifteen years of faithful supplication, Monica's request was answered. Augustine was in Rome, where he heard a sermon by Saint Ambrose. A short while later, he sat in a garden reading the Christian scriptures and tearfully gave his life to God.

Through all the years she had prayed for her son, little did Monica realize that Augustine would later become one of the preeminent theologians in Christian history; his writings on sin, grace and salvation remain cornerstones of the faith.

Saint Monica died in Rome on August 27, 387. Given her North African roots, many artists depict her as a black woman. Although her race is uncertain, new black Catholic parishes in the United States have often been named after her. Of course, if Monica was black, her son, Saint Augustine of Hippo, would also have been of black descent.

≡ Bayard Rustin: "If We Got To, We Got To Go!"

Wherever injustice, racism or war appeared, Bayard Rustin seemed to be there. Rustin spent a lifetime organizing, marching, protesting and fighting for equality, peace and justice. He was raised among Quakers, and their commitment to nonviolence and peace remained with him his entire life. When he went to New York in the 1930s, he saw communists on the front line of every struggle for human dignity and workers rights. Their devotion to justice drew him in, and Rustin became a stalwart member of the Youth Communist League from 1936 to 1941.

Many speculate that Ruskin's identity as a gay male in a time of staunch homophobia heightened his sense of compassion and fairness toward others. In fact, opponents often threatened to discredit him by exposing his gay lifestyle.

When A. Philip Randolph sought to organize the famous 1941 March on Washington, he asked Rustin to work on it. A few months later, Rustin went to California to help protect the private property of interned Japanese Americans. Attracted by the Fellowship of Reconciliation's (FOR) ardent work for peace, Rustin signed on as a member. The FOR, founded in 1915 by Quakers, social gospel ministers and others, was a Christian social reform and peace group often at the forefront of nonviolent protests. As a member of the Fellowship, Rustin was a tireless ambassador for peace and justice.

But Rustin did not just speak of peace; he lived it. In 1943, he was sentenced to a federal penitentiary for refusing to fight in World War II. When he was released, Rustin continued where he had left off. He helped coordinate the 1955 Montgomery bus boycott, shaped the Congress of Racial Equality's (CORE) activism, met Gandhi in India and Nkrumah in Africa, and was constantly on the front lines of justice. Rustin's devotion to peace and justice culminated at the age of fifty-three when he became one of the primary organizers of the 1963 Civil Rights March on Washington.

For this unceasing activist, whose primary vocation was community organizing and political work that paid twenty-five dollars per week, life was never easy. He was arrested on twenty-three separate occasions, and in the South he was often beaten and stomped. Nevertheless, Rustin never quit. Once during a march in Alabama, a burly white sheriff threatened him with arrest and jail. Rustin responded, "If we got to go, we got to go." That simple proclamation was the foundation of his life: He did whatever was necessary to fight racism, war and inequality.

Peace activist and Civil Rights Movement organizer Bayard Rustin died in New York on August 24, 1987. He worked with the Youth Communist League (YCL), the Fellowship of Reconciliation (FOR), the Congress of Racial Equality (CORE), and was one of the primary organizers of the 1963 Civil Rights March on Washington, D.C.

☰ The Brotherhood of Sleeping Car Porters
Birthplace of Black Activism

Luxury trains cruised effortlessly across the American landscape, and travelers basked in the comfort of first-class rail travel. The sleeper cars were especially desirable: good food, good wine and good service awaited those with money. Train travel offered a great trip—unless you were a Pullman porter.

In many respects, these porters were uniformed slaves. They were expected to serve, polish, clean, carry and smile their way into the good favor of white travelers. The vast majority of the porters were black, and they earned far less than their white peers. Pullman porters lived in almost inhuman conditions. To make the trip pleasant for others, they lived like animals. They worked fifteen to twenty hours a day and curled themselves into the smoking room of the men's bathroom for their three-hour allotted nap. For four hundred hours of work per month, these porters received $67.50.

Despite these harsh conditions, Pullman porters had status in the black community. They traveled across the country transmitting news from place to place, and they were the foundation of a black professional class. Black college graduates rejected by other employers became Pullman porters. When porter Theodore Welden died in a rail accident, his body was identified when the police found his Dartmouth College "Class of 1922" pen in his vest.

In 1925, black socialist A. Philip Randolph and his partner, Chandler Owen, met secretly with several porters in Harlem to consider what they could do to get the Pullman corporate giant to hear their requests for decent treatment. Though blacks were generally suspicious of organized labor, they decided to form a union—with a difference. Instead of the usual racist union leadership, this would be an organization of porters representing themselves. They decided to call themselves The Brotherhood of Sleeping Car Porters and elected Randolph as their president.

Organizing the porters was difficult because Pullman officials transferred, demoted or fired anyone they suspected of unionism. Still, under the courageous leadership of Randolph and others, the Brotherhood grew from a few hundred in 1925 to several thousand. More importantly, by 1934, after nine years of negotiations, conflict and struggle, the Pullman Company was forced to recognize the Brotherhood.

The significance of the Brotherhood extends beyond wages and working conditions for porters. The Brotherhood of Sleeping Car Porters is the birthplace of black activism. Out of the bosom of the Brotherhood arose Randolph's dream of the proposed 1941 March on Washington, which, though called off, gave inspiration to the famous 1963 March on Washington. When Rosa Parks was arrested for refusing to move to the back of the bus, Brotherhood member E.D. Nixon helped organize the Montgomery bus boycotts. Oakland Brotherhood leader C.L. Dellums preceded future radical congressman Ron Dellums. Today's black gains are yesterday's struggles of The Brotherhood of Sleeping Car Porters.

A. Philip Randolph, Chandler Owen and others created The Brotherhood of Sleeping Car Porters on August 25, 1925, at St. Luke's Hall in Harlem. It was the first labor union organized and led by blacks in the United States.

The Basilica of the National Shrine of the Immaculate Conception in Washington, D.C., is a powerful tribute to the Blessed Virgin Mary. It houses beautiful chapels dedicated to Our Lady of Perpetual Help, Our Lady of Mount Carmel, Our Lady of Guadalupe and other manifestations of the Mother of God. One of the most recent additions to the shrine is Our Mother of Africa. This beautiful chapel plunges the spectator into what the Catholic Church calls a "sacred conversation."

Three sculptures in the chapel speak of the divine drama of African-American life. The bronze sculpture of Mary, the Mother of Africa, is holding the Christ Child and looking straight ahead. She peers directly at a sculptural representation of African-American history from the darkness of slavery to a future hope. The figures march forward under the watchful gaze of the Mother of Africa. Between the Mother of Africa and the drama of black history is the crucified Christ. The woodcarving of Jesus' death is a vivid reminder that Christ is in the midst of black suffering.

As visitors meditate in Our Mother of Africa Chapel, God's presence is almost palpable. Mary and the Christ Child reach forward, as if to touch black people trudging forward from darkness into the light. In the center stands Christ crucified, demonstrating that no human pain is beyond God's love. As visitors gaze at the Mother of Africa, then toward the black struggle, and then back to the center at the Christ on the cross, they are engaged in a sacred conversation. The inescapable message is that God, Christ and the Mother of Africa are in the midst of the pain, trauma and anguish of black life. The Mother of Africa watches over her children, Christ feels our pain in his cross, and in the midst of all is God, bringing life and light out of despair and darkness. Every visitor to Our Mother of Africa Chapel becomes part of this conversation with God.

On August 30, 1997, 3,000 members of the National Black Catholic Congress dedicated Our Mother of Africa Chapel at the Basilica of the National Shrine of the Immaculate Conception. Since the chapel's dedication, thousands have come every year for a sacred conversation with God.

≡ W.E.B. DuBois: Black Genius

The vast expanse of W.E.B. DuBois' life contains traces of every black political impulse. There is no strategy in African-American liberation that DuBois has not shaped, informed or enhanced. As the great Cornel West wrote, "The scope of his interests, the depth of his insights, and the sheer majesty of his prolific writings bespeak a level of genius unequaled among black intellectuals." DuBois' life is, in fact, a black American memoir. He was born six years after the end of slavery and died on the eve of the 1963 March on Washington. When DuBois was born, Frederick Douglass worked for equality; when he died, Martin Luther King, Jr., proclaimed his dream.

The writings, teachings and organizings of W.E.B. DuBois focused on but one thing: the liberation of black folk. His books were not recitations of dry history; they were brilliant analyses of the past intended to inspire activism. *Black Reconstruction*; *The Souls of Black Folk*; *Suppression of the African Slave Trade*; *The Philadelphia Negro*; *The Negro, Color and Democracy*; *The World and Africa*; his works of poetry, sociology, history and prose; his insightful articles in *The Crisis* and elsewhere—all sought the full emancipation of DuBois' people.

As an integrationist, DuBois helped found the National Association for the Advancement of Colored People (NAACP); as a Pan-Africanist, he helped form the Pan-African Congresses; as a socialist and pacifist, he spoke out against monopoly wealth and belligerent foreign policy. Through his immense contributions, W.E.B. DuBois transformed African-America's sense of self, understanding of struggle and collective knowledge of Africa. He is arguably the most significant black activist/scholar to have graced the earth.

Writer and teacher W.E.B. DuBois died in Accra, Ghana, on August 27, 1963. He is widely regarded as one of the most significant black activist/scholars in U.S. history and was the author of the seminal book, **The Souls of Black Folks.**

≣ Umbanda: The Spirits Are with Us

When the sun rises in Brazil, morning breaks with a glory that contrasts with the grim poverty in Rio de Janeiro. At daybreak, followers of the Umbandan faith walk, bike or drive to their churches, known as *centros* or *terrerios*, where they sing, dance, drum and call on the gods to possess their souls. A spiritual counselor sits among them and listens as they talk of their sickness, wayward children, poverty, loneliness, broken promises and shattered dreams. For many Afro-Brazilians living in the *favelas* of Brazil, the Umbanda faith is a source of healing and strength.

Spirits populate Umbandan theology. There are African deities known as *Orixa*, spirits of Brazilian Indians called *cabolcos* and spirits of enslaved "old blacks" called *pretos velhos*. These are not abstract spirits, but spirits who can heal, offer wisdom and advice, and bring good fortune. The *Orixa* combine Yoruban gods with Catholic saints to give black Brazilians Afro-Catholic blessings. The *cabolcos* are respected as proud and courageous for having resisted slavery. The *pretos velhos* lived through the horrors of slavery and therefore are wise enough to help Umbandans survive poverty and oppression. Two popular *pretos velhos* are Father Joaquim and Mother Conga—two "old blacks," whose altar depicts them sitting back with pipes in their hands, dispensing wisdom to their followers.

Life for many in Brazil may be difficult, but when followers of Umbanda attend *terreiro*, their lives are transformed. Their road is straightened and their burden is lighter, aided by the wisdom of slavery's survivors, Indian warriors and African gods.

Twenty million Brazilians follow the Umbandan faith, which combines African religion, Roman Catholicism and European spiritism.

≣ Benjamin J. Davis: Black Red

Benjamin Davis was born in Dawson, Georgia, a descendent of ten generations of enslaved ancestors. His father, Ben Davis, Sr., was a proud black man who never buckled to racism and Jim Crow laws. He edited a black independent newspaper, opened his home to debt-ridden sharecroppers and resisted segregation whenever it raised its ugly features.

Young Ben Davis watched closely and learned from his father. After Davis, Jr., graduated from Morehouse and earned a Harvard University law degree, he sought to open a practice to help blacks achieve civil equality in Atlanta, Georgia. Although Davis had always been impressed with his father's courage, he did not believe that bravery alone was enough. As he wrote in his book, *Communist Councilman from Harlem*, he saw his father struggle for fifty years without ever realizing his dream. Unlike his father, whom he deeply respected and loved, Davis, Jr., was not going to spend his days fighting without results.

When black communist Angelo Herndon was arrested in 1932 for "inciting insurrection," Davis offered to represent him. Herndon's "crime" against America had been leading black and white workers in a march against unemployment in Atlanta. The charge, if upheld, could lead to the electric chair.

Davis' encounter with Herndon and the Communist Party changed his life. In Herndon and his colleagues, Davis saw a solution to the problem of poverty. Despite overwhelming odds, Party members never wavered in their work with the poor. At the trial's conclusion, Ben Davis decided to join them. He immediately wrote his father that he had found the answer to inequality and injustice. For Davis, Jr., class struggle explained it all: racism, Jim Crow, imperialism and war. He devoted himself to social change, working toward a socialist society where all would contribute to the common good and, out of the common good, would receive the basics of life.

The great A. Philip Randolph often asked Ben Davis why he added the handicap of being "Red" to the inescapable burden of being Negro. Davis replied that being Black and Red was a benefit, not a handicap. Blackness gave him anger against oppression, and Marxism provided the organization and theory necessary for the struggle. Like Angelo Herndon before him, Davis, too, was later prosecuted and jailed for "advocating revolution"—a revolution where peace, equality and unity replaced racism, poverty and war.

Attorney and civil rights advocate Ben Davis died on August 22, 1964. He explained his belief in communism in his book **Communist Councilman from Harlem.**

≣ Boukman and the Haitian Revolution
"Listen to the Voice of Liberty"

AUG 30

On August 22, 1791, a tropical storm brought ominous clouds over Haiti. The tension and violence of that slave island were mirrored in the skies above. Fierce winds, heavy rain, booming thunder and crackling lightning created a stunning spectacle. For Boukman and the slaves of Haiti, the storm was God's sign to strike for liberty. Boukman was a *Papaloi*, or Voodoo High Priest, whose physical height and spiritual practices made him a giant in the eyes of the slaves.

Black historian C.L.R. James wrote that such religious devotion was crucial to the Haitian revolution: "The rising was…a thoroughly prepared and organized mass movement…. Voodoo was the medium of the conspiracy." Boukman secretly organized slaves across the island, using religious gatherings as a cover for their plans. In spite of strict prohibitions, slaves would travel miles to sing, dance and pray, and few white masters knew that their prayers, chants and sermons contained the seeds of uprising. Yet the slaves' faith was not merely a cover; it was their inspiration and strength. On the night of the great storm, Boukman told the slaves gathered around him:

> Our God, though hidden in the clouds, he watches us. Our God who is good to us orders us to throw away the symbol of the god of the whites who has often caused us to weep and to listen to the voice of liberty that speaks in the heart of all.

That night was the beginning of a long struggle for freedom from slavery, and from France. The preaching and prophecy of Boukman ultimately culminated in the establishment of the Republic of Haiti in 1804. It was a remarkable movement: A group of illiterate slaves stood up to fight one of the great European powers. It was not an easy struggle. The overthrow of slavery's violence came with its own violence. Yet Boukman's faith in the God who heard their cries, who cared for them and who stood with them in struggle was at the heart of their revolution. For Boukman, faith in God and love for freedom were one and the same. His God, "though hidden in the clouds," still empowered their fight for liberty.

On August 22, 1791, Boukman and several other Haitian slaves began the Haitian revolution. Dessalines, Toussaint L'Overture, Boukman and many others would continue this fight for the next twelve years.

AUG 31   ≣ Trinidad: The Holy Trinity

Christopher Columbus gazed at the three mountains towering over the bay, and the three pillars reminded him of the Father, Son and Holy Ghost—the Holy Trinity. It was 1498, Columbus' third trip to this exotic and new world. He called the land, "*La Isla de la Trinidad,*" Spanish for "The Island of the Holy Trinity." The Spanish invader was unaware that he had stumbled upon a place that would later produce African-influenced culture and intellectuals who would transform the world.

Since Columbus' intrusion upon the Carib and Arawak peoples, Trinidad has hosted a vibrant culture influenced by Africa, India and Europe. Two hundred years after Columbus, other "adventurers" brought black people from West Africa to work the cacao plantations. This was the origin of a black population that grew from 310 in 1783 to 505,000 today.

Despite its small size, black Trinidad transformed the Western hemisphere. Calypso music and steel bands now grace the landscapes of America and Europe, and brilliant thinkers have emerged from that island nation. C.L.R. James, Pan-Africanist George Padmore and political leader Eric Williams are all from Trinidad. Few nations of Trinidad's size have produced such richness of intellectual thought and social activism.

Located ten miles off the coast of Venezuela, Trinidad has an unmistakable African imprint. Dragged across the ocean in chains, African people threw off the yoke of slavery, freed themselves from English colonialism and fought for constitutional reforms on the island of "The Holy Trinity." Movements such as the Trinidadian Workingmen's Association, the Trinidad Labour Party, the People's National Movement and the National Alliance for Reconstruction Party all worked for democracy, equal rights and justice. Trinidadians who immigrate elsewhere bring an African dignity born of a tradition of struggle. Long live Trinidad and their beautiful children of Africa.

Trinidad achieved independence from England on August 31, 1962. The nation now boasts one of the most diverse populations in the Caribbean, with descendants of the original Carib peoples joined with descendants of and influences from East India, Africa, France, Spain, China and the Middle East.

SEPTEMBER

Daisy Lee Bates

"Amen! Tell it! Uhh huh. Speak the Word!" Every Sunday black Christian preachers straddle the pulpit in cathedrals, churches and storefronts across America to proclaim the good news of salvation. Men and women with Ph.D.s and those with "No-D's"; full-time ministers and part-time pastors who also work full-time as janitors, construction workers, postal workers, teachers and bus drivers—black preachers bring the Bible to life.

The black preacher is a unique creation of Africans in America. Guttural cries, eloquent rhythms, sing-song climaxes, sweating foreheads and swaying congregations mark their sermons. They are the messengers of hope, the conduits of redemption for millions of believers. They are the answer to the New Testament question, "How shall they hear, without a preacher?" (Romans 10:14, KJV). Whether hidden away in the swamps where slaves gathered, standing defiantly in abolitionist meetings, shouting in ghetto storefronts, or elucidating the word in America's most prestigious chapels, they are the bearers of good news to the people.

Black preachers often speak of a compelling desire to preach, a burning deep within that cannot be contained. Their zeal calls to mind Jeremiah, the Hebrew prophet who lamented, "If I say, 'I will not mention him, or speak any more in his name,' then within me there is something like a burning fire shut up in my bones; I am weary holding it in, and I cannot" (Jeremiah 20:9).

Black preachers do not speak for themselves; they always bring forth the Word of God, deep from their souls Like Jeremiah, they must speak, they must preach, for the word is a "fire burning" in their hearts, a fire that blazes forth Sunday after Sunday, inspiring black Christians all over the world.

Look at the list of some of the black Christian preachers who have delivered the word: Martin Luther King, Jr., Rev. C.L. Franklin, Rev. James Forbes, Bishop Absalom Jones, Rev. Henry Highland Garnet, Dr. Howard Thurman, Rev. Gardner C. Taylor, Rev. Jeremiah Wright, Rev. Vashti Murphy McKenzie, Rev. Dr. Renita J. Weems, Rev. Calvin Butts and many other men and women who continue to bring life to their congregations. Sociologists and historians note the black preacher may well be the single most significant figure in U.S. black history. They held the community together during slavery, called for moderation during a time when overt resistance meant death, supported abolition and the Underground Railroad, initiated the Civil Rights Movement and now are leaders in the black community's fight against drugs, violence and the spread of AIDS. Today, black Christian preachers speak the word of life and work for salvation throughout the U.S. and indeed the world.

Every Sunday, black Christian preachers of all denominations—Catholic, Episcopal, Pentecostal, United Church of Christ, Baptist, Methodist, AME, AME Zion, Holiness, Presbyterian, Disciples of Christ and many others—preach the word as faithful servants of God.

≣ Reverend Peter Williams Cassey: Man with a Mission

In the mid-1800s, many Americans moved west for land, fame or fortune. It was no different for black folks. Many migrated to the Bay Area surrounding San Francisco, searching for a better life after slavery. One in particular, Peter Williams Cassey, believed that God had called him to help his people adjust to this new life. Cassey was ordained an Episcopal minister at Trinity Church of San Jose, California.

As Rev. Cassey listened carefully to the woes of his parishioners, he soon realized that parents had no place to educate their children. The school district refused admission to nonwhites, so black parents were forced to leave their children to the streets while they searched for work. Cassey took action: He solicited donations, built a schoolhouse, recruited teachers and created the St. Phillip's Mission School for Negroes. At St. Phillip's, black children uprooted from the South and East learned math, reading and writing. They also learned about Jesus Christ, the Holy Scriptures and Christian living. The newly arrived migrants were overjoyed, for they knew their children would be cared for, educated and prepared for life in the world. In 1868, the school gave birth to the St. Phillip's Mission, the first Episcopal Church for African Americans in the Bay Area. A few months later, Rev. Cassey and his parishioners started a Sunday school at St. Phillip's Mission.

Cassey's vision for a ministry started in a schoolhouse, grew into a church school and eventually became a full-service parish. Years later, when San Francisco's black Episcopalians were looking for a church home, Rev. Cassey helped them found St. Cyprian's Mission and Christ Mission. Even today, black Episcopalians in the Bay Area are indebted to Peter Williams Cassey for their religious roots and fundamentals of faith.

Rev. Peter Williams Cassey was ordained at Trinity Church in San Jose, California, in September 1862. His ordination was the beginning of a magnificent ministry among Bay Area black people.

≣ Private Spottswood Rice: "Don't Be Uneasy, My Children"

Spottswood Rice had an agonizing choice: If he ran away from the plantation, he would be leaving his children in slavery's clutches; but if he stayed, he and his family would be in bondage forever. If he stayed, he and his children would die as slaves; if he escaped, someday he could return for them.

Spottswood Rice chose escape. With tears in his eyes and an ache in his heart, he ran away from the plantation in Missouri, thinking of his beloved children. Though they were his, they were owned by someone else.

In February of 1864, Rice joined the U.S. Colored Troops in Glasgow, Missouri, and became Private Spottswood Rice. In the fall, he learned that his regiment was headed for his former master's county. Private Spottswood Rice sat next to the dim kerosene lamp and began to write, with his own idiosyncratic grammar, spelling and punctuation:

> My Children, I take my pen in hand to rite you A few lines to let you know that I have not forgot you and that I want to see you as bad as ever. Don't be uneasy my children, I expect to have you. Be assured that I will have you if it cost me my life.

Rice also wrote his children about the mistress of the plantation:

> As for her cristianitty, I expect the Devil has such in hell.

Then he addressed another letter to this very same mistress:

> The longor You keep my My Children from Me, the longor you will have to burn in hell and the Qwicer Youll Get Their.

Rice signed his name to both letters and mailed them off to the plantation. He then gathered up his rifle and his gear, and marched forward with his regiment. History does not record whether Private Spottswood Rice and his children were ever reunited. We do not know if his agonizing search was in vain. We do know, however, that Spottswood Rice was, above all, a devoted and loving black father.

Private Spottswood Rice, a member of the U.S. Colored Troops in Missouri, wrote letters to his children and to the plantation mistress who held them in slavery before embarking on his regiment's mission in Missouri on September 3, 1864. His intention was to free his children from bondage. We do not know whether or not he succeeded.

SEP 4 ☰ James Alexander Spencer: Standing as Equals

Ever since he was a child, James Alexander Spencer had believed the Catholic Church's teachings. He believed in Jesus Christ, the resurrection, the power of the Mother of God, the sacraments, the presence of Christ in the Eucharist and the communion of saints. Spencer was born a free black during slavery in South Carolina, and the racism he encountered did not diminish his faith in God or the Roman Catholic Church. In fact, whenever Spencer read pronouncements from Rome, his faith in the church was renewed, because the words from the Vatican underscored what he already read in the Bible: that, despite persistent discrimination, God created all men and women equal. Whenever Spencer took the Eucharist, his faith in the equality of humanity was restored by the words of the ritual: "Take this all of you, and eat, this is my body, broken for you." If Christ had given himself for all, then Spencer knew he was precious in the sight of God.

Spencer became a schoolteacher and Reconstruction legislator in Charleston, South Carolina. When Reconstruction was overturned and black hopes were crushed, he looked to the church. While the federal government and the white South might betray black aspirations, he expected more from his church. America might not live up to her Declaration of Independence and Constitution, but he counted on his church to live up to Christ. Spencer's devotion to the Catholic faith made him a leader in the famous Black Catholic Congress movement.

As one of the black Catholic elders, James Alexander Spencer presided over the Fourth Congress held in Chicago in 1893. This was a significant Congress; speakers and resolutions were calling for dramatic changes in the church, demanding a greater role for blacks in the American Catholic Church.

One of Spencer's peers described him as "one of the advanced civil rights men...who wants all: blacks and whites, to stand on equal footing, at least in the churches, if it cannot be done anywhere else." This was the faith of James Alexander Spencer. This was the faith that catapulted him above disappointment and led him to preside over the Fourth Black Congress. He believed with all his heart, soul, mind and strength that God created everyone as equals and that, even if no one else in the world was behaving that way, the church of Christ must.

James Alexander Spencer, a black Catholic layman from Charleston, South Carolina, presided over the Fourth Black Catholic Congress from September 4-9, 1893, in Chicago, Illinois. He was a leader in calling upon the American Catholic Church to support desegregation and promote justice for all people.

SEP 5   ≡ **Black Women: A Mother's Commitment**

Sometimes it is hard to fathom the sheer determination of the common folk in the Civil Rights Movement. It is difficult to comprehend how men and women ignored death threats, endured beatings and pushed on in the face of pervasive and arbitrary violence. We cannot imagine the extent of the risks and sacrifices made by people in struggle. What was the source of their capacity to risk their own safety, security and life for the cause?

Anne Moody, a Congress of Racial Equality (CORE) worker in Mississippi, once explained why she devoted herself to the fight for equality:

My whole childhood came to life again. I thought of how my mother suffered with us when we had been deserted by our father; how she labored as a field hand every day but Sunday.

For Anne Moody, the Civil Rights Movement was a memorial to her mother, a way to honor her and create a world where her children's children would not suffer. And Moody was not alone; many other African-American women honored their mothers in their commitment to the Movement. Sallie Mae Hadnot of the NAACP once wrote:

> My mother cooked white people's food but ate only the soup, and dragged herself out of bed to work at a local cafe.... She later scrubbed for a white woman who worked her so hard that she always came home griping about backaches.

The memory of her mother's anguish fueled Hadnot's commitment to equality. In Tennessee, Georgia Mae Turner once told an interviewer:

> My mother did all she could, making dresses out of cotton sacks and picking cotton in those raggedy pieces of shoes.

For these women and countless others, the image of their mothers slaving in cotton fields, silently enduring humiliation as maids and nannies, working from dawn until night, energized their struggle for freedom. They were not working for abstract justice; they were fighting so their sisters, daughters and granddaughters would not have to endure the same indignities as their mothers had done.

No statistics or numbers exist for how many black women have participated in the Civil Rights Movement. Many acknowledge, however, that women have been the backbone of the struggle. Without doubt, many were inspired by the courage and quiet dignity of their mothers.

SEP 6 ≡ **Dorothy Dandridge: Black Star**

Dorothy Dandridge loved the stage. Even as young girls, she and her sister—"The Wonder Kids"—sang, danced and acted in local performances. Dandridge carried her theatrical passion into adulthood. Her thespian talents catapulted her to heights seldom attained by black actresses. In 1954, she won an Academy Award for Best Actress for her performance in the classic *Carmen Jones*. Three years later, she starred in the powerful story of self-loathing and romance, *Island in the Sun*. Shortly thereafter, Dandridge took home a Golden Globe Award for her role in *Porgy and Bess*.

Talent enabled Dorothy a luxury few black actors and actresses could afford: the ability to reject the demeaning roles commonly relegated to hungry black actors. Further, she pushed for integrated seating in previously white clubs when she performed. Many clubs set new attendance records when Dandridge performed, and because of her popularity club owners often had to accommodate her demand to admit both white and black customers.

For her excellence on stage, her uplift of black roles and her advancement of integration, Dorothy Dandridge is indeed the quintessential Black Star.

Academy Award-winning actress Dorothy Dandridge died on September 8, 1965, in Hollywood, California, after taking an overdose of Tofranil, an anti-depressant. During her illustrious career, she demanded that places where she performed provide integrated seating for blacks and whites.

SEP 7   ≡ Holy Family Society: "Here, We Are All Free"

A fictitious letter that might have been written by a member of the Holy Family Society of St. Peter's Cathedral in Baltimore, Maryland, in the 1840s:

Sunday, 7 p.m., and its meetin' time again. Every Sunday without fail, I gather with over one hundred other black Catholics here in the basement of Calvert Hall. This dingy little place is part of the massive St. Peter's Cathedral, the biggest Catholic Church in Baltimore. I've been coming to the meetin' for two years, and I love it. Me and a whole group of black Catholics met during Advent, two years ago. It was 1843, I believe. We decided us black Catholics needed a place to pray to Jesus in our own way. Father Hickey was a big help to us. He usually is the only white person present and often preaches us a sermon.

At our second meetin', we decided to call ourselves the Holy Family Society. I remember that first meetin' like it was yesterday. We were so excited to be taking matters in our own hands. The cruel white world out there treats us so bad, but in here we are our own masters. Some of us are slave, some are free, but in the Holy Family Society, we are all free.

At the third meetin', we elected John Noel from Haiti as president and Mary Holland as first counselor. I voted for both of them, as they are hardworking, good Catholic people. Our service is longer than the white folks' Mass. We sing several songs, pray a lot longer and usually are here for about two hours. Everybody pays dues of about six cents a month. From that money we take care of our poor, and last year we started a lending library. You can't imagine how excited we were when we purchased our first books. White folks may discourage us from learning, but here we can learn and read on our own.

Sometimes the priest, that Father Hickey, does a whole Mass with the Eucharist and everything. Then when we take the body of Christ into our bodies, we know that we are special. White folks can call us names and put us down, but we know that Christ lives inside us.

Like I said, I love this meetin'. No matter what happens to me during the week, I know I can walk down these steps to this basement and feel like a human being. I can sing, pray, hear God's Word and be with people who know how I feel. Here, more than anywhere else on this earth, I know God loves me, God is with me and God welcomes me into the kingdom.

The meetin' is about to start. I've got to go now. Pray for me.

On September 7, 1854, the Holy Family Society of St. Peter's Cathedral in Baltimore, Maryland, met for the last time in the parish hall. The Society was one of the first associations of lay black Catholics in the United States.

SEP 8   ≣ **Cheik Anta Diop: The Glory of African People**

Cheik Anta Diop of Senegal, West Africa, helped destroy the myth of black inferiority with force of will and utter genius. For centuries, white academicians had justified and buttressed white superiority, arguing that Africa was populated by subhumans incapable of creating culture or value. They believed that black people deserved to be slaves, servants, janitors, butlers, shoeshine boys and maids because nothing in their history indicated otherwise. And they taught that everything African with merit was of Greek, Asian or other non-African origin. Egypt was a classic case in point. Scholars contended that the magnificent Egyptian culture, with its religions, pyramids, social structure and dynasties, was a Euro-centric civilization.

Then Cheik Anta Diop stepped onto the stage. In works such as *The African Origin of Civilization: Myth or Reality; Civilization or Barbarism: An Authentic Anthropology* and *Precolonial Black Africa*, he dropped bombshells on the academic world. Diop argued that Egypt and other Nile Valley civilizations were created by black Africans. Even more startling, Diop argued that black Africans were, in fact, humanity's primary guide on the road to civilization, that the culture of black Egypt served as the basis for the later European civilizations. This revelation was startling. If Eyptian black people had built the Sphinx and developed advanced theories on medicine, astronomy, hygiene, mathematics and religion, then racism was permanently undermined.

Black historian John Henrik Clarke recounts a story where Diop attended an international symposium on Egyptology. White anthropologists and historians salivated at the chance to debunk Diop's heresy. But, one-by-one, Diop drew upon his impeccable historical sources to destroy their assaults on his theory. By the end of the conference, the white academics were forced to admit, reluctantly, that Africa was home to a multitude of cultural advancements.

The logical conclusion, Diop taught, was that if blacks have produced civilization and culture, then they cannot accept second-class and degrading circumstances. Cheik Anta Diop's theories provided the self-respect and communal solidarity necessary to fuel future black liberation movements and human rights struggles in both America and Africa.

In September of 1956, Cheik Anta Diop attended the First International Congress of Black Writers and Artists at the Sorbonne in Paris, France. The Senegalese scholar held the audience spellbound when he pronounced, "While pursuing this research, we have come to discover that the ancient Paraonic Egyptian civilization was undoubtedly a Negro civilization."

SEP 9   ≡ Paul Cuffee: The Traveler

Paul Cuffee's story is one of determination and triumph. In the late 1700s, his father, Kofi, who had been renamed Cuffee by his slave master, was able to purchase liberty for his children. Young Paul Cuffee grew up in maritime Massachusetts and quickly learned that most of the jobs and much of the wealth of the world came from the ocean. Cuffee taught himself mathematics and navigation, and soon secured work on the high seas. He worked harder and learned faster than all his peers. Rising through the ranks of maritime duties, Paul Cuffee became a capable sea hand, then a captain.

After several years of work, Cuffee did the unbelievable in 1800: He started his own shipping line. Long before Marcus Garvey, the Nation of Islam and the Black Power Movement, Paul Cuffee's crews were exclusively black. He helped many black boys learn the dangerous, yet prosperous, shipping industry. Both his fleet and his wealth grew, but Cuffee did more for his race than provide a few jobs.

Despite his wealth, Cuffee continued to experience racism as if he were still a slave or an uneducated black domestic. Further, after years of abolitionist work, he was convinced America would never end slavery. By 1810, Cuffee was certain that black salvation lie in emigration to Africa. On January 11, 1811, he set sail to West Africa to build a home for ex-slaves.

His ship, appropriately named *The Traveler*, made its first successful voyage to Africa. A few years later, Cuffee made a second voyage, this time with thirty-four African Americans to settle in Sierra Leone. Though Paul Cuffee died before he could organize mass resettlement of blacks in Africa, he was a forerunner of black emigration from the United States. Not only did he advocate a return to Africa, but he also possessed the means to make it happen. For Cuffee, "Back to Africa" was not an abstract theory; he built and sailed the ships to make the journey. Many consider Paul Cuffee "the father of black nationalism."

Black shipping magnate Paul Cuffee died on September 9, 1817, in Westport, Massachusetts, and was buried in a Quaker cemetery. Attracted by the abolitionist fervor of the Quakers, he had become a Quaker in 1808 and funded construction of their Westport Meeting House. He transported the first African Americans back to Africa in the early 1800s and is considered by many to be "the father of black nationalism."

SEP 10 ≣ Reverend Alexander Crummell: Knowledge and Duty

Theologian; activist; scholar; missionary; intellectual; ordained Episcopal priest; founder of schools in Africa; pastor of black churches in New York and Washington, D.C.; author; leader; preacher—Alexander Crummell was all of these. It seemed there was no path to racial uplift he did not travel.

The two pillars of Crummell's life were education and good deeds. An early event in his life galvanized his uncompromising zeal for education. In 1835, Crummell, along with future militant preacher Henry Highland Garnet and their friend Thomas J. Sidney were to attend Noyes Academy, an abolitionist school in Canaan, New Hampshire. However, before they could begin classes, three hundred whites attacked the school, tied oxen to the building and urged the beasts forward to bring the structure down.

Crummell left Canaan—ironically, the Old Testament name for the Promised Land—to attend school elsewhere. Rather than give up, however, he reasoned rightly that if whites were so opposed to black learning then education must be the key to racial equality. He committed himself not only to learning but also to expressing his knowledge in good works for his race.

Such was his motivation for founding a school for Africans at Cape Palmas, Liberia, for teaching at Monrovia's Liberia College and for creating the American Negro Academy in the United States. A forerunner of black nationalist thought, Crummell linked the struggle for equality in America to the fight against colonialism in Africa. He saw the struggle on both sides of the ocean as one and the same, and he moved across the Atlantic with ease.

There was also a spiritual foundation in Crummell's commitment to his work. For him, Christian salvation meant more than accepting Christ; it meant action. It meant feeding the hungry, clothing the naked and bringing freedom to those in chains. Alexander Crummell was a spiritual giant who shaped the contours of African-American activism for generations to follow.

Theologian and activist Rev. Alexander Crummell died on September 10, 1898, in Red Bank, New Jersey. He helped found and taught at schools in Africa and America and became a forerunner of black nationalist thinkers.

≣ Viola Winters: "I'm Still in There"

Visitors to the home of Viola Winters were greeted with portraits of Dr. Martin Luther King, Jr., and Jesus Christ. Both images told much about her life. Born and raised in Holmes County, Mississippi, Winters was one of the many foot soldiers in the Civil Rights Movement. Her name was never in the papers, but her courage helped topple the walls of segregation. She registered blacks to vote in Holmes County, integrated the railroad station and forced Durant Hospital to drop its policy of requiring a fifty-dollar deposit before admitting black patients.

These acts were not without consequences, for whites in Holmes County took such actions seriously in the 1960s. Viola Winters was once asked if people were ever killed for resisting racism in her county. She replied:

> They sho' were, but I still didn't get afraid. That didn't stop me. I asked the Lord to take care of me and just went on out there. I overcome fear by keep goin'.

Despite lynchings, cross burnings and threats, Mrs. Viola Winters did indeed "keep goin'." She and other activists gathered at the Second Pilgrim Rest Baptist Church for song and sermon, and moved from there to marches and protests. Years later, she said about the struggle:

> It was new…something we never did before, and I'm still in there. I done get to age, but I'se a still strugglin' there til God call me.

Viola Winters looked racism, death and violence in the face, and never flinched in her quest for equality. The portraits of Jesus Christ and Martin Luther King, Jr., must have smiled upon her as she gave of herself so others could live free.

Viola Winters of Holmes County, Mississippi, exemplified the common folk who fought for human rights in the South. Her faith in God gave her courage to do the right thing despite the dangers.

≣ Steven Bantu Biko: Bigger Than Life

Steven Bantu Biko was one of the great heroes of Africa, a man who faced violence with love and oppression with dignity. Outspoken and articulate, Biko worked tirelessly with his fellow black Africans to dismantle apartheid. For Biko, the worst crime of racism was not the passbook, the township or the Security Police; it was the message that blacks were inferior and subhuman. If the outward restrictions of racism vanished, Biko believed blacks would still be shackled by dependency, apathy and self-hate. To counter this internal vulnerability, he created the Black Consciousness Movement to celebrate the humanity and beauty of blackness. He envisioned a black self-confidence independent of white liberalism, unbroken by white supremacy.

A fountain of energy, Biko was one of the founders of the South African Students Organization (SASO), and in 1968 he became its first president. His work in SASO, and later in the Black People's Convention (BPC), led black students and workers to understand that they were responsible for their own freedom. Biko taught that blackness was not a badge of degradation but rather a call to hard work and sacrifice.

Steven Biko's liberation of the black mind was dangerous to the white establishment, and on August 18, 1977, he was detained under Section 6 of South Africa's Terrorism Act. Special Branch agents manacled, tortured and beat him. He lay in his own blood and vomit, naked and handcuffed, and he later died of a fractured skull and other wounds inflicted by his jailors. Biko once wrote:

> In my view the truth lies in my ability to incorporate my vertical relationship with God into the horizontal relationships with my fellow men; in my ability to pursue my ultimate purpose on earth which is to do good.

Steve Biko knew correctly that his cause was bigger than his life. True to his prediction, his murder galvanized the global anti-apartheid movement; the divestment movement flourished and black South Africans resumed their struggle. Special Branch agents could kill Steve Biko, but they merely hastened their own destruction. The South African group, Sweet Honey in the Rock, sings it well in their musical tribute "Biko": No matter what, the powers of the State could not kill the ideas, legacy and spirit of Steven Bantu Biko.

Steven Bantu Biko died of torture inflicted by the South African apartheid government on September 12, 1977, in Port Elizabeth, South Africa. He was 22 years old when he founded the South African Students Organization (SASO). His vision of black self-determination and pride led thousands of black youth into the freedom struggle in South Africa and around the world..

SEP 13   ☰ Tupac Shakur: "Life Goes On"

Years after his premature death, young people across America still nod to the hip-hop sounds of Tupac Shakur. He is regarded as perhaps the ultimate "gangsta' rapper," a poet with the hardest sound and lyrics that blow the cover off hard truths.

Tupac was for many a man who saw clearly what was happening in the world and wanted people to know about it. He lived in a world of poverty, racism and violence uniquely reserved for young African-American males. Despite signs of equality and a rising black middle class, there yet resides a neglected core of young black men with unbelievable incarceration rates, high unemployment, early death through homicide and hypertension, high dropout rates—who have a much different view of America. This was the world Shakur knew and brought to life in his lyrics.

Shakur's mother was Afeni Shakur, one of the "New York 21" (Black Panther Party members accused of conspiring to bomb utilities in New York City in 1971). She served jail time, and when released she soon became addicted to crack. The family was poor and transitory, and some accounts note that by the time Shakur was in high school they had moved twenty times.

Tupac Shakur was a talented poet and writer. As a boy he had performed in neighborhood theater ensembles. In later years he became an avid reader, devouring Thomas Merton, James Baldwin, Maya Angelou and other writers. However, like most of his peers, Shakur learned about his world through his experience. His music is a portal into the world of black urban youth, into eyes that see the truth about American justice, equality and fairness with unrelenting clarity.

Yet, like the Hebrew prophets of the Old Testament, Shakur's exposure to the evil around (and within) him was balanced with songs of hope and struggle. The powerful "Keep Ya Head Up" encouraged and inspired. He also wondered aloud if there was to be a heaven for him and his partners. Perhaps his most powerful work is "So Many Tears," a song with lyrics that go right to the streets, where drugs and guns are more prevalent than education and jobs; right to the pavement, where chalk lines outline the dead bodies. In his classic "Life Goes On," Shakur talks about "niggas" someday coming out on top. In a world where black men are perpetually on the bottom, this was a stunning affirmation of faith.

Tupac Shakur's music and life, in many respects, mirrors the relentless search for dignity and self-respect most black men in America must endure. He not only "told it like it was" but also pointed forward to how it could, and should, be.

Rap artist Tupac Amaru Shakur was murdered when a barrage of bullets riddled his car on a Las Vegas avenue. He died six days later, on September 13, 1996. His lyrics remain among the most powerful in hip-hop and rap music.

SEP 14   ≣ Bishop Desmond Tutu: Transfiguration

In the fall of 1986, Desmond Tutu was installed as the Anglican Archbishop of Cape Town, South Africa. His flock, however, was more than Cape Town: His diocese included South Africa, Lesotho and Namibia. This was not a peaceful time in South Africa—far from it. In June, the apartheid government had instituted a state of emergency that gave broad and arbitrary police powers to security forces. Twenty-five thousand human beings, mostly black South Africans, had died in the political violence.

Apartheid appeared invincible, as the forces of reaction relied increasingly on violence and brutality. The new archbishop's black parishioners were the victims of persistent racism, treated as subhumans and nonentities, and white parishioners were losing their humanity in the process of degrading others. "Coloreds"— those of mixed race—were better off than blacks but worse off than whites.

On September 7, 1986, Tutu stepped into the pulpit at St. George's Cathedral to announce the focus of his ministry. He preached that morning on the Transfiguration of Jesus Christ, an event in which Christ was physically changed before his disciples to show his divine glory. For Desmond Tutu, the Transfiguration was a symbol of the renewal of South Africa. Just as the body of Christ was transformed into a dazzling figure, so too would God's power change South Africa from violent inequity to peaceful solidarity.

Tutu proclaimed from the pulpit, "The principle of transfiguration says nothing, no one and no situation is 'untransfigurable.'" The new bishop would not accept that humanity's sinful actions of racism, inequality, torture, malnourishment and death would have the last word. He preached that God could transform South Africa into something beautiful. He concluded:

We shall be free, all of us, black and white, for it is God's intention. He enlists us to help him to transfigure all the ugliness of this world into the beauty of his kingdom. We shall be free, all of us, because the death and resurrection of Jesus Christ assures us that life has overcome death, light has overcome darkness, love has overcome hate, righteousness has overcome injustice and oppression, goodness has overcome evil, and that compassion and caring, laughter and joy, sharing and peace, reconciliation and forgiveness have overcome their awful counterparts so that in God's kingdom, God is all in all.

Desmond Tutu was installed as the Anglican Archbishop of Cape Town, South Africa, on September 7, 1986, in St. George's Cathedral. He also served as General Secretary of the South African Council of Churches, was a winner of the Nobel Peace Prize, and became the chair of the Truth and Reconciliation Commission in South Africa after the fall of the apartheid regime.

SEPT 15   ≣ **The 16th Street Baptist Church: Not Just Another Sunday**

It was another beautiful September Sunday morning in Birmingham, Alabama, with black folk strolling down boulevards toward their places of worship. The 16th Street Baptist Church was particularly popular among Birmingham's black Christians. Not only famous for its charismatic preaching and inspirational singing, it was also a meeting place for civil rights marchers. Across the street from the church was the Kelly Ingram Park, often the staging area for desegregation marches. Located between downtown and the neighborhoods of black Birmingham, the 16th Street Baptist Church was a visible symbol of black activism.

On the morning of September 15, 1963, black boys and girls streamed down the steps into the church basement for their Sunday school classes. Excited talk of weekend play and frequent laughter filled the hallways. Summer was over, school doors had just opened, and the great Martin Luther King, Jr., had stunned the world with his "I Have a Dream" speech one month earlier. Upstairs, the adults prepared for worship and spoke with hope that the March on Washington might—just might—bring change to America. Maybe white and black could build the equal society America so often claimed it was. Some could hardly contain their optimism, but the old folks warned them not to "count their chickens" yet.

As the adults gathered in the sanctuary upstairs and the children listened to their lessons downstairs, an explosion rocked the building. Smoke and screaming replaced prayers and Bible stories. Broken bodies stumbled through broken glass and burning wood. Suddenly, without warning, an idyllic scene of religious devotion had become a massacre. Deacons, ushers and choir members ran downstairs amid the smoke and confusion to search for their children, nieces, nephews and grandchildren. They found all but four. Rescuers later dragged the lifeless corpses of Denise McNair, Carole Robertson, Cynthia Wesley and Addie Mae Collins from the rubble. A building usually reserved for singing and preaching now reverberated with cries and moans.

These four black girls would never grow into the women God intended them to be, for terrorists had determined they should die. The hope of the March on Washington the previous August was blasted away on the morning of September 15.

Let us never forget Denise, Carole, Cynthia and Addie Mae; may we not rest until the racism that destroyed them is forever crushed.

On September 15, 1963, white terrorists murdered four black teenage girls in the cowardly bombing of the 16th Street Baptist Church in Birmingham, Alabama. The event galvanized the Civil Rights Movement with a new sense of urgency throughout the country.

≣ John W. Bate: "A Gift from Heaven"

Young John W. Bate, a slave since birth, did not know what "freedom" meant. He had sometimes heard quiet talk of freedom, but for a nine-year-old, the word had little meaning. All he knew was that suddenly, after the Civil War, he had to leave his shelter, friends and all that was familiar. Like the four million other slaves freed after the Civil War, the Bate family had no land, education or assets. They were cast alone into their "freedom"—a status worsened by white hostility and violence.

With his mother and siblings, John Bate moved to Louisville, Kentucky, where his mother sought to provide for her family. These hopes were dashed when scarlet fever and smallpox ravaged Goose Alley, where the ex-slaves lived. Mama Bate was left paralyzed, and all her children but John died. In order to survive, he begged for scraps in alleys and backyards to feed himself and his mother.

One afternoon, a white missionary named Kate Gilbert asked John if he would like to come to her classes nearby. John knew nothing of school and told Gilbert no. She persisted, and young John finally agreed. Slowly, John Bate began to see a world beyond Goose Alley. As he learned of foreign lands, big cities, mechanical inventions and social progress, he was captivated and wanted to know more. In a later radio interview he said:

> I had never heard of Christopher Columbus, or Queen Victoria, or people living over in a place called China. It was like discovering a new world. When I found out how men had fought and worked all over the world hundreds of years just to make men free and enjoy life, I was more sure than ever I had to do something like that, too.

Bate later attended Berea College in Kentucky, a school so committed to racial fairness that half the students were black. When he left Berea, he sought to give what he had received. Moving to the small town of Danville, Kentucky, Bate founded a one-room school where ex-slaves learned to thrive in freedom. Day after day, Bate walked to the school, thinking of new ways to challenge and encourage his students. Despite obstacles that would have broken others, he persisted. His one-room school grew into Danville's best high school for blacks, and from 1915 to 1964, hundreds graduated from the Bate School to become teachers, doctors, social workers, professionals and productive citizens. Respectfully called "Professor" by his students, John Bate was a teacher and principal for over fifty years. He once called his education "a gift from heaven," and hundreds of Kentucky families were forever transformed because of his willingness to share that gift.

Former slave John W. Bate, great-grandfather of the author of this book, died on September 8, 1945, in Danville, Kentucky, at the age of eighty-nine. He ran the Bate School in Danville, Kentucky, for almost fifty years.

≣ Margaret Walker: "For My People"

In 1942, Margaret Walker published *For My People*, an extraordinary volume of poetry and only the second to be published by a black woman in the U.S. (The first was Georgia Douglas Johnson's work in 1918.) It was Walker's first book, and in many respects it remains her signature work.

Walker's parents had moved north from Birmingham, Alabama, at the urging of the great poet Langston Hughes. Hughes had seen young Walker's poetry and had been so impressed that he urged them move to where her skills could blossom. When the family relocated, Margaret Walker developed as Hughes had hoped. The poem for which the book *For My People* was named marked a seminal point in Walker's career and became for many the lyrical anthem of black America.

Critic Eugenia Collier wrote:

We knew [that] poem. It was ours.... And as [it] moved on, rhythmically piling image after image of our lives, making us know again the music wrenched from our slave agony, the religious faith, the toil and confusion and hopelessness, the strength to endure in spite of it all, [it] went on mirroring our collective selves and we cried out in deep response.

Collier spoke for all black America when she said the poem was "ours." For many blacks—myself included—the poem crystallizes experiences we've had but could not express. Even as Margaret Walker describes the wounds of racism and poverty, she calls for "a new earth" to rise, for "full of healing." The unmistakable beauty of black life in America pulses in Walker's words.

Poet Margaret Walker died on September 15, 1998, in Jackson, Mississippi. She is the author of* For My People, *only the second volume of poetry published by a black woman in the United States.

≣ Hezekiah Grice: The First Negro Convention

One rainy fall evening of 1830, Hezekiah Grice walked the streets of Baltimore in search of an answer. Though a free black man, Grice was subjected to taunts and jeers, and he was restricted from earning a decent living. He looked around and saw similar mistreatment of blacks everywhere. He had sat quietly through many debates by free blacks and abolitionists in the North. Some believed that America was incorrigible and advocated emigration to Canada or Liberia. The most militant argued for the violent overthrow of southern slavery. Still others were convinced that hard work, thrift and quiet determination would melt away racism.

These ideas churned in Grice's mind. He did not know which was right. Further, even if he had an opinion, it would matter little, for he was merely a black apprentice. He did not have the status of famous preachers, abolitionists or leaders, such as Richard Allen, Nathaniel Paul and others.

Yet that drizzly evening, Grice had an idea. Despite his anonymity, he decided that he would call together the first Negro national convention in America. He would invite black leaders, preachers, abolitionists and writers—anyone concerned for the future of the race. In April of 1830, he sent letters to every black leader he could find. But several weeks passed and nothing happened. He did not hear a word from anyone, and Grice thought his idea was a failure.

Then, a few weeks later, he received a letter from the great Rev. Richard Allen inviting Grice to come to Philadelphia. Allen wanted to implement Grice's plan for a national meeting! From that humble beginning, Allen and Grice began working together to gather leaders for the first Negro Convention in Philadelphia.

On September 15, 1830, black delegates from several northern cities converged to discuss the future of black America. They met at Allen's Mother Bethel Church, an appropriate location since the church was considered both a black refuge and a landmark. The delegates discussed emigration, revolution and separation as possible strategies for black survival. A black newspaper covered the event:

> In looking to the important results that grew out of this Convention, the independence of thought and self-assertion of the black man are the most remarkable.... [These] black brethren in bonds did manfully fight in the days of anti-slavery, which tried men's souls, when to be an Abolitionist was, in large extent, to be a martyr.

The paper rightly noted that those black men who stood up in search of solutions had already risked their lives for their race. But their courage was rewarded ten-fold. That first Negro Convention, born in the mind of a lone a black worker from Baltimore, set the stage for all future organized manifestations of black resistance.

September 15, 1830, Hezekiah Grice, Richard Allen, Austin Steward and many other black leaders gathered at Mother Bethel Church in Philadelphia, Pennsylvania, at the first Negro national convention, where they began a movement for black self-determination that lasts to this day.

SEP 19   ≣ Jimi Hendrix: "Purple Haze"

The haunting rhythms of the blues danced in young Jimi Hendrix's ears. Captivated by those riffs and melodies, little Jimi Hendrix taught himself to play the guitar. At first, he sought to sound like his idols, but later he developed his own unique style. Muddy Waters, B.B. King and other blues masters were his guidepost, but he soon traveled paths beyond the blues. He went to New York as the "Jimmy" in Jimmy James and the Blue Flames, and he was influenced by the folk sounds of Bob Dylan. Hendrix also backed up soul singers such as Wilson "Wicked" Pickett and Sam Cooke.

Like the great tenor sax player John Coltrane, Jimi Hendrix was never content with a singular musical style; he always stretched beyond himself for more. He loved blues, R & B and folk, and he blended those traditions with rock to create an astonishing sound. When Jimi Hendrix took a band called "The Jimi Hendrix Experience" to England, his virtuosity and flamboyance stunned London audiences. Britain's best guitarists came to hear him and left shaking their heads, in awe of an artist they believed was better than anyone on the planet. Trumpet great Miles Davis admired Hendrix, and later in his career infused his jazz sound with rock and pop.

Hendrix, in many respects, shaped the sixties and the music of that turbulent era. In his classic performance at the Monterey Pop Festival, he became a rock mega-star. Hendrix performed magnificently, blowing through "Purple Haze," "Red House" and "Voodoo Child" and ending in a cacophony of blazing electricity. He later formed an all-black rock group, The Band of Gypsies, with Buddy Miles on drums and Billy Cox on bass.

Jimi Hendrix streaked across our earth like a shooting star, quickly gone but burned in our memory forever.

Guitarist Jimi Hendrix died on September 18, 1970, in London, England, of barbiturate intoxication at 27 years old. He was considered by many to be the greatest guitarist of his generation and broke new ground in the fusion of many music genres.

SEP 20   Amy Euphemia Jacques Garvey: "Ethiopian Queens Will Rise Again"

Amy Euphemia Jacques Garvey was much more than "the wife of Marcus Garvey." She had her own dignity, not one conferred by her husband. Garvey was a regular columnist in the Universal Negro Improvement Association's (UNIA) paper, *The Negro World*, and her editorials urged racial pride, economic solidarity and African unity. Garvey was a black nationalist before she ever met Marcus Garvey. She believed that the mental slavery, self-hate and self-destructive behavior among some blacks could be eradicated by devotion to African culture. She considered Africa as not only the home of her race but also the birthplace of humankind, and she believed that Africa's secrets held the solution to injustice and inequality.

In her quest to promote Africa, Amy Garvey was one of the few women delegates to the famous 1945 Pan-African Congress in Manchester, England. Traditionally, nationalist movements have minimized the leadership role of women, but Garvey confronted that propensity for patriarchy. Her participation in the Congress was critical, as she added her wisdom gained by years of work in the black nationalist movement. In 1963, she wrote "Garvey and Garveyism," a summary of the power of the UNIA's commitment to black nationalism. Garvey had been writing, promoting and fighting for black pride and black self-help since the 1920s, and now, forty years later, despite all the efforts toward integration and inclusion, she was still promoting black nationalism.

Her 1925 article, "Be Not Discouraged," sums up Amy Garvey's lifelong dedication to all things black:

> Be not discouraged...but push forward, regardless of the lack of appreciation shown you. A race must be saved; a country must be redeemed.... Africa must be for Africans, and Negroes everywhere must be independent. God being our guide...Ethiopian queens will rise again.

Amy Euphemia Jacques Garvey, wife of black nationalist Marcus Garvey, was an author and leader in her own right. She was a delegate to the 1945 Pan-African Congress in Manchester, England, and wrote many influential articles promoting black nationalism.

SEP 21   ≡ **Ida Ball Robinson: Women in the Pulpit**

The Holy Spirit fell upon Ida Ball Robinson when she was a teenager in Pensacola, Florida. While other young black girls her age were dating, babysitting and studying, Ida was holding prayer meetings in her parents' home. Carrying her tattered Bible everywhere, she talked so much about God's love that many were astonished. But what truly set her apart was her sincere belief that the Holy Spirit lived in her. This conviction fired her zealous prayer life, her evangelistic fervor and her desire to preach.

As an adult, Ida Robinson felt called by God to preach and was selected as pastor of the Mt. Olive Holy Church. This congregation was part of the black Pentecostal United Holy Church, a body that was generally opposed to women in the pulpit. Robinson found little support for her ministry, so she left the United Holy Church in order to "loosen women from the bondage of male domination." In 1924, she founded the Mt. Sinai Holy Church of America, a Pentecostal denomination that believed the Holy Spirit anointed women as preachers.

Within a few years, Robinson's dream of a denomination open to the Holy Spirit's gifts in men and women was growing. She opened eighty-four affiliate churches in Pennsylvania, Florida and as far away as England. Ida Ball Robinson would eventually ordain one hundred and sixty-three ministers, one hundred and twenty-five of whom were women. Her faith in the power of the Holy Spirit enabled her to build a denomination where both men and women could share their gifts from God.

In 1924 in Philadelphia, Pennsylvania, black preacher Ida Ball Robinson founded the first large Pentecostal denomination headed by a woman, the Mt. Sinai Holy Church of America.

≡ The Blues: "What Did I Do, To Be So Black and Blue"

We cannot trace the beginnings of the blues. There is no written musical score, no formal concert, no school or teacher that locates its origin. Somewhere in a southern shack, far from the master, the overseer, the cotton field and the whip, slaves chanted and hollered and groaned away life's pain. Using African rhythms and instruments made from memory, these Africans planted the seeds of the blues. The great Son House once told an interviewer, "In the fields, we made up our songs about things that was happenin' to us at the time, and I think that's where the blues started."

Though slavery ended, black pain did not. Disrespect, violence, Jim Crow laws, sharecropping and racism built a world that magnified human misery; a world where all humans suffered from broken hearts, lost loves and ongoing hardships; a world where black anguish was multiplied. And out of those woes came the sound we call "The Blues." Blues man Charlie Patton called it "a mean, black moan." No book or dissertation could describe the Mississippi Delta or a Chicago tenement as the blues could.

The genius of the blues lies in both the lyrics and the riffs. Through guitars, harmonicas and pianos, black souls poured out their troubles, and their blues connected with their audiences' acquaintance with grief and loss. Who among us cannot identify with some aspect of the blues? Theologian James Cone (*The Spiritual and the Blues*) and Marxist Amiri Baraka (*Blues People*) brilliantly conveyed the power of this original music in their classic books.

The legacy of the blues lives in the artists, the men and women who created the music: Robert Johnson, Leadbelly, Muddy Waters, Lightin' Hopkins, Blind Lemon Jefferson, John Lee Hooker, Robert Nighthawk, Bessie Smith, Koko Taylor, Howlin' Wolf and hundreds of others brought a language, style and presence to the blues that no other musical genre can match. The blues may have roots in Africa, but it is born, shaped and transmitted by the saga of American lives, and it has transformed American music.

Blues music is considered the first authentic black folk art form in America. Further, without the blues there would be no gospel, no jazz, no rock & roll music.

SEP 23 ☰ George Padmore: The Life and Struggles of Negro Toilers

George Padmore had seen the light. From his native Trinidad to the American South and on to Washington, D.C., Padmore had finally found in international communism what he thought was the answer to his people's pain. Since he had left Trinidad in 1924 and come to the United States, Padmore had tried to understand why blacks were poor and exploited. He had seen first hand how the quest for capital accumulation, open markets, high profits and cheap labor fueled white supremacy. He saw how the ruling class used racism as tool of subjugation, repressing people of color, soothing exploited white workers and dividing the working class. When he found the Communist Party in Harlem, he began to understand how the degradation of black peoples—from colonialism and slavery to discrimination and segregation—was rooted in capitalism. He came to believe in a classless society where all would be employed, educated and healthy; where all would contribute equally and receive equally; where there would be no privileged elites or suffering masses.

Once converted to communism, Padmore had the passion of an ardent zealot, seeking to change the entire world. He left the United States, never to return again, and moved to the Soviet Union. In Moscow, his organizational brilliance catapulted him to leadership positions in the international communist movement.

Devoted to black liberation, George Padmore became the Secretary of the International Trade Union Committee of Negro Workers (ITUC-NW). This group was the vanguard of black worker movements everywhere, from Johannesburg to Harlem. Working long days and nights, he could glimpse the dawn of a better future for his people. In his book *The Life and Struggles of Negro Toilers*—a brilliant compendium of information about black workers around the world—Padmore told the story and plight of black workers in the West Indies, America and Africa with facts, statistics and anecdotes.

In 1934, however, things changed. Josef Stalin sought alliances with western colonial powers and consequently sacrificed black liberation on the altar of political expediency. Padmore's ITUC-NW was disbanded, and he was asked to drop his support for anti-colonial movements and black liberation. For George Padmore, race loyalty trumped his love for the Communist Party. Communism was for him a means to an end, and to the extent the Party abandoned his cause he would abandon the Party. Padmore was not a communist because he loved Marx and Stalin; he was a communist because he loved his people and saw in that ideology a means to black self-determination and dignity.

Padmore, however, never stopped working for black elevation. His heart, aim and vocation were forever with the life and struggles of the "Negro toilers." He moved to London where he became a leading organizer of the Pan-African movement. Later he was friend and advisor to Kwame Nkrumah's independent government in Ghana.

International political organizer George Padmore died on September 23, 1959, in London, England. He spent most of his later years in Ghana as Nkrumah's advisor on African Affairs. He wrote The Life and Struggles of Negro Toilers, *a compendium of information on black workers throughout the world.*

SEP 24 ≡ Margaret Murray Washington: "There Are Too Many of Us Down"

Margaret Murray Washington slowly approached the podium at Old Bethel AME Church in Charleston, South Carolina, where black churchwomen had packed the building to hear her speak. Washington may have been the wife of Booker T. Washington, but her fame was due to her own merits as a powerful speaker and perceptive organizer. Margaret Washington was not afraid to speak her mind, and that day was no exception. She got right to the point, no messing around with superfluous accolades and ingratiating comments. She stood upright and began to speak:

> If we wish to help each other, let us not only praise ourselves, let us also criticize. Plain talk will not hurt us. It will lead each woman to study her own condition, that of her own family and that of her neighbor's family.

The audience began to shift uncomfortably, but Washington had only just begun. She proceeded to say that it was not enough for comfortable middle-class black families to bask in their accomplishments. She challenged prosperous black folks to look around and lift up their race:

> We are…too ready to say: Oh well, I keep well, my boys and girls behave themselves, and I have nothing to do with the rest of the race! No…race has ever come up by entirely overlooking its members who are less fortunate…. We cannot do it…. There are too many of us down.

Margaret Washington continued for an hour, urging the crowd to live by an ethic that lifted up the less fortunate members of the race. The audience knew this was not just talk, for they had watched Washington on the frontlines for years, building women's organizations and giving time and money to help others. They had watched her rise to become the first president of the National Federation of Afro-American Women, founded in 1895. They knew she was not shy or retiring but in every place and at all times urged black folk to live virtuous, caring and moral lives. It was not enough to rely on personal success, Margaret Murray Washington would remind her people, because "there are too many of us down."

On September 12, 1898, Margaret Murray Washington, wife of Booker T. Washington, addressed a crowd at the Old Bethel AME Church in Charleston, South Carolina. Her speech later appeared in local newspapers around the country and led to middle-class black women getting more involved in black self-help movements.

SEP 25   ≣ Miles Dewey Davis: "So What"

A portrait of Miles Dewey Davis lounging with his trumpet is one of the more compelling images in black history. It isn't just about the music, though his music is beautiful; it is also about the man. People respond to Miles Davis because he made his own statements in his own way. No matter what era he played, no matter where or with whom, Miles was Miles. He was not always generous; often, in fact, he was ill-tempered and enigmatic. What others thought, how others reacted, whether he was seen as an angry black man or a militant musician, was not important to Davis. Most important to him was being Miles.

This was evident in his musical transformations. Despite success with a particular genre, Davis often moved on to other styles. In the forties and fifties, he was one of the pioneers of bebop. In the late fifties, he startled the jazz world with his classic "Birth of the Cool," a work that inaugurated a new form of jazz. In the sixties, his quintet with Wayne Shorter, Herbie Hancock, Ron Carter and Tony Williams created what was called "modal jazz." This classic quintet went on to record albums considered among the greatest in jazz history.

But Davis was not content to rest on bebop, cool or modal. In 1969, he stunned the jazz world with his extraordinary *Bitches Brew* album, which combined jazz and rock to inaugurate an entirely new paradigm in music. Some fans were elated, others infuriated, but Miles still was Miles.

In the eighties, Davis once again explored new ground. His 1988 recording, *Miles Davis: Live Around the World*, carried popular tunes ("Time After Time") and political causes ("Amandla" and "Tutu") on an electric jazz excursion. Backed by the funky rhythms of young musicians, Davis blew his muted trumpet all around the world.

The lasting legacy of Miles Davis is not so much his musical genius as it is his refusal to rest on his accomplishments. Davis was constantly growing, and the world is better off for it. The whole history of music was transformed because of Miles and bebop, Miles and cool, Miles and fusion. Many would argue that Davis' *Kind of Blue* album was his greatest work. Some would further say that the most popular song on that album, "So What," was also the theme of his life. To his critics, to the disapproving glare of others, to prevailing trends, to self-appointed interpreters of music, Miles Davis would always reply with a resounding, "So what."

Miles Dewey Davis was a profoundly influential jazz musician. His albums, such as **Birth of the Cool, Kind of Blue, In a Silent Way** *and* **Bitches Brew,** *changed the very shape of jazz. He died on September 25, 1991, in Santa Monica, California*

SEP 26   ≣ Alberto de Barros de Assis Boavida: Health Brigades

Alberto de Barrios de Assis Boavida was considered by his contemporaries to be a selfless and heroic militant in the Angolan fight for independence. Angola had been a Portuguese colony for five hundred years, and the subjugation of the Angolan people had become increasingly brutal. The Portuguese dictator Salazar and his secret police tortured, exiled and murdered Angolan citizens with impunity.

Alberto Boavida was one of the few Angolans able to study medicine abroad. He mastered tropical diseases, gynecology and other specialties, and he returned to practice medicine among his people. In 1960, he joined the *Movimento Popular de Libertação de Angola* (MPLA), the Popular Movement for the Liberation of Angola. Portuguese authorities had waged war against the MPLA, and many members had been arrested, exiled or executed. After years of struggle, most of the leadership of MPLA was dead or in hiding. Nevertheless, Boavida risked his medical career to join the MPLA.

Plunging into the cause, Boavida brought healthcare to Angola's poorest peasants. During the MPLA's armed fight for independence, he was one of the first doctors to provide medical care on the battlefront. His most enduring contribution, however, was the creation of Angola's Health Brigades. These formations were so successful that they have been emulated in revolutions around the world. As regions of Angola were liberated from Portuguese rule, Boavida and his Health Brigades immediately set up camp. These brigades taught hygiene, nutrition and preventative care, and conducted mass vaccinations. Boavida trained many of the nurses and auxiliaries who cared for Angola's poor and injured.

Boavida was widely regarded as a talented member of the MPLA, and his love for the people was evident in his demeanor, presence and character. In the liberated zones and within the ranks of the MPLA, he was revered for his contribution. The Health Brigades were a reflection of his sacrifice, and they saved hundreds of Angolan babies, children, soldiers and elderly.

When Portuguese colonialists killed Boavida in 1968, the people of Angola mourned. The revolution continued, however, and so did the Health Brigades—teaching, dispensing, vaccinating and healing.

Dr. Alberto Boavida, founder of Angola's Health Brigades, was killed on September 25, 1968, during a Portuguese helicopter attack on the Movement for the Liberation of Angola base near the river Lueti in Angola.

SEP 27

Daisy Lee Bates: The Little Rock Nine

Violence intruded upon Daisy Bates at a very young age: Just as she was learning to walk and talk, three white men brutally murdered her mother. The drunken gang surrounded Mrs. Bates in the darkness, and when she resisted, they raped her and beat her to death. The outraged black community sought justice from the sheriff and the courts, with Daisy's father leading the protest. Soon, however, rumors spread that if he kept it up, he would be lynched. Just a step ahead of the lynch mob, he cradled his daughter one last time and left town. The family that Daisy Bates' parents had worked a lifetime to build had been destroyed by racism in just a few days.

Friends and family raised Bates, and they somehow instilled in the young girl a self-respect that never faltered. Rather than collapse into a heap of self-pity, Bates overcame cruelty and grew into a courageous and generous woman. The pride she had learned from family and from the wrong inflicted on her parents fueled an unquenchable passion for justice. She was a selfless worker and organizer, and she later became President of the Little Rock NAACP. In 1957, she was catapulted onto the national scene by leading the integration of Central High School. Bates personally escorted the brave "Little Rock Nine" students, as they were called, through a daily gauntlet of hatred, taunts, threats and foul obscenities into the school.

As the angry mobs hounded them, Bates surely recognized this hatred as the same evil that had killed her mother and threatened her father, but she resisted the urge to strike back, to repay the hate with hate. Daisy Bates pushed on, even when the cause seemed hopeless. She kept believing, even when the mobs appeared unrelenting.

The story of Bates' walk into history, grasping the hands of frightened black students, is one of the remarkable tales in black American history. It is long past time we honor the courage and compassion of this brave woman. Daisy Bates overcame her past so that others might walk proudly into the future.

Daisy Bates was an advocate and protector of the Little Rock Nine, nine black students who integrated Central High in Little Rock, Arkansas. In September of 1957, accompanied by Bates, they walked through the doors of Central High amidst virulent threats. Bates recalled the struggle for integration in her book, **The Long Shadow of Little Rock.**

SEP 28   ≣ Bessie Smith: Empress of the Blues

The solid rock upon which all women's blues and jazz vocals rests is the incomparable Bessie Smith. Many consider her to be the greatest of the blues singers of the 1920s. The creativity, energy, freedom and vitality of her music influenced later singers who built upon her legacy.

Smith blazed a way out of no way. At the time she came along in the 1920s, black singers were dismissed and ignored. The twenties marked one of many low points in black history: Lynching was common; unemployment, segregation and race hate were rampant; and white preachers, judges and scholars were proclaiming black inferiority. At the bottom of the heap was the black woman. Since even white women were second-rate citizens, it was obvious that a black woman was the lowest of the low.

Bessie Smith burst from the bottom unafraid and undaunted. Black fans loved her music and her style. She sang the blues with such depth and feeling that audiences could sense their own pain lifted. When she sang "Downhearted Blues," "Jailhouse Blues" or "Nobody Knows When You Are Down and Out," black folk across America heard their pain validated. They were not crazy after all; their aches and sorrows were confronted and comforted in the sounds of Bessie Smith.

Blacks were not her only fans. Remarkably, despite the disdain in which blacks were held at the time, whites flocked to hear her. Historians note that her contract with Columbia Records saved that label from extinction. Unbelievably, her first recording, *Downhearted Blues*, sold 780,000 copies—a remarkable number for the 1920s.

Smith was the consummate proud black artist. When she performed in white clubs, she did not change her mood, demeanor or performance. Blacks loved the way she was herself and refused to bow to critics, white audiences or record companies. She wore the title "Empress of the Blues" with a flair and style that lives on in the music of the many great black women vocalists who followed in her footsteps, including Billie Holiday, Sarah Vaughn and Nancy Wilson.

Blues vocalist Bessie Smith died in an automobile accident on September 26, 1937, in Clarksdale, Mississippi. She was the "Empress of the Blues." Her first recording, **Downhearted Blues,** *sold 780,000 copies in the 1920s.*

SEP 29
≡ Hosea Hudson: "The Water's Deep"

Hosea Hudson was but one of the many black men who eked out a meager existence from the steel mills of Birmingham, Alabama. The Stockham Foundry was a hot, dangerous cauldron where the lives of black workers were expendable when compared with the owner's profits. Hudson and his peers worked harder and longer than their white counterparts, but received far less money and infinitely less dignity. Hudson seethed each time he heard "nigger get this" and "nigger do that," and thought to himself that the Foundry was no different than his grandparents' slave plantation. Company housing fit for cattle, unannounced cuts in pay, mangled and smashed limbs—the life of black steel workers was hell on earth.

Hudson had a rich tenor voice, and he often sang away his troubles in the church quartet on Sundays. Yet the troubles relieved on Sunday would return every Monday. He often thought to himself, "Where is a black man to find some dignity in this world?" In September of 1931, he found an answer. Co-worker Al Murphy invited him to a meeting one evening after work. With sweat and grime covering his body, Hudson and others listened to Murphy outline the program of the Communist Party, explaining, as Hudson later wrote:

> How the Scottsboro case [was] a part of the whole frame-up of the Negro people in the South—Jim Crow, frame-up, lynching—all that was part of the system. So I could understand that all right, how speed-up, the unemployment, and how unemployed people wouldn't be able to buy back what they make.… That was the beginning.… When it come ready to join, I join, that night.

From the time Hosea Hudson joined Alabama's Communist Party that night until his death in 1988, he worked steadfastly for black rights. Though he lacked formal education or financial wealth, Hudson nevertheless sacrificed what little he owned for equality and justice. He became the President of Steel Workers Local 2815, a leader in the Right to Vote Club and the Vice-President of the Alabama Political Education Association.

For Hosea Hudson, the Communist Party was the vehicle through which he could express his passion for justice. The Party gave him what the Christian church could not: the ability to fight for his dignity as a human being. He understood that the call to build a just society was no shallow gesture, that it required courage and discipline few could match. He once wrote, "When I started in, it's like you got water a foot deep here, and you don't know way out yonder the water's deep."

Hosea Hudson, illiterate black steelworker, became a fearless leader in the Communist Party in Alabama. Threats, lynch mobs, arrests, corporate goon squads and racist labor leaders could not deter his quest for human dignity. Not knowing what he might face in that "deep water," Hudson nevertheless walked straight into the unknown depths of racial pride, worker solidarity and economic justice.

Steelworker Hosea Hudson became a communist in September of 1931, in Birmingham, Alabama. He died in 1988 after a lifetime fighting for the rights of all working people.

SEP 30   ≡ Mother Eliza Davis George: "When God Says Go"

Eliza Davis George grew up in segregated Texas. To be poor was hard enough, but to be black and poor was a double portion of sorrow. George looked out on a world where the rich lived well and all whites lived better than blacks. As a young girl, she found a balm for her pain, and the pain she felt for others, in church. Singing songs such as "His Eye Is on the Sparrow," "What a Friend We Have in Jesus" and "Blessed Assurance" not only made her world tolerable, but they also told her Jesus was with her through all things.

As George grew older, she believed Jesus was the only salvation, both from sin and from woe. She took seriously the gospel's call to leave behind all distractions and imitate the selfless love of Christ. Unlike many of her peers, Eliza George was educated and had the opportunity to escape Texas' crushing poverty. She could have moved west or north or to any big city for opportunity, but she heard the voice of Jesus say otherwise.

Rather than pursuing opportunities and personal gain, George left Texas to find even greater suffering. Following the call of God, she joined a missionary society and sailed to Africa. There she ministered to young girls condemned to abusive marriages and to young boys forced into military service. Her heart aching with the pain she saw, George rescued many young boys and girls from their misery.

The military authorities and irate wife abusers hated George's work and threatened her with death. Escaping detection and capture, she spent months in West Africa helping brutalized girls and boys find refuge and shelter. Many African children looked to her as an ever-present protector, and they renamed her "Mother."

Years later, Mother George would tell how she had to choose between financial success and loving Jesus. She once had held a ticket out of poverty, but she declined to use it, choosing instead to follow the call of God. Her statement to those who questioned her said it all: "When God says go, you just go."

Mother Eliza Davis George of Texas ministered in Africa for several years. She returned to Texas, where she lived to be over 100 years old. She died in 1979.

OCTOBER

Sister Elizabeth Lange

Alice Moore Dunbar-Nelson was a talented black woman whose many gifts made a difference in the struggle for equality and justice. During her lifetime, she was an accomplished violinist, cellist, actor, writer, scholar, teacher and poet. Her interests ranged among many endeavors, and she excelled at each. Dunbar-Nelson was especially committed to racial and gender justice, and she expressed her commitment through her teaching, speeches and writings. In a 1927 speech, "The Negro Woman and the Ballot," she urged her sisters to action:

> To those colored women who worked, fought, spoke, sacrificed, pleaded, wept, cajoled, all but died for the right of suffrage for themselves and their peers, it seemed as if the ballot would be the great objective of life.... When the Negro woman finds that the future of her children lies in her own hands— if she can be made to see this—she will strike off the shackles she has allowed to be hung upon her and win the economic freedom of her race.

Dunbar-Nelson did not just talk about what to do; she lived her convictions. She was an agitator for justice and was once fired from her teaching position because the school district prohibited instructors from outside political activity.

Her first book of poetry, *Violets and Other Tales*, was published in 1895 when she was just twenty, and she went on to publish other literary works, including the great *Masterpieces of Negro Eloquence* in 1914. Her 1920 poem, "I Sit and Sew," with its juxtaposition of the horrors of war with mundane domestic tasks is considered a classic in American poetry:

> *I sit and sew—my heart aches with desire—*
> *That pageant terrible, that fiercely pouring fire...*
> *There in that holocaust of hell, those fields of woe—*
> *But—I must sit and sew.*

Alice Dunbar-Nelson was a talented black woman, and she used those talents to help elevate her people. She urged black women to vote, she organized and fought for equal rights, and she wrote poetry to enlighten and transform.

Musician and poet Alice Moore Dunbar-Nelson was married to the black poet Paul Laurence Dunbar. After he died, she married the black journalist Robert Nelson. She edited and published the book **Masterpieces of Negro Eloquence** *in 1914. This gifted black woman died in 1935.*

The West African nation of Guinea has a very rich history. Evidence of human presence in Guinea dates back thirty thousand years, and the savannahs, forests and rivers of Guinea have witnessed both the tragedies and glories of human life. Northern Guinea was the heartland of great African empires such as Ghana and Mali, and Guinea was also home to Fouta Djallon, the longest autonomous Islamic theocracy in history. Like the rest of West Africa, Guinea was victimized as many of its strongest and brightest were kidnapped and dragged away to slavery.

When Europe carved up Africa, the French gobbled up the piece known as Guinea, but the people of Guinea, particularly those from the Fulani of the Fouta Djallon, met the masters from Paris with stiff resistance. Samory Toure of the Mandinka, a West African freedom fighter from the 1880s, successfully fought the French for over twenty years. He laid the foundation for the later struggles of Sekou Toure and others. After World War II and the rise of the Pan-African movement, Guinean peasants and workers demanded their independence from France.

Activist and future president Sekou Toure led a popular movement that crippled the French will to govern, and Paris finally agreed to a popular vote. On September 28, 1958, Guineans decided their own future as a nation. When the votes were counted, 1,134,324 had voted for freedom from France, while only 58,981 were opposed. On October 2, Guinea became the first African French colony to gain independence.

Though the nation of Guinea is currently gripped by illiteracy, poverty and disease, the African spirit of community and joy remains among the common people. Travelers there remark about the generosity and humility of the children, families and workers. From their beginnings thirty thousand years ago, the Mandinka, Fulani and other Guineans continue their arduous journey toward dignity and peace.

On October 2, 1958, Guinea became one of the first independent nations in Africa since the European colonization. It was home to great freedom fighters, such as Samory Toure and Sekou Toure.

≡ Sister Elizabeth Lange: "Imitation of Christ"

What a disconcerting sight: black women, the lowest gender of the most despised race, walking around clad in garments of holiness. It was 1831 in Baltimore, Maryland, and most Africans in the South were slaves. The few free ones, both North and South, were considered low in intellect and devoid of spirit. Yet here was a group of black women walking down a Baltimore street in habits worn by holy women of God. How could this be? How could these black women have attained such a sanctified status?

Sister Elizabeth Lange, also called "Mother Lange," was the courageous spiritual leader of this black community of nuns, called the Oblates of Providence. In 1831, her community was officially recognized by the Pope, enabling them to operate a full-fledged religious order with specific obligations. The Oblates of Providence were authorized to "renounce the world to consecrate themselves to God and to the Christian education of young girls of color."

This mandate opened the door for the Oblates to teach slaves, which was an illegal and criminal act in the South at that time. It was feared that blacks who could read and think would undermine the foundations of white supremacy. Yet here were the Oblates, black women arrayed in the innocence of religious garb, toppling the fundamental assumptions of racism.

The Order's motto, "Imitation of Christ," symbolized the essence of their devotion and work: They followed Christ and Christ alone. Their belief in Christ transcended the power of immoral laws, and they were determined to do as they believed God called them. If Christ called them to reach out and teach girls of color, then that was what they intended to do.

Their home, the St. Frances Convent and Chapel, became an educational center for black girls and the spiritual home of black Catholics. Mother Lange and the Oblates of Providence modeled themselves after their Savior, and their holiness brought education and dignity to hundreds of black girls.

On October 2, 1831, the Pope officially recognized the Oblate Sisters of Providence. They were the first order of African-American nuns to be recognized by the Roman Catholic Church. Sister Elizabeth Lange was their first Mother Superior.

≣ Ruby Doris Robinson: Young Revolutionary

The embers of activism smoldered deep within Ruby Doris Robinson. When she was only thirteen years old, the images of the Montgomery bus boycott had been seared onto her soul. She could not shake the images of black grandmothers, maids, janitors and school children walking as empty buses rolled by. Their resistance had taught her that blacks could lift themselves from second-class treatment, and the passion young Ruby felt as she watched the boycott never left her. As a student at Spelman College, seventeen-year-old Ruby Robinson joined a lunch counter sit-in and was hauled away to jail in downtown Atlanta, Georgia.

Imprisonment only fired up Robinson's kindling passion for justice, and she returned to campus as a founding member of the Student Nonviolent Coordinating Committee (SNCC). Robinson emerged as a brilliant student leader, and her uncompromising positions led SNCC into direct confrontation with southern racists. She crafted the "jail, no bail" policy of SNCC, a move intended to draw media and public attention on their cause. In 1966, she became SNCC's first and only woman executive secretary.

The Civil Rights Movement suffered a tremendous loss when Ruby Doris Robinson died of leukemia at the young age of twenty-five. In her short lifetime, she expended more energy on behalf of justice than many do in a full lifetime. May we capture but a portion of Ruby Robinson's passion to build a just and peaceful society.

Student leader and activist Ruby Doris Robinson died of leukemia on October 7, 1967, in Atlanta, Georgia. She was a founding member of the Student Nonviolent Coordinating Committee (SNCC) and crafted that organization's "jail, no bail" policy on non-violent civil disobedience.

≣ Sutton Griggs: "A Way Out of No Way"

Sutton Griggs felt God's hand rest upon him. Like other blacks freed from slavery, Griggs understood God as a liberator. He believed with all his heart that God delivered blacks from the evils of bondage just as God rescued the Hebrews from Egypt, and Griggs devoted his life to Christian ministry. He graduated from Richmond Theological Seminary, and in 1895 he was called to serve a black Baptist congregation in Tennessee.

After several months as pastor, Rev. Griggs wanted to write as well as preach, but this seemed absurd. After all, slavery had ended a mere thirty years earlier, and ex-slaves were illiterate, unschooled and uneducated. Besides that, few black Americans had time to read, consumed as they were with the responsibilities of liberty and the hostilities of white people. And who would publish a black writer? You had to be famous, like black writers Paul Laurence Dunbar or Charles Chestnutt to be published by the white press. There was no black press, no black capital, few black readers and no encouragement. After slavery, book publishing was the last enterprise many thought worth pursuing.

But Griggs was not discouraged. He served a God who watched over the oppressed, opened the eyes of the blind and made "a way out of no way," as Griggs used to say. So he did the audacious: He came home from serving his church and sketched the outlines of a novel. Realizing few publishers would consider his work, Griggs formed his own company, Orion Publishing. Orion was one of the first black self-publishing companies in America. In 1899, Sutton Griggs published his first novel, *Imperium in Imperio (Empire within an Empire)*, a work about the worsening conditions of blacks in the South.

When the National Baptist Convention reneged on its promise to help with distribution, Griggs sold his books door to door throughout the South. Griggs went on to publish four other novels. His work was so powerful that eventually more black folks read Sutton Griggs than Dunbar and Chestnutt! Sutton Griggs lived and acted like a man who indeed served a God who made "a way out of no way."

Sutton Griggs founded Orion Publishing Company, one of the first black self-publishers in the nation. His vision and energy enabled him to publish and distribute five of his own books in post-slavery America.

OCT 6   ≡ Fisk Jubilee Singers: "Safe in the Arms of Jesus"

On October 6, 1871, nine black men and women left Nashville, Tennessee, and sang their way into history. The Fisk Jubilee Singers went on a concert tour to raise funds to save their school, Fisk University. Not only did they rescue their school from financial ruin, but they also brought gifts to America still enjoyed to this day. Slavery had ended just six years prior, and America was anxious to forget it had ever happened. Yet the Fisk Jubilee Singers believed that the songs of the slaves—the spirituals—were important wellsprings of faith to be preserved. Many who survived slavery did so because spirituals had nurtured their souls. The Jubilee Singers decided that America was as much in need of hope as were the slaves. They were right. Audiences across the nation filled concert halls to hear "Rock My Soul," "Steal Away," "Deep River" and other classics.

The Singers accepted an invitation from President Grant and became the first black choir to perform at the White House. On a second visit to the White House, their song, "Safe in the Arms of Jesus," moved President Chester Arthur to tears. Ironically, the evening before their performance, they had been denied lodging by every hotel in Washington, D.C.

Yet the Jubilee Singers did not give up, and they continued their historic tour. When they traveled overseas, European audiences were astonished at the beauty of the slave spirituals. Many on the continent saw slave spirituals as an authentic American art form, because it was music not borrowed or modified from Europe but created in the cauldron of the New World alone.

The Fisk Jubilee Singers accomplished much more than saving their university; they brought the gift of the black spiritual to the world.

On October 6, 1871, the Fisk Jubilee Singers began their historic tour of America. Under the leadership of George Leonard White, the Singers introduced the black spiritual as an American art form.

OCT 7 ≣ Emma B. Delaney: Duty Calls

Emma B. Delaney spent twelve years at Spelman College in Atlanta, Georgia. She graduated from the high school department in 1894, the mission department in 1896; she completed nurses' training in 1900. Later, reflecting on her life, she wrote:

> *After entering Spelman Seminary and spending twelve years there, where our duty to God and humanity, both home and abroad, is daily set forth, the mere desire for the work was changed to duty…a longing for the work that nothing else would satisfy.*

For Delaney these words were not abstract platitudes; they articulated her commitment and the very core of her calling. Upon graduation, she enrolled to be a missionary in British Central Africa. At that time, most women who served as missionaries to Africa primarily went with their husbands, though a few single white women had served limited duty before returning home. Few single black women had ever served, but no one, of any color, was as intrepid as Emma Delaney.

But once she got to Africa, her troubles were not over. During the next three years, Delaney contracted fever almost monthly. On top of that, British authorities treated her with suspicion and viewed her work as "inciting the natives to revolution." As with most black missionaries, Delaney was also often without money or resources. Compounding her woes were the accusations of many Africans that she was spreading the white man's culture. When Delaney returned to the United States in 1905, she had lost fifty pounds and was suffering from fatigue and stress.

Delaney was not through, however; her duty to "the work" was relentless. When she regained her health, she raised funds for a return to Africa, and in 1912 she boarded a ship for her beloved continent. For the next eight years, she worked among the Liberians, teaching children about Christ, showing women new skills and educating families about basic healthcare. Delaney persisted through poverty, famine and smallpox, and she spent a total of twelve years in two assignments serving in West Africa. In 1920, Delaney returned to the United States. She died two years later, but the results of her commitment did not die with her.

One of the young Africans Delaney converted was Daniel Malekebu, a boy she considered her "son" in the faith. He came to the United States and studied medicine at Meharry University in Nashville, Tennessee, and then returned to Africa, where he healed hundreds of Africans. Those who lived because of Malekebu, and the others touched by Delaney's mission, are the eternal legacy of Emma Delaney's duty to "the work that nothing else would satisfy."

Missionary Emma B. Delaney died of hematuric fever on October 7, 1922, at her mother's home in Fernandina Beach, Florida. Her commitment to "duty" left its mark at Spelman College, West Africa and everywhere else she served.

OCT 8 ≡ James Albert Ukawsaw Gronniosaw: The Most Remarkable Particulars

In 1710, Ukawsaw Gronniosaw was born an African prince in present day Nigeria. Though born to a life of royalty and privilege, Gronniosaw was victimized by betrayal, hatred, slavery and poverty. His classic book, *A Narrative of the Most Remarkable Particulars in the Life of James Albert Ukawsaw Gronniosaw*, published in England in 1772, recounts his life in Africa, America and England. As a teenager, Gronniosaw traveled to Ghana to visit his family and explore the country. A local king got word of his visit and assumed he was spying for an enemy, the King of Bornou. The king arrested Gronniosaw, and he was judged and scheduled for execution the following morning. The next day, however, the king decided not to kill the boy but to sell him into slavery instead.

Ironically, Gronniosaw was grateful when he was sold to the Europeans, for certain death awaited him in Ghana. He was able to survive the harrowing journey to America and had the good fortune of being bought by a relatively kind master. He learned to speak and write English and was exposed to his master's Christian religion.

While at prayer one evening, Ukawsaw Gronniosaw was overwhelmed by a vision. He recounted it in his *Narrative*:

> *I was so drawn out of myself, and so fill'd and awed by the Presence of God that I saw (or thought I saw) light inexpressible dart down from heaven upon me…. I continued on my knees, and joy unspeakable took possession of my soul.*

Gronniosaw was later freed by his master and moved to England to start a new life. To dramatize his new beginning, he added "James Albert" to his name. He later married and had a child, but tragedy struck when his child died soon after birth. His pain was multiplied when local churches refused to bury a black baby. Months later, both Gronniosaw and his wife were laid off prior to a particularly harsh winter. Still grieving for his baby, Gronniosaw was homeless and hungry, with no place to turn.

Still, he never succumbed to despair. He had survived death threats, slavery, the death of his child and poverty. Near the end of his *Narrative*, Gronniosaw described himself and his wife as "pilgrims, very poor pilgrims, traveling through many difficulties toward our heavenly home." Ukawsaw Gronniosaw experienced pain unknown to most of us, yet he never wavered in his faith in God and in himself.

In the fall of 1772, James Albert Ukawsaw Gronniosaw's A Narrative of the Most Remarkable Particulars in the Life of James Albert Ukawsaw Gronniosaw *was published. It not only described his remarkable life but also became a tool in the abolitionist fight against slavery. His royal birth was often contrasted with his subsequent enslavement and poverty.*

OCT 9 ≡ Catherine (Katy) Williams Ferguson: Mother to Motherless Children

In 1774, a pregnant slave woman was sold by her master to a new owner in New York City. While aboard the northbound schooner, the young woman gave birth to a baby girl she named Catherine. Little did anyone know that Baby Catherine, born as property aboard a sailing ship, would profoundly change the lives of hundreds of New York City's children.

When Catherine (Katy) Williams was a young girl, her mother helped her memorize scriptures from the Bible, and she faithfully attended the Murray Street Church in New York City. Though she was later separated from her mother, young Williams maintained her faith in God. When she was eighteen, two abolitionist women helped free her from slavery. Once freed from slavery, Williams married a man named Ferguson and had children.

Freedom, however, did not mean all was well. By age twenty, Katy Ferguson had gained her freedom but lost her mother, her husband and two children. She faced these crises with a faith in God and love for others that few could match.

Still with an ache in her heart, she opened her modest home to the poor black and white children in her neighborhood, where once a week she taught Bible lessons, reading and survival skills. Her pastor was so impressed with this work that he suggested she move her school to the Murray Street Church basement. In that poorly lit and ill-furnished basement, New York's first Sunday school was born.

For forty years, Ferguson changed the lives of hundreds of children. She taught lessons from the life of Christ, gave advice on surviving in a merciless world and was mother to hundreds of motherless children. Word got around: If you can't read, go see Katy Ferguson. If you are hungry, Katy can help you. If you need a place to stay, Katy will find you shelter.

For forty years, Katy Ferguson cast aside her own pain and gave her time, energy and money to children who suffered as she did. When she died of cholera in 1854, hundreds attended her funeral. Ferguson embodied the scripture her mother had taught her as a child: "You shall love the Lord your God with all your heart…and your neighbor as yourself" (Luke 10:27).

Teacher and activist Catherine (Katy) Williams Ferguson died of cholera in New York City in 1854. She ran the first Sunday school in New York City at the Murray Street Church. In 1920, New York City opened a home for unwed mothers named The Katy Ferguson Home.

OCT 10 ☰ Tommie Smith and John Carlos: "Not the Triumph but the Struggle"

The image is etched in the minds of any who saw it: Two finely tuned athletes, the best in the world at their craft, standing in defiance of all that would negate their humanity. With Olympic medals draped around their necks, Tommie Smith and John Carlos held black-gloved fists aloft during the national anthem. These two dedicated men had just beaten the entire world at the two-hundred-meter dash. Now they challenged white supremacy as the world watched in disbelief. Rather than salute the flag and anthem, Smith and Carlos protested America's treatment of their people.

An estimated two hundred million people witnessed this exercise in black militancy. Many remember that Smith and Carlos wore black gloves and held their fists aloft. Few, however, were aware of the full meaning of their protest. One glove was worn on the right hand for black power, the other on the left for black unity. Further, neither wore socks, a symbolic show of solidarity with the poor.

Politicians and the press crucified Tommie Smith and John Carlos for their brazen protest. Newspapers, congressmen and countless others spewed hatred upon them. They were stripped of their medals and expelled from the Olympic Games, and that was merely the beginning. Running had been their life. Since they were children, they had honed their minds and bodies to accept the discipline of track. Now, angered white officials excluded them from racing. All the harshness and brutality of America crashed down upon them.

Ironically, America's reaction to their defiance merely confirmed the truth of their protest. Tommie Smith later recalled his thoughts the moment he heard the "Star-Spangled Banner":

That's my flag…but I couldn't salute it in the accepted manner, because it didn't represent me fully; only to the extent of asking me to be great on the running track, then obliging me to come home and be just another nigger.

Smith and Carlos were true heroes that day: They stood by their conviction and paid the price of reminding the world of America's racial shortcomings. Though it was lost on those who criticized them, Smith and Carlos lived the Olympic Creed: "The most important thing in the Olympic Games is not to win but to take part, just as the most important thing in life is not the triumph but the struggle."

Tommie Smith and John Carlos transformed personal triumph into communal struggle and left a lasting mark on the movement for black equality.

On October 16, 1968, black track and field athletes Tommie Smith and John Carlos won medals for the 200-meter dash in the Summer Olympic Games in Mexico City. During the playing of the U.S. national anthem, they protested America's racism with a black-gloved salute. Their act energized the Black Power Movement as the two became cultural icons in the black community, even though they were stripped of their medals.

OCT 11   ≣ Claude McKay: The Beauty of the Catholic Church

Claude McKay, extraordinary poet, ex-communist and literary genius, was back in America. He had been abroad for a dozen years and had returned to New York. But things were different. No one wanted to publish his poetry, and high blood pressure and influenza had left him sick and poor. When his few remaining friends urged him to leave New York, McKay took their advice and caught a train out of Harlem to Chicago. In the Windy City, he met Catholic activist Dorothy Day of the Catholic Worker Movement and saw firsthand how these genuine radicals were living with the poor and empowering them to fight for their rights and dignity.

Through Day and others, McKay was introduced to Catholicism, and much to the dismay of his Marxist friends he was baptized into the Catholic Church on October 11, 1944. He later wrote that he had fallen in love with the Catholic way of life. He told his friend Max Eastman that becoming Catholic was "like falling in love…you love her…for her Beauty, which cannot be defined."

Here was a man immersed in black struggle, literary excellence, Marxist thought and political action. His ideals had led him to Harlem, France, Russia, Morocco and England. All his writings, all his travels, were for one aim: to create a world where humans could live together in dignity and peace. This man who searched the world for human solidarity finally found it. In an unpublished article, "Right Turn to Catholicism," he declared that the Catholic Church was the only "international organization where all people were a family."

Claude McKay had searched for a place where all were welcome and loved. After looking for such solidarity in the Harlem Renaissance, the Communist Party, the Comintern (Communist International) and black nationalism, he finally found his home in the Roman Catholic Church.

On October 11, 1944, black activist Claude McKay was baptized into the Roman Catholic Church. He believed his conversion changed his life, and he proclaimed that from then on the kingdom of God was "within him."

OCT 12 ≣ Nossa Senhora Aparecida: Our Blessed Lady of Blackness

Submerged under the Paraiba River, the sculpture of the Virgin Mary had slowly darkened as sediment and mud collected over its smooth surface. The white face of Mary had already been shaded from decades of burning candles at her feet. Now, at the river bottom, the browned face had turned a rich black. For reasons now unknown, the sculpture of Mary had been taken from the chapel and hurled into the river. Decades later, the sacrilegious dumping of the Virgin was about to become a blessing for black Brazil.

In 1717, Domingos Garcia, Filipe Pedroso and Joao Alves were fishing in the river Paraiba. To their surprise, the weight in their net was not a load of fish but the sculpture of a Black Virgin Mary. Soon afterward, a chapel was built near Aparecida, the site where the fisherman found the sculpture. Slowly, word began to spread through the state of Sao Paulo and across the entire nation, and the story was always the same: In the chapel at Aparecida, Our Blessed Lady of Blackness awaits pilgrims in need of aid; anyone with a burden, ailment, debt, sorrow or sin can be comforted by the Blessed Mother; if Mary the Mother of God is black, then Jesus her Son is black; and if Jesus is black, then he surely feels our burdens and aches.

Hundreds heard the story and responded, traveling to Aparecida to pray before this black Mother of God. They left Mary's presence with strength, healing and blessing, returning home to tell others of their journey.

For over three hundred years, the black image of Mary has looked down with mercy on the woes of Brazilians. "Hail Mary, full of grace, the Lord is with thee," say the pilgrims. This simple prayer to *Nossa Senhora Aparecida* (Our Lady of Aparecida) continues to bring miracles, blessings and comfort to black Brazilians.

Though pilgrims come daily to the chapel at Aparecida, Brazil, the most significant day for **Nossa Senhora Aparecida,** *Our Lady of Aparecida, is October 12, the date fishermen pulled the statue from the river in 1717.*

Angela Yvette Davis' entire life has been devoted to justice for African Americans, the poor, indigenous people, prisoners, women and those relegated to the fringes of our world. In school, young Davis organized interracial study groups in response to the unfairness around them. When she was fifteen, her family sent her to New York's progressive Elizabeth Irwin School, where teachers urged their students to analyze the roots of injustice, to question assumptions and to view history from the perspective of the oppressed. Angela Davis' early activism and progressive education were significant factors in her development.

She was further shaped by the times. The four girls murdered in the 1963 Birmingham church bombing had been her friends. Also, while studying in Paris, Davis had bonded with Algerian students fighting French occupation in their homeland. In 1968, when capitalist hegemony was being rocked by revolution, assassinations and protest throughout the world, Davis joined the Communist Party. She was hired by UCLA to teach philosophy, but Governor Ronald Reagan and the UC Board of Regents terminated her employment because of her radical political views.

Still she did not retreat. She became part of an effort to free the Soledad Brothers during the late sixties. In particular, she befriended George Jackson, and when his brother, Jonathan, was killed in an unsuccessful escape attempt—along with the trial judge and three others—Davis was charged with kidnapping, conspiracy and murder, though she was nowhere near the incident. She went into hiding, and several months later the FBI arrested her. Her raised fist and beautiful Afro hair became the symbol of chained black aspirations. "Free Angela" posters and slogans covered the ghettos and universities of America. She was later exonerated and freed, and since then has remained a ringing voice for black freedom, prison reform and gender equity. The passion that had begun in Birmingham and was fueled in New York and Paris has been ablaze in the life of Angela Davis ever since

FBI Special Agents arrested Angela Yvette Davis in New York City on October 13, 1970. She was on the FBI's Ten Most Wanted list following the shootout in San Rafael in which the guns used were reportedly registered in her name. She has been considered by many black Americans and political progressives to be a beautiful manifestation of black pride and self-determination.

Not often are we graced with such remarkable human beings as Julius Nyerere. As a Roman Catholic, Nyerere's commitment to the poor was unwavering; he spent his life working on behalf of others. In the 1950s, he forged the Tanganyika African National Union (TANU) into that nation's largest anti-colonial organization. When Tanganyika gained independence from England, Nyerere was elected to lead the nation into its future. He looked boldly forward, took significant risks and did whatever was necessary to lead his nation out of poverty and dependency. While other leaders might have chosen to be chauffeured around in luxury bulletproof cars, Nyerere drove around the capital of Dar es Salaam in a common vehicle.

His accomplishments were stunning. Nyerere created the nation of Tanzania by merging the island of Zanzibar with Tanganyika. Despite the presence of over one hundred different ethnic groups, he made Kiswahili the national language to facilitate economic and political unity. His literacy and health campaigns vastly improved the lives of Tanzanian peasants.

Nyerere saw all of Africa as his calling, and he also served as chair of the Frontline States, an organization that supported liberation movements in Angola, Mozambique, Namibia and South Africa. Their independence is due in large part to his work. A force in the Organization of African Unity, Nyerere was a vigilant advocate for human rights and economic justice.

In 1967, Nyerere astonished the world with his revolutionary Arusha Declaration. In an epic speech, he announced that Tanzania was dedicating itself to *ujamaa*, or "familyhood." Nyerere proposed that the future of Tanzania and Africa lay in "collective villages," where resources could be equitably managed and distributed.

By 1985, however, with the failure of many of these village ventures and slow economic growth in his country, Nyerere voluntarily stepped down as president. When he left office, he honestly assessed both his successes and his failures. Despite his admission of failed economic policies, Nyerere remained a beacon of African leadership. Continuing his commitment to justice. Nyerere continued to work for peace in Burundi, supported sustainable policies by the World Bank and International Monetary Fund, and sought to end the genocide in Rwanda.

Julius Nyerere was truly one of the remarkable black leaders of our time. Little wonder that many Tanzanians, from workers in Dar es Salaam to peasants in the countryside, still refer reverently to him as *Mwalimu*, Swahili for "teacher."

Former President of Tanzania, Julius Kambarage Nyerere, died in London on October 14, 1999. His passing was recognized by people the world over, from Fidel Castro to the Radical Black Congress to the Catholic Maryknoll missionary order. He was hailed for his commitment to communal human development and his opposition to war and excessive private property. His devotion to the Catholic faith and belief in the goodness of common folk grounded a lifetime of good works and service. He also wrote a catechism for his fellow Tanzanian Catholics.

≣ Thomas Sankara: "We Must Have a New People"

Thomas Sankara was the progressive President of Burkina Faso, West Africa, from 1983 to 1987. He promoted education for the poor, equality for women, healthcare for the sick and education for the illiterate. He stood up against Western economic and cultural imperialism and demanded global justice in trade and aid.

In his earlier years, Sankara had studied communism and Marxism in Europe. Upon his return to Burkina Faso, he was anxious to translate revolutionary theory into a better life for his people. After his appointment in 1983 as President by the new *Conseil National de la Révolution*, Sankara devoted himself to transforming his country. His nation was one of the poorest on earth, shackled by infant mortality, illiteracy, low agricultural production, traditional patriarchy and countless other woes.

Under his leadership, rural medicine was improved and infant mortality dropped from 208 per 1,000 to 145; irrigation and literacy programs brought education and agricultural improvements to the poor; and he undermined crippling patriarchy by encouraging men to do household chores.

Sankara knew that building a new nation required selfless dedication to a higher cause. He often spoke directly to the masses about their responsibilities and duties. During a rally celebrating the fourth anniversary of the revolution, he proclaimed:

> For a new society we must have a new people; a people that has its own identity, that knows what it wants and how to assert itself…and understands what will be necessary to reach the goals it has set for itself…. A democratic revolution needs a convinced people, not a conquered people—a people that is truly convinced, not submissive and passively enduring its destiny.

In four short years a president, Thomas Sankara improved the lives of women, children and the poor of his nation, Burkina Faso, which is translated as "Land of the Upright People." Sankara sought to build a new society with his "upright" people and so made his mark as a remarkable revolutionary leader.

President Thomas Sankara was assassinated in a coup on October 15, 1987, in Ouagadougou, Burkina Faso, West Africa. For several weeks after his death, thousands of the poor honored Sankara's gravesite.

☰ The Million Man March: A Public Commitment

On October 16, 1995, over nine hundred thousand black men gathered in Washington, D.C., to publicly affirm their commitment to live as complete human beings. They came from all across America, from college campuses, corporate boardrooms and ghetto streets—from every city, suburb or town where blacks lived—to proclaim their manhood.

Conceived by Nation of Islam leader Louis Farrakhan, the Million Man March captured the imagination of black men. The march was not an end, but it was a means to an end. Participants saw the march as the first day of a long pilgrimage, a journey where they would assume responsibility for themselves, their families and their communities. As sons, brothers, fathers, boyfriends, grandfathers, voters, workers, citizens, Christians and Muslims, they dedicated themselves to live in the fullness of their manhood.

Rosa Parks, Jesse Jackson, Louis Farrakhan and Maya Angelou were among the speakers who energized the thousands. Critics say the March resulted in no sustained organization. Those who were there, however, will tell you that lives were transformed and that thousands returned home as better men, with a commitment to create better homes and communities.

The Million Man March was conceived by Nation of Islam leader Louis Farrakhan and organized by Ben Chavis. It intended to encourage black men to accept their responsibility for their families and community. It was held on October 16, 1995, in Washington, D.C.

☰ Dangerfield Newby: "Come without Fail"

Dangerfield Newby carried in his pocket a tattered, fading letter from his enslaved wife. He could not read very well, but he had seared each word of his wife's letter in his heart: "Oh dear Dangerfield, come this fall without fail.... I want to see you so much that it is the one bright hope I have before me." Harriet Newby had written these words just as she had been sold from the Shenandoah Valley to the rice plantations of Louisiana. She knew that once she was in Louisiana she might never see her beloved Dangerfield again, so she pleaded, "Come."

Dangerfield Newby wondered how he could possibly see his wife again. He knew that any visit to the plantation would have to be in secret and most likely be confined to a few moments on a dark night. If he were caught, his wife and children would be punished severely, and he could be re-enslaved. But he also knew that if he did not act soon, he would never, ever, see his wife and children again. Such pain was too much to bear.

Newby decided to join abolitionist John Brown and twenty other black and white freedom fighters in an assault on slavery. Their plan was to raid the federal arsenal at Harper's Ferry, Virginia, and, once armed, to march through the South, their ranks swelling with newly-freed black slaves. Dangerfield knew his wife's plantation was close to Harper's Ferry, and he hoped his family would be among the first to be liberated from slavery's grasp.

Newby's dream died in a hail of bullets as federal troops surrounded the rebels trapped in the armory. Of John Brown's twenty-one revolutionaries, five were black: Dangerfield Newby, Sheridan Leary, John Copeland and Shields Green all died in the raid or were hung afterward; Osborne P. Anderson escaped and later fought in the Civil War. Each had families in slavery, and all had known that their gamble for freedom could mean death.

Yet for Dangerfield Newby and the others, love compelled them to act. Newby could no longer abide the suffering that his wife and children were enduring. He knew that, as another's property, they had no protection from sale, whippings, rape and abuse. Indeed, he had no choice but to "come without fail."

Abolitionist John Brown's black associate, Dangerfield Newby, died on October 17, 1859, when he and other freedom fighters were trapped by thousands of federal troops at the U.S. Armory at Harper's Ferry, Virginia. They had intended to spark a rebellion of slaves throughout the South.

☰ Cyril Valentine Briggs
OCT 18 — "The Renaissance of Negro Power and Culture"

The "New Negro" political movement that Harlem birthed after World War I was full of luminaries. "New Negroes" such as Marcus Garvey, W.E.B. DuBois, A. Philip Randolph and others were among the great activists of this time. None, however, were as radical as Cyril Valentine Briggs and his companion, Richard Moore.

Cyril Briggs was fair-skinned enough to pass for white, and he was also burdened with a speech impediment that hindered his public speaking. Yet neither of these prevented him from emerging as a powerful Harlem advocate for revolutionary change. Born on the West Indian island of Nevis, Briggs had moved to Harlem, where he had become a respected political leader. He and fellow West Indian Richard Moore believed that the severity of black poverty required drastic remedies.

Together in 1918 they founded *The Crusader*, a paper dedicated to "the renaissance of Negro power and culture." The pages of *The Crusader* demanded an end to World War I, proclaimed the dignity of black folk and urged cooperation with other progressive workers.

Briggs also founded the African Blood Brotherhood, a secret organization devoted to armed self-defense and allied with the Communist Party, USA (CPUSA). The African Blood Brotherhood gathered most of Harlem's most radical blacks into one revolutionary body. Later, as the Communist Party demonstrated their commitment to black rights, the African Blood Brotherhood disbanded and many of its members joined the CPUSA, including Cyril Briggs, Richard Moore, Lovett Fort-Whiteman and Grace Campbell.

Believing that communism was the only hope for black American justice, Cyril Briggs rose to become one of the first great black communists in America. He also helped organized the American Negro Labor Council and the League of Struggle of Negro Rights, and he wrote for *The Harlem Liberator*. His commitment paved the road later trod by many other African Americans who worked for a classless and just society, including W.E.B. DuBois, Fred Hampton, George Jackson, Langston Hughes and Angela Davis.

Black activist Cyril Briggs was committed to communism as the only hope for black justice in America. He helped organize the "New Negro Movement" in Harlem after World War I. He died on October 18, 1966, in Los Angeles, California.

OCT 19   ≡ **Prime Minister Maurice Bishop: "Forward Ever!"**

Maurice Bishop was one of the founders of Grenada's New Jewel Movement (NJM), a revolutionary party that took power on that Caribbean island nation in 1979. The NJM overthrew the existing dictator and ran the country until a bloody coup ended its progressive reign in 1983. What happened during those four years is one of the significant untold stories of our time.

After the 1979 revolution, Maurice Bishop became the Prime Minister of Grenada. With the fervor only revolutionaries can muster, his NJM dramatically changed the lives of Grenada's one hundred thousand black citizens. Unemployment, which had hovered at a staggering forty-nine percent, plummeted to twelve percent as the Bishop government restored workers' rights and revitalized unions. One-third of the national budget was spent on education and healthcare. Agricultural production increased, volunteers ensured that poor families had milk and vegetables, literacy increased dramatically and medicine was provided to the poor.

Bishop and the NJM sought not only to change living conditions but also to transform the souls of the people. Colonial culture had created dependency, apathy and individualism, which had collectively undermined the social fabric of Grenada. The NJM radically set out to build a new humanity on the island. At his famous 1983 speech at Hunter College in New York City, Bishop said:

The point I am making, brothers and sisters, is the nature of the struggle we have undergone: not only to raise production and productivity but to instill new values in our people. As we struggle on the road toward creating a new man and a new woman, living a new life, the old habits, the old culture, the old prejudices, are always struggling against the shoots of the new. That is a struggle that we have to resolutely wage every day of our lives.

Such talk was too dangerous for the United States. The image of English-speaking black folks building a revolution on the doorstep of America was too much. Years of American destabilization ended in a reactionary coup and a U.S. invasion. Yet the glory of the Grenadian revolution and the leadership of Maurice Bishop is a testament to the ongoing fight for human dignity. He often ended his speeches with a rousing, "Forward ever!" Though his revolution was crushed by an unrelenting enemy, Maurice Bishop's commitment and example live on in those working for equality and change.

On October 19, 1983, Prime Minister Maurice Bishop of Grenada, along with Jacqueline Creft, Unison Whiteman, Fitzroy Bain, Norris Bain and Vincent Noel, was murdered by counter-revolutionaries supported by the U.S. government. Through his New Jewel Movement, he had sought to transform Grenada into a just society.

OCT 20   ≡ **President Samora Machel: Poder Popular**

Samora Machel is a beloved figure in Mozambique's history. Trained as a nurse, he joined the Front for the Liberation of Mozambique (FRELIMO) in 1962. For the next seventeen years, he rose through the ranks until he became President of Mozambique following the assassination of President Eduardo Mondlane. Machel had been a close comrade to Mondlane, and both had always known that their commitment could cost their lives.

Machel was a Marxist, well-versed in the history and theories of socialist ideology, yet he also believed that the source of liberating knowledge was not from European books but rather the soul of working people. Machel taught that Marxism-Leninism was a science whose validity was tested in the practice of political action. He once wrote, "A science belongs to its creator. Who is the creator of Marxism-Leninism? It is a science of class. It belongs to its creator, the working class."

Machel taught his followers that their revolution against the Portuguese was grounded in their experience. His organization, FRELIMO, believed that the concrete conditions of their suffering, the world of their pain, was the laboratory that taught the principles of revolution. FRELIMO held firmly to the principle that the people, indeed, knew what a just society looked like and, what's more, knew how to create it. This view was the basis of Machel's *poder popular*, or "people's power."

After the overthrow of the Portuguese colonialists in 1975, Machel orchestrated mass rallies to energize the reconstruction of Mozambique. For years, South Africa and the United States supported counter-revolutionary movements to overthrow FRELIMO. South Africa accused Machel and FRELIMO of building "sophisticated weapons" and threatening South African security. Yet Machel always responded with his customary reliance on *poder popular*. He said:

> *Mozambican society defines people and their fulfillment as its strength. In Southern Africa, where the scars of colonialism…are still felt…we have built a Party, a nation, a way of life in which colour does not matter, race does not matter, religion or tribe does not matter. Everything that causes unnecessary division has begun to fade from the people's consciousness. This is the sophisticated weapon that threatens apartheid.*

Machel gave his life for the political, cultural and mental liberation of the people of Mozambique. Though a Marxist, his inspiration came not from Karl Marx and Frederick Engels, but from the wisdom of the people: *Poder Popular!*

Samora Machel died in a plane crash on October 19, 1986, in Mbuzini, South Africa. At the time, South Africa waged a secret war against the legitimate government of Mozambique by supporting the Mozambican National Resistance. South Africa was frightened that Mozambique would inspire revolution by their black majority. Many suspect that South Africa was responsible for the crash and murder of Samora Machel.

OCT 21　　　　　　　　　　≡ **Crystal Bird Faucet: Power to the Sisters**

Crystal Bird Faucet sat at her metal, government-issue desk in Philadelphia, Pennsylvania, and looked over the latest unemployment numbers. It was the height of the Great Depression, and Philadelphia, like the rest of the nation, staggered from layoffs and bread lines. Faucet knew that the official unemployment figure was only part of the story. She knew that behind the statistics were malnourished children, frail elderly and hopeless parents.

Crystal Bird Faucet also knew that the official unemployment percentage was usually double in the black community, sometimes triple for black women. Staring out the window, she wondered what more she could do for her sisters. How could she help those standing in the bread lines, dragging themselves from one fruitless interview to another or waiting on corners hoping to be somebody's maid for a day?

Faucet was the head of the Philadelphia Women's and Professional Project of the Works Progress Administration, an agency created to find employment for women on public relief. The misery of black women surpassed any single group in America in the best of times, but during the Depression the suffering was horrific. Crystal Bird Faucet scanned the numbers of black women unemployed and then looked at the number of sisters her agency had helped that past year. "It's just not enough," she thought. "We have to do more than this."

The Women's Professional Project had a quota of black women they could help each year. "The Project," as it was called, required that one-third of their clients be black women. For Faucet, this was not nearly enough, given that black women earned less, bore more burdens and received less help than anyone else. She decided that whatever power she had was useless unless she could use it on behalf of her sisters. Without seeking permission or going through committees or wading through bureaucratic red tape, Faucet decided to raise the quota for black women from one-third to one-half. She sat upright and penned a memo to all her caseworkers: "Effective immediately, 1/2 of our clients will be black women." She signed the memo and sent it out.

No one questioned her motives or authority, and the agency began a more determined outreach to black women. By the time she left the Project, thousands of black women had found work through her efforts. More importantly, after she raised the quota to one-half, three thousand additional black women moved from relief lines to work. Crystal Bird Faucet's actions model for us how the effective use of bureaucratic power can give life and dignity to others.

Crystal Bird Faucet was the head of Philadelphia's Women's and Professional Project of the Works Progress Administration, an agency created to ensure that women received assistance during the Depression. She raised the percentage of black women served by her agency from 33% to 50%.

≡ Reverend Benjamin F. Chavis: Christ the Center

The young United Church of Christ minister Rev. Benjamin F. Chavis had already spent two years in North Carolina prisons, where he and his fellow activists were confined to filthy, rat-infested, ten-by-five-foot cells. Prior to his arrest, Chavis had been sent by the United Church of Christ to advocate and organize for racial justice in Wilmington, North Carolina. He had spent hours at the Gregory Congregational United Church of Christ with black students, workers and preachers. But the police and sheriff were constantly watching him, waiting for an excuse to destroy his ministry.

In 1971, Wilmington erupted in rioting after a black church was fired upon and a white store burned down. Without evidence or witnesses, Rev. Chavis and nine black students were charged with "unlawful burning" and conspiracy to assault, and they were sentenced to two hundred and eighty-two collective years in prison. The "Wilmington 10," as they were called, symbolized America's penchant for punishing victims and rewarding the guilty.

Though only thirty, Chavis had been in the freedom struggle since he was fourteen. He hated the way black folks were treated, and for years he had worked in the NAACP and SCLC to change America. Now, in a tiny cell, sharing space with his comrades, Chavis questioned his faith. "Does God matter? If the Klan goes free and black activists are terrorized, is there any hope? Is this struggle worth fighting if all that awaits is despair?"

Searching for words to capture his agony, he found that despite all evidence to the contrary he still believed. That night in the darkness of his putrid cell in the Hillsboro State Prison, using scraps of toilet paper, corners of his mattress and pieces of paper napkins, Ben Chavis began to write *Psalms from Prison*. In one of the poems from the book, "Christ the Center," he proclaimed that even in the midst of violence, imprisonment and despair, Christ was both the center of his life and of the freedom struggle. Despite the sounds and smells of failure and despair all around him, he held strong his belief that victory was certain with Christ at the center.

Chavis' words of hope burst forth from his cell like a thunderbolt. Racist power structures, violent war-makers and relentless poverty could not break his spirit. Despite the Vietnam War, the assassinations of King and Kennedy, and ongoing repression, Rev. Ben Chavis held strong his belief that "Christ is the center!"

On October 18, 1971, Rev. Benjamin F. Chavis and the rest of the Wilmington 10 were sentenced to 282 collective years in prison for allegedly inciting a riot in Wilmington, North Carolina. In April of 1980, the Fourth Circuit Court of Appeals overturned this blatantly political conviction. Chavis' book, Psalms from Prison, *records his struggle to maintain his faith while in prison.*

≣ **Handmaids of the Most Pure Heart of Mary: Black Nuns of Harlem**

In 1916 in Savannah, Georgia, life was harsh for black Americans. Lynchings were common, and black families were bound to servitude through the unforgiving debts of tenant farming. Though they were fifty years removed from slavery, in many respects the lives of black people had not improved. In the midst of this agony, a few black Catholic women gathered to discern God's voice. They knew the pain of black Georgians, for they felt a full measure of it themselves. Yet they also knew that Christ had called them to holiness. They were drawn to the ministry of the great St. Francis of Assisi, the Italian saint who many believed most closely embodied the life of Christ. Like St. Francis, they believed that the gospel demanded they serve the poor.

After months of study and prayer, these black Catholic women received permission to become the third black order of nuns in the United States. In October of 1916, the Franciscan Handmaids of the Most Pure Heart of Mary were commissioned by the Pope. They lived simply and in poverty, yet their generous hearts held riches for all. Eight years later, Cardinal Patrick Hayes heard of their selfless service and asked them to come to minister in Harlem.

In 1924, the Franciscan Handmaids moved to Harlem and opened a day nursery for working parents, the St. Benedict Day Nursery. The black migration to the North had left the black extended family in crisis, and parents were comforted to leave their children with these caring black nuns.

Few know of these selfless women; their names are not proclaimed in the list of black scholars, writers and ministers who illuminate black history. Yet they served the poor of Harlem and brought the love of St. Francis into the lives of black immigrants. During their peak in Harlem, over eighty black women were members of the Franciscan Handmaids of the Most Pure Heart of Mary.

In October 1916, the Catholic Church recognized the Franciscan Handmaids of the Most Pure Heart of Mary. They were the third black order of nuns in the United States, following the Oblate Sisters of Providence in Baltimore and the Sisters of the Holy Family of New Orleans.

Late afternoon sun cast shadows across Ebbetts Field. Half the field glistened in sunlight, and the other half rested in shaded darkness. The Brooklyn Dodgers needed a win to stay in the pennant race, and time was running out. August humidity sapped the players of both energy and hope. Number 42 was dancing off third base. If he made it home, the Dodgers would win the game.

Jackie Roosevelt Robinson stood on third base, staring down the pitcher. Robinson's coal black arms contrasted sharply with the creamy-white wool home jersey of the Dodgers. His skin differed from that of every player on the field— and that of most of the people in the stands. Standing on third, Robinson was not just the potential winning run for the Brooklyn Dodgers. He represented hope, justice and equality for every black person in America. If he failed, if he faltered, if he erupted in anger or collapsed in weakness, a bony white finger would wag and say, "I knew you people were no good. You can't be our equal. We are better than you."

Could he do it? As he shifted back and forth on third base, did Robinson know the weight he carried? Did he realize that the self-respect of millions of black Americans rested on his every step? Jackie Robinson was, indeed, the Black Messiah.

The pitcher glanced over to third. Robinson darted back and forth. The pitcher tensed up. The fans begin screaming as he threw the first pitch toward home.

"Ball!" yelled the umpire. The crowd hooted in delight.

Robinson kept taking bolder steps toward home. Finally, the pitcher wound up again and in a flash Robinson took off. The pitcher hurled the ball to the catcher and watched helplessly as the ball, the catcher and Robinson disappeared in a cloud of dust.

The umpire stretched out both arms and yelled, "Safe!"

Jackie Robinson was safe at home, and Brooklyn had won the game, but blacks in Brooklyn and across America were ecstatic. Jackie Robinson had registered a victory for dignity, pride and self-respect: "If Jackie can compete and win on a national stage, then surely I can get that job, rent that apartment, pass that test, and ride that bus."

Jackie Robinson died on October 24, 1972, in Stamford, Connecticut. He was elected to the Baseball Hall of Fame on the first ballot. He finished his brilliant career with a .311 batting average. His poise and competitiveness changed baseball forever, and he opened the doors for many to follow, including Frank Robinson, Willie Mays, Hank Aaron and Barry Bonds. Many believe that Jackie Robinson's integration of baseball laid the foundation for the Civil Rights Movement. His number, 42, is the only number that has been permanently retired throughout all of Major League Baseball.

☰ The Women of Langston, Oklahoma: Education for All

A remarkable tale of community pride, social obligation and educational achievement arose out of Langston, Oklahoma. Following the Civil War, the town was founded as an all-black haven. Ex-slaves and their children came seeking new life during the Land Rush of 1889. By 1892, six hundred African Americans had settled in Langston.

The women of Langston were determined to make education a priority. They had seen the destructive consequences of illiteracy and ignorance on their race; they had seen how blacks were cheated out of land, money and rights because they could not read. The black women of Langston knew that their town's survival was dependent upon their children's reading, writing and math. Since everyone in Langston was black—the mayor, newspaper, businesses, realtors, undertakers, sheriff and judge—the town itself could all disappear without education.

In 1892, Langston's black women persuaded city leaders to build a public school from kindergarten through the eighth grade. A few years later, the town added a high school. The women of Langston met often to ensure that the teachers were teaching and the students were learning. If any student faltered in school, women in the community came together to see how they could help. If a family was too poor and needed a child to work, women in the community found a way to help so the child could remain in school.

Frontier towns such as Langston were typically characterized by low educational standards, poor schools and illiteracy, but the black women of Langston came together to change that dismal trend. A few years after the school's founding, seventy percent of Langston residents could read and write. Even more stunning was the fact that ninety-five percent of all the women and girls of Langston were literate in the 1890s. Their newspaper, *The Langston City Herald,* was so popular that even when the town population was only six hundred, the newspaper had four thousand subscribers throughout Oklahoma. The black women of Langston proved to America what social gains await those who came together for the common good.

By insisting on education for all, the black women of Langston, Oklahoma, changed not only the future of their town but also the future of education for all black children in the last years of the nineteenth century.

≣ Reverend Rebecca Cox Jackson: Struck by Lightning

Gray and black clouds swarmed overhead as Rebecca Cox Jackson walked the lonely dirt road home from work. Worn out from working long hours as a seamstress, she barely looked up. Had she done so, the thirty-five-year-old black woman would have seen the darkness of an approaching thunderstorm. Suddenly, torrential rains and violent winds turned the landscape into a chaotic swirl of leaves, dust and branches. Rebecca Jackson began to run, but she was too late. Lightning bolts flashed and lit up trees all around her, and she fell to the ground in a crumpled heap. As she lay still amid the chaos, she heard the voice of God: "Rebecca, repent of your sins and go preach my gospel of life to all people."

The storm passed, and Jackson arose to a new life. True to her divine calling, Rev. Jackson went about preaching and teaching the gospel of Christ. Her impact was so profound that the AME Church sent Bishop Morris Brown to investigate the validity of her call. After hearing her preach, Brown returned with a report that noted, "If ever the Holy Ghost was in a place, it was in that meeting."

Jackson believed that God had made her equal to anyone. Shortly after her conversion, she left the AME Church and joined the Shakers. A little known but devoted group, the Shakers believed that God was both Father and Mother and therefore both men and women could lead the church. This theology suited Jackson's calling, and she became a leader and pastor in her congregation.

In later years, however, white Shakers failed to embody their own teachings about equality, and Jackson joined other black women to form a black female Shaker community. They lived in communal simplicity, praising God in song and dance.

After she died, Jackson left behind teachings and writings that were rediscovered by black novelist Alice Walker in 1981. The progressive feminist perspectives of Rev. Rebecca Cox Jackson stunned Walker and other activists, who could not believe such radical religious thought existed in the 1800s. Jackson heard the call of God to preach; but she also heard the call to be fully female, fully black and fully human.

Rev. Rebecca Cox Jackson was struck by lightning and heard a call from God outside Philadelphia in 1835. She became a preacher in the AME Church and then joined the Shakers. Although she died in 1871, the black female Shaker community she founded was to last another 25 years.

☰ General Benjamin O. Davis, Jr.: Leader of the Tuskegee Airmen

Benjamin O. Davis, Jr., followed the hallowed footsteps of his father, Benjamin O. Davis, Sr., who had completed his military career during the U.S. Armed Forces' most bigoted epoch. Overcoming opposition at every turn, the father had been the first African American to achieve the rank of general in the United States Army. Benjamin Davis, Jr., once wrote, "My father taught me to be strong and to endure adversity; he did it, and so could I."

Davis needed his father's lessons to survive his ordeal at West Point. He enrolled in 1932 and was only the second black to attend the academy after Ossian Flipper, who had graduated sixty years earlier. America was in the throes of white supremacy at that time, and few places could match the military's devotion to whiteness. Davis endured four lonely years; no one spoke to him, except for official reasons, during his entire student career. He suffered personal abuse and physical hardship from both cadets and faculty, who secretly longed for his failure. He had no study partners and sat alone wherever he went. At West Point football games, Ben Davis had a complete bleacher section all to himself.

Yet Davis never complained and kept focused on his goal. In 1936, he graduated thirty-fourth in a class of two hundred and seventy-six. Many of his tormentors had themselves flunked out, and Davis had accomplished under duress what many could not do under ideal conditions. Years later, several of his classmates wrote letters of apology, praising his achievements in light of their own ill-wishes and abuse.

Captain Benjamin Davis went on to enter the Army Air Corps, and he led the all-black 99th Pursuit Squadron into battle in North Africa, Italy and France. Ben Davis, Sr., had taught his son to be strong and endure adversity, and Ben Davis, Jr., emulated his father's example fully.

Captain Benjamin O. Davis, Jr., became the first black Army Air Corps General on October 27, 1954. When he graduated from West Point in 1936, he was only the second black graduate from the academy and the first in sixty years. Davis was the leader of the Tuskegee Airmen, who later formed the core of the famous 99th Pursuit Squadron and the outstanding 332nd Fighter Group.

A letter as it might have been written by a volunteer in the 1st Kansas Volunteer Colored Infantry during the Civil War:

> *Me and my fellows formed a line just where sergeant pointed his sword. The rebs were coming fast, and we hadn't much time. My heart was racin' and my palms sweatin'. I had seen many things in my life. I had been a slave, I seen whippins, and I even seen people die. But nuthin was like this. Crazed, yelling white men, screamin' and runnin' up toward us. But none of us moved. This was going to be our first fight with them rebs. They kept on comin'.*

> *We had to stand and fight. There could be no runnin', no surrender and no losin'. Ol' Jeff Davis already declared any black soldier captured by the rebs would be executed on the spot. Us colored troops stood firm while the Confederates advanced. Closer and closer, the line advanced on us, slowly, out of the woods, across the field, now just a few feet away. They were almost on top of us, and we still awaited the order to fire. "What's he waitin' for?" we thought. Finally came the shout, "Fire!" and our muskets discharged in one loud volley. Smoke and screamin' was everywhere. We kneeled down to re-arm, and the line behind us fired over our heads. Their volley sounded louder than ours. The rebs fired back, and I was sickened by the thudding sound of bullets entering flesh and bone. Men around me cried out and dropped to the ground. Our sergeant screamed "Fire" once again, and we did. It was a devastatin' blow as reb bodies fell right in front of us. The screams and cries were so loud, we barely heard the reb trumpet call for retreat. We couldn't believe our ears.*

> *Most of us had been slaves, with masters who told us when to work, where to live, and some even took our wives or daughters for unspeakable acts. And now we had them on the run. Maybe we could beat this slavery thing after all. But it was no time to celebrate. We had our own killed and wounded to tend to. We beat them rebs this time, but we all knew the fight wasn't over. We wouldn't stop fighting until every last one of us was free.*

The 1st Kansas Volunteer Colored Infantry was created in spring of 1862 when Abraham Lincoln agreed to recruit black troops. On October 28, 1862, the 1st Kansas defeated a Confederate force at Island Mound, Missouri. They lost 10 men in that battle. Fighting alongside Native Americans and white militia, they distinguished themselves a year later by defeating Confederate troops at Honey Springs in Indian Territory.

Lizzie Woods Roberson loved to read the Bible. Though born a slave, she had secretly learned to read, and her favorite book was the Holy Scriptures. Even as young as eight, she would open her Bible the moment she returned from the fields.

At the end of the Civil War, Roberson's family was freed, along with the slaves from across the South. For several years, she continued in her family's Baptist faith. As a young woman, however, Lizzie Roberson felt something was lacking in her life. The sermons were great, the songs inspiring, but something was still missing.

One Sunday afternoon she visited a local Church of God in Christ (COGIC), the black Pentecostal denomination, and there she found what she was missing. Roberson had read about the Holy Spirit, but she had never understood it. Now, sitting in this small country church, she not only understood, she *felt* it. The Holy Spirit was not God looking down on her; it was God inside of her. This was what she had been missing!

Roberson immersed herself in the Pentecostal faith and soon became a pillar in the church. She led prayer bands for women, often arriving in church early for their "prayer hour." Soon she was a Bible teacher, evangelist and prayer leader for Pentecostal churches all over the South.

The Church of God in Christ was a young denomination, and Bishop Charles Harrison Mason, the founder of COGIC, saw the faith of women as vital to their future. Bishop Mason asked Roberson to lead the Women's Department of the COGIC. This may have been one of his wisest decisions, for Roberson transformed the Women's Department into a powerful ministry within the church. The women of COGIC strengthened churches, raised families, taught children and brought the Holy Spirit's power to black Christians all over America.

Roberson's impact on the church was so powerful that most knew her simply as "Mother." As an evangelist, she preached sermons that converted and edified many. As a prayer warrior, Mother Roberson was incomparable, spending hours in prayer to her God. But she did not pray alone, for Mother Roberson trusted that the Holy Spirit lived in her. Her faith, her prayer and her preaching made the Church of God in Christ the vibrant denomination it is today.

Mother Lizzie Woods Roberson led the Women's Department of the Church of God in Christ (COGIC) after the Civil War. She was known for her powerful preaching and praying. She died in 1945.

≡ Paul Bogle: National Hero of Jamaica

As a young man in Jamaica, Paul Bogle sometimes heard Jesus speaking to him. At first, Jesus told him to "come unto me" for forgiveness and salvation. As Bogle matured, he heard Jesus calling him to something more. He heard Christ telling him that the Holy Spirit rested in him, and that he must give sight to the blind, freedom to the enslaved and life to the dead. He heard Jesus saying that the gospel meant good news—not just in theory, but in reality—and that good news for Jamaica's poor was respect, dignity and justice. Paul Bogle took what he heard very seriously, and he became a preacher in the Native Baptist Church of Jamaica, proclaiming God's goodness to all who would listen.

Black folk in Jamaica were living under tough conditions at the time. Although slavery had ended in 1834, Jamaican authorities had created an "apprenticeship" system that resulted in the virtual re-enslavement of blacks to the white sugar planters. The wages, working conditions and debt arrangements were so onerous that it was nearly impossible to distinguish apprenticeship from slavery.

Black suffering had become so intolerable that Bogle's preaching seemed feeble and ineffectual to him. Searching for a practical solution to black pain, he led a march on the Morant Bay Courthouse to demand an end to apprenticeships. The showdown between angry peasants and colonial troops erupted in a riot, and many protestors were killed. The Morant Bay riots were the beginning of widespread protests, and colonial authorities moved to crush the opposition. Five hundred blacks were whipped, one thousand cottages burned and five hundred blacks, including Paul Bogle and his comrade George Gordon, were executed.

But the murder of Bogle did not end his impact on black Jamaicans. In death, he became the symbol of black pride and resistance, and later leaders such as Marcus Garvey, Bob Marley and others looked to Bogle for inspiration. In 1965, the Jamaican government declared Paul Bogle a national hero.

Baptist preacher and black activist Paul Bogle was executed on October 24, 1865, in Morant Bay, Jamaica, for leading a march protesting the practice of black "apprenticeship." Reggae artists such as Burning Spear and others refer to him in their songs as an important martyr and freedom fighter, and he was declared a national hero by the Jamaican government in 1965.

Susan Paul: Memoir of James Jackson

Susan Paul's teaching was inflamed with a passion for black youth. Her every lesson was a building block upon which her children could create their own destiny. Though slavery did not exist where she taught in the North, blacks were nonetheless treated as subhuman brutes, as if they were unable to learn or earn, able only to serve white people. Cleaning, cooking and serving were all that blacks could hope to attain.

Susan Paul had other ideas, and her lessons were the key that opened the doors of equality. Paul captured her passion for black youth in her book, *Memoir of James Jackson, The Attentive and Obedient Scholar, who died in Boston, October 31, 1833, Aged Six Years and Eleven Months*. Although James Jackson had died prematurely, in his short life he had exhibited a zest for learning. Undaunted by segregation, restrictions and poverty, the young boy did his school work and followed instructions as one on a mission to change the world. For Susan Paul, this young child, anxious to break his bonds and stand upon his own feet, symbolized the black community.

Aware that education could unlock doors previously closed to her people, Susan Paul sought every means available to promote excellence and diligence in school. Knowing that white Americans, both in the North and in the South, discouraged schools for blacks, she countered that as often as possible. She wrote *Memoir of James Jackson* to pass the word in her community that learning and knowledge could enable them to overcome racism and achieve equality in America.

Teacher and author Susan Paul died in 1841. She was an abolitionist who promoted black pride and educational excellence. In 1832, she formed the Garrison Juvenile Choir, a group of students who performed at antislavery gatherings to raise money for the abolitionist movement. She was the author of the influential book on black education, Memoir of James Jackson.

NOVEMBER

Sojourner Truth

Florinda Muñoz Soriano couldn't take it anymore. Poverty, illness and deprivation were all around her, and she would have no more of it. There had to be more to life than what she had thus far seen and heard. Life in the Dominican Republic was hard; few could escape, and promises of land reform and economic justice withered and died fruitless deaths. Soriano was tired of weeping over the graves of neighbors' children, of watching fellow peasants be abused and degraded. Heilo Viejo, where she lived, was one of the toughest areas on the island. Like her neighbors, Florinda struggled to hold her family together under the weight of crushing poverty. Yet she realized nothing would change unless she attacked the roots of their condition.

Soriano began talking with her neighbors and friends about changing the system, about organizing for the struggle ahead. She turned every place into a meeting, and soon marketplace, fields, churches and shacks were hosting peasant forums. After several weeks of organizing, Soriano and hundreds of other peasants demanded that the landowners and government redistribute lands and end unfair practices. These gatherings evolved into the Federation of Christian Agrarian Leagues, groups of peasants who agitated for basic human rights.

The rich, with their unbridled profits, felt threatened, of course. Soriano had become a danger to their privileges, and they tried to frighten her into submission. But *"Mama Tingo"* (which means "one who brings happiness"), as the peasants began calling her, did not back down, even when threatened by the planters' armed patrols.

On behalf of the peasants of the Dominican Republic, the poet Blas Jimenez wrote a poetic tribute to Soriano, describing her as black, brave and beautiful, leading the way to freedom with her machete and her pride. Mama Tingo's work with the peasants and her courage in the face of danger are unforgettable. She brought hope into places familiar with grief and despair. Though burdened with her own troubles, she saw beyond her problems and confronted the real enemy: an economic system that used the poor to support obscene wealth. Florinda Soriano sacrificed herself so others could live with some measure of joy.

On November 1, 1974, Florinda Muñoz Soriano was assassinated by a gunman as she traveled home from a meeting of the Federation of Christian Agrarian Leagues in the Dominican Republic. She was known as "Mama Tingo"—the "one who brings happiness"—by the peasants for whom she fought and died.

☰ Pelé: A National Treasure

In his prime, Pelé was perhaps the most recognizable black person in the world. From Kenya to Japan, from Italy to Chile, people could identify his picture. In his own country of Brazil, he was known and beloved by all. When he was twenty-two, the Brazilian Congress declared him a "non-exportable national treasure." For years, Brazilians considered him their true leader and dubbed him "King Pelé."

Pelé was more than the greatest soccer player of all-time; he was a source of pride for blacks and others living on the margins in the Third World. In the 1950s and 1960s, parts of Africa were still colonized, Central and South America were dominated by the United States and black heroes were scarce. Onto this global scene stepped Pelé. Wearing the white jersey of his Santos team, with number "10" on his back, Pelé electrified the world. The Santos team was unbeatable in Brazil, and when Pelé joined the national team, they won an unprecedented three World Cups. Black, brown and white children all over the world wanted to be like Pelé. Seldom has anyone been so loved and revered, not only for what he did on the field but also for what he did for international black pride and self-esteem.

A prolific black Brazilian soccer player, Pelé scored 1279 goals in 1362 games. He dominated the game of soccer during his reign as "King Pelé."

☰ Saint Martin de Porres: Black Saint of Peru

Even as a child, Martin de Porres expressed God's love for the poor and sick. When he was twelve, church members and priests were amazed at his compassion and generosity, and many wondered aloud why he was so holy. Martin de Porres was born in Lima, Peru, son of a Spanish nobleman and a free black woman from Panama. Since his parents were not married, Porres carried the twin burdens of illegitimacy and mixed race. He did not complain about his origins, however, and the stares, whispers and closed doors he encountered did not diminish his confidence. Instead, Martin de Porres gave himself to the sick and the poor on a scale never before seen in Peru.

At fifteen, he joined the Third Order of Saint Dominic and was part of a community of priests, with whom he would spend the next forty-five years. Because the Dominican Order excluded black men from full participation, he joined the Third Order without the full rights of membership accorded to others. His love for the poor, however, convinced the Order to change their policy and admit him with all privileges.

As Martin de Porres ministered to African slaves and opened orphanages for homeless children, he ignored racial slights and obstacles. His spirituality became legendary around Lima and, in time, over all of Peru. No one was too sick, too poor, too disfigured or too wretched for his loving touch. Peruvian Catholics began spreading the word that he could lay hands upon the sick and heal their illnesses. Martin de Porres did whatever he could for those in need. Though he knew discrimination and exclusion, he focused his life on the good he could do for others.

Martin de Porres died in Lima, Peru, on November 3, 1639. He was canonized a saint in 1962 by the Catholic Church and has become the patron saint of racial justice and compassion for the poor.

NOV 4   ≣ **Dr. Rayford W. Logan: The Transforming Power of History**

Lieutenant Rayford W. Logan was thoroughly disgusted with his country. He and his fellow black soldiers of the 92nd Infantry Division had risked their lives in the muddy trenches of Belgium and France. They faced the same German bullets and artillery shells as their white countrymen, yet their own government treated them as pariahs. When southern congressmen felt that French reporters were too complimentary of black combat bravery, they compelled U.S. Army officers to warn the French not to speak highly of black troops in front of white Americans—or to allow black men anywhere near French women. Within their own ranks, black soldiers fared no better. White soldiers freely called them "nigger," even if they were officers, such as Rayford Logan. The final blow of humiliation came when England and France allowed African soldiers in the victory march through Paris, while America excluded her own black citizens.

For Rayford Logan, enough was enough. A Phi Beta Kappa member from Williams College, Logan saw that black military service and war wounds did nothing to reduce white hatred, and he became convinced America would never change. Once the war was over, he vowed to remain in France, where he stayed for five years and helped establish the fledgling Pan-African movement.

Years later, he had a change of heart. He returned to America in 1924 to participate in the work for civil and human rights. For Logan, understanding was the first step toward transformation, and he chose history as his weapon for change. Lt. Logan became Dr. Logan, and this history professor began to teach in a way that students could use it to shape their future.

Logan put his own encounters with American racism into the context of history. Rather than wallow in self-pity, he explored the roots of America's shame and worked to change it. One of his most important books, *The Betrayal of the Negro*, explores the period between 1877 and 1918 to reveal the growth of white supremacy. In addition to his lectures, Logan was a leader in Carter G. Woodson's Association for the Study of Negro Life and History and later participated in the 1963 March on Washington.

For almost thirty years, Dr. Rayford Logan taught at Howard University, and many future leaders studied under his tutelage. For Dr. Logan, history was not a worn-out tale shelved away in a dusty library but a means for grappling with and overcoming obstacles for a better future.

Dr. Rayford W. Logan taught history at Howard University from 1938 to 1965. He died on November 4, 1982, in Washington, D.C., his birthplace 85 years earlier. He was the author of **The Betrayal of the Negro.**

NOV 5 ≣ **Revolutionary War Slaves: Black Loyalists to the English**

When the Revolutionary War broke out in America, black slaves wondered which side would deliver the freedom they so longed for. Although the "Founding Fathers" used all the right words, their deeds fell short of their rhetoric. George Washington, Thomas Jefferson, Patrick Henry and the others talked of the evils of tyranny and the blessing of liberty, yet they went home to their plantations to be waited on by their slaves. As a result of this duplicity, many black slaves flocked to the British Crown. And it turned out to be for good reason. For on November 7, 1775, Lord Dunsmore of England declared, "I hereby declare that all indebted Negroes or others, free, that are willing to bear arms."

When cries rang out, "The British are coming," slaves could almost taste the sweetness of liberty, and they risked their lives to run away from their masters and take up arms. Here are some of the brave black souls who stood as an indictment against the hypocrisy of the Christian roots of the American Founding Fathers: Quanimo Dolly helped the English defeat the Americans at Savannah; Thomas Peters was a sergeant in the British Black Pioneers and a political leader in the community at Nova Scotia; Ralph Henry ran away from his master Patrick, author of the famous line, "Give me liberty or give me death." There were many others. Thirty of Thomas Jefferson's slaves ran away to the British when General Cornwallis approached. The slaves of George Washington and James Madison escaped to join the English. Some estimate that during the Revolutionary War thirty thousand slaves left Virginia alone. Boston and Violet King, David and Phyllis George, Hannah Jackson, Chloe Walker, British Freedom, Benjamin Whitecuffe, Isaac Anderson, David George, Cato Perkins and thousands of others fought with the British, sought refuge in their camps, traveled to Nova Scotia or Sierra Leone and displayed tremendous courage in their fight for liberty.

When the war ended, George Washington tried to negotiate the slaves' return to slavery, but these black slaves went wherever freedom awaited. They courageously built homes in Nova Scotia, Sierra Leone and London. Between the border of South Carolina and Georgia, ex-slaves built a fortified community of twenty-one homes on Bear Creek. They resisted American attacks for several years, hiding deep in the swamps and wetlands. Though the war was over and the English were defeated, they continued to call themselves "The King of England's Soldiers." For these and thousands of other slaves, England represented the possibility of freedom, while America sought only their continued dehumanization and bondage.

The book **Rough Crossings: Britain, the Slaves and the American Revolution** *is a stunning account of the courage and dedication of these early freedom fighters. On November 7, 1775, the British promised freedom to any slave who would fight for the crown. In contrast, the Americans resisted black enlistment, finally relented under pressure and then re-enslaved the soldiers as soon as the war was over.*

NOV 6　　　　　　　≡ **William Wells Brown: "Now Go and Get Your Liberty"**

William Wells Brown overcame the brutality of slavery to become a writer, abolitionist and defender of human rights. His beautiful memoir, *Narrative of William Wells Brown, A Fugitive Slave, Written by Himself*, describes the heartbreak of his life as a slave. He saw family and cabin-mates beaten and abused, and often witnessed slaves murdered at the master's whim or on the slightest pretext.

As a young man, Brown saw his mother, sister and brothers sold to a cotton plantation in the Deep South. His narrative portrays in bitter detail the scene of his last words with his mother. Brown watched as his mother—the woman who had held him when he was sick and taught him how to survive—was chained with fifty other slaves like animals. Unable to touch or embrace, Brown and his mother spoke for what they knew would be the last time. Brown said his heart was so broken, "It struggled to free itself from human form." As his mother was pulled away, she told William, "You have ever said that you would not die a slave, that you would be a freeman. Now go and get your liberty!"

With those words, his beloved mother was dragged away. Brown later wrote that he pretended his mother and siblings were dead; this thought brought him more peace than imagining their suffering under a harsh and lustful master.

That night, he determined to seek his liberty, just as his mother had admonished. On New Year's Eve, 1834, at the age of twenty, William Wells Brown escaped to the North. Instead of letting pain paralyze him, he transformed himself into the embodiment of human freedom. Brown founded several Underground Railroad stops and became a powerful voice for abolition. In 1847, he published his *Narrative*, a compelling testimony against slavery. It became the talk of the abolitionist movement in the North, Canada and Great Britain; in the South, copies were destroyed on sight.

His novel, *Clotel, Or the President's Daughter*, was published in 1853. It was the first novel written by an African American, and it shocked America. There had been talk among the abolitionists that former President Thomas Jefferson had fathered children by his slaves, and Brown dared to tell that story in the pages of *Clotel*.

Throughout his life, William Wells Brown's followed his mother's advice to "go and get your liberty." Once he had tasted the sweetness of liberty himself, he sought to extend its blessings to as many as he could. He made the horrors of slavery real to thousands and fueled anti-slavery sentiment. But he didn't stop there. It was as though suffering had expanded Brown's heart. He cared not only for black causes, but he also fought for women's rights and was a delegate at the 1849 Paris Peace Conference.

Author and human rights advocate William Wells Brown died in Chelsea, Massachusetts, on November 6, 1884. He was author of the **Narrative of William Wells Brown, A Fugitive Slave, Written by Himself** *and* **Clotel, Or the President's Daughter,** *the first novel published by an African American.*

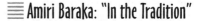

NOV 7 ≣ Amiri Baraka: "In the Tradition"

Amiri Baraka is a prolific black artist, but his path to literary brilliance was obscured in his early years: He flunked out of Howard University and was dishonorably discharged from the United States Army. After a time as a "beat poet" in Greenwich Village, Baraka, then known as LeRoi Jones, visited Cuba. Much of his literary work had been apolitical, but in Cuba he saw the common people politically mobilized by art. After his trip to Cuba, Jones was transformed. He changed his name to Amiri Baraka and became a militant voice in the Black Arts Movement. Located primarily in Newark and the East Coast, the music, art and poetry of the Black Arts Movement is often compared in influence with the Harlem Renaissance.

Baraka was not just an artist, and his activism was expressed in many ways, most notably his work on the 1972 National Black Political Convention in Gary, Indiana. While many activists from the sixties became more conservative in later years, Baraka became more radical. In the seventies, he turned away from America's material temptations and diversions to join a Marxist-Leninist Party, the League of Revolutionary Struggle (LRS), a multi-racial formation of activists who believed both in socialism and in art as tools in the fight for equality.

Baraka expressed black solidarity with internationalism brilliantly in his poem "In the Tradition." On the album *New Music, New Poetry*, Baraka and tenor saxophonist David Murray perform the poem and describe the liberation struggle of the oppressed classes. They talk of how Harriet Tubman, Langston Hughes, Malcolm X, Jacob Lawrence, Bessie Smith and others fought for black liberation through art and action; and how Irish literature, Puerto Rican music and Appalachian culture does the same for other oppressed people.

Another of Baraka's contributions is his work to highlight black artists from around the world. He has written and lectured about Mikey Smith of Jamaica, (author of the classic poem "Mi Cyaan Believe It"), Lynton Kwesi Johnson of England, Ngugi wa Thiongo of Kenya and others. Through them, he links the struggle of African-Americans with global black aspirations for freedom.

Baraka's politics and art have never stagnated, and he has continually opened himself to new perspectives and transformed his art accordingly. His evolution from beat poet to nationalist to Marxist internationalist reflects his search for solutions to poverty and oppression, and he continues to perform and write on behalf of blacks and working people around the world.

On November 3, 1983, black poet and activist Amiri Baraka, formerly known as LeRoi Jones, addressed the Michael Smith Memorial in Brixton, London, where he condemned the murder of black intellectuals and activists such as Mikey Smith, Walter Rodney and Maurice Bishop. Baraka's classic works include, Black Music, Blues People, Daggers and Javelins, Black Fire, The Music: Reflections on Jazz and Blues, Tales of the Out and the Gone *and* Somebody Blew Up America.

NOV 8 ≣ Edward (Eddie) Robinson: "Coach"

The interview had gone well; all Eddie had to do was wait. After several anxious days, he received word to return to Louisiana Negro Normal and Industrial Institute to discuss the job. To Eddie Robinson's relief and excitement, the Negro Institute asked him to be their football coach and athletic director. He had long dreamt of coaching young men at the Negro Institute, and now his vision was fulfilled. The administrators at the Institute were glad to have him and hoped he would stay long enough to help create a first-rate black school in Louisiana.

They would not be disappointed, for Eddie Robinson stayed fifty-six more years, beginning in 1941. Coach Robinson's first year was a great success as the team went undefeated at 8-0. Yet his greatest contribution was not the team's victories, but his transformation of Negro boys into black men. Many boys who enrolled at Grambling State University, as the school was later renamed, became adults under the tutelage of Coach Robinson. His influence was so pervasive that when people referred to "Coach" everyone knew they were talking about Robinson.

"Coach" became a legend not only at Grambling but throughout the circuit of historically black colleges. His teams, records and the men he produced brought pride and honor to all black Americans, and to Grambling in particular. Over two hundred Grambling players were drafted by the National Football League (NFL), more than any other college in the United States. Buck Buchanan, Tank Younger, Doug Williams and Willie Davis are but a few of the stars whom Robinson prepared for the NFL.

Other schools may have had more money, richer donors, better stadiums, newer equipment and more media coverage, but none of them had Eddie Robinson. That a black school in Louisiana could send more men to the NFL than powers such as Ohio State, Notre Dame and University of Southern California is a testimony to Grambling's "Coach," the incomparable Eddie Robinson.

Edward "Eddie" Robinson began coaching football at Grambling State University in 1941. He coached his last game on November 15, 1997, and died on April 3, 2007. His focus on athletic excellence and high moral standards were recognized by the nation. He sent over 200 Grambling players to the National Football League.

NOV 9   ≡ Sergeant William H. Carney: The Altar of Freedom

William H. Carney struggled to make sense of his life. The black teenager and his parents had recently been freed from slavery, and his life of torment had finally ended. But what did it mean? Could his life have meaning after such a terrible beginning? These questions lead him to devote his life to Christ and to use his freedom for the salvation of his race. He attended "secret schools" in Virginia, and when his family moved to New Bedford, Massachusetts, he joined a church led by a Reverend Jackson.

While Carney was preparing for the ministry, the Civil War erupted and his plans changed. Carney later wrote:

> *Previous to the formation of colored troops, I had a strong inclination to prepare myself for the ministry; but when the country called for all persons, I could best serve my God by serving my country and my oppressed brothers. The sequel is short; I enlisted for the war.*

Carney enlisted in the 54th Massachusetts Volunteer Infantry, the famed colored regiment, and shortly thereafter was promoted to sergeant. The new non-commissioned officer was assigned responsibility for a squad in Company C. He risked his life at the assault on Battery Wagner in South Carolina and led his troops in several other engagements in the South.

Though he could have been a pastor, evangelist or teacher in New Bedford, safely ensconced from the battlefield, Carney's chosen ministry became working for the freedom of his people. He embodied the qualities of a true minister in his service and sacrifice. He may have been free, but he felt his freedom was incomplete until all his people were free. He followed the call of his Christ to risk his life on the altar of freedom as a Union soldier.

On November 6, 1863, Sergeant William H. Carney of the 54th Massachusetts Volunteer Infantry wrote a letter to the abolitionist paper The Liberator *about the life of black soldiers. Under pressure from soldiers such as Carney, abolitionists and others, Congress finally authorized equal pay for black and white Union soldiers in 1864.*

NOV 10   ≣ Ken Saro-Wiwa: "The Moral Victory"

Ken Saro-Wiwa sat alone in the darkness of his Nigerian jail cell. His execution was set for the following morning, and he was spending his last evening recounting his life. He had been the Commissioner for Works, Land and Transport in Nigeria and a celebrated political journalist for the Lagos daily newspapers *Punch, Vanguard* and *Daily Times*. He had written for Nigeria's most successful soap opera, *Basi & Company*, which had been watched by millions of Africans, and his book, *Sozaboy: A Novel in Rotten English*, had delivered an insightful satire on Nigeria's corruption.

Saro-Wiwa's talents had offered him opportunities and comfort unknown to most Nigerians, yet he had turned his back on his own success and cast his lot and talents with his oppressed Ogoni people. One of Nigeria's two hundred and fifty tribes, the Ogoni people had the misfortune of living atop Nigeria's rich oil reserves. Multi-national oil corporations' quest for drilling sites had turned the Ogoni's fertile farms into an ecological wasteland. Formerly quiet farmlands had been transformed by oil spills, gas flares and the stench of sulphur.

Ken Saro-Wiwa had used his considerable abilities in politics, journalism, entertainment and literature to expose the illicit collaboration between the Shell Oil Company and the Nigerian government. His videos, articles and speeches had exposed the devastation of his people and their beloved land. Not content to merely document injustice, Saro-Wiwa and others had gone on to found the Movement for the Survival of the Ogoni People (MOSOP).

In the 1990s, MOSOP had become increasingly militant, marching on government buildings and disrupting Shell's operations. Saro-Wiwa's visibility had brought support and respectability to MOSOP, but as the organization had grown, so had the repression. Activists had been murdered and homes burned to the ground. Saro-Wiwa was ultimately arrested for the murder of four Ogoni military collaborators, despite the fact he was elsewhere at the time of the murders.

So now, Ken Saro-Wiwa sat in his cell, awaiting his execution. The courts had set the next day, November 10, for his hanging, and Saro-Wiwa used his last night to write letters to his friends, among them William Boyd:

> I'm in good spirits…. There's no doubt that my idea will succeed in time…. The most important thing for me is that I have used my talents as a writer to enable the Ogoni people to confront their tormentors…. My writing did it, and it sure makes me feel good…. I think I have the moral victory.

Nigerian author and journalist Ken Saro-Wiwa was hung in Port Harcourt, Nigeria, on November 10, 1995. Massive international outcry could not stop the execution of Saro-Wiwa and eight of his comrades by the Nigerian government. Saro-Wiwa had exposed the corrupt dealings between the Shell Oil Company and the Nigerian government over land occupied by his Ogoni people for centuries.

NOV 11   ≣ Nat Turner: "The Last Should Be First"

When Nat Turner was born, his mother knew he was special. There was something about his countenance and expression that set him apart from other children. Nat was a slave, just like his mother, brothers and sister, but he acted as if he were free. As a child, Turner declared that God was his only Master and that no man owned him. As he grew older, his relationship with God deepened. He preached to slave gatherings long after sunset and far from the ears of the master. He preached about struggle: God against the Devil, light against darkness, freedom against slavery, black against white.

One spring afternoon Nat Turner was working in the fields when a vision from God seized him. As he recounted his experience:

> I heard a loud noise in the heavens, and the Spirit instantly appeared to me and said the serpent was loosened and Christ had laid down the yoke he had borne for the sins of man and that I should take it on and fight against the serpent; for the time was fast approaching that the first should be last and the last should be first.

This was not the only time Turner heard God's voice urging him to act on behalf of his people. In February 1831, he saw a solar eclipse that he believed was a sign that the very heavens were demanding a change on earth. The following August, he led five other slaves in a revolt that horrified the South and stunned the nation. As they marched from plantation to plantation, killing slaveholders and freeing slaves, the revolution grew to sixty slaves. Under Turner's direction, their goal was the military arsenal in Jerusalem, Virginia. For Turner, the destination of "Jerusalem" confirmed God's hand upon his mission. After three days of fighting and fifty-seven casualties, however, white militia and vigilantes defeated the rebellion. Though Turner was able to hide for several weeks, the authorities finally captured him. The court declared to Nat Turner "that you be hanged from the neck until you are dead! dead! dead!" On November 11, 1831, the sentence was carried out.

As a black man bold enough to strike against the violence of slavery, Nat Turner exploded the myth of black docility. Many consider his rebellion the first blow of the Civil War. Turner has since become a symbol of black resistance. From black Union soldiers in the Civil War, to marchers in the Civil Rights Movement, to ghetto youth in the Black Panther Party—all remember Turner as a courageous black human being who acted on behalf of his people.

Nat Turner was executed on November 11, 1831, in Southampton, Virginia, along with 100 other black slaves after he led a revolt against slavery. The whole South lived in morbid fear that somewhere out there lurked "the next Nat Turner." He is the subject of William Stryon's Pulitzer Prize-winning novel, **The Confessions of Nat Turner.**

NOV 12   ≣ Wilma Glodeau Rudolph: Run for Your Life

Frail and sickly, young Wilma Glodeau Rudolph struggled just to walk. Her knees weak and swollen, her lungs holding more fluid than air, Rudolph managed just a few shuffling steps at a time. Unable to run, play and jump rope like other children in the neighborhood, she was further isolated by a scarlet fever-induced rash. She wore leg braces until she was nine and could not walk until she was ten. Scarlet fever, double pneumonia and polio ravaged her young body. Family members, doctors and nurses doubted if she would ever be healthy.

Not content just to walk, however, Wilma Rudolph began to run. To the astonishment of those who watched her struggle, she began to outrun friends on the way to school. By the time she was twelve, she was the fastest runner in her school—not the fastest *girl*, but the fastest *runner*.

Thus began one of the remarkable stories of our time. In junior high, Rudolph set the school basketball record for total points scored. A few years later, she attended Tennessee State University and became a cornerstone of the famed Tigerbelles track squad. Rudolph and her teammates toured the South, defeating all comers. The running career of Wilma Rudolph culminated in the 1960 Summer Olympics in Rome. Under the gaze of the whole world, she took gold medals in the hundred-meter and two-hundred-meter dashes and the hundred-meter four-team relay.

Wilma Rudolph was the first woman in Olympic history to win three gold medals in track. Her transformation from a stricken girl in braces to the fastest woman in the world is a stunning example of the power of persistence. Though born with little physical stamina, she made herself an athlete by sheer determination and will. Her courage to strengthen her legs and lungs to overcome her childhood weaknesses is a source of inspiration and encouragement for anyone who faces seemingly insurmountable obstacles.

Black track and field runner Wilma Rudolph died on November 12, 1994, in Detroit, Michigan at the age of 53. She won three gold medals in the 1960 Summer Olympics in Rome and spent her post-Olympic life teaching and performing community service.

NOV 13   ≡ Lerone Bennett: The Challenge of Blackness

At some point in life, every black American faces not only the question of what it means to be black but also what it means to be black in America. Few are more qualified to speak on blackness than senior editor of *Ebony* magazine, black studies lecturer and member of the Institute of the Black World, Lerone Bennett. At the first national conference of the Institute of the Black World, Bennett delivered his remarkable address, "The Challenge of Blackness," and his insights that afternoon still resound in the black community.

Bennett began by quoting philosopher Jean-Paul Sarte, "Truth is the perspective of the truly disinherited," and expanded this to say that an American history that excludes blacks is inherently false. He noted, for example, that "George Washington and George Washington's slaves lived different realities." For history to be complete, he argued, black reality had to be told in its fullness. He went on to proclaim that blackness is a challenge to America and all its values: "For if black reality is what America really is, then obviously America is not what it claims to be."

This statement has profound implications. To the extent that blacks live an altogether different reality than whites, then whites live an illusion. If black reality is the truth, then America has lived a lie, and black folks are obligated to confront the nation as the bearers of truth—not with self-righteous pettiness but with an openness that exemplifies what justice and democracy truly mean. Bennett extended this into a challenge for his people:

The first challenge of blackness is defining blackness. We believe that this challenge will require the long and careful collaboration of many minds, and that we can no longer afford the luxury of doing our own thing in our own private pastures. By this...we say we believe in the community of the black dead and the black living and the black unborn. We believe that community has prior claim on our time and our talent and resources, and that we must respond when it calls.

Bennett concluded where he began, emphasizing that black folks' experience with pain prepares them for the salvation of their race and their nation:

It is the challenge...of letting our light shine, not only because it is our light, but also because in the world in which we live, the black light we reflect is the only light left.

Lerone Bennett has been the Senior Editor of Ebony *magazine, a prolific writer and lecturer and a member of the Institute of the Black World. He gave his "Challenge of Blackness" lecture in November of 1969 at the first national conference of the Institute of the Black World.*

NOV 14 ≣ **Captain Grant Reynolds: Chaplain, United States Army**

Captain Grant Reynolds walked back to his office following his usual Sunday sermon in the chapel. Usually he walked alone, but this Sunday several black soldiers followed close behind him. It was a beautiful spring morning, but Reynolds was oblivious to the sun's warmth. All of his attention was focused on what the black soldiers were saying: They simply couldn't take it anymore. As they each recalled incidents of degradation and insults from white officers, soldiers and citizens, their anger rose to a crescendo. They asked Reynolds how long they could risk their lives for a country that treated them like brutes. They all knew the stories: that Nazi prisoners of war had been treated better in United States prison camps than black American soldiers; that innocent black soldiers were often jailed on the spurious word of white citizens; that words such as "nigger" and "spear-chucker" were used against them at every turn.

The men were at their boiling point, and Captain Reynolds knew it. "You're a captain and a minister," they said, "and you've got to help us. These red-necks are running a plantation here, and we can't take it anymore." After the soldiers left, Reynolds could not shake the images they had presented; he was all too familiar with their frustration. Even though he was a chaplain and an officer, most whites referred to him, too, as a "nigger." Reynolds longed to make things right, but he was haunted by the helplessness he felt, even as a United States Army Captain.

In January 1944, Chaplain Reynolds decided to resign his commission and join the NAACP's campaign on behalf of Negro soldiers. He wrote several brilliant articles condemning the United States government and the War Department for perpetuating white supremacy. He pointed out the hypocrisy of asking the victims of racism to risk their lives for the perpetuators of their degradation.

In one particularly devastating article, Reynolds noted that in many southern Army camps black troops discovered that the South was "more vigorously engaged in fighting the Civil War than in training soldiers to resist Hitler." Reynolds was relentless in his criticisms:

> The War Department has sold the Negro soldier a rotten bill of goods.... The Negro...is given stark evidence each day of the War Department's unqualified disrespect for his status as an American citizen.

Reynolds may have ended his official ministry as chaplain to black troops, but he lived the gospel of liberation wherever he traveled. His articles were read by the Roosevelt Administration, and many suspect that his work played a role in destroying America's segregated Army shortly after World War II.

Captain Grant Reynolds, a chaplain in the United States Army, joined the Washington Bureau of the NAACP and wrote several articles for their magazine, The Crisis. One particular investigative report—a series published in September, October and November of 1944—was studied by key figures in the U.S. government and led to eventual changes in Army policy.

NOV 15   ≡ Stokely Carmichael: "Black Power!"

Stokely Carmichael traveled the black world as few others have. He was born in Trinidad, grew up in the Bronx, studied philosophy at Howard University, served time in Mississippi's Parchman State Prison, marched in Alabama and died in Guinea, West Africa. Carmichael's travels mirrored his love for black people and his passion for their freedom. Whether in the university, in a jail or on the streets, Carmichael demanded that black people live as free and respected citizens of the world.

After his graduation from Howard University, Carmichael helped organize the famous Student Nonviolent Coordinating Committee (SNCC). SNCC was a powerful organization, mobilizing students into a political force that could not be ignored. One of their projects was a voter registration drive in Lowndes County, Alabama, where they helped found the Lowndes County Freedom Democratic Party. A movement comprised of students, farmers and workers, the Freedom Democratic Party used a Black Panther as its symbol, which was later adopted by Oakland's Black Panther Party.

In August of 1966, Carmichael became a folk hero among militant African Americans. Wearing dark shades and sporting a short Afro, Carmichael demanded not handouts or integration but "Black Power!" Almost instantly, this declaration energized younger militant blacks who were tired of turning the other cheek to violent racists. "Black Power" became a rallying cry that frightened white liberals and intimidated black moderates.

By 1969, Carmichael had focused his attention on the liberation of Africa. Changing his name to Kwame Ture, he founded the All-African People's Revolutionary Party, which denounced U.S. imperialism and promoted Pan-Africanism and socialism. Whether at Howard, in SNCC or in Guinea, Stokely Carmichael held fast to one central commitment: freedom for his people.

Political activist Stokely Carmichael, who changed his name to Kwame Ture, died of cancer in Conakry, Guinea, West Africa, on November 15, 1998. He was 57 years old. He helped form the Student Nonviolent Coordinating Committee (SNCC) and popularized the phrase "Black Power."

NOV 16   ≡ The Black Slaves' Church: Foundation of Faith

In America's early years, many white Christians were so immersed in slavery and racism that it is hard to imagine how they reconciled their actions with the gospel of Jesus Christ. Their beating, raping, selling and abusing of human beings contradicted every one of Jesus' teachings to love God and others. To complete the utter hypocrisy, some white Christians actually forbade blacks to engage in their own worship.

With this horrific backdrop, some historians now argue that the only real Christians were the slaves. Some posit that without the religion of the slaves Christianity as an authentic faith could not have survived slavery. Certainly, the slaves' narratives and their spirituals stand as testimonies to their love of God.

We know that slaves went deep into the woods for prayer and song that would last for hours. One slave would start singing a Psalm or a hymn, and others would join in, adding new verses, moaning new melodies and giving birth to new songs of freedom. They believed not in a distant Christ but in one who had come in the flesh and suffered, as they did, at the hands of cruel oppressors. They embraced a Christ who was with them in the cotton fields, on the rice plantations and on the auction block. Their church was not a building but the presence of God wherever they gathered. Mary Reynolds, an ex-slave, once said:

We never heard of no church, but us have praying in the cabins. We'd set on the floor and pray with our heads down low and sing low, but if Solomon [the slave driver] heared, he'd come and beat on the wall with the stock of his whip. He'd say, "I'll come in there and tear the hide off you back…." Once my maw and paw taken me and Katherine after night to slip to another place to a prayin-and-singin'…. We prays for the end of tribulations and the end of beatings and for shoes that fit our feet.

Slaves had no power, protection, education or money; they did not own their own bodies, nor could they protect their families from the ravages of the owner. But they did have their faith. In Christ they found a Savior who felt what they felt, who could deliver them from every evil. For many, that was enough. Their faith led them to survival, resistance, family and community, and their faith lives on in the bosom of black America today.

There are over 65,000 black Christian churches in the United States today. There are 23 million African-American Christians, including 11.1 million Baptists in three different conventions, 3.7 million members of the Church of God in Christ, 3.4 million in the African Methodist Episcopal and African Methodist Episcopal Zion churches, 2 million Roman Catholics and 3.5 million in smaller black communions and predominately white Protestant groups. They all owe their faith to the foundation laid by slave Christians.

NOV 17 ≡ Audre Lorde: "Poetry Is Not a Luxury"

Audre Lorde's writings are a window into a world often neglected and diminished by our society. Her solitary body contained many identities, and she balanced them all in perfect wholeness. She was black, lesbian, feminist, mother and lover, a woman who saw no contradiction in her identity. Her self-understanding was evident in her work *Sister Outsider*, a collection of essays and speeches in which she described how society tried to force her to the margins.

Audre Lorde was, by nature and identity, at odds with the dominant powers of her day. A black lesbian feminist was perhaps the single most neglected and least considered entity in America. Yet through her poetry and essays, Lorde courageously took her stand as a human being. Her most quoted poem, "Coal," makes the claim that her color, her blackness, emerges from the depths of the earth, and that her words, beginning in blackness, become jewels in the brilliance of light.

In 1984, Lorde wrote the classic essay "Poetry Is Not a Luxury," in which she urged her fellow sisters to speak their minds:

These places of possibility within ourselves are dark because they are an-cient and hidden; they have survived and grown strong through that dark-ness. Within these deep places, each one of us holds an incredible reserve of creativity and power, of unexamined and unrecorded emotion and feeling. The woman's place of power within each of us is neither white nor surface; it is dark, it is ancient, and it is deep. For women then, poetry is not a luxury. It is a necessity of our existence.

Audre Lorde wrote not as a frivolous aside but as an essential element of her survival. For her, poetry was not a luxury, for through it she spoke her mind, enlightened her sisters and changed her world.

Poet Audre Lorde died on November 17, 1992, in St. Croix in the Virgin Islands. She was the author of Sister Outsider, *a collections of essays and speeches, and the influential essay, "Poetry Is Not a Luxury," which urged women to speak their mind through poetry.*

NOV 18 ≡ Female Benevolent Society of St. Thomas: "What I Have Is Ours"

Grace Bustill and Sarah Allen, two black churchwomen in Philadelphia, were but two of many black women who fueled a successful self-help movement at the end of the eighteenth century. In 1793, Bustill and Allen were active in the forma-tion the Female Benevolent Society of St. Thomas in Philadelphia, Pennsylvania.

The women of the Society were devoted to helping those less fortunate than themselves. Times were difficult, money was scarce and life was rough even for whites, and family and church were the only places people could turn for help during financial or personal crisis. Yet it was black women—who were considered the lowest of the low, who were treated the worst, who were able to earn the least—who came together to help others. They collected dues and pooled their resources for families in dire need. Their clerk would receive requests for help from people who were sick, hungry or dying, and the Society would decide how much each person would receive. They also determined which of their members would make pastoral visits in the black community.

Some of the women of the Society were free from birth; others were recent refugees from slavery. Yet all shared a desire to uplift the race. Meeting weekly in a church basement, the Society worked for the social betterment of black Phila-delphia. Educating the untrained, hiding fugitive slaves and feeding the hungry were critical parts of their program.

The women of the Society of St. Thomas may have been oppressed themselves, but collectively they were strong. They had little, but together they gave much. They lived by the creed that what they owned as individuals was to be shared with all. "I may not have much," said the members of the Society, "but what I have, is ours."

The Female Benevolent Society of St. Thomas was one of the hundreds of black self-help societies in Philadelphia and other northern cities. Most were created by black women and existed for the social betterment of the community.

NOV 19   ≣ João da Cruz e Sousa: The Black Poet

His name, João da Cruz e Sousa, declared his origins, suffering and destiny. His mother had grown up in slavery but was freed by the time he was born. Exhilarated by the birth of her son, she named him João da Cruz, after the Spanish Catholic mystic St. John of the Cross, who had penned magnificent descriptions of his quest for God. Likewise, João da Cruz used poetry in his own quest for liberty. Like John of the Cross, he too was a teenager when his first works were published.

He was also named Sousa, in honor of the Brazilian liberator, Marshall Sousa, who had freed his father. João da Cruz e Sousa lived into the full meaning of his name. As playwright, essayist and poet, he protested Brazil's slave system. He became known all over Brazil as "The Black Poet," writing of freedom and Brazilian abolitionism. His poems, such as *"Violes que choram"* ("Weeping of Guitars"), *"Cancao negra,"* ("Black Song") and *"Pandemonium,"* testified to an uncompromised black humanity.

In João da Cruz e Sousa, poetry, freedom and art were forged into a coherent celebration of human dignity.

Black poet João da Cruz e Sousa died of tuberculosis on November 19, 1898, in Sitio, Minas Gerais, Brazil. Though only 37 when he died, he was a seminal figure in South American literature and opposition to slavery.

Deep in the Pernambuco region of Brazil, beyond the influence of cities and towns, lay the African nation of Palmares. No one professed to know the exact location, and anyone who claimed to know was called a liar. The Portuguese army searched in vain for years, chasing rumors and trails but finding nothing. But somehow, despite its secrecy, runaway African slaves knew how to find it. Though no black—slave or free—claimed to have any idea where Palmares was, black runaways managed to end up there. Once they found Palmares, they found freedom. In Palmares, African slaves were transformed from Portuguese property into liberated human beings.

By 1670, over twenty thousand escaped slaves called Palmares home. Their charismatic leader, Zumbi, built Palmares into a functioning nation. Deep in the Brazilian jungle, Zumbi and his people organized agricultural ventures, developed political systems and built a military. For nearly one hundred years, Palmares was the most significant Maroon community in the Americas. Maroon, derived from the Spanish word *cimarron*, which originally referred to domestic cattle that had taken to the hills, began to be applied to runaway slaves and ultimately was used to describe the many fiercely independent ex-slave communities in the Americas. Though Palmares was the most significant, other Maroon communities existed in Brazil and such places as Jamaica, Venezuela and Florida.

Formed to protect themselves from re-enslavement, Maroons allowed runaways to live as free as their courage would allow. The Maroon community made it possible for black babies to be born in Palmares and live their entire lives in freedom, never tasting slavery's bitterness. Zumbi and his people did what many thought was impossible: They built, from nothing, institutions and values based on self-determination and dignity.

Zumbi, leader of the Palmares Maroon Community in Brazil, was captured by the Portuguese army and beheaded on November 20, 1694. To destroy the legend of his immortality, his murderers publicly displayed his head for months afterward. Ironically, the date of his death has since been proclaimed Brazil's National Day of Black Consciousness.

≣ Henriette Delille and Juliette Gaudin: Sisters of the Holy Family

"Who do you think you are? You are proud…too proud!" This was the reaction of the Archbishop of New Orleans in 1872 when he realized that the woman who stood before him, wearing a nun's habit, was a black woman.

That traumatic episode was typical of the obstacles encountered by Henriette Delille and Juliette Gaudin, creators of the Sisters of the Holy Family in New Orleans. Racism in the South and in the Catholic Church was so pervasive then that black people were not even allowed to be considered "holy." Only one order of black nuns had ever been recognized—the Oblate Sisters of Providence, in 1831.

The South in the 1840s was so arrayed against black humanity that even expressions of faith and love were crushed. Blacks were thought to lack a soul, spirit and any other characteristics of humans. Despite this, Delille and Gaudin met with white nuns, talked with priests, visited archbishops, wrote letters and studied with black women to build a community of black nuns. Their desire for holiness overcame the constant refrain of discouragement they heard, and they sought the prayerfulness, devotion and discipline of the convent.

But they did not desire separation from the world; rather, they sought to educate, serve and nurse the black community around them. Delille and Gaudin believed that Christ had called them to serve the poorest of their people, and they were not about to wait for an official blessing to carry on their work. No pro-hibition, custom or rule would stand in their way. These two women, Delille from New Orleans and Gaudin from Cuba, believed that the sacraments and teachings of the Catholic Church brought them closer to God and to their people, and they took action, founding a shelter for the homeless, teaching the uneducated and caring for orphans.

On November 21, 1842, on the Feast of the Presentation of the Blessed Vir-gin Mary, the Catholic Church finally recognized their order and allowed them to wear habits—the defining clothing of women religious. On the insistence of Delille, they were called the Sisters of the Holy Family.

The order attracted other women, including Josephine Charles from Balti-more. Each of the sisters was a light of Christ and a servant of the people. Each time they taught a child, sheltered the abandoned or prayed for others, they exemplified both the love of God and the spirituality of black people. For many blacks, a black nun was the defining proclamation that blacks were both human and holy.

The Sisters of the Holy Family of New Orleans was only the second order of African-American nuns to be recognized by the Roman Catholic Church. Co-founder Sister Henrietta Delille died on November 17, 1862; early recruit Sister Josephine Charles died in 1885; and co-founder Sister Juliette Gaudin died in 1887.

≣ Charles Waddell Chesnutt: "Scholar, Worker and Freeman"

Charles Chesnutt is a significant figure in black literary history. In many respects, he was a bridge between the slave narratives and the Harlem Renaissance. More importantly, Chesnutt was master of the short story. His carefully woven tales described black life as few writers have, before or since. At a time when blacks were considered subhumans without soul or insight, Chesnutt portrayed the full range of black emotion. No subject was beyond his reach; he wrote about blacks who passed for white, interracial sex (both forced and consensual), racism and family traumas. Until Chesnutt, few dared explore the open secrets of the racial divide: miscegenation and "passing."

Chesnutt's commitment to truth in fiction superseded his desire for popularity. Though many counseled him to compromise his writings in exchange for increased popularity, Chesnutt refused. Between 1897 and 1905, he published several collections of short stories, including *The Conjure Woman*, *The Goophered Grapevine*, *The Wife of His Youth*, and the novels *The House Behind the Cedars*, *The Marrow of Tradition* and *The Colonel's Dream*. Each work viewed black reality from a different vantage point.

Although Chesnutt's writing received some critical literary acclaim, its major impact was the tool it provided the black struggle for freedom. During his heyday as a writer, Chesnutt's stories could be found in black homes across America. He validated the daily skirmishes with racism and reminded blacks of their dignity and humanity. In 1928, the NAACP awarded Chesnutt their Spingarn Medal for "his pioneer work as a literary artist depicting the life and struggle of Americans of Negro descent, and for his long and useful career as scholar, worker and freeman."

Black author Charles W. Chesnutt died on November 15, 1932, in Cleveland, Ohio. His writing was a bridge between the slave narratives and the literature of the Harlem Renaissance. In 1928, the NAACP awarded him the Spingarn Medal for his "useful career as scholar, worker and freeman."

≣ Albert Ayler: "Truth Is Marching In"

Many view music as a reflection of the politics and movements of the time, but not so with Albert Ayler's music. In 1966, when he recorded his classic "Truth Is Marching In," his sound transcended current events and temporal movements. His soaring, explosive tenor sax screeched and wailed, not about his time but about a time that was not yet. His music reached beyond boundaries to create a world better than what was.

By 1966, Malcolm X had been assassinated, the Vietnam War was underway and political lies abounded. Yet at the Village Vanguard, Ayler was recording "Truth Is Marching In," a different song that began with a slow cadence of truth rising from the earth and then erupted into both beauty and chaos. Ayler later wrote of the song:

> When there's chaos, which is now, only a relatively few people can listen to the music that tells of what will be…. Truth is marching in…and that truth is that there must be peace and joy on earth.

Ayler's music was not about racism, violence, hatred and injustice; it was about the gathered human community building a place where all could share in the bounty of peace. Jazz critic Nat Hentoff once took a friend to hear Albert Ayler in a New York jazz club. When the quartet's stunning set was done, Hentoff asked his friend what he thought. The friend replied, "That doesn't seem to matter so much as the fact they opened me up. It's like I heard only part of what it's possible to hear before."

Ayler had accomplished his vision. He believed that we all hear less than we should, that we live our lives below what is possible. His compositions, including "Truth Is Marching In," "Holy Ghost," "Our Prayer," "Light in Darkness" and many others, lead us beyond what is, so we can create the "not yet."

Jazz saxophonist Albert Ayler produced amazingly beautiful music during the tumultuous 1960s. In November of 1970, he was found dead in the East River. Authorities assumed his death was a suicide, though that has never been verified. His greatest song is considered by many to be "Truth Is Marching In."

NOV 24   ≣ Solomon Northup: Twelve Years a Slave

The tale of Solomon Northup is so remarkable that for years it was thought to be fiction. Born free in New York, Northup nevertheless endured the discrimination common in the North. Despite being a farmer and craftsman, he was denied opportunities because of his race. He could not vote, own property, serve on a jury or appear to be equal to any white person. He was called "nigger," despised by many of his neighbors and considered subhuman by teachers, preachers and policemen. Despite all this, Northup was at least free—until one horrific day in 1841 when he was taken by kidnappers posing as circus recruiters.

They grabbed him, locked him in a slave pen and whipped him unmercifully. Solomon Northup, a free black man, the husband of Anne Hampton and father of three, was ruthlessly stripped of his family and his freedom. Just as his ancestors in Benin and Senegambia had experienced capture, Northup also had his life snatched away. He later wrote:

It could not be that a free citizen of New York, who had wronged no man, nor violated any law, should be dealt with thus inhumanly. The more I contemplated my situation, however, the more I became confirmed in my suspicions. It was a desolate thought, indeed. I felt there was no trust or mercy in unfeeling man; and commending myself to the God of the oppressed, I bowed my head upon fettered hands and wept most bitterly.

For twelve long years Northup endured slavery's wrath. He felt the master's whip, he heard women scream as they were staked and whipped, and he listened to children wail, "Don't go, Mama," as their mothers were sold away. But slavery would not have the last word in his life. Twelve years after his capture, in 1853, Solomon Northup was reclaimed by the efforts of his wife and friends in New York and granted his freedom. He returned home and wrote his autobiography, *Twelve Years a Slave*, a vivid portrayal of the terrors of slavery that helped incite fiery opposition to slavery in the North. He told his story so that his brothers and sisters in slavery—those born there and expecting to die there—could taste the liberty that he savored in the North.

On November 19, 1852, Anne Hampton Northup wrote a letter to the Governor of New York requesting his help in securing Solomon Northup's freedom. That letter was instrumental in the liberation of her husband from the Red River plantation in Louisiana. He later wrote the book, Twleve Years a Slave, which was used by abolitionists to organize opposition to slavery.

NOV 25   ☰ Reverend William Henry Sheppard: Prophet of the Congo Free State

Rev. William Henry Sheppard, a newly ordained minister in the Presbyterian Church, was called to pastor the Harris Street Church in Alabama, but he quickly became dissatisfied with his new church. White ministers ostracized him, white Presbyterians hated him and sometimes even his black parishioners misunderstood him. He soon realized that his gifts could never be fully utilized in the Presbyterian Church in Alabama.

Sheppard had heard of missions in Africa—how preachers evangelized the natives, built schools, taught children and healed the sick—and he petitioned the Presbyterian Church to send him to Africa. Unfortunately, though claiming to follow Christ, the Presbyterians were like every other Christian denomination at the time (except perhaps the Quakers) in their denial of fundamental black dignity: They refused to send Sheppard unless he found a white minister to lead the delegation. Sheppard reluctantly agreed, and he and his white partner, Rev. Samuel Lapsley, sailed to the Congo Free State in 1890.

They set up a mission in the Kasai Valley, and there built the Luebo Missionary Station. Sheppard was excited and met the challenges of poverty, disease and language with a zeal unmatched by most missionaries. He was respectful of the natives and worked to learn their language, customs and religious beliefs. But after a few months, Sheppard began noticing something was wrong. Late one evening, after preaching, teaching and dispensing medicine all day, he saw a child without hands stumbling out of the woods. He ran to help and brought the child back to the church. To his horror, Sheppard heard from villagers that people without hands were nothing new. They told him how Belgium's military proxy, the *force publique*, cut off the hands of any villager who refused to work on the rubber plantations.

This incident led Sheppard to deeper investigations. What he found allowed him to become the voice of the abused in the Congo. He discovered that King Leopold II of Belgium was engaged in the systematic plunder of rubber, ivory and minerals from the Congo and was perpetuating horrific abuse and terror on the black population to gain compliance. Sheppard responded in a fury. In 1907, he wrote the powerful "Personal Observations of Congo Misgovernment," an indictment of European colonialism and racism:

> As a result of this forced labor system, the rubber and ivory have been pouring into the port of Antwerp, and the blood of thousands of innocent men and women in Africa has been freely shed to satisfy the greed of the man who poses as their benefactor.

For the next twenty years, Sheppard preached against the system of abuse that destroyed the lives of black Africans. He wrote books and articles, testified to European parliaments, wrote letters to the American press and fought Belgium's reign of terror. With his tireless advocacy for African people, William Sheppard helped bring about the end of Leopold's atrocities. Even today, the Presbyterian Church is the largest Protestant denomination in the Congo, a testament to the devotion Sheppard had for his people.

Rev. William Henry Sheppard died on November 25, 1927, in Louisville, Kentucky. He had led the Prebyterian mission in the Congo for many years and lobbied against the system of abuse by the Belgian colonialists under King Leopold II.

☰ Sojourner Truth: "Is God Dead?"

For thirty years, during the height of slavery and oppression, Sojourner Truth was perhaps the most powerful abolitionist in the nation. It is difficult to imagine a black woman living so boldly without being mobbed or lynched. Yet the history books record her unmatchable bravery and unshakeable convictions. Who was this immensely courageous black woman who marched out of the mists of history?

From the 1840s until her death in 1883, Sojourner Truth was white America's worst nightmare: A fearless black woman who spoke her mind and could not be frightened, bought or compromised; an itinerant preacher who boldly denounced slavery and slavers and promoted black equality; a feminist who upheld women's rights and demanded women's suffrage; a civil rights advocate who spoke truth everywhere she traveled.

Sojourner Truth was born Isabella Van Wagenen and worked as a slave in New York. Like many women slaves, she was overworked and victimized by beatings and sexual abuse, and she suffered the horror of watching her son sold away from her. In 1827, however, she experienced a spiritual awakening. She had a dramatic vision of a mysterious visitor who burned bright with holiness, radiant with love. In her autobiographical book, *The Narrative of Sojourner Truth*, she described herself in the third person, recalling the impact of this vision:

> *Previous…she heard Jesus mentioned in reading or speaking, but had received from what she heard no impression that he was any other than an eminent man, like a Washington or a Lafayette. Now he appeared to her…so every way lovely, and he loved her so much! And, how strange that he had always loved her, and she had never known it!*

This vision changed Van Wagenen forever. She knew that, despite the abuse heaped upon her and her people, despite the taunts, abuses and pain, Jesus loved her. For her this was no ordinary love because it changed her from victim to victor. She shed her slave name in 1843 and called herself "Sojourner Truth" for the rest of her life.

When she was freed from slavery in 1828, she began her ministry. Clutching a Bible in one hand and a cane in the other, Sojourner Truth preached about God, redemption and equality with a relentless intensity that few could match. Once the great Frederick Douglass told an audience that he was tired of ineffectual prayers and in frustration proclaimed that abolition could come only through violence. When he finished, Sojourner shouted from the rear of the church, "Frederick, is God dead?" These three words, "Is God Dead?" are inscribed on her tombstone.

Sojourner Truth believed that Jesus loved her and would stand with her through everything. The "transcendent loveliness" she saw in Jesus enabled her to love every person she encountered and empowered her to uphold the beauty of all humans, regardless of race or gender.

Sojourner Truth, born Isabella Van Wagenen, was a former slave, women's rights advocate and abolitionist. She died on November 26, 1883, in Battle Creek, Michigan. Her autobiography, The Narrative of Sojourner Truth, *told of a dramatic vision that had given her the courage to fight slavery her entire lifetime.*

NOV 27   ☰ **Reverend John Berry Meachem: Living the Gospel of Salvation**

John Berry Meachem was born a slave in Virginia. After years on a plantation, he was sold to a Kentucky planter from whom he later purchased his freedom. As a young man, he experienced two events that transformed him forever. First, he fell in love with a woman whom he later married. Unfortunately, she was still a slave, the property of another and unable to live with the man she loved. The second event was his conversion. Meachem responded to an evangelist's call to a new life in Christ and devoted his life to God. He began spending a good portion of each day praying and telling others of the goodness of God.

After a while, John Meachem felt called to the ministry. His dreams of building a church in Kentucky were shattered, however, when his wife was sold away to a new master in Missouri. Meachem followed her and silently vowed that his wife would never again be taken from him. Working feverishly at his carpenter trade, he eventually earned enough money to purchase his wife's freedom. They were finally able to settle in Missouri as a free black couple, and Meachem sought to build a church where black folk could experience the love of God and the fellowship of the Holy Spirit.

After many grievous struggles, Rev. Meachem and his wife founded the St. Louis First African Mission Church. The church quickly grew to two hundred and twenty members, two hundred of whom were slaves. Meachem was a fine pastor to his church, serving diligently through prayer, preaching and music. In addition, his carpenter business flourished, and he became one of the wealthiest blacks in Missouri.

For Meachem, the gospel meant a glorious liberation from sin and a practical liberation from unjust bondage. He believed that the good news of Jesus was something both to proclaim and to practice. So he began to use his money to purchase the freedom of some of the slaves in his congregation. Eventually, he rescued twenty of his parishioners from slavery's darkness.

In order to continue his ministry, Rev. Meachem arranged for those he rescued to pay him back over time. The ex-slaves gladly complied, for with their freedom came a responsibility to help others like themselves. The St. Louis First African Church became a place where people were truly free, both from sin and from slavery.

Rev. John Berry Meachem became pastor of the St. Louis First African Mission Church in 1827. He also owned and operated a river vessel he named "The Temperance Steamboat." He rescued many from slavery with money made from his successful carpentry business.

NOV 28   ≣ Richard Wright: Native Son

In Richard Wright's novel *Native Son*, Bigger Thomas' mother angrily confronts her son: "Bigger, sometimes I wonder what makes you act like you do."

This bewilderment was an expression of Richard Wright's own quest to understand and harness black rage. Born in Mississippi, abandoned by an alcoholic father, witness to virulent racism in Memphis, Arkansas and Chicago, Wright wanted the world to see life as he saw it. Further, he wanted to find the answer to the question, "What makes you act like you do?"

White America has asked that question of black folks since slavery. As blacks have responded to racism with rage, to exclusion with bitterness and to repression with self-destructive behavior, America has stood by piously and asked, "What makes you act like you do?" This question immediately places blame on the victim and avoids studying the effects of white racism, poor education systems and political scapegoating. Instead of soul-searching, white America looks only at victims as the source and cause of their own misery.

Richard Wright took up his pen and waged war against this cruel inquiry. He forced his readers to look at Bigger Thomas as a person reacting to a world that sought to destroy black males, as a human being in revolt against a civilization that excluded him from its benefits. Though he may have been misguided, though his actions may have been destructive or violent, Bigger Thomas' actions were a rebellion against society. Wright's character was uneducated, but he knew enough to understand that whites attended good schools, had money and lived in quiet neighborhoods, and that blacks were denied work, relegated to the worst neighborhoods and packed into poor schools. Unable to change the system, Thomas became both destructive and self-destructive.

To the question his character faced— "What makes you act the way you do?"—Richard Wright's answer was, "Racism!" Wright never excused or glorified the victim; he simply wanted people to see Bigger Thomas as a symbol of black America, existing in the context of a racist culture where only the strongest escape destructive consequences.

Novelist Richard Wright was the author of black classics such as **Native Son, Black Boy, Uncle Tom's Children** *and other powerful works. He died on November 28, 1960, in Paris, France. The annual Hurston/Richard Wright Literary Award for College Writers was established by novelist Marita Golden to honor excellence in fiction writing by students of African descent enrolled full time as undergraduate or graduate students in any college or university in the United States.*

NOV 29   ☰ Reverend Sister Sara Ann Hughes: Called to Preach the Gospel

Sara Ann Hughes prayed for hours that night. All she wanted to do was to serve God and live a life of holiness. She already could preach the word of Christ, she knew, but she wanted to do more. In several tent meetings in North Carolina, her sermons had brought attendees streaming down the aisles for conversion. Yet she begged God to expand her ministry and use her as a vessel. That night she prayed particularly hard because the following day, November 29, 1885, African Methodist Episcopal (AME) Bishop Henry M. Turner would ordain her, along with eleven men, as deacons of the church. In just a few short hours, she would be added to the rolls of the ordained and be known as "Reverend Sister."

Despite fierce opposition from the men in the AME Church, who were bitterly opposed to Hughes' ordination, she was ordained. At the AME North Carolina Annual Conference of 1885, Hughes stood before Bishop Turner to publicly receive the anointing of God's Holy Spirit. Bishop Turner told the crowd that although a woman had not been ordained in fifteen hundred years of church history he knew this ordination would redound to the glory and honor of God.

The next five years proved Bishop Turner right. Hundreds of parishioners were blessed by their new deacon. The Reverend Sister's sermons, counseling and teaching helped many AME members to grow in Christ. When somehow officials of the AME Church managed to "de-ordain" her, she continued to serve God, witnessing, ministering and praying until she died. Oppressive church structures could not quench the Rev. Sara Ann Hughes' desire to live and preach the gospel. People could keep her from being a deacon, but no one—absolutely no one— could keep her from loving God and preaching the word of Christ.

On November 29, 1885, Sara Ann Hughes became the first woman ordained a deacon in the AME Church. This historic event took place under the leadership of Bishop Henry McNeal Turner at the North Carolina Annual Conference. She was later "de-ordained" by officials of the same AME Church, yet she continued to witness, minister and pray until she died.

NOV 30   ≡ **"Old" Elizabeth: "Nobody to Look to but God"**

Elizabeth lived to be almost one hundred years old, a truly remarkable lifespan for a woman born into slavery in 1766. When she was a young girl of eleven, her master sold her away from her parents, brothers and sisters. Little Elizabeth would never again have the hugs, laughter, sharing and tears of her family—an anguish almost impossible to imagine.

Once at her new plantation, she begged her overseer to let her walk several miles to visit her family. The overseer refused, but Elizabeth went anyway. Barely remembering the way, she walked twenty miles before she found her old plantation and her family. It was a beautiful but quiet reunion; they could not celebrate too much lest they be caught and punished. Before she left, Elizabeth's mother squeezed her daughter tight and whispered into her ear, "You have nobody in the whole wide world to look to but God."

Elizabeth's mother hated saying those words, but she knew that her child would die heartbroken and distraught otherwise. She wanted her child to be able to rest in God's arms, despite the loneliness of slavery. Elizabeth walked home repeating those words over and over for twenty miles, and her mother's advice changed her life. Elizabeth later wrote:

> *After this time, finding as my mother said, I had none in the world to look to but God, I betook myself to prayer, and in every lonely place I found an altar. I mourned sore like a dove and chattered forth my sorrow, moaning in the corners of the field.*

The day she left her mother marked the beginning of Elizabeth's transformation. She was eventually freed from slavery and went on to become an evangelist. Though some hated the idea of a "colored woman preacher," she was allowed to preach at camp meetings all around the South, bringing faith and hope to many.

Elizabeth's mother had given her the gift of faith. Even at age ninety-seven, Elizabeth remembered her mother's grip on her arm and the words in her ears: "You have nobody in the wide world to look to but God."

The evangelist and former slave named Elizabeth was later called "Old Elizabeth," since she lived well into her nineties. She preached among Quakers, Methodists and other denominations all over the South.

DECEMBER

Rosa Parks

≣ James Baldwin: Go Tell It on the Mountain

The theme of James Baldwin's most famous novel was also the theme of his life; he did, indeed, "tell it on the mountain." His mission was to tell what he saw, what he heard and what he felt so deeply that he could transfer his experiences to his readers. Above all else, Baldwin wanted them to feel life as he and others in pain had experienced it. Baldwin the teenage Harlem preacher, Baldwin the abused son, Baldwin the gay expatriate—this was the Baldwin who wrote about what it means to be a human being. His work and his words are difficult, for he told it like it was and asked each reader to struggle for a better self, a better community and a better world. As he wrote in *No Name in the Street*: "We are responsible for the world in which we find ourselves, if only because we are the only sentient force which can change it."

James Baldwin was no idle dreamer or conveyer of wistful hopes. He lived in Harlem and saw how white supremacy wasted black humanity; he walked with Martin Luther King, Jr., and Amiri Baraka and the Black Panthers. Baldwin knew…and still he hoped. His insistent urge, his continual cry, was that we live as humans and treat others as if life really mattered. Though he left the black store-front church, the culture of black belief in a crucified and loving Jesus stayed with him. The titles of his writings paid constant homage to his black church roots, as evident in his controversial essay, "The Fire Next Time," which opens with the title "Down at the Cross." The theology that fueled his writing was essentially the fundamental element of all black theology: that all people, no matter how poor, enslaved, addicted or mistreated, have dignity.

Baldwin's constant message was his plea for us to stay human, to be real to ourselves and act as if others are real. As he expressed in his brilliant essay "The Devil Finds Work," the absence of "being real" was the presence of evil:

> For, I have seen the devil…and have seen him in you and me: in the eyes of the cop…in the eyes of some junkies, the eyes of some preachers, presidents…in the eyes of some orphans, and in the eyes of my father, and in my mirror. It is that moment when no other human being is real for you, nor are you real for yourself.

James Baldwin was the definitive and consummate artist, and his passion and honesty confronts us on every page of his writings. His work draws out our humanity, making us angry, distressed and inspired enough to work toward a better world.

Author James Baldwin died of stomach cancer in St. Paul-de-Vence, France, on December 1, 1987. He is the author of the novel* Go Tell It on the Mountain, *one of the undisputed classics of black literature.

≣ Rosa Parks: "I'm Not Moving"

Rosa Parks was tired that day. Not just tired of working as a seamstress at Montgomery Fair, but tired of being pushed aside by whites. It wasn't just that blacks had to sit at the back of the bus; it was a lot more than that. Blacks had to pay in the front, step off the bus and re-enter through the back door. Once seated in the black section, the indignity was not done. If the front section filled and some whites were left standing, the white section was simply expanded. Each bus had a "no-man's land" that blacks were allowed in—as long as no whites were standing. Any whites who needed a seat could displace blacks in this section.

Rosa Parks and three other blacks were seated in this "no-man's land" when more whites boarded the bus. The bus driver, endowed with powers of arrest by the City of Montgomery, ordered the four to move so the whites could sit. Three of the blacks obeyed, but Parks did not move. The driver reminded her of his police powers and threatened to arrest her if she did not move.

Still she did not move. Blacks in the back and whites in front looked on in disbelief. Here was a working-class black woman defying the foundation of white privilege. Blacks cast their eyes away, and whites pretended not to notice the challenge to their superiority. The bus driver glared at Parks and again demanded that she move.

She looked up at him and said, "You can have me arrested, but I'm not moving."

The driver called the Montgomery police, who hauled Parks off to jail. Rosa Parks, however, was not through. Friends and some members of the NAACP reminded her that she could pay the fine and drop the whole thing. Others, however, encouraged her to challenge the law that degraded all Montgomery blacks.

Park's decision changed the course of civil rights across the nation: She refused to pay her fine. Her stand sparked the famous Montgomery bus boycott, a boycott that lasted three hundred and eighty-one days. E.D. Nixon and the NAACP, JoAnn Robinson of the Women's Political Caucus and Rev. Martin Luther King, Jr., of the Montgomery Improvement Association, were key figures in the boycott, but none of them would have become involved without Parks' courageous decision.

Only months before Parks stood up to segregation, she had attended Myles Horton's Highlander Folk School in Tennessee, where she had learned about non-violent protest. But she had been so quiet there that fellow students doubted she could stand against injustice. Fortunately for us, and anyone who benefits from equal rights today, they were wrong.

Rosa Parks was arrested on December 1, 1955, for not moving to the rear of the bus as ordered by the driver. Following her refusal, Montgomery blacks organized the famous bus boycott in which 42,000 protestors walked and carpooled for 381 days until bus company officials changed their racist practices. She died on October 24, 2005, in Detroit, Michigan, at age 92. She was called "the mother of the new Civil Rights Movement" by U.S. Representative John Conyers.

DEC 3   ≡ Daniel Rudd: "All Will Be Well"

Daniel Rudd was born in Bardstown, Kentucky, just before slavery came to its long-awaited end. His parents were devout Catholics, a rarity among America's slaves, and Rudd loved the saints, sacraments, tradition and spirituality of the Catholic faith. He saw beyond the European façade of the church into the roots of its faith, and he believed that the Catholic Church was the source for eventual black salvation. However, while others looked to Rome and Ireland for truth, Rudd looked to Africa. There he found saints such as Benedict the Moor, Augustine, Monica and Cyprian.

Rudd believed that his beloved church could not only save black folk from their own sins but also from the sins of white racists. In his newspaper, *American Catholic Tribune*, he proclaimed the message of black pride and Catholic salvation. The weekly *Tribune* was the first and only national black Catholic newspaper in America, and it carried news of black life, openly debated the merits of political strategies and showed how the Church could join that struggle. In his own words, Rudd sought to:

...give the great Catholic Church a hearing and show that it is worthy of at least a fair consideration at the hands of our race, being as it is the only place on this continent where rich and poor, white and black, must drop prejudice at the threshold and go hand in hand to the altar.

His newspaper, however, was not enough. In 1889, Rudd and other black Catholics founded the National Black Catholic Congress movement. Between 1889 and 1894, five Congresses were held. The first was in Washington, D.C., from January 1 to 4, 1889. On January 4, one hundred delegates from the Congress were catapulted to the national stage when they met with President Grover Cleveland. After this euphoric beginning, each Congress brought black Catholics from across America to support each other, petition for equality in Catholic schools and suggest strategies for black self-help. The last Congress of Rudd's time was held in Baltimore in 1894.

Yet Rudd's dream of black Catholic unity did not die, for in 1987 black American Catholics revived his vision and renewed the Congress movement. Daniel Rudd was both a visionary and a doer. Long before talk of black theology and before the Catholic Church understood its racial justice obligations, Rudd lived the good news of self-respect and communal love.

For Rudd, the Catholic Church was not a cold cathedral with dry rituals and meaningless ceremony. It was the very place were black liberation could occur. Within his "Mother Church," men and women could encounter Christ, become the people of God and together build the kingdom of heaven. One of Rudd's final admonitions was:

> Our Catholic young…should stand up for the faith that is in them. Get close together…fling personal ambition to the winds, work for the general good, and all will be well.

Daniel Rudd's vision lives on in black Catholics who see the Church as a way to both personal and communal salvation.

Black Catholic publisher and organizer Daniel Rudd died in Bardstown, Kentucky, on December 3, 1933. He helped found the National Black Congress Movement in the late nineteenth century in the United States.

In 1967, when Fred Hampton was nineteen years old, the United States government took a manila folder, put his name on it and added him to the "Agitator Index." Over the next two years, that file grew to twelve volumes, totaling four thousand pages. What exploits of a single black man could fill that many pages, ten-fold longer than a novel, approaching encyclopedic proportions?

At the age of nineteen, Fred Hampton was an articulate and passionate advocate of black freedom. From his hometown of Maywood, Illinois, just outside Chicago, he wanted nothing more than to improve black living conditions. Police brutality, unemployment, mental despair, frustration and rage plagued the residents of Chicago's West Side. Martin Luther King, Jr., had observed that Chicago's racism trumped even that of Mississippi, and Fred Hampton sought to change that.

In 1967, Hampton joined the Chicago branch of the Black Panther Party, and within months he became the chair of the Illinois Black Panther Party. FBI scribes soon had a lot more to write about. Hampton seemed to be everywhere at once, organizing Panther meetings, teaching classes at their "Liberation School," serving free breakfasts at their "Serve the People" programs and protesting police excesses. He and other Panthers also went to Chicago's South Side to transform the dangerous Blackstone Rangers gang into allies in the struggle.

By the time he was twenty-one, Hampton had become a powerful black leader in Chicago and was gaining national prominence, but his rise was too much for the powers at the FBI and the Chicago Police Department. On the night of December 3, 1969, Fred Hampton had just concluded a political education class at the Church of the Epiphany. Not far away, however, elements of the FBI and the Chicago Police Department were checking their weapons for their planned raid on Hampton's apartment.

Hampton, his fiancée Deborah Johnson, Mark Clark and other Panther leaders returned to Hampton's apartment at 2337 W. Monroe Street, where they went to sleep around 1:30 a.m. At 4 a.m. on the morning of December 4, government agents crashed through the door and killed both Mark Clark and Fred Hampton as they slept. Few single incidents reveal America's ferocity as this cowardly act. Fred Hampton was murdered in his sleep for loving his people too much.

The Chicago Police Department and the FBI murdered Fred Hampton, Chair of the Illinois Black Panther Party, along with Mark Clark, on December 4, 1969. Panthers Ronald Satchell, Blair Anderson and Verliner Brewer were injured. An informer had given the police a floor plan of the Hampton's apartment, and they knew exactly where to shoot after breaking down the door. At least 98 rounds were fired that night, none by members of the Black Panther Party.

DEC 5 ☰ Gwendolyn Elizabeth Brooks: "I Know Who I Am"

By 1967, Gwendolyn Elizabeth Brooks was already a published black poet. Living on Chicago's South Side, she found material for her poems everywhere. The South Side was a black metropolis, a place where black people had built a self-sufficient community. Black churches, bookstores, schools, dentists, musicians, restaurants—the neighborhood permeated Brooks' poetry, and the street corners came alive in her verse and meter. Her poems also brought perspective to racial dynamics, as she relived Emmett Till's murder, the Little Rock school integration and other episodes in story of black America.

In the spring of 1967, Brooks walked onto the campus of Fisk University in Nashville, Tennessee, already recognized as an important black American poet. Fisk was hosting the Second Black Writer's Conference, and luminaries from the black literary world graced the campus. Despite her credentials, awards and publications, Gwendolyn Brooks was always open to learning from others. In Nashville, she encountered black cultural activists such as Don L. Lee, Amiri Baraka, Larry Neal and others who expanded her vision and helped her find her identity. Brooks wrote of her time at Fisk, "If it hadn't been for these young people, these young writers who influenced me, I wouldn't know what I know about this society. By associating with them, I know who I am." Out of this experience of finding herself came her classic poem, "In the Mecca," which focuses on a mother searching for her lost child.

Secure in herself, Brooks shunned larger white publishers to support small and struggling black firms. This cost her both money and exposure, but she valued helping her people more than accumulating personal wealth. She also produced small, inexpensive volumes of poetry so working class folk could afford to buy them.

Gwendolyn Brooks knew who she was. Rooted in her community, she learned from and gave back to the people.

Poet Gwendolyn Brooks was the first black woman to win a Pulitzer Prize for her book **Annie Allen.** *She made her work available through small black-owned publishing houses. In Chicago, she taught classes for the Blackstone Rangers, a South Side street gang. She died on December 3, 2000.*

DEC 6 ☰ Frantz Fanon: "Not Dead"

Frantz Fanon was born of descendants of slaves on the island of Martinique. Intellectually brilliant and sensitive to the suffering of others, Fanon went to Lyon University in France to study psychiatry in 1948. His first post after graduation was a hospital in Bilda, Algeria, where he served as chief of psychiatry. His encounters with patients there changed his life.

At the time, France was engaged in a brutal occupation of colonial Algeria, and French Parachute Divisions and Foreign Legion troops were particularly barbaric. Fanon treated many French soldiers who suffered psychological trauma because of their actions as perpetrators of torture. He also treated, on his own time, Algerian victims of that same torture. So he knew the harm caused by colonialism on both torturer and victim. Every day he saw the effects of the French campaign of violence and abuse. Every day he saw the results of this oppression on the Algerian people. And what he saw led him to participate in the Algerian revolution.

Fanon quit his job and went into exile as a member of the *Front de Liberation Nationale* (FLN) or National Liberation Front. For the rest of his life, Fanon was devoted to the cause of Algerian freedom in particular and African liberation in general. Though his degree opened to him vistas of comfort unavailable to others, he chose life among the exploited.

Fanon's classic book, *Les Damnes de la Terre (The Wretched of the Earth)*, presented his conviction that the worst crime was to steal a person's dignity and freedom. He believed that, without the capacity to choose and determine their own future, people ceased to be human.

Fanon was not a black nationalist, an Algerian revolutionary or a Martinique scholar. He was, instead, a sensitive black man who experienced the grotesque manner in which racism distorts and violates the human personality. In one of his early writings, he mused:

> I want only one thing: an end to the enslavement of man by man…. May it be granted to me to discover and to will man where ever he may be.

In a later writing, he said:

> Yes to life. Yes to love. Yes to generosity. But man is also a no. No to scorn for man. No to the indignity of man. No to the exploitation of man. No to the murder of what is most human about men: freedom.

Though Frantz Fanon died young at the age of thirty-six, he lives on in the actions of those who struggle for human dignity. It is fitting, then, that his biographer, David Macey concluded his book with the triumphant, *"Fanon, pas mort"* ("Fanon, not dead").

Author and supporter of Algerian independence, Frantz Fanon, born in Martinique, died of leukemia in a Washington, D.C., hospital on December 6, 1961. He had never wanted to travel to America, as he viewed it as a "nation of lynchers," but friends persuaded him to go there for medical attention. His book, The Wretched of the Earth, originally written in French, is still widely read today.

Mary Prince was born a slave in Brackish Pond, Bermuda, in 1788. For much of her life, she experienced the sadism of slavery. Her brilliant narrative, *The History of Mary Prince: A West Indian Slave*, is a stunning tale of brutality and human dignity. When it was published in 1831, Prince became the first black English female author. Her scathing tale exposed churches, literary salons and respectable homes to the horrors of slavery. She held nothing back.

Prince recounted a chilling tale of a master who whipped a slave, "poor Hetty," to death for allowing a cow to escape. The horror of the tale escalated because the whipping caused "poor Hetty" to miscarry her baby, a child Prince said was the master's. Prince sought to awaken the conscience of England not through fiction, but with history—her history. Prince had been sold from Bermuda to the Turks Islands to Antigua. It seemed each new master was as cruel as the former.

She recalled the first time she was sold away from her family: "I cannot bear to think of that day. It is too much…. All that we love taken away from us—Oh it is sad, sad!" In writing of her various masters, she noted, "I hoped when left I should have been better off, but I found that it was going from one butcher to another." Often beaten and sexually abused, she wrote of one particular time, "I cannot recall how many licks [with a bullwhip] he gave me, but he beat me until I was unable to stand, and till he himself was weary."

Prince, however, was not destroyed by such butchery. When her mistress moved from Antigua to England, Prince petitioned the Anti-Slavery Society and with their help gained her freedom. There was a price, however. She could remain in England as a free woman or return to her beloved husband in Antigua as a slave. As much as she wanted her husband, she could not bear subjecting herself again to the sexual whims of her master. With inconsolable sorrow, she stayed in England.

"I have been a slave—I have felt what a slave feels, and I know what a slave knows." By writing these words down, Mary Prince not only kept her own history alive but also aroused anti-slavery sentiment in England, which, in turn, helped bring down slavery in the Americas. Her history reaches us today, helping us to "feel what a slave feels" so we will never again treat another human being that way.

In December of 1826, black slaves Mary Prince and Daniel James were married at the Spring Gardens Moravian Chapel in Antigua, a Caribbean colony of England. Prince had become a Moravian because the church welcomed her while she was a slave. Two years later, her mistress moved Prince to England. She was eventually freed from slavery, but she never saw her husband again. She told her story in **The History of Mary Prince: A West Indian Slave,** *which was the first book published by a black English female author.*

≣ Blessed Sister Marie-Clementine Anuarite Nengapeta
"I Forgive You"

Young Anuarite Nengapeta carefully watched how the nuns carried themselves. Growing up in the village of Wamba in the Democratic Republic of the Congo, Nengapeta was an observant and sensitive girl, and no group caught her eye more than the small order of nuns who lived in her village. She was so captivated by their grace, demeanor and kindness that she wanted to follow them into the convent and become a nun.

Her family did not want her to leave, but she persisted. One afternoon, a truck arrived to pick up girls and women who were leaving to enter the convent at Bafwabaka. Anuarite Nengapeta climbed aboard the truck to join them.

On August 5, 1959, she took her vows and fulfilled her life's desire. She consecrated her life to God and took the name Sister Marie-Clementine. She soon became a steadfast member of the community. She was both gentle and courageous, serving and counseling those in need and fearlessly chasing away hostile men who sometimes harassed the nuns.

In 1964, the Mulele rebellion erupted, engulfing the Congo in civil war. On November 29, 1964, trucks loaded with soldiers stopped in front of the Bafawbaka convent. The armed men dismounted and ordered all forty-six nuns into the trucks. The following day, Sister Negapapeta and Sister Bokuma Jean-Baptiste were separated from the others and taken away in a car with a group of Simba soldiers led by a Colonel Olombo. When the nuns were ordered to have sex with the soldiers, they refused and were beaten without mercy. Sister Jean-Baptiste's arm was broken in three places, and she fainted. Sister Negapapeta courageously resisted, but she was overcome and raped. The soldiers then bayoneted her and shot her in the chest.

During this brutal encounter, Negapapeta shouted, "I forgive you, for you know not what you are doing." She lingered on past midnight and died at one o'clock the next morning. Sister Negapapeta had followed Christ from village to convent to death. Her companion sisters remembered her as a model of love, modesty, fidelity and valor.

Sister Marie-Clementine Anuarite Nengapeta was raped and murdered by rebel soldiers in the Congo on December 1, 1964, for her faithfulness and commitment to Jesus Christ. She was the first Congolese woman declared "Blessed" (the final step before canonization) by the Catholic Church in 1985.

≡ A Love Supreme: "It Is All with God"

On a cold winter afternoon, four musicians gathered in a dimly lit studio to record some music. That afternoon, they created more than just another record; they made history. With Jimmy Garrison on bass, Elvin Jones on drums, McCoy Tyner on piano and John Coltrane on tenor saxophone, the John Coltrane Quartet recorded *A Love Supreme,* one of the greatest jazz sessions in history. Like most of Coltrane's later compositions, *A Love Supreme* is a memoir of the Spirit, a proclamation of the soul's quest for God.

Musically, each composition reflects distinct parts of the spiritual journey. With increasing intensity and depth, the works "Acknowledgment," "Resolution," "Pursuance" and "Psalm" describe the human relationship with God. The progression moves from acknowledging God's presence, to resolving to live a life of devotion, to pursuing that life with intensity and, finally, to singing a psalm of adoration and thanks. Within the scope of one musical masterpiece, Coltrane clarifies what generations of preachers, theologians and saints have proclaimed: that God loves us and awaits our response.

The music on the album matches John Coltrane's words on the album cover:

During the year 1957, I experienced the grace of God, a spiritual awakening which was to lead me to a richer, fuller, more productive life…. This album is a humble offering to Him. An attempt to say, "Thank You God." May we never forget that in the sunshine of our lives, through the storm and after the rain, it is all with God, in all things and forever. All Praise To God.

Thousands have been uplifted and blessed by the sounds of *A Love Supreme.* To the extent that most of us are on a spiritual journey, we can relate to John Coltrane's quest to love and praise God. With each hearing of *A Love Supreme,* we can renew our quest for enlightenment and a deeper faith.

The John Coltrane Quartet recorded the album* A Love Supreme *on December 9, 1964, for Impulse Records. It is considered by many to be one of the most spiritual jazz albums ever recorded.

≡ Dr. Lena Edwards: "In Giving We Receive"

Lena Edwards was a black woman who loved St. Francis of Assisi. The Italian saint's love for God, people, peace and the earth resonated with her spirituality. She had been raised in middle-class America and trained in obstetrics and gynecology. She served for thirty years in Jersey City as a doctor, where she was renowned for her patient care. After this much-heralded career, Edwards retired from medicine to take a prestigious teaching position at Howard University.

Yet university life did not satisfy her zeal to emulate the teachings of St. Francis, who had washed the wounds of lepers when no one else would touch them. Dr. Edwards wanted to follow his way of humility and service. She had long been a devoted Catholic whose faith was at the core of her life and destiny. Before coming to Howard University, Edwards had joined the Third Order of Franciscans, where she and her colleagues had taken vows of poverty, discipline and spiritual devotion.

After much prayer and contemplation, Edwards left Howard University and went to Hereford, Texas. In this impoverished county, Mexican migrant workers were among the poorest and least cared-for humans in America. Edwards used her personal savings to build a maternity hospital for these workers. She shared in their poverty, living and working among them, and she trained volunteers in maternal care and basic medicine. Here at last Edwards fully lived the spirituality of St. Francis of Assisi. Though her medical career had been rewarding, she felt that, in this distant Texas county, she was doing what her mentor, St. Francis, had taught: "In giving we receive, and in dying we are born to eternal life."

A follower of the teaching of St. Francis of Assisi, Dr. Lena Edwards died on December 3, 1986, at the age of 85. After careers as a doctor, a university professor and a worker among migrants, she continued her ministry by raising money for African-American female medical students and serving on a number of groups promoting human welfare and development.

DEC 11   ≣ Salem Poor: "A Brave and Gallant Soldier"

African Americans have fought without hesitation in each of America's foreign wars. At San Juan Hill, France's Belleau Wood, Iwo Jima, Khe Sanh, Baghdad and in hundreds of other battles, black soldiers have courageously given their blood for their country. Salem Poor, the first African-American war hero, planted the seeds of this black courage.

On June 17, 1775, Salem Poor and a group of revolutionary soldiers confronted the might of the British army at the battle of Bunker Hill. Under intense musket and artillery fire, Poor distinguished himself by standing his ground amidst fierce fire and killing or wounding several British soldiers breaking through the colonial ranks. On December 5, 1775, fourteen American officers present at Bunker Hill commended Poor for his courage: "We declare that a Negro man called Salem Poor behaved like a brave and gallant soldier."

Whatever racism existed among the white troops at Bunker Hill, Salem Poor had tempered it by his valor. He later fought in several other battles and was with George Washington at Valley Forge. Salem Poor was indeed the forerunner of all black heroes to come, and his memory lives on in black soldiers' deeds of courage.

Black soldier Salem Poor was commended for his courage at the Battle of Bunker Hill on December 5, 1775. The black soldiers at Bunker Hill also included Barzillai Law, Cuff Whittemore, Titus Coburn, Peter Salem, Ceasar Brown and many others.

DEC 12 ≡ Phyllis Wheatley: A Poet with a Forgotten Name

Who was this African girl brought to the shores of America? What was her name? Who were her parents? What future had been denied her when she was stolen from Gambia in West Africa?

We will never know, for when she was only seven years old, the African girl later known as Phyllis Wheatley was shipped like cargo to Boston. In America, she became the property of and house servant to John and Susanna Wheatley, who gave her the name Phyllis Wheatley: "Phyllis" was the name of the ship that transported her; and the Wheatleys were her owners.

Susanna Wheatley, however, soon realized that Phyllis Wheatley was gifted beyond her prescribed domestic duties. When the Wheatleys allowed Phyllis to learn, they altered the future of African-American literature. Phyllis Wheatley, a girl whose name was forgotten, whose parents grieved for her in Gambia, became the first slave and the first African American to publish a book of poetry, *Poems on Various Subjects, Religious and Moral*. Since no publisher in the United States would print her work, Wheatley and her supporters went to England, where her book was published in 1773. This distinction, aside from the merits of her work, makes her forerunner to Paul Laurence Dunbar, Langston Hughes, Maya Angelou, Sterling Brown, Gwendolyn Brooks, Amiri Baraka, Sonia Sanchez and every other black poet arising from the soil of America.

With all odds against her, Wheatley produced poetic works that astounded colonial readers. Critics were amazed when they learned she was a black slave. Many, including the Governor of Massachusetts, repeatedly tested her to prove that she could, in fact, author such a beautiful work.

Some scholars claim that Phyllis Wheatley's visit with George Washington made him question the morality of slave ownership. She wrote poems about Christianity, George Washington, black artists and many other subjects. Her classic poem, "To S. M., a young African painter, On Seeing His Works," is a celebration of African art. Her homage to "S.M.," a slave painter she knew named Scipio Morehead, was a tribute to African dignity at a time when blacks were treated as property and cattle.

Wheatley was emancipated by her owners after the publication of her book. She tried unsuccessfully to sell a second manuscript, which has never been recovered. *Poems on Various Subjects, Religious and Moral* was not printed in the United States until 1786.

Poet Phyllis Wheatley was the first slave and the first African American to publish a book of poetry. She died on December 5, 1784, while giving birth to her second child. She died in poverty and obscurity, but her legacy lives on in her writing and that of her black successors. Memoir and Poems of Phillis Wheatley, a Native African and a Slave. Dedicated to the Friends of the Africans *was published in 1834 and includes a biographical sketch of Wheatley in addition to a collection of her best-known verse.*

DEC 13   ≣ Ella Baker: Radical Visionary

Ella Baker sat quietly as black preachers, with their confident southern cadence, spoke their minds. She listened carefully as they sought to outdo each other in eloquence, wit and theological insight. With forty years of struggle behind her, Ella Baker was respected, but she was not in the "inner circle" of black leadership. Nevertheless, when the preachers were done, she spoke up.

"The trouble with you men," she said in a measured tone, "is that you think you are the movement. You are not; the movement is the people."

The room fell silent. No one wanted to take on Ella Baker, for her words and wisdom were grounded in her work on the frontlines. Her words were not an academic abstraction or a hollow slogan; she lived those words through a lifetime of unparalleled struggle for equality and justice.

Unlike many activists, Baker's passion for human rights did not begin in the sixties and end in the seventies. Her entire adult life, beginning as a student at Shaw University in Raleigh, North Carolina, was devoted to creating a better life for others. She organized for the Young Negroes Cooperative in the thirties, the NAACP in the forties, and the Southern Christian Leadership Conference and Crusade for Citizenship in the fifties.

When she was fifty-seven, Ella Baker invited student leaders to a meeting that birthed the Student Nonviolent Coordinating Committee (SNCC). Their name was a testament to the vision of Ella Baker. Not a leadership council, nor a collection of preachers and messiahs, they allowed the whole group to coordinate nonviolent student activism. Baker believed passionately that the Civil Rights Movement was the people and that the more people who were involved, the more vibrant the Movement would be.

Baker constantly challenged women, the young, the poor and local people to learn more about their conditions, organize themselves and participate in their collective enhancement. Her generosity and commitment to democracy helped shape the black freedom movement: the Black Panthers, the Students for a Democratic Society, the Mississippi Freedom Democratic Party—all had roots in the work of Ella Baker. Even today, as local people organize and empower themselves, they pay homage to Baker's radical democratic vision.

A tireless worker for civil rights, Ella Baker died on her 83rd birthday, December 13, 1986, in New York City. She helped organize the Student Nonviolent Coordinating Committee (SNCC) when she was 57 years old.

DEC 14   ≣ **Wole Soyinka: Man of Commitment**

As a playwright, poet, essayist, novelist, theater director and critic, Wole Soyinka is a major black African literary figure. When he won the 1986 Nobel Prize in Literature, Soyinka finally received global recognition for his work furthering the cause of human liberty. A proud Nigerian and a member of the Yoruba people, Soyinka transcends nation and culture to speak peace around the globe.

Many of his plays, books and essays are brilliant observations on European colonialism, African dependency and crippling corruption. He does not limit his message, however, to a critique; the true core of his message is that our actions can make a difference. For Soyinka, art is not neutral; art takes sides. In societies divided into rich and poor, powerful and powerless, strong and weak, theater and literature must choose sides. He once said, "Social commitment is a citizen's commitment and embraces equally the carpenter, the mason, the banker, the farmer…the critic." Soyinka sees himself as a socially committed citizen, an artist whose work enlightens and inspires.

Such a stance often makes the artist an enemy of the state, and Soyinka is no exception. He was arrested and jailed for two years for criticizing the Nigerian civil war and persistent corruption. After imprisonment he wrote, "Books and all forms of writing have always been objects of terror to those who seek to suppress truth."

While in prison, he wrote the classic *The Man Died*. The first chapter concludes with this powerful statement:

(The government's) present excesses and mutual condonment of crime have made necessary the uncompromising contents of this book, for the first step towards the dethronement of terror is the deflation of its hypocritical self-righteousness. It is only the first step. In any people that submit willingly to the "daily humiliation of fear," the man dies.

Terror, prison, corruption and war have not deterred Wole Soyinka from speaking truth. In his commitment to truth and social justice, Soyinka writes what he believes, lives what he writes and urges us to do the same.

Noble Prize-winning Nigerian author and playwright Wole Soyinka has written more than twenty major works and has had a forty-year career in literary activism. The first essay in his book The Man Died *is titled "Letter to Compatriots" and was written on December 14, 1971, two years after his release from prison for criticizing government corruption.*

DEC 15 ≣ Septima Poinsette Clark: Change Is Coming

Black ministers sat around the smoke-filled room talking about the upcoming march. Between the jokes and laughter, they had some serious discussion about their plans. Dr. Martin Luther King, Jr., would lead the march, as was often the case. A few minutes later, a civil rights leader from another town asked King to lead a march in that city the following week. Septima Poinsette Clark sat quietly in the corner, the usual place for women at a Southern Christian Leadership Council (SCLC) meeting. Quietly but firmly, however, she addressed those who asked King to lead the marches: "*You're* there. You're going to ask the leader to come everywhere? Can't you do the leading in those places?" The room froze and tension was palatable.

Dr. King broke the silence, "It's all right, Mrs. Clark. My schedule can handle it." Laughter broke the tension and the meeting continued.

Septima Clark, however, was not done. Afterward, she wrote Dr. King to ask that he not lead all the marches and that he challenge local ministers to take responsibility in their respective cities. She pointed out that there was a lot of potential out there, but people needed experience to grow. This was typical of Septima Clark, constantly challenging the Civil Rights Movement to be more democratic, inclusive and progressive.

Persistent struggle was not new to Clark, for all her life she had fought to improve the lives of common folk. When she realized that the NAACP fought for black dignity in the South, she joined and became an active member. When the South Carolina School Board fired black teachers for NAACP participation, she refused to hide her membership. Despite the consequences, she listed "NAACP" on the "loyalty form" all teachers were forced to sign. She was immediately fired.

Later, she taught at the radical Highlander Folk School run by the great Myles Horton. She ran the Citizenship Schools and taught people how to read, organize and work for justice.

As a teacher, organizer, member of the NAACP, leader at the Highlander Folk School and executive member of the SCLC, Septima Clark was a driving force in the black freedom struggle. After retirement, she wrote:

I don't ever expect to see a utopia. No, I think that will always be something that you are going to have to work on, always. That's why, when we have chaos and people say, "I'm scared, I'm scared, I'm concerned," I say, "Out of that will come something good." It will too. They can be afraid if they want to…. Things will happen, and things will change. The only thing that is really worthwhile is change. It is coming.

Teacher and civil rights activist Septima Clark died on December 15, 1987, in Charleston, South Carolina, the city in which she had been born 89 years earlier. She challenged the leaders of the Civil Rights Movement to encourage indigenous leadership in the places it was organizing.

DEC 16 ☰ Sarah Parker Remond: A Century ahead of Her Time

While still a teenager, Sarah Parker Remond joined her brother Charles on the antislavery speaking circuit. The summer she turned sixteen, in July of 1842, America was on the verge of collapse. Talk of war, threats of succession, fears of armed slave uprisings, draconian anti-black laws and virulent hatred were tearing the young nation apart. Into this chaos Remond stepped fearlessly, raising her voice against the evil of slavery.

Southern slavery was not her sole concern, for she also chastised the North for their segregated churches, theaters and schools. Parker bravely confronted every law, philosophy or government that limited human growth. Even though she was only in her twenties, she was a century ahead of her time. Future generations would stumble over the question of loyalty to race or gender, but Remond embraced both without wavering. In 1858, she was instrumental in creating the National Women's Rights Organization, a group committed to granting women the right to vote.

Her most important contribution, however, came overseas. During the Civil War, Great Britain's abolitionist movement had waned as they argued with wealthy Britons who benefited from southern cotton. Sarah Remond, her brother Charles and other black radicals went to England to bolster the courage of their British comrades in the struggle. Black historian Benjamin Quarles later described Remond and the other black Americans who convinced the English to support the North as "ministers without portfolio."

Remond's travels throughout Great Britain helped revitalize British abolitionism, and her agitation eventually influenced the outcome of the Civil War. Without the support of the English, the South became isolated and was doomed to lose to the more industrial, populated and wealthy North. Speeches such as the one she delivered at Manchester, England, swayed the course of history:

When I walk through the streets of Manchester and meet load after load of cotton, I think of…twenty-five millions of dollars' worth of cotton which supply your market, and I remember that not one cent of that money has ever reached the hands of the laborers.

After the Civil War ended, Remond returned to America and continued her fight for human dignity by helping to lead an unsuccessful fight to include women's suffrage in New York's Constitutional Convention. Later, she moved to Italy, became a medical doctor, married an Italian and practiced medicine in Rome. Sarah Parker Remond was a black woman who spoke courageously for the downtrodden, proclaimed that women must vote and swayed the foreign policy of the world's greatest empire.

An advocate for equal rights her entire life, Dr. Sarah Parker Remond died in Rome, Italy, on December 13, 1894. She led an effort by blacks to gain the support of England for the cause of the North in the Civil War.

DEC 17

Maria W. Stewart: "I Am Able"

Maria W. Stewart was an outspoken, principled and progressive woman with great passion and faith. Born in Connecticut, orphaned at five, a house servant until age fifteen, she had moved to Boston and married James Stewart in 1826. There she also befriended, and was mentored by, the great David Walker, author of the classic book, *Appeal to the Colored Citizens of the World.*

Three years later, in 1829, James Stewart died suddenly, and a year later David Walker was poisoned. Maria Stewart was inconsolable. With both her husband and her friend abruptly gone, she was paralyzed with grief. A widow with nowhere to go, Stewart turned to Jesus Christ. She had a profound religious conversion and dedicated her life to God. She believed with all her heart that God was calling her to preach the good news and that the Holy Spirit would empower her to work toward spiritual, social and political liberation. Ignoring racist and sexist restrictions, she could be heard from platforms all over Boston. She was possibly the first American black woman to address audiences of both men and women.

Maria Stewart was an enigma: an outspoken woman when females were supposed to be subservient; a black radical when African Americans were considered inferior; a Christian abolitionist when many believers supported slavery. She condemned racism and colonization schemes before white audiences, and she challenged black men to live according to Christian principles. She urged black women to stand up and "distinguish yourselves" in education and politics. She demanded that all blacks live holy lives and work toward racial uplift, and she preached an uncompromising message of personal salvation, self-respect and black unity.

No matter where she spoke, Stewart was wholly devoted to God's truth. Her confidence in the Spirit's presence was evident in her pamphlet, "Religion and the Pure Principles of Morality, the Sure Foundation on Which We Must Build." Some audiences howled at her message, and black men in one audience threw tomatoes at her, but Maria Stewart gave no ground. She once said:

> O, had I received the advantages of an early education, my ideas would, ere now, have expanded far and wide; but alas! I possess nothing but moral capability—no teachings but the teachings of the Holy Spirit.

Maria W. Stewart is considered by many historians to be the first female black nationalist and the first woman political writer. The farewell speech she gave when she moved from Boston stands as a testament to the source of her strength:

> I found myself sitting at the feet of Jesus.... I thought I heard a spiritual interrogation, "Are you able to drink of the cup that I have drank of?"... And my heart made this reply: "Yea, Lord, I am able."

Maria Stewart, a passionate preacher and political writer, died on December 17, 1879, in Washington, D.C. She is considered by many to be the first female black nationalist and the first woman political writer in the United States.

≣ Edmonia Highgate: "I Trust Fearlessly In God"

Edmonia Highgate left New York at the end of the Civil War to help educate black people out of slavery's ignorance. Though she had been free all her life, her aunts, uncles and cousins had belonged to white owners across the South, and she had seen the oppression they endured. Though she was a good schoolteacher with a stable future in the North, she could not rest in New York's relative safety while her race suffered for lack of education. She also knew the value of learning; she had seen how it opened tightly-shut doors for her in New York. So she hired a carriage and made the long arduous trip south, past deserted plantations, smoldering battlefields and long lines of freed blacks with nowhere to go. Determined to help, she went where she heard the need was greatest, rural Louisiana, to give ex-slaves an education and a future.

Racist whites hated educated blacks, and some of their worst nightmares were northern teachers such as Edmonia Highgate. On December 17, 1866, she wrote a letter to a friend in New York:

> *There has been much opposition to the School. Twice I have been shot at in my room. My night scholars have been shot but none killed. The rebels threatened to burn down the school and house.... The nearest military protection is two hundred miles distant.... But I trust fearlessly in God and am safe.*

How was this woman able to be so brave in the face of death? The answer lies in her letter. She believed in her safety because she believed what the Psalmist wrote: "The Lord is my light and my salvation; whom shall I fear?" (27:1). Her God was greater than the threats, gunshots and nightriders of the South. Despite danger all around, she trusted "fearlessly in God."

When we are cornered by invincible odds, when we are threatened by forces beyond our strength, let us remember the indomitable courage of Edmonia Highgate.

Black teacher Edmonia Highgate moved to the South after the Civil War to teach freed slaves and their children in New Orleans, Louisiana. On December 17, 1866, she wrote a letter to a friend in New York City that documented how her students were fired on while walking to school, as was her classroom while school was in session. But she courageously persisted, despite the danger.

DEC 19 ≡ "Black Harry" Hosier: "One of the Best Preachers in the World"

Harry Hosier was born a slave in Fayetteville, North Carolina, around 1750. As a young man, he was freed from slavery's bondage and lived the precarious life of a free black in the South. Attracted by the power of the gospel message of the Methodist Church, Hosier converted to the Methodist faith. He quickly became absorbed, devoting himself to their basic "method" of holiness: scripture reading, prayer and worship. Though uneducated, he taught himself to read the Bible, and after several years of study, he had memorized large portions of scripture.

Soon after his conversion, Harry Hosier heard God's voice calling him to preach the gospel of Jesus Christ. It quickly became apparent to all that Hosier had been blessed with the gift of preaching. While whites had called him a slave or a second-class citizen, God had called him to be a preacher. And what a preacher he was. With vivid detail, he could bring Jesus Christ to life through his sermons. In the melodious sound of his voice, people could almost hear Jesus' calling to repentance and holiness.

His peers affectionately called him "Black Harry." Thomas Coke, a respected leader of the English Methodist Church, described him as "one of the best preachers in the world and one of the humblest persons I ever saw." A popular minister who was asked to speak at Methodist churches across the country, "Black Harry" was equally effective when preaching to slaves, free blacks, poor whites or affluent whites. Each audience came away believing that God had spoken directly to them. Much of the growth in the Methodist Church in the late 1700s was due to the powerful preaching of "Black Harry" Hosier.

Methodist preacher Harry Hosier died in 1806 at the age of 56. In 1781, in Adams Chapel in Fairfax County, Virginia, he was the first black to preach to a congregation of Methodists in the United States. His sermon, "Barren Fig Tree," urged believers to stir up the gift within them and live their lives according to the good news of salvation.

☰ Mother Matilda Beasley: "For God's Glory"

All signs spoke of despair and failure. Matilda Beasley had no money, little shelter, no books, no building—almost nothing that indicated her ministry would work. She was, in fact, a person few believed existed: a black Franciscan nun in the post-Civil War South. In 1890s Georgia, most blacks were not Catholic, and whites did not believe that Negroes had souls. Further, blacks had little capital to donate to her cause, and whites had no regard for her efforts at all.

Yet Beasley had a dream: She wanted to build a community of dedicated black women religious who would feed the hungry, clothe the naked and heal the sick. Every day she walked the streets of town, she saw black orphans rummaging in alleys, ex-slaves suffering for lack of medicine and families in dire need of food. She believed that a community of black nuns, committed to the ideals of the legendary St. Francis, could serve God and their people. St. Francis had taken a vow of poverty and had preached the gospel of Jesus Christ everywhere, and his oft-quoted statement, "Preach the gospel always; when necessary, use words," became the vision that Beasley followed.

But Mother Beasley's dream was beginning to crumble. Her convent was no more than an architect's sketch, and the orphanage was but a wish. She had no members ready to take vows of poverty and faced the dubious task of telling a people just out of slavery that the road to freedom was through voluntary poverty. Still, she did not give up and spent several more years writing letters requesting financial help from Catholic archbishops and even Katherine Drexel, the founder of the Sisters of the Blessed Sacrament, who eventually became one of the first American saints to be canonized. Beasley contacted Drexel because of that white Catholic woman's devotion to ministry to black Americans. Records show that Beasley wrote six letters to Drexel between 1893 and 1895. Unfortunately, Drexel could not contribute, for she was already giving to other black ministries all across the country. When weeks passed with no word from Drexel or the archbishops, Mother Beasley felt as if she waited in vain for confirmation that she was following God's will.

She then wrote to Fr. John Slattery, informal supervisor of African-American Catholic missions in the United States. In one letter, she asked him to send books or anything else that might be done "for God's glory." Slattery, however, like so many others, was unable to provide enough support. After years of prayers, letters and tears, Beasley's dream collapsed in a heap of unpaid debts, unbuilt architectural plans and unmet needs. In her last letter to Fr. Slattery she wrote, "My health has failed me, and I can no longer carry on the work and have not been able to raise a community."

For Mother Matilda Beasley, remaining faithful to the vision was more important than anything else. Nothing could dissuade her, not even failure itself. Although she did not attain her vision in her lifetime, another order of nuns started a community precisely on the location selected by Beasley. Her faith was the foundation upon which others fulfilled their calling to serve Christ and the people.

Mother Matilda Beasley died on December 20, 1903, in Savannah, Georgia. She was found one morning after missing Mass, lying dead in a state of prayer in front of a statute of the Virgin Mary. She had tried, and failed, to organize a community of black Franciscan nuns to serve the poor in the South, but her faith was the foundation upon which others later succeeded.

≣ Angela Dawson: The Massacre on North Preston

Angela Dawson grew up in the rough part of Baltimore, and her early years were marked by the multiple traumas that afflict the poor in America: underemployment, drug addiction, low self-esteem, poor schools, vanquished hopes and gang violence. The block Dawson lived on was surrounded by tough streets where the strong survived, the weak were preyed upon and the fortunate escaped. But she stayed because she had no choice, and she stayed because she loved her community. Her friends were there, her memories were there and, as she grew older, her children were born there.

Those blocks were her home, and so Angela Dawson confronted the crack dealers who menaced the neighborhood. Her house sat on the corner of North Preston and North Eden, which was the preferred hangout for local drug dealers. She began by politely asking them to leave. When that failed, she called the police whenever deals were going down. Dawson simply wanted a community where her children could play outdoors or walk home from school without being solicited or caught in crossfire. Drug dealers laughed at her efforts, however, and on occasion, cursed her out. But she never backed down; for the sake of her five children, she never backed down.

In the pre-dawn hours of October 16, 2003, however, someone kicked in her front door, poured gasoline inside and lit a match. The three-story row house ignited like a torch. The assailants certainly meant to kill, for they had filled the only exit from the house with gasoline. Angela Dawson awoke to flames and smoke and desperately tried to save her children. Neighbors, awakened to the noise, could hear her screaming, "God, please help me!"

Angela Dawson, 36; her husband Carnell Dawson, 43; her daughter Lawanda Ortiz, 14; her son Juan Ortiz, 12; their son Carnell, Jr., 10; and twin sons Keith and Kevin, 9—all perished in that deliberate slaughter. One week later, 21-year-old Darrell Brooks, who lived across the street, was arrested for the crime.

Angela Dawson died trying to build a better life for her children. She stood up against those willing to destroy others for addiction and profit. God bless this courageous black woman and her family, and may their memory compel us to prevent such future atrocities.

Lifelong Baltimore, Maryland, residents Angela and Carnell Dawson were married on December 31, 1998. Carnell was employed as a handyman refurbishing schools, and Angela volunteered in her children's classrooms. Each of the children was doing well in school when their home was burned to the ground and the entire family was killed for opposing drug dealing in their neighborhood.

≣ Gertrude Pridgett "Ma" Rainey: Moanin' the Blues

Gertrude Pridgett "Ma" Rainey was the first nationally-known female blues singer. Her career peaked between 1923 and 1928, when she recorded ninety-three classic blues songs. During the five-year period that Paramount Records produced her songs, Rainey's voice captivated white and black listeners across the nation. Her first recording, *Moonshine Blue,* set the pace for her later works.

Rainey was not just a singer; she was an artist in the fullest sense of the term. Her earlier groups—Bunch of Blackberries; Rainey and Rainey: Assassinators of the Blues—combined music, word and dance in a dazzling display of black creativity. But in 1928, Paramount dropped her because they felt her down-home style and gutbucket bluesy moan were outdated. Yet among black folk, "Ma" Rainey remained the Queen of the Blues; few singers could articulate their anguish as she did. Long after she passed, "Ma" Rainey remained an icon of the blues.

Although her musical career lasted only five years, her influence on both music and black culture was profound. Some blues singers, including Koko Taylor and others, adopted her style with great success. Since Rainey sang at a time when black culture was considered inferior and black music was largely unknown in the white world, she is viewed by many as a courageous pioneer. In fact, the great poet Sterling Brown dedicated a poem to her, and her life inspired August Wilson's play, *Ma Rainey's Black Bottom*. The celebration of "Ma" Rainey's life in theater and verse signify her status in the eyes of black America.

Blues singer Gertrude Pridgett "Ma" Rainey died on December 22, 1939, in Columbus, Georgia. She is called "The Queen of the Blues," and her life inspired black author August Wilson's play, **Ma Rainey's Black Bottom,** *which was nominated for a Tony Award for Best Play in 1985.*

≣ Prince Hall: Grand Master of the African Lodge

Before Prince Hall immigrated to Cambridge, Massachusetts, his home had been Barbados, where some of the cruelest forms of slavery existed in the Americas. Hall forever carried the memories of these sadistic punishments and tortures. When he arrived on the shores of the United States, he came with a desire to liberate his race from slavery's clutches.

Hall was different from many early black abolitionists in that he was a Mason. Like every other element of American culture, the Masons were stained with racism. Yet in 1787, Hall secured approval from the Grand Lodge of Ireland to form African Lodge No. 459. Prince Hall became the Grand Master and led the black Masons in countless acts of service and advocacy.

As a Mason, preacher and abolitionist, Prince Hall was an outspoken advocate for black freedom. He was especially inspired by the Haitian slave revolution. He believed that God was with the Haitian quest for freedom, and it inspired him to work for freedom in the United States. One Sunday evening at the Grand African Lodge, Hall preached to his fellow Masons:

> My brethren, let us remember what a dark day it was with our African brethren, six years ago in the French West Indies.... But blessed be God, the scene is changed.

Hall went on to say the scene had changed because Toussaint L'Overture, Dessalines, Boukman and hundreds of Haitian slaves had acted to free themselves. They did not wait for outside benevolence or their masters' eventual enlightenment; they struck a blow for themselves. For Prince Hall, this act of self-determination was evidence that God gave humans the ability to free themselves from oppression.

Wherever he went, Prince Hall preached the gospel of self-liberation. He lobbied the Massachusetts legislature for a school for black children. When they refused, he started one himself. His sermons, speeches and writings demanded the immediate emancipation of the black race. For him, being a Mason and a preacher were but vehicles to accomplish his real goal: the physical and mental liberation of black people in the Americas.

Preacher and abolitionist Prince Hall was born in Barbados. He was the first black Mason in the United States and served as Grand Master of African Lodge No. 459 in Cambridge, Massachusetts. He died on December 4, 1807.

DEC 24 ≡ Art Ensemble of Chicago: Great Black Music

In the late 1960s, several young black musicians gathered to explore the deep roots of ancient black music. As accomplished jazz players, their ears and souls were nourished with the multi-layered sounds of black music. Muddy Waters' blues, Paul Robeson's baritone, Mahalia Jackson's gospel, James Brown's soul, storefront church choirs, Duke Ellington's big band, New Orleans march tunes and West African drums—all formed a single tapestry of black music. To them the sound was one; there were no mutually exclusive categories, genres and styles. They called themselves the Art Ensemble of Chicago, and their motto was "Great Black Music: Ancient to the Future."

But it was more than music; it was art. Their shows combined face paintings, African dress, world instruments, dance and poetry. And then there was the sound. Even now, listening to the Art Ensemble is a soul-cleansing event. Their sound strips away tension, stereotypes and assumptions and leaves listeners with a deeper sense of themselves and their connection to the universe.

Roscoe Mitchell, a member of the Art Ensemble, said it well:

I think that music is the highest science in the world. We want to be as high into the music as we possibly can, so we always try to stimulate the highest thought that we can. The thing about us is, if we're being honest and trying to do our best to keep this music as high as we can, then we automatically elevate or expand people's thoughts. It is definitely a mind-opener.

Each solo, each composition, each concert of the Art Ensemble of Chicago is different from the previous one; each stands on its own as an offering to the Spirit. Famoudou Don Moye on drums, Malachi Favors Maghoustut on bass, Joseph Jarman on reeds, Roscoe Mitchell on reeds and Lester Bowie on trumpet produce some of the greatest music of all time. It is global, African and personal. It is liberating, stimulating. Above all, it is Great Black Music.

The Art Ensemble of Chicago was formed in 1969 and has produced dozens of classic avant-garde compositions. Fanfare for the Warriors, Nice Guys, Full Force *and the* Dreaming of the Masters *series are among their many excellent recordings.*

DEC 25   ≣ Jupiter Hammon: "An Evening Thought"

The gaiety and joy of Christmas day were almost over, and darkness signaled evening's arrival. Jupiter Hammon had been busy the entire day, for as slave to the prosperous Lloyd family of Oyster Bay, New York, his job had been to prepare the decorations, clean the mansion and serve the steady stream of relatives and guests. Now that his chores were done, Hammon closeted himself away in his room for quiet reflection.

At the age of forty-nine, Hammon had known nothing outside of slavery. Yet unlike many slaves, he had the good fortune to be owned by a wealthy and kind master. Though his life, decisions and future were not his own, Hammon had enjoyed benefits most slaves could only dream of. He had worked as a clerk in the family business, learned to be an artisan and a farmer, and attended local schools.

Years earlier, he had also dedicated his life to Jesus Christ, and his faith was more important to him than anything else. So on this Christmas night, while many took pleasure in gifts, families and friends, Hammon thought of his Savior. Overwhelmed with joy, he sat on the edge of his bed and excitedly wrote his deepest yearnings.

The poem he created that night, "An Evening Thought, Salvation by Christ, with Penitential Cries," was not just a tribute to Jesus Christ; it was also the first poem published by an African American. The very next year, 1761, "An Evening Thought" was published, and Hammon became the forerunner to hundreds of future black writers. He wrote:

Salvation come by Jesus Christ alone,
The only Son of God;
Redemption now to every one,
That love his holy Word.

Dear Jesus we would fly to Thee,
And leave off every Sin,
Thy tender Mercy well agree;
Salvation from our King....

Jupiter Hammon's love for Christ surpassed both his degradation as a slave and his good fortune for having a kind master. To Hammon, nothing was more important than the grace of God. Further, he not only praised his Savior, but he also led the way for black poets such as Countee Cullen, Sonia Sanchez, Sterling Brown, Maya Angelou and hundreds of others. All are indebted to the pioneering work of Jupiter Hammon that Christmas evening.

On December 25, 1760, black slave Jupiter Hammon wrote the first poem published by an African-American writer in the United States. He died in 1806 in Oyster Bay, New York.

DEC 26   Ellen and William Craft: "We Are Safe"

In a tale almost stranger than fiction, Ellen and William Craft escaped from the grasp of slavery with an ingenious plan. Ellen was the daughter of a black slave and a white slave-owner. With a complexion closer to white than black, and with features similar to white children, she soon provoked the ire of her mistress. In a fit of rage, the white mistress sold Ellen away from her mother and siblings. William's story was different in detail but similar in misery:

My old master had the reputation of being a very humane and Christian man, but he thought nothing of selling my poor old father, and dear aged mother, at separate times, to different persons, to be dragged off never to behold each other again.

When Ellen and William met and fell in love, they spent weeks agonizing whether they should marry or not. Each had mourned the loss of family to an owner's whim, and they never wanted to feel that pain again. Nevertheless, the two married, but with the understanding that together they would plot an escape from slavery. Years passed, and no feasible plan or opportunity came. They later wrote, "After puzzling our brains for years, we were reluctantly driven to the sad conclusion that it was almost impossible to escape from slavery in Georgia."

In December of 1848, the two fashioned a plan, a risky plan, in which failure would bring torture and execution. Near-white in complexion, Ellen Craft would disguise herself as William's injured owner traveling North in search of medical attention. For eight days Ellen Craft would have to convince everyone she met that she was not only white, but also a man. William's job was to be the illiterate slave—an easier task, since that is what he was. Arrayed in costume and armed with wit, Ellen and William Craft slipped off the plantation one moonless night. Traveling northward, they convinced hotel clerks, railroad conductors, steamer crews and border guards that a white man and his slave were in their midst.

Ellen wore a top hat and glasses, bandaged her face to cover her beardlessness and put her right arm in a sling to hide the fact she could not write. In escapades that defy reality, the Crafts traveled from Georgia to Charleston, then on to Wilmington to Richmond, and finally, from Baltimore to Philadelphia. On Christmas Day they arrived in Philadelphia. Once inside their destination, Ellen grasped her husband's hand and exclaimed, "Thank God, William, we are safe!"

William and Ellen Craft later wrote in their classic narrative, *Running a Thousand Miles for Freedom*:

> When we reached the house, she was in reality so weak and faint that she could scarcely stand alone. However, I got her into the apartments that were pointed out, and there we knelt down, on this…Christmas-day—a day that will ever be memorable to us—and poured out our heartfelt gratitude to God, for his goodness in enabling us to overcome so many perilous difficulties, in escaping out off the jaws of the wicked.

On December 25, 1848, black slaves Ellen and William Craft completed their thousand-mile journey to freedom. Their escape from slavery was so dramatic that southern slave-catchers vowed to capture them and end their victorious saga, but the couple spent the rest of their lives in freedom.

DEC 27 ≡ Curtis Mayfield: "People Get Ready"

During the tumultuous sixties, many people felt as if society were unraveling. Black self-assertion was met with FBI surveillance, white backlash and police brutality; black communities were divided on their strategies for survival. Some urged escape and separation from "the Devil"; others sought accommodation and integration; still others believed that equality would come only through violence, bloodshed and armed revolution. The vast majority of black families were simply trying to survive—working, praying and struggling to make it in racist America.

Into this confusion floated the melodious, gospel-tinged voice of Curtis Mayfield. Just as black America was pondering which way to go, Mayfield came with an answer through music: He told us to get ready to get on board the freedom train. His lyrics proclaimed that we didn't need a ticket or baggage. Simple faith would enable us to climb on. Once there, our faith and gratefulness toward God would lead us to liberty.

"People Get Ready" became an anthem for black people working for liberation. It was a song of hope, faith and love—the very qualities that enabled black folks to survive slavery, Jim Crow laws, sharecropping, the Klan, the ghetto and every other evil the demon of racism cast in their paths. "People Get Ready" urged that if we kept the faith, stayed alert and loved our people, the train of black redemption would arrive on our doorstep. Mayfield once said, "'People Get Ready' was taken from my church or from the upbringing of messages from the church…. I must have been in a very deep mood when I wrote that song."

Curtis Mayfield encouraged the Civil Rights Movement, and the Movement in turn uplifted him. "We're a Winner," another of his inspiring songs, gave hope to black people amidst race riots, the Vietnam War and continued white repression. Once again, Mayfield convinced us that we were winners, that we were moving on up and no one could tell us we could not triumph.

Mayfield later wrote that "We're a Winner" was "locked in with Martin Luther King, it had an inspiring message." For over forty years, Curtis Mayfield made memorable, gorgeous and thought-provoking soul music that inspired and empowered. As few artists have done before or since, he articulated the soul and spirit of a people.

Singer and songwriter Curtis Mayfield died on December 26, 1999, in Roswell, Georgia. His song, "People Get Ready," became one of the anthems of black people during the 1960s.

DEC 28 ≣ Moses Kotane: Book of Life

During the 1920s, Moses Kotane was like millions of other South African black men, shoved to the margins of their country and forced to choose between starvation and dangerous employment. Stripped of dignity, self-respect and humanity, these men had to accept any affront white racists put upon them. Kotane, however, resisted with every ounce of his being.

In 1928, while working at Quinn's Bakery in Johannesburg, he heard mention of the African National Congress' *Book of Life*. He was intrigued, for all he knew was sorrow, tears and blood. When Kotane learned that the names of Africans who committed themselves to working for liberation and justice were inscribed in the *Book of Life*, he immediately joined the African National Congress (ANC) and devoted himself to study, work and activism. He also joined the Industrial and Commercial Union (ICU) in its quest for safer working conditions and equal pay.

One afternoon, a member of the South African Communist Party asked Kotane to consider joining the Party. Kotane hesitated, noting that he already belonged to two organizations, the ANC and the ICU. He realized, however, that many of the most dedicated people in both the ANC and the ICU were communists. Wherever black dignity was assaulted, whenever protest was needed, whenever a stand was necessary, it seemed the communists were there. That was enough for Moses Kotane. During a lifetime of struggle, he became a beloved figure in both the Communist Party and the ANC. He told his followers:

> *Fellow Africans, it is time you realized your true position and followed the lead of the Communist Party. It is time you renounced the oppressor's yoke and strive for your liberty and freedom. Now is the time of crisis and I appeal to you…to act as a united people and test your national strength.*

For forty years, Kotane led the Communist Party in South Africa as a radical, multi-racial party. His courageous stand on behalf of black liberation sowed the seeds for Steve Biko, Nelson Mandela, Walter Sisulu and the other heroes of black South African freedom and equality.

Political activist Moses Kotane joined the African National Congress and the Communist Party in Johannesburg in 1928 and became one of South Africa's great leaders for the cause of liberty. He died in May of 1978 at age 73.

DEC 29 ≡ Bohoro Nyagakon: God Have Mercy

Gunfire and grenades came closer and closer. Bohoro Nyagakon, her husband and their children huddled together in their home, hoping the battle would pass. It didn't, and the sounds and screams grew nearer. The horror of war swirled right outside their home; smoke, cursing and gunshots surrounded them. Suddenly, the door was trampled and five sweaty, wild-eyed soldiers burst through. They grabbed Bohoro Nyagakon's husband and shoved him in another room, tossing the children outside. The soldiers, each one in turn, raped her, even though she was eight months pregnant. Nyagakon later said, "Five of them came at me. I closed my eyes…. Then they each had sex with me, five of them. Afterwards, I was so bruised and my mind was shutting down."

Bohoro Nyagakon, like thousands of Congolese women caught in the violence of civil war, was raped so brutally that she suffered from vaginal fistula, a frighteningly paralyzing condition wherein the vagina is so ruptured that bodily functions are uncontrollable. The victim literally sits in her own urine and excrement. Bohoro Nyagakon lost her baby and, for the next ten months, lay stunned in a bed, surrounded by the stench of her own bodily discharges. When her husband took her to Bukavu for vaginal reconstruction, they were shocked to find hundreds of other Congolese women in the same horrible condition.

Soldiers high on cocaine, drunk with palm wine and frenzied with the violence of war still roam the Congo today in search of females to rape. Age, pregnancy, disability—nothing matters to them. They rape girls as young as eight and women as old as seventy-five. They leave their victims traumatized by rape, infected with AIDS or brutalized by vaginal fistula.

God have mercy on the victims, the perpetrators and those of us who know what is going on and still do nothing. God have mercy on Bohoro Nyagakon.

Bohoro Nyagakon is one of the thousands of Congolese women rebuilding her life after the trauma of gang rape during the civil wars of the 1990s and the early 21st century.

DEC 30   ≡ Kwanzaa: "I Pray for the Life of the People"

Created in the 1960s by black nationalist Ron Karenga to celebrate African communal principles, Kwanzaa is observed by thousands of African-American families. The celebration and rituals resurrect what slavery tried to destroy: a cultural connection to Africa. The Ashanti, the Yoruba, the Thonga and other African peoples celebrated the first fruits of a new year with several days of thanksgiving. For example, the Ashanti king always opened each year with the prayer: "The edges of the year have met, I pray for the life of the people."

In similar fashion Kwanzaa conveys the five themes present in most African celebrations: the ingathering of the people, the reverence of the Creator and Creation, a commemoration of the past, the recommitment to cultural ideals and celebration of the good.

Kwanzaa interweaves aspects of the black experience in America with these ancient African traditions. The *mkeba* (mat), the *kinara* (candleholder) the *Kikombe cha umoja* (unity cup) and the *nguzo saba* (seven principles) symbolically recreate an African culture on American soil. In the midst of a sometimes hostile culture, black folks cling to each other and the beauty of Africa to commemorate the past year and to anticipate the next. Kwanzaa calls forth the wisdom of the ancestors to enlighten future generations.

May the seven principles of Kwanzaa forever guide our path, we pray for the life of our people.

Kwanzaa lasts from December 26 through January 1. Each of the seven days is devoted to one of the Nguzo Saba. In order, they are Umoja (Unity), Kugichagulia (Self-Determination), Ujima (Collective Work and Responsibility), Ujamaa (Cooperative Economics), Nia (Purpose), Kuummba (Creativity) and Imani (Faith).

≣ Roberto Clemente: "The Great One"

Roberto Clemente's athletic talents were superseded only by his magnificent courage and generosity. He was, by all accounts, a significant figure in the history of baseball. Decades after his death, he remains a beloved figure in Puerto Rico, Pittsburgh and around the world. Roberto Clemente—his name is synonymous with grace, selflessness and racial pride. However, as great as he was on the baseball field—and he was truly great—his humanity exceeded his athleticism. Many who saw and knew Clemente called him "The Great One."

Just how talented was he? League batting title champ for four seasons, National League Most Valuable Player in 1966, outstanding performer in the Pirates' 1960 and 1971 World Series wins, Roberto Clemente is considered by many to be the best right fielder in baseball history. That alone was enough to enshrine him in the hearts of Puerto Rican and American fans. Yet baseball exploits were only a shadow of his real greatness. His true glory was his indomitable compassion and racial solidarity.

One of baseball's first Latin stars, he was proud of his blackness and his Latin heritage, but he was ignored, misquoted, mocked and demeaned by a white media intolerant of language and racial differences. Clemente, however, would not allow sportswriters or anyone else to define him. When some insisted on calling him "Bobby" Clemente, he retorted, "Don't call me Bobby." He took other Latin players under his tutelage, spoke Spanish whenever he felt like it and demanded simple respect.

In the last game of his baseball career, he got his three thousandth hit, a milestone considered certain to ensure automatic entry into the Hall of Fame. Several months later, he died in a plane crash while taking humanitarian supplies to his fellow Latino brothers and sisters in earthquake-torn Nicaragua. While his last ball game was a historic milestone, his last act as a person represented the pinnacle of sacrifice and solidarity. Roberto Clemente, both on the diamond and in life, was truly "The Great One."

Roberto Clemente died on December 31, 1972, in a plane crash while taking supplies from Puerto Rico to Nicaragua. For days afterward, grieving Puerto Ricans stood on the shore near the crash site in hopes he had somehow survived. The next year, Clemente was voted into the Baseball Hall of Fame with 93% of the vote on the first ballot after that conservative institution waived the mandatory five-year waiting period.

INDEX